A COMMUNIST IN THE FAMILY

To my fellow travellers, April 2017

'Every traveller wants to find the place where being what he is will matter, and that place is home.' ROBERT DESSAIX, *CORFU*

'Wasn't that the definition of home? Not where you were from but where you were wanted.'
ABRAHAM VERGHESE, *CUTTING FOR STONE*

'It is not hard to do a bit of good; what is hard is to do good all one's life.'
WANG BINGNAN, PRESIDENT OF THE CHINESE PEOPLE'S ASSOCIATION FOR FRIENDSHIP WITH FOREIGN COUNTRIES, SPEAKING ABOUT REWI ALLEY[1]

'What is it about China that *gets* people from the rest of the world? The answer is a single word – warmth.'
REWI ALLEY DIARY 1952–55

A Communist in the Family

SEARCHING FOR

Rewi Alley

ELSPETH SANDYS

OTAGO

Published by Otago University Press
Level 1, 398 Cumberland Street
Dunedin, New Zealand
university.press@otago.ac.nz
www.otago.ac.nz/press

First published 2019
Copyright © Elspeth Sandys
The moral rights of the author have been asserted.

ISBN 978-1-98-853160-1

Published with the assistance of Creative New Zealand

ARTS COUNCIL OF NEW ZEALAND *TOI AOTEAROA*

Editor: Jane Parkin
Index: Diane Lowther
Design/layout: Fiona Moffat

Cover: Rewi in Shandan, 1982. From *Rewi Alley*, a commemorative photo album compiled by the
Research Office for Rewi Alley's Works of the Chinese People's Association for Friendship with
Foreign Countries and *China Reconstructs* magazine, 1988, Beijing: China Reconstructs Press.

Printed in China through Asia Pacific Offset

CONTENTS

AUTHOR'S NOTE

This is the story of a relationship with a man, Rewi Alley, as family member, writer, humanitarian and unwitting myth-maker. It is also the story of a relationship with a country, China, where he lived for 60 years, from 1927 to 1987, about which I now know enough to acknowledge how little I know. Whoever said 'You can never come to the end of China' said a true thing.

Rewi Alley's long life in China has been the subject of many books, films and documentaries, in both Chinese and English, yet he remains known to only a few in the West. That this man, friend of peasants and presidents, founder of the movement known internationally as Gung Ho, honoured as one of the top ten foreign friends (*guoji youren*) of China, has been largely ignored by the English-speaking world is the puzzle I have set out to try to solve.

As an excuse (explanation?) for my audacity in writing this book, I could offer up the fact that it was a condition of the costs of my trip to China being paid, but that begs the question of why I should think I am in any way qualified to write about the country, home to over a quarter of the world's population, that I have visited only once. All I can say in my defence is that Rewi Alley, my mother's first cousin, has always loomed large in my life. And I can't write about him without writing about China.

'A person goes to China for a week and writes a book. A person goes to China for a year and writes an article. A person goes to China for two years and stays silent.' Words often quoted by old China hands, quoted here in acknowledgement of the impossible task I have set myself.

*

In the interests of creating a dramatic narrative I have taken some liberties in my depiction of Rewi's relationships with friends and family. At times, based on what I know of the facts, I have imagined meetings and conversations, but I have been careful not to stray from the written record. 'Imagine it,' Richard Ford instructed his readers in his 2017 memoir of his parents, *Between Them*. 'You have to, because there is no other way.' So that, as a writer, is what I have done. I hope readers will forgive any mistakes made in daring to imagine Rewi Alley's life in a country so far from his birthplace, and mine.

A note on the English form of Chinese words

When Rewi Alley went to China, the system in use for expressing Chinese words in English was the one devised by the British after the Opium Wars. It was known as the Wade-Giles system. Not surprisingly it didn't survive the War of Liberation (capital letters will be used for this war, in which the communists triumphed, as they are in China). In the early 1950s Chinese linguists started working on a new system that would come to be known as Pinyin. Adopted by the Chinese government in 1958, it was acknowledged as the international form of the romanisation of Chinese words in 1982.

Ahead of his times in so many ways, Rewi Alley never quite managed the transition from Wade-Giles to Pinyin. So as late as 1980 he is still calling Beijing Peking, and Baoji Paochi. So when I quote him, it's the old system I'll be using. Elsewhere, apart from in quotes from the pre-Pinyin period, the modern form will be used. Though contradictions, especially in the spelling of personal names, linger on. Mao Tse-tung became Mao Zedong when the Pinyin system was adopted, but the old spelling persists, as does the form Mao Tsetung. The same applies to Zhou Enlai (Chou En-lai, Chou En lai), Soong Chingling (Soong Ching-ling, Soong Qingling) and Jiang Jieshi (Chiang Kaishek, Chiang Kai-shek). Jiang Jieshi is the correct Pinyin form for China's defeated nationalist leader but because he is mostly known in the West as Chiang Kaishek that is the form I will use.

Other variations in spelling occur as a result of crossovers from Mandarin to Cantonese and vice versa. When quoting I will use the form given in the quoted passage; otherwise I have tried, as far as possible for a non-Chinese speaker, to standardise to Pinyin.

Acronyms, the blight of so much modern journalism, are kept to a minimum. I have, however, used: CCP for the Chinese Communist Party; Corso for the Council for the Organisation of Relief Services Overseas; CPNZ for the Communist Party of New Zealand; ICCIC for the International Committee for the Promotion of Chinese Industrial Co-operatives; INDUSCO for the fundraising arm of ICCIC founded by Ida Pruitt; KMT for the Chinese nationalist government, the Kuomintang (also spelt Guomintang); NZCFS for the New Zealand–China Friendship Society; and NZSIS (shortened to SIS) for New Zealand's Security Intelligence Services.

TIMELINE OF THE LIFE OF REWI ALLEY

1897   *2 December*: Born Springfield, Canterbury, New Zealand.

1898   *January*: Family moves to Amberley.

1902–05 Attends Amberley Primary School where his father Fred is headmaster.

1906   Family moves to Christchurch. Fred Alley becomes headmaster of Wharenui School, which Rewi now attends.

1912–16 Attends Christchurch Boys' High School.

              16 February: Enlists in New Zealand Expeditionary Force.

1917   *July*: Sails for Britain on the *Ulimaroa*.

              December: Sails for France (based at Étaples).

1918   *New Year*. Meets the Chinese soldiers from the British Labour Corps.

              Shrapnel wound to the shoulder while fighting in the Ypres Salient.

              August: Seriously wounded at Bapaume. Evacuated to England.

              November: Returns to New Zealand.

1920   Begins farming at Moeawatea, Taranaki.

1926   *November*: Walks off the farm. Returns to Christchurch.

              December: Leaves New Zealand for Australia.

1927   *January–March*: Employed in fertiliser factory in Sydney before sailing to China.

              21 April: Arrives Shanghai.

1927–38 Employed as fire fighter (later factory inspector) by Municipal Council in the British International Settlement.

1929   *July*: Travels to Salaqi in Inner Mongolia to help with famine relief work. Meets Edgar Snow.

              September: Adopts his first son, Alan (Duan Simou).

1932   Japanese bomb Shanghai (the January 28 Incident).

              February: Travels to Wuhan in Hubei province to help with

flood relief. Instrumental in saving thousands of Chinese from execution by the nationalist KMT.

March: Return trip to New Zealand with Alan.

September: Arrives back in Shanghai. Finalises adoption of second son, Mike (Li Xue).

December: Meets Agnes Smedley and makes contact with progressives.

1933 Meets Soong Chingling (Madame Sun Yatsen) and Dr George Hatem (Ma Haide).

1934 Joins international political study group in Shanghai. Regular meetings held. Members include Edgar and Peg Snow, Soong Chingling, James Bertram, Agnes Smedley, Ma Haide, Ruth Weiss, Israel Epstein, Manny and Grace Granich and Dr Hans Mueller.

1936 Writes articles for the fortnightly *Voice of China*. Becomes involved in the communist underground.

September: Travels to Xi'an and Taiyuan to launder money for the Red Army.

December: Capture of Chiang Kaishek in Xi'an.

Signing of the United Front between the KMT and the communists.

1937 *January–October*: Visits family in New Zealand then tours the US inspecting factories.

August: Start of the War of Resistance against Japan. Mike and Alan caught up in the second bombing of Shanghai.

November: Mike and Alan leave for Yan'an where the Red Army is based following the end of the Long March (October 1934–35).

1938 The Shanghai study group comes up with a plan for Gung Ho.* Rewi involved in setting up the committee for Promotion of Industrial Co-operatives.

---

* Gung Ho – Work Together – was a co-operative movement founded by Rewi Alley and others in 1938 to help the Chinese in the war against Japan. Based on the principles of co-operation, it succeeded in establishing over 500,000 co-operatives throughout unoccupied China that produced goods essential to the survival of the 8th Route Army

May: Resigns from Shanghai Municipal Council. Meets with Zhou Enlai to discuss Gung Ho. Travels to Wuhan to meet with Soong Meiling (Madame Chiang Kaishek), W.H. Donald (Chiang's Australian adviser) and H.H. Kung (finance minister). The KMT government gives permission for Gung Ho to begin operations.

Summer: Meets George Hogg in Wuhan. Meets Christopher Isherwood and W.H. Auden.

May–December: Travels to many places in northwest China on Gung Ho business.

August: Appointed technical advisor to Gung Ho's Executive Yuan.

1939   Throughout the year travels widely on Gung Ho business.

February: Meets Mao Zedong in Yan'an.

May: Hospitalised in Ganzhou with typhoid and malaria.

1940   Continues Gung Ho travels, setting up new co-operatives and inspecting existing ones.

February: Second meeting with Mao.

July: Hospitalised with recurring typhoid and malaria.

October: Visits the Philippines to raise money for Gung Ho.

1941   Further travels on Gung Ho business. Works on establishment of Bailie training schools.

1942   *New Year*: George Hogg becomes headmaster of Shuangshipu Bailie School in Shaanxi province.

September: Discharged by the KMT as Technical Advisor to the Executive Yuan.

Continues to work as field secretary for ICCIC.

1943   *Autumn*: Meets Joseph Needham. Travels with him to Gansu province to look for a new school site away from Japanese bombs. Settles on Shandan.

December: Leads advance party from Shuangshipu to Shandan.

1944   *February*: George Hogg undertakes his 'little Long March', transporting students and equipment to Shandan from Shuangshipu.

Rewi travelling to raise funds for the Shandan school.

1945   *May*: War in Europe ends.

July: Death of George Hogg. Rewi takes over as headmaster of Shandan Bailie School.

September: Japanese surrender, following the bombing of Hiroshima and Nagasaki.

1945–49 Running the school. Dealing with threats from the KMT. Supporting the communists in the civil war.

1949   *September*: Shandan liberated.

1949–51 Rewi's position at Shandan becomes increasingly tenuous. The school is taken over by the army, then transferred to the Oil Ministry.

1951   *May*: Attends memorial service for Agnes Smedley in Beijing.

June: Meeting in Beijing to wind up Gung Ho.

1952–87 Rewi the writer and translator publishes more than 60 books.

1952   Clara Alley (Rewi's mother) dies.

June: Appointed delegate to Peace Conference of the Asian and Pacific Regions.

October: Attends Beijing Peace Conference.

Yo Banfa! (Rewi's first book) published in Shanghai.

1953   Appointed headmaster of Lanzhou Oil and Technical School – a mainly titular position.

Takes up residence in the old Italian Legation in Beijing. Later shares staff – secretary, cook, chauffeur – with Anna Louise Strong who has an apartment in the same building.

1954–60 Attends peace conferences. Publishes books. Travels as a peace delegate to Vietnam, Korea, Finland, Sweden.

1960   *February*: Visits New Zealand. Addresses public meetings. Shadowed by the SIS.

1960–76 Travels as peace delegate to India, Cuba, Korea, Vietnam, Indonesia, the Philippines, Japan, Poland.

Writes poetry and prose. Translates. From 1966–76 *Travels in China* is the only one of Rewi's books published in China. Other books are published in New Zealand and Australia.

1964–65 *December–February*: Visits New Zealand. Refuses invitations to speak publicly.

1966–76 Chinese Cultural Revolution. Rewi under constant threat but protected by Zhou Enlai.

1971 *October*: Home trip to New Zealand. Shadowed by SIS.

1972 *March*: Undertakes speaking tour of Australia at end of New Zealand stay.

May: Honorary doctorate conferred on him (in absentia) by Victoria University.

1973 Brief visit to New Zealand. Addresses Ministry of Foreign Affairs.

1976 *January*: Death of Zhou Enlai.

July: Death of Zhu De (Chu Teh), hero of the Liberation struggle.

September: Death of Mao.

October: Overthrow of the Gang of Four.

1977 *December*: Celebrates eightieth birthday in Great Hall of the People, hosted by Deng Xiaoping, China's new paramount leader.

1978 *May*: Death of Pip, Rewi's brother.

1979–82 Travels. Writes. Translates.

1980 *December*: Soong Chingling hosts a party in her Beijing residence for Rewi's eighty-third birthday.

1981 *May*: Death of Soong Chingling, Madame Sun Yatsen.

1982 *June*: Returns to Shandan to open Exhibition of Cultural Relics which he donated.

December: Made Honorary Citizen of Beijing.

1983 Revival of Gung Ho. Rewi made Honorary Advisor to the Association of Chinese Industrial Co-operatives.

1984 *September*: Visits Shandan to attend opening ceremony of library built in memory of George Hogg.

1985 *December*: Presented with medal of the Queen's Service Order at New Zealand embassy in Beijing.

1987 *27 December*: Rewi Alley dies.

CHINESE POLITICAL CHRONOLOGY

1839–42	First Opium War
1850–64	Taiping Rebellion
1856–60	Second Opium War
1899–1901	Boxer Rebellion
10 Oct 1911	Double Ten Day. Wuchang Uprising, which led to the final overthrow of the Qing dynasty (1644–1911)
29 Dec 1911	Republic of China established under provisional presidency of Sun Yatsen
10 Mar 1912	Yuan Shikai replaces Sun Yatsen as provisional president
25 Aug 1912	Sun Yatsen founds the Kuomintang (Nationalist) Party (KMT), subsequently dissolved by Yuan Shikai
1913	Sun Yatsen goes into exile
25 Oct 1915	Marriage of Sun Yatsen and Soong Chingling in Tokyo
Nov 1915	Yuan Shikai dissolves Chinese Assembly and declares himself emperor.
1916–28	Warlord era
Jun 1916	Yuan Shikai dies
1917	Sun Yatsen returns to China
4 May 1919	Student march on Tiananmen Gate, protesting against the terms of the Treaty of Versailles. Founding of May 4th Movement
10 Oct 1919	KMT reinstated under leadership of Sun Yatsen
1923	First United Front between KMT and communist forces formed to defeat warlords
12 Mar 1925	Sun Yatsen dies. His deputy, Chiang Kaishek, becomes the effective leader of China
1926–28	First (successful) Northern Expedition against warlords
12 Apr 1927	April 12 Incident: KMT forces massacre thousands of suspected communists throughout China. Beginning of period known as the White Terror

1927–34	Chiang launches repeated encirclement campaigns against communist forces
Sep 1931	Japanese invasion of Manchuria triggered by the Mukden Incident
28 Jan 1932	January 28 Incident: Japan bombs Shanghai
1 Mar 1934	Japanese install the deposed Qing Emperor Pu Yi as puppet emperor of Manchuria
16–22 Oct 1935	The Long March of the Red Army from Yudu in Jiangxi province in the south to Yan'an in Shaanxi province in northern China.
7 Jul 1937	Marco Polo Bridge Incident leading to full-scale invasion of China by Japan, starting the second Sino–Japanese War
24 Sep 1937	Battle of Pingxingguan: first Chinese victory against Japan Jan 1941 New Fourth Army Incident: Chiang orders KMT troops to attack the communist New Fourth Army, effectively ending the wartime United Front
2 Sep 1945	Japan surrenders following bombing of Hiroshima and Nagasaki. Soviet Union invades Manchuria. Allies order Japanese troops in China to surrender to Chiang Kaishek
10 Oct 1945	Double Tenth Agreement between communist forces and KMT
Jul 1946	Full-scale war breaks out between communist forces led by Mao Zedong and KMT led by Chiang Kaishek
1946–49	Civil war. Communist forces win decisive victories in Liaoshen, Huaihai and Pingjin campaigns
1 Oct 1949	Mao Zedong proclaims the founding of the People's Republic of China at Tiananmen Square, Beijing
Dec 1949	The Great Retreat: Chiang Kaishek and his defeated forces withdraw to Taiwan
1958–62	The Great Leap Forward
1966–76	The Cultural Revolution
9 Sep 1976	Death of Mao Zedong
6 Oct 1976	Overthrow of the Gang of Four
1 Oct 1978	Deng Xiaoping becomes paramount leader
14 Mar 2013	Xi Jinping elected president of the People's Republic of China

PROLOGUE

IT'S called the Breakfast Room, though no one ever eats breakfast there. It's large and oddly shaped, with hidden corners and curved windows and a ceiling decorated with laurel leaves. From the large bay window seat you look out on a goldfish pond, favourite haunt of both kingfishers, with their eyes on the fish, and my cat Basil with his eyes on the kingfishers. Beyond the pond is my father's greenhouse where he grows – and I suspect talks to – his prize begonias.

There's a fireplace in the room, active, of course – this is 1952. The Romans invented underfloor heating 2000 years ago but I doubt my parents know this. Even if they did they would have considered this expensive alternative to a good fire indulgent. In this house children grow up wearing hand-knitted jerseys and scratching their chilblains. Opposite the window is an alcove with a built-in, L-shaped seat. It's my favourite place in the house, the place I escape to when I want to read, or hide. It has an overhead light and a curtain that can be drawn to shut it off from the rest of the room.

Right now my hiding place is occupied. My mother is entertaining – no, that's the wrong word – my mother is talking earnestly to a man called Colin Morrison. He's the head of an organisation called Corso. I don't know at age 11 what this stands for, but I know it's something to do with sending money and sheep to China.

I'm not supposed to be in the room. My job is to answer the door, then disappear to make tea. I'm mostly an obedient child, but there are times when something stronger than the fear of disapproval takes over. Today it's the word Rewi that has me rooted to the spot. Rewi is my uncle. (So I believed at the time: later I would learn he was my mother's first cousin, not her brother; later still I would work out that, as an adopted child, I wasn't related to him at all. Not that this made any difference. In his diaries he refers to me as his 'writer niece', and I, to this day, think of him as 'Uncle Rewi'.)

Your uncle, my mother has told me, is doing heroic work in China, saving hundreds if not thousands of lives. Uncle Rewi has two adopted sons, Alan and Mike. Mike is my pen-pal. He's told me my name in Chinese means Shining Lake. But there's another name, one that is spoken only when my father is out of the room. *Communist*. I don't know what it means. All I know is it makes my father unhappy – and gets me into trouble. 'Your uncle's a filthy commie!' In attempting to defend my family honour in the school playground I have suffered a bloody nose. Other insults have followed, but so far no more blood has been spilt.

Ours is a Presbyterian household. Pictures of a blue-eyed, fair-haired Jesus surrounded by multi-coloured children, of the Eye of the Needle Gate in Jerusalem, of Mary and Joseph and the baby Jesus in the manger at Bethlehem, line the walls of the corridors and living rooms. There are also – because this is a Scottish Presbyterian household – pictures of Highland cattle, of the mist-bound mountains of Glencoe, of tartan-clad emigrants boarding a sailing ship at Greenock. But there are other things not on such prominent display – a chest carved out of mulberry wood, a tiny jade horse, a lidded vase designed to hold singing crickets – trophies of my father's travels as a young man, when the 'lure of the Orient' drew him to Shanghai, the 'Paris of the East', and Peking, the ancient imperial capital. These tucked-away treasures, and their accompanying pictures – a strange building that looks like lots of beehives one on top of the other, a garden with an arched stone bridge and trees laden with blossom, a scroll painting of huntsmen with bows and arrows – are my mother's favourite things in the house. The mostly unused (and unheated) living room in which they are stored is her hiding place. It's where she goes to read *Millions Know Him – Do You?*, a booklet about Uncle Rewi with the word Corso on the cover, and *China Reconstructs*, the magazine founded by Madame Sun Yatsen, a very important lady. There have only been two issues so far but there will be more. They are very shiny, with lots of pictures of smiling people working in factories and hospitals and schools.

Mr Morrison is talking now. He's telling my mother how cold it is in Shandan, where Uncle Rewi lives. 'Minus 40 some days,' he says, in the kind of voice preachers use to scare you into being good. Pictures start to form in my mind: Uncle Rewi's school, dwarfed by the snow-covered mountains of Shandan; the boys in their padded coats and caps with long ear flaps, learning how to make tools and tractors; the games of basketball when lessons are over; the horses and camels; the starving children – Uncle Rewi calls them 'ants' because of their stunted growth – rescued from coal mines; the dusty mud-brick buildings that might have sheltered Marco Polo seven centuries ago when he went to meet Kubla Khan, the Mongol ruler of China; the river where, in summer, the Shandan boys swim naked, something I would never be allowed to do; the Buddhists temples converted to workshops. '"Out come the Buddhas, in comes the boiler",' my mother quoted, reading one of Uncle Rewi's poems aloud. My eye travels to the sideboard where a tiny brass Buddha – 'my little fat daddy', my uncle's first gift to me – sits in solitary splendour. Had the Buddha come from anyone but him it would, out of deference to my Presbyterian father, have been hidden away as idolatrous.

'... almost impossible to find out what's happening,' Mr Morrison is saying. 'Seems Rewi's been moved on, or the school has ...'

My mother's hushed voice fills the gap Mr Morrison has left. 'Is he in trouble?'

'I don't think so. I think we'd know if ...'

'There's been nothing in his letters. Just the usual things. The cold, the shortages, news of the boys ...'

'I think we just keep going. That's what I'm telling my committee. Unless we hear otherwise we assume the school is still operating and Rewi is in charge.'

A silence opens up. I can't do anything about my heart, which is acting as if a firecracker has been lit under it, but I can at last get my feet moving. As I carefully open the door to the kitchen I hear my mother say, 'Make no mistake, Rewi can be pig-headed. I know him too well. If what's he's doing is pitting himself against the government ...'

Mr Morrison makes a spluttering sound, the kind it's okay for adults to make but if children do it they're accused of being rude. 'Well, he is an Alley. What can you expect?'

*

So who are the Alleys? And why, as an adopted member of the family, am I so drawn to them? My father once told me I'd be glad when I grew up to know I didn't have Alley blood in my veins. He was, of course, thinking of my mother, whose mental breakdowns blighted my childhood and – in ways I've struggled to imagine – his marriage. He may also have been thinking of my grandfather, Henry Alley, a fierce Old Testament figure whose only love seems to have been for horses – he broke in the famous racehorse Phar Lap – and the unforgiving God he worshipped. I doubt he would have been thinking of Rewi's father. Frederich Alley, like his brother Henry, was a stern disciplinarian, but unlike Henry he was a rationalist, with a strong sense of justice and a keen political awareness. Henry published one small book in his lifetime – *The Education of the Horse*. Frederich, who earned his living as a teacher and part-time farmer, published several, in which he addressed the problems of land reform, social justice and education. Rewi, whose relationship with his father was anything but warm, clearly owed much to his father's ideas. As I, brought up by an unloving mother, owe much to her ideas. Both, to paraphrase Rewi, were 'socialists before their time'.

Frederich and Henry were in a direct line of descent from Captain John Alley, whose four sons emigrated to the New World in the mid-1850s, two to the United States – both fought in Lincoln's Army in the Civil war; a grandson went on to become a general in the US National Guard – two to New Zealand. If this were fiction I would want to say that Captain John, progenitor of the Alley diaspora, whose bones lie buried in the Lough Hill Vaults in Kings County, Ireland, was a staunch supporter of Irish independence. It would fit so neatly with Rewi's eventual rejection of imperialism. But the opposite is almost certainly true. Kings County, now known as Offaly County, was part of the notorious Tudor plantations set up during the reign of Elizabeth I to re-establish England's control over Ireland. The population introduced in the wake of that invasion would have been staunchly loyal to the Crown.

The name Alley suggests that the family were originally French, possibly, like my adoptive father's family, arriving in Britain as part of the Norman invasion. Seven centuries later France was no longer a conquering power but a country haunted by the guillotine and the blood-curdling cries of the mob. Captain John, an officer in the British Army, who had fought against the French following the revolution of 1789, would have regarded the rag-tag collection of Irish revolutionaries opposing British rule as little better than the French sans-culottes. And since we know he is buried in the Lough Hill Vaults, it follows that he was not impoverished. There may not have been enough land to support his family – why else would four of his sons have had to emigrate? – but there can be little doubt that this was a middle-class, Anglo-Irish, Protestant family. Indeed, Rewi's sister Gwen remembers their grandmother, a widow who never wore anything but black, and made her abhorrence of sex apparent at every opportunity, talking wistfully of titled relatives back 'home' in Ireland. My own mother told me with what sounded like pride that she was related to a bishop. (That my closet-communist mother should have thought this a matter of pride is not something I can explain.)

Again, if this were fiction, I would be tempted to characterise Rewi's great-grandfather as either a rebel – which he clearly was not – or a tenant farmer reduced to near starvation by the disastrous potato famines of the

mid-nineteenth century. The parallels, given Rewi's passionate commitment to the cause of the Chinese peasantry, would have made for a pleasing symmetry. But this is not fiction. Rewi's background was one of Anglo-Irish respectability, not suffering on a mythical scale.

What did come down through those three generations is something far more subtle than worldly fortune or inherited political views. It's something I saw in my tormented mother and recognised in others in the family. I see it still in my cousins. Independence is the obvious word, but that fails to convey the feistiness, the occasional bloody-mindedness that, in my mind, typifies the genus Alley. 'I don't care,' the child Rewi would say when he got into trouble, as he frequently did. 'Well, that's it, I don't care.'[1] A mantra that would serve him well through the years of war and revolution in China when trouble of a more serious nature came calling. Rewi's sister Kath once told me that it was all very well to keep a clean and tidy house, as my mother commanded, but if you didn't sweep the dirt under the carpet from time to time you weren't really living. It was one of several lessons in subversion (another name for bloody-mindedness) subtly conveyed to me by my Alley relatives.

I can't claim to have inherited Alley characteristics, though my mother routinely described me as 'cussed' and 'uppity', but I like to think that some at least of the Alley talent for overcoming obstacles and failing to follow orders has, along with their (more recent) left-leaning politics, rubbed off on me. They certainly rubbed off on Rewi. In the rebellious child raging at the injustices of his father's punitive regime lay the seeds of the revolutionary raging against the injustices of imperial China. The famous 'Alley temper' – I can still see Kath's infant son Bruce kicking the wall, screaming, 'I've got the Alley temper!' – would occasionally get Rewi into trouble, but more often it would do the opposite, overcoming whatever or whoever stood in his way. 'Rewi gets things done,' his friends in China boasted. I suspect they were being polite. What they were really saying was, 'When Alleys want you to do something, they just keep talking till you give in and do it': words I had heard before, and would hear again on our journey across China.

CHAPTER ONE

Auckland, 8 April 2017

I'M standing, as instructed, by the Cathay Pacific check-in sign, searching the faces of passers-by to see if any of them are my Alley cousins. Ten of us, 21 if you count spouses, partners and family friends, are headed for China to attend the celebrations marking 90 years since Rewi Alley's arrival in Shanghai. (Nine is a sacred number in Chinese lore, being one of two numbers – nine and five – associated with the majesty of the emperor. There hasn't been an emperor in China for over a century, but the significance attached to those numbers remains.)

I'm an hour early. A friend recently predicted that the day would come when my fear of missing planes – and trains and buses – would take off into the stratosphere, and I'd end up sleeping at the airport to be sure I didn't miss my flight! Even when, as today, the journey has been meticulously planned, not by me but by my redoubtable first cousin Jocelyn, anxiety hovers like a threatened headache. Have I packed the right clothes? Did I remember to bring a sleeping pill for the journey? My cellphone is where it's supposed to be in my handbag but where did I put the charger? Did I even pack it? (I needn't have worried. The Great Firewall of China will render my phone redundant.)

That this journey, three years in the planning, is happening at all is something of a miracle. 'When Alleys want you to do something they just keep talking till you give in and do it' probably had something to do with it. Jocelyn may not have had the same hurdles to surmount as our famous cousin, but she was dealing with a bunch of highly independent individuals with built-in resistance to doing what they're told! That she got us all into line with our fares paid and visas stamped is testament to her good-natured persistence. Whether we will come up to scratch over the next two and a half weeks is not so certain. We've been told to pack formal gear for a banquet in the Great Hall of the People and other official occasions. Some of us have agreed under pressure to give speeches. I suspect it's going to be a bumpy ride.

Still no sign of the familiar Alley face: the long nose (Rewi was called high nose, *gao bizi*, in China); the spiky red-gold hair; the intense gaze (many people remarked on Rewi's intense blue eyes). On my mother's side, the Alley side, I have 56 first cousins. The Alleys are famous, some might say notorious, for many things, including an enthusiasm for breeding. My grandfather sired 18 children, which I used to think was a world record till I discovered that Johann Sebastian Bach had 20. Four of my 56 cousins should be appearing any minute: Jocelyn and Zeke (Philip), children of Uncle Digger, my mother's youngest brother; and Carol and Christine, daughters of the next youngest, Uncle Bert. Digger's youngest son, Ross, a music lecturer and pianist who lives in England, will join us, along with his friends Peter and Irene, in Beijing. Also on the trip are four cousins less closely related to me: Maurice, son of Rewi's brother Pip (Philip), a professor at Massey University and active member of the New Zealand–China Friendship Society (NZCFS); Maurice's niece Sarah; Rachel, granddaughter of my mother's brother John; and Alison, who is related to Rewi on both sides of the family tree.

Together we will travel, by plane, bus and train, from one side of China to the other, a distance of 6000 kilometres. We will stay in Beijing, Shanghai, Xi'an, Fengxi'an, Lanzhou, Zhangye and Shandan. Multiple events are planned for every day. We will have almost no free time. My anxiety, usually associated with travelling on my own, has shape-shifted to a worry that I won't be up to the task that has been allotted to me. Most of my costs have been paid (see Acknowledgements) on the understanding that I will write a book. Not a travelogue, but a book about Rewi, the man to whom we are all, in our different ways, connected, in whose footsteps we are ostensibly walking. (In fact we will be following a circuitous route of our own, ending in Shanghai where Rewi started, doubling back on our tracks to meet the requirements of a complex schedule.) For the last six months I have been reading everything I can lay my hands on by and about him. I have put myself through a crash course in Chinese history. Not enough, the voice in my head accuses. You will never know enough …

Someone is waving. Zeke and his wife Judy. Hurrah! Two hours and some panicked moments later – Carol and Christine couldn't be found: they'd disobeyed instructions and checked in early – we are all assembled in the departure lounge. Jocelyn does a head count. With the addition of Maurice's wife Dorothy, Rachel's husband Stewart, Carol's husband Laurie, Alison's partner David, and friends Maurice Beeby, Betty Gray and Helen Foster, the number is 21. This ritual of counting will be repeated every day from now on. On two occasions people will go missing – not for long, but long enough to conjure up images of police searches and diplomatic embarrassment.

We're a motley lot. Clutching bags and bottles of water, we rummage for our boarding passes and talk, in the way of people who don't know one another very well, about things common to travellers – past experiences, the best ways to get to sleep in economy class, the prospect of catching up on a film or two. Ahead of us is a 12-hour flight to Hong Kong, a two-hour stopover, then a four-hour flight to Beijing. As it turns out, 18 hours of travel stretches to 22 and we reach Beijing four hours behind schedule. We have five hours to shower and rest before kick-starting our itinerary at noon Beijing time.

On the other side of the world the Chinese president, Xi Jinping, has just arrived at Palm Beach to meet with the American president, Donald Trump, in his opulent summer residence, Mar-a-Lago in Florida. The *New York Times* is describing it as 'a vital meeting for the two nations, the Asia and Pacific region, and the globe as a whole'. The focus of these high-level talks was to have been trade, but the situation has changed. Top of the agenda now is North Korea.

CHAPTER TWO

REWI was born in the small Canterbury settlement of Springfield on 2 December 1897. There were two older siblings, Eric and Gwen. Four more would follow: Geoff, Pip, Kath and Joy. 'Mother never wanted to have so many children,' the adult Rewi writes in his memoir, 'but Dad was the wife-possessive kind, old style, that allowed the woman no say.' No say about conjugal rights, perhaps, but Clara Alley (née Buckingham) was no victim. She was a passionate suffragist, one of the first to sign the petition to parliament which led, in 1893, to the passing of a Bill giving adult women the right to vote. That New Zealand was the first country in the world to introduce female suffrage was due in large part to a regular visitor to the Alley family home – Kate Sheppard, leader of the suffrage movement. (One report I read claimed that Clara was the movement's secretary, but I've not been able to verify this.)

'The wife-possessive kind'. Running beneath that characterisation of his father is something Rewi never openly expressed but several times implied – criticism of the man who, according to Rewi's younger brother Pip, was capable of hating his own children. Pip never lost the conviction that his father, having dismissed him as a disappointing specimen, not tall enough, not obedient enough, insufficiently malleable, hated him. 'I Was Fortunate in My Parents' is the title Rewi gave to the first chapter of his memoir. Fortunate in his mother, yes – he described her in a poem as 'more than food, more than all else'[1] – but in his father Frederich, whose legacy shaped so much of his life? I'm not so sure.

'Dad was a good bloke according to his lights,' the adult Rewi wrote in a letter to his sister Gwen, qualifying that ambiguous statement with, 'I guess the stock was a bit in-bred, easy to fly into rages'.[2] It's the nearest he gets to open criticism of the man who regularly thrashed his sons, sometimes twice for the same offence, once as headmaster of the school they attended, and again, after school was out, as a father. 'But if one hollered a bit [the thrashings] were always a bit lighter,' Rewi joked, turning what could have been a source of bitterness into a story told to raise a laugh.[3] As adept at escaping punishment by making himself scarce as he was at lining his trousers with rabbit skins to soften the blows, he also made light of being locked in the tool shed – another regular punishment. Time away from the list of chores and exercises devised by his disciplinarian father, even if it had to be spent locked in an outhouse, was time gained for the imagination.

Not that Fred Alley had everything his own way. When, on one occasion, he lifted his hand to Gwen, his usually placid wife leapt to her child's defence. 'If you ever touch her again I'll leave you,' she said in a voice that left no room for doubt.[4] Likewise 10-year-old Rewi, the designated 'scamp' of the family, catching his father about to thrash Pip, threatened to cut his throat if he went ahead. There must have been something fierce not just in Rewi's words but in his demeanour, because Fred stopped what he was doing. Though he didn't stop the insults. Rewi would always be the 'no-hoper', the 'Norfolk dumbbell'.

A few years later the boys would combine to attack their father, just as my uncles combined to attack *their* father, Henry. 'Look what my sons have done to me!' Fred yelled at Clara as he walked into the house, blood streaming from his nose.[5] No one knows what Clara, accustomed to making excuses for her husband, said or did. But Fred never thrashed the boys again. (In the case of my grandfather his sons threw him off his horse and told him never to darken their mother's doorstep again. He never did.)

So what, apart from the regular beatings, was Rewi's childhood like? Can we see the man in the boy? A case could be made for seeing Rewi, the middle child, as the outsider. Since more attention is often paid to the older and younger members of the family, a middle child is frequently left to his own devices. He, or she, becomes adept at creating an alternative universe into which he can conjure up the family he wishes he had. Though Rewi in many ways fits this profile – he was a rebellious school pupil and an errant family member, skilled at hiding in trees or in the riverside cave he and his older siblings had erected – everything he has written about his childhood makes it clear he never felt neglected by his mother, nor did he ever want to run away from her. 'A few words from her would do wonders,' he says in his memoir. 'How often as a boy she has taken me by the hand and drawn me over to show me the tracery of twigs against the winter sky, the beauty of a rosebud, or the glory of apple blossoms.'

But Rewi did run away, many times. As a runaway child myself, I can understand the complex emotions that jolted him into these dangerous acts of defiance. If found in one of his many hiding places by one of his siblings he would explain that he wasn't running away at all, he was 'just finkin'.[6] So long as Fred didn't get wind of it, nothing more would be said.

Did Clara sense in her rebellious son a love of beauty that would find expression years later in his enthusiasm for the art of China's past? Did she know when she encouraged him to cut out pictures of the old masters from the magazines, *Windsor* and *Graphic*, that she was nurturing a passion that would last a lifetime?

When the New Zealand politician Warren Freer travelled to China in 1955 – only the second Western politician, post-Liberation, to do so (the first was British Prime Minister Clement Attlee) – he visited Rewi at the Peking Hotel where he was then living. 'I was amazed to find that it resembled a museum more than living quarters,' Freer wrote. 'It was simply crammed with artefacts of every possible type.'[7] Rewi the lover of beautiful things, who as a boy described a new silk blouse his mother was wearing as 'the most wonderful and beautiful garment ever', is not the Rewi of the public record.[8] But just as he learned, under Clara's indulgent eye, to appreciate the beauty of apple blossom, distinguish a Raphael from a Rubens, a Titian from a Tintoretto, so he would learn, as a settler in China, to identify a jade seal from the Han dynasty, a pottery horse from the Tang, a bronze warrior from the Ming …

I am drawn to this Rewi. I see him holding a jade thumb protector from the Qin dynasty, picked up, more than likely, from the ruins of a Buddhist temple, or from beneath the walls of one of the many abandoned imperial palaces, and dreaming his way back into the past. One of the things he collected was a porcelain baby-shaped pillow from the Ming period. What dreams did that poignant object release? Ancient maps of China, thousand-hand Buddhas, a bronze dragon from the Warring States period, neolithic stone axes, Qing dynasty snuff bottles, scroll paintings, a bronze Tang dynasty dancer discovered in the dust of Shandan – Rewi's appetite for the past seems to have been as boundless as his belief in the future. 'One could look at it for hours,' he wrote of a Buddhist reliquary carved on a portion of elephant tusk.[9]

'I am very glad I never grew up,' Rewi confided to his first biographer, Willis Airey. What he meant was that the boy who was moved by the beauty of trees and sky, who could be absorbed for hours looking at paintings, who noticed when his mother wore a new silk blouse, was part of the man. As was the teenager who skipped school so he could sneak into the city museum to gaze at its wonders.

This is the man I want to get to know: a man who saw the past in the present and the old in the new. A man who would become an art ambassador for China, following the lead of his friend Zhou Enlai, who championed people's diplomacy over militarism. What motivated Rewi – apart from the pleasure he got from temporary ownership – was not a collector's pride in his collection, but a passionate belief in the power of art to bring people closer together. The champion of the co-operative movement, the 'can-do' fixer of everything from flood-damaged dykes to broken-down trucks, the writer of sometimes tedious books and poems about the New China, is there for all to see. But the man who loved beauty, a man of his time who may well have felt that such love was indulgent so not to be paraded, remains in the shadows. I think of my father, who spent hours contemplating the wonder of the begonias in his glasshouse but never talked about his feelings, and I feel how alike, despite the labels and the politics, the two men, heroes of my childhood, were.

> Old women with headdresses
> like those of ancient England,
> faces filled with strength
> and wisdom, so that one thought of one's own mother:
>
> children gay as the wild-flowers
> of the grasslands under
> a summer's sun: great herds
> of horses, cattle, sheep
> growing among the richness:
>
> and the strumming of a guitar
> in the felt tent at night,
> voices raised in song – lad then lass
> replying, song that lifted
> out into the night, and lost itself
> among the snowcaps glittering
> above the dark firs
> in the moonlight.[10]

*

Springfield today is the site of a magnificent statue commemorating Rewi's birth, by the Chinese/New Zealand sculptress Lu Bo (wife of Rewi's foster son Deng Bangzhen). But Springfield was Rewi's home for only a month.

Early in 1898 the family moved to Amberley in North Canterbury, where Fred took up the post of headmaster of the district high school.

Growing up in a small community in which his father was a leading figure, Rewi's innate resistance to authority was bound to get him into trouble sooner or later. Tasked with finding the runaway Rewi, his older siblings would discover him hiding in the walnut tree behind the chook-house, or sitting on the cowshed roof, or chatting to a tramp who'd taken shelter in the riverside cave. Despite being frequently thrashed for these disappearances Rewi did nothing to change his behaviour. It was enough for him that he sometimes got away with it. 'I don't care I don't care,' he would shout, falling back on his mantra. 'It's not a good slogan,' he admitted years later in his memoir. 'But it certainly helped me in various tough spots of my life to simply say, "Well that's it, I don't care."'

'You can't be cross with him – it's just a waste of time,' the home help, Edna Pengelly, whom the children called Pen, is recorded as saying, making excuses for the little boy whose red-gold curls and vivid blue eyes gave him an air of innocence that could not be said to fit the facts. 'He's a scallywag all right, but he's got a good heart,' she asserted in his defence when he was caught poking holes in the water tank for no other reason than the joy of watching the water spurt out.[11]

Was this ability to win people over to his side the key to Rewi's later success in garnering support and raising money in the most unlikely places? Did the blue eyes charm people into giving him the help he needed to launch his scheme to save China's industry and help win the war? Or was it his way of speaking – whether in English or Chinese – that drew people to him? His father, an elocution enthusiast, had instilled in his children the necessity of speaking not just clearly and concisely, but melodiously. Having spent many hours listening to recordings of Rewi, and as someone quick to fall under the spell of 'melodiousness', I can attest to the appeal of his speaking voice. He could sound angry. He could sound opinionated. He could (and often did) sound amused. He could even sound upper-class – viz his constant use of 'one' as a personal pronoun – but that was a reflection of his upbringing, not his outlook on life. But more than anything else, he sounded warm, as if he wanted to be your friend.

The dictionary defines charisma as 'compelling attractiveness or charm that can inspire devotion in others'. That Rewi possessed this quality – inherited from his father, whose Irish red hair, blue eyes and powerful voice commanded attention if not devotion – has been widely acknowledged, even if some believe he put it to dubious use. A man with 'the build of a football hooker and the soul of a poet', New Zealander James Bertram, the first European to interview Mao Zedong, wrote in recommending Rewi for an honorary doctorate in 1972.[12] To Edgar Snow, the first Western journalist to interview Mao Zedong, Rewi was a 'blitzbuilder', a man of 'sainted patience' – an unusual compliment for an Alley![13] Rewi 'never lets insult or affront interfere with the vision of a distant horizon which some people claim they see in his sky-blue eyes,' he asserted in a collection of tributes published for Rewi's seventy-fifth birthday.[14] Rewi's biographer Geoff Chapple, who spent many weeks travelling with him in the summer of 1979 and formed a close bond with him, considered Rewi to be a man who had 'thrown himself totally into the balance on the side of the good'. His most outstanding characteristic, in Chapple's opinion, was his ability to 'make you feel you were the person he most wanted to talk to'.[15] Having corresponded with my cousin over many years I can attest to this quality, evidenced in his interest in me as a writer and his impatience with me as a political thinker. To my great disappointment only one of his many letters to me has survived my peripatetic life.

Amberley's population at the turn of the century was solidly European – the Alley children never saw a Māori – with blurred but still visible distinctions between the working and middle classes. Despite its small population it boasted a shop, two pubs, a church, a bank, a police station, a courthouse, an Oddfellows Hall and, of course, the school, ruled with an iron fist but an open mind by headmaster Frederich Alley. The two largest houses in the settlement were the schoolhouse, where the Alleys lived, and the adjacent vicarage, but you only had to shift your gaze a little for those buildings to become mere dots on the landscape, dwarfed by the magnificent Southern Alps. Prone to earthquakes, Amberley would play an unwitting part in Rewi's decision decades later to establish his school in earthquake-prone Shandan.

Fred, who attended church regularly – though he stopped going in later life – would not allow his children to attend Sunday school because he wanted them to think for themselves. In the same perverse spirit he wouldn't allow the village children to come to the house to play, not because he considered them inferior but because he didn't want his children's minds 'contaminated'. What he meant by this, his daughter Gwen believed, was that he didn't want them contaminated by talk of sex. 'Never touch your tiddler unless you have to,' Rewi's fiercely puritan Alley grandmother instructed her impressionable grandson. 'Never think about it. Always keep it covered.'[16]

But not even Fred could police his children 24 hours a day. On Saturdays, when Fred routinely visited his mother 80 kilometres away in Christchurch, Rewi and his siblings would, under the benignly watchful eye of their mother, let rip, stripping off in summer to swim in the river, testing each other's mettle in a game they called Stoics, designed to see how much torture each of them could endure. If older brother Eric told Rewi to 'scat', as he frequently did, he would wander off on his own, collecting broken glass, rusty nails and old bottles to add to his growing collection, evidence of his fascination, even as a child, with the buried evidence of the past.

At the end of the day Fred would reappear, exhausted from the long ride back from the city, to find his children sitting quietly, studying the day's text. 'The world is my country, to do good is my religion.' 'The drunkard and the glutton shall come to poverty and drowsiness shall clothe a man in rags.' Rewi seems to have taken the first lesson to heart but not the second. When he was discovered, at secondary school, trying to dispose of a stash of empty beer bottles, the punishment from his teetotal father was swift and brutal. Not even Clara, a committed member of the Women's Temperance Union, could excuse her son for that particular crime.

Every morning before breakfast, regardless of the weather, the children would be pushed out the door to run around the block. Rewi became adept at running only part of the way, peeling off to think his own thoughts or, given his appetite for the forbidden, to smoke a cigarette. Later, after school, there would be exercises involving dumbbells and chest expanders. Fred's disappointment in both Rewi and Pip, neither of whom grew to the six feet he expected of his sons, was compounded by Rewi's failure to achieve academic distinction. 'All you'll be suited for in life, Alley, is to break stones,' his maths teacher at Christchurch Boys' High School predicted, an opinion endorsed by Fred, who was convinced his middle son, the 'Norfolk dumbbell', would 'never amount to anything'.[17]

No wonder Rewi referred to himself throughout his life as a 'country bumpkin' and 'an ordinary New Zealand plug'.[18] The successful son was Geoff, six foot three inches tall, holder of a first-class arts degree, founder of the Country Library Service, and an All Black – more than enough to delight his father and win the approval of his fellow Kiwis. To Rewi's great disappointment Geoff – whom he once described as 'so good a man and so big a one' – never visited him in China.[19] 'We've achieved things in New Zealand too,' Geoff would remind people every time his older brother's successes in China were held up for admiration.[20] Sibling rivalry is to be expected in a family where expectations are high, but as with so many things, the Amberley Alleys carried it to excess. 'Pip has quarrelled with Geoff.' 'Gwen has quarrelled with Cath.' 'Joy has quarrelled with Gwen.' 'Geoff has quarrelled with Rewi.' I would overhear these whispered confidences – I was an enthusiastic eavesdropper – in my far more sedate household, where quarrelling was confined to the paddocks, far from adult ears. How exciting, I would think. Wish they were my family … (Rewi hated these family quarrels. 'Next time I come I do not want to run into family rows,' he wrote to Pip from China. 'I cannot stand scenes, rows, bickering …'[21])

Despite Fred's Irish blood, the Alleys of Amberley were in many ways solidly 'English'. Clara, whose homesickness for her native Norfolk was a constant theme in her conversation, made sure that the idea of Home was kept alive in the minds of her children. When Fred's sister Amy came back from a trip to the north with tales of the 'wonderful big dark [Māori] men' she'd gone riding with, Clara advised her children to take what she said with a grain of salt.[22] Clara disapproved of Amy. Her free and easy manner marked her, in Clara's opinion, as a 'colonial'. Yet it was the unmarried Amy (Fred maintained she was 'too good' for any man) whom Fred tasked with finding a name for their third child. What Clara thought when her sister-in-law announced the baby was to be called Rewi, after the famous Māori chief Rewi Maniapoto, leader of the Kīngitanga rebellion against the British, is not recorded. But Amy was never asked to name another child.

The children born after Rewi, like the two born before, have names that could have come straight from English novels of the period. What could be more English than Gwendolen? Rewi stands out. Perhaps that was what his Aunt Amy intended. Naming the new golden-haired baby after the legendary defender of Ōākura Pā was nothing if not provocative. No one has ever suggested Amy saw in the child Rewi the legend he would become, but Rewi – called 'Doody' because of his habit of doodling – wore his name with pride for the rest of his life. 'New Zealander with a Maori name it is a privilege to bear,' he wrote.[23] When, in China, it became politic for Europeans living there to adopt Chinese names, Rewi chose not to. 'Luyi Aili' he was and 'Luyi Aili' he would remain.

CHAPTER THREE

IN 1906 the Alleys moved to Christchurch where Fred had been appointed headmaster of Wharenui School in Riccarton. Rewi, nine years old, his skill as a rebel by now finely honed, announced that he would not go unless there was a river. I had always assumed the watery playground Rewi was leaving behind was one of Canterbury's braided rivers whose shallow, fast-running water and patchworks of small bush-studded islands make them magical places for children. Not so. Visiting Amberley in 2017 for Rewi's one hundred and twentieth birthday commemoration I saw his 'river' for the first time. Not much more than a metre across, dribbling its sluggish way through bush and trees, the only word to describe it is 'creek'. But to nine-year-old Rewi it was a place of wonder. History doesn't record how he was persuaded to accept the inevitable and move with his family but I imagine another thrashing was involved.

Reading about these years in Rewi's memoir I'm struck by the way he dismisses setbacks and suffering – not just the thrashings, but the loneliness of the little boy banished to the tool shed or hiding in the walnut tree – as part of normal growing up. One of Fred's more wide-sweeping rules was that his sons had to work during their holidays on the farm he'd acquired in Southland. When a teenage Pip refused this order he was thrown out of the house. Nothing so drastic happened to Rewi, who reluctantly obeyed his father, but he does record, in passing, that he was bullied by the farm manager, Charlie.

It's typical of Rewi, an optimist by nature, to skip over this part of his story. He assures us he was happy at Christchurch Boys' High, despite being seen by most of his teachers as a washout. (His science teacher called him a 'delinquent'.) Perhaps his real life was being lived when he was 'doodling' or 'just finkin'. An avid reader, he devoured everything he could lay his hands on, from the penny-dreadfuls *Dick Turpin* and *Buffalo Bill* to Alexandre Dumas' *The Three Musketeers*, Jules Verne's *Twenty Thousand Leagues Under the Sea*, Macaulay's *History of England*, Walter Scott's *Ivanhoe*, and the *Complete Works of Shakespeare*. He learned Coleridge's 'Kubla Khan' by heart, using it as his poem of choice whenever he had to write lines as punishment, a frequent occurrence given his liking for cigarettes and beer, and his habit of roasting chestnuts over the school's Bunsen burners.

Thirty years later, when it came to the setting up of Gung Ho, Rewi would remember *The Three Musketeers* and find in it the motto for his nascent co-operative movement – 'One For All and All For One', the oath taken by the musketeers. Soon those words, written in Chinese characters, would appear wherever Gung Ho offices were established. And Rewi, travelling back and forth across the desert lands of Gansu province and Inner Mongolia, would find himself repeating the verses he'd written out as punishment, seeing in the world around him the fabled country conjured up by Coleridge.

> In Xanadu did Kubla Khan
> A stately pleasure dome decree,
> Where Alph, the sacred river, ran
> Through caverns measureless to man
> Down to a sunless sea ...

*

In 1914 the security of both the real world of school, home, siblings and schoolmates, and the imaginary world in which 16-year-old Rewi spent so much of his time, came to an abrupt end. On 4 August Germany, in defiance of the treaties that had kept Europe free from war for almost a century, invaded Belgium. Great Britain, as guarantor of Belgium's neutrality, immediately declared war. The Dominion of New Zealand, steadfastly loyal to the Mother Country, was quick to follow suit. Within days Eric Alley, who'd given up university to work on the family farm, had volunteered for the army. No one, apparently, tried to stop him.

Early in 1915 Eric, who had joined the 2nd Battalion of the Otago Mounted Rifles, sailed with his horse Percy to Egypt. Wounded at Gallipoli, he found himself, in one of those coincidences beloved of novelists, in a hospital near London being nursed by his former 'nanny' Edna Pengelly. For the rest of her life Pen would regret not recommending that the seriously wounded Eric be repatriated back to New Zealand. He went on to fight in France, dying of wounds received during the battle for Armentières.

A relative of Clara's recently told me a story about Rewi and Eric that I'd not heard before. Dorothy Waymouth, whose mother, like Clara, was a Buckingham, related how at the end of the war Rewi went to find his brother's grave in Armentières. Discovering the cross that had been made for him – as for every Kiwi soldier killed in France – lying in the grass, he picked it up and brought it back to New Zealand, where he lodged it in the church at Lumsden, near the Alley farm in Southland.

Rewi doesn't record the effect the news of his older brother's death had on him. As with so much else, his feelings have to be deduced from his actions. What we do know is that from this time on he was determined to follow in Eric's footsteps. Others had lied about their age. He could too. But he would have to wait. He was still only 16.

*

The Christchurch home to which Fred and Clara retired was called Westcote. Visiting it as a child I thought I'd been transported to an enchanted kingdom. It was, to quote from a letter of Rewi's, an 'adorable' place – a hundred-year-old house, with the wide, creeper-covered veranda typical of colonial homesteads, surrounded by orchards and paddocks in which the grass came up to my chin. The house itself was honeycombed with rooms that seemed, to my six-year-old eyes, to hold mysteries greater than the stars. There was even a room with a concealed entrance, a perfect place to hide. This windowless room became my secret place, a refuge from adult scrutiny – though I'm sure, looking back, my great aunt knew perfectly well where I went when I disappeared from view. (Years later, on being shown, in one of England's country houses, the priest hole where Catholics were hidden from Elizabeth I's Protestant policemen, I was instantly transported back to that secret room in Westcote, Rewi's last New Zealand home.)

So haphazard was the house's design, or rather lack of it, the children complained that the house made them feel 'woozy'. Perhaps what they were trying to say was that they, like me, had fallen under its spell. To be in the kitchen with Great Aunt Clara, breathing in the scent of baking bread, listening to her soft Norfolk voice as she answered my endless stream of questions, was to glimpse a world where people and places seemed to belong to one another. Clara was white-haired by this time, but even at the age of six I could see she was beautiful. I never knew Uncle Fred – he'd died some years earlier – nor do I remember, during that first childhood visit to Westcote, talk of Rewi, who had by this time been living in China for nearly 20 years. But I remember the bust of him sitting in pride of place on the sideboard, and I can still see the beautiful painted scroll hanging on the wall, a gift (I would learn much later) from Madame Sun Yatsen, widow of the founder of the first republic of China, to the mother of her dear friend Rewi Alley.

I need to qualify that phrase 'I remember'. Until recently I believed Rewi had stayed with my family when I was a schoolgirl. I would often tell the story of the house being besieged by journalists wanting to speak to him, and my mother having to hold him back because he'd been allowed into the country only on condition he stayed away from the press. The Cold War was heating up. Rewi was an avowed communist. Who knows what retribution would fall on him if he broke the terms of his agreement? So my mother, a match for Rewi in so many ways, bustled him into the large oak wardrobe in her bedroom and turned the key.

It's a wonderful story, but I was not part of it. When I first began to research Rewi's life for my Radio New Zealand play *Broken China*, I discovered he made only six trips back to New Zealand – in 1932, 1937, 1960, 1964–65, 1971–72 and, briefly, in 1973. In 1954 he was living in Beijing – he was certainly not locked in my mother's wardrobe! I can only assume this story was seeded by something my mother told me – an incident from Rewi's 1937 visit perhaps – and in my enthusiasm for information about this mysterious 'uncle', I'd absorbed the details and made them my own.

There is, however, another possibility. In September 2018 I attended a lecture in Dunedin given by Dr Richard Bullen of the Canterbury Museum. The subject was Rewi's art collection, gifted over many years to the museum he loved to visit as a teenager. To my astonishment there was mention of a 'secret' visit Rewi made to New Zealand in 1954. I was cock-a-hoop. So my memory was true after all! Only it wasn't. Consultation with the family quickly quashed my claim to have been a reliable witness to the wardrobe incident. The Alley family was – is – close. Its networks extend across the country, and indeed the world. There's no way Rewi could have travelled to New Zealand, even under the radar, without leaving a trace. My head accepts the truth of this. My heart, knowing how close Rewi and my mother were, wants that childhood memory to be true.

When Clara died in 1952 she was buried, at her request, not with her husband but with her beloved father, Tom Buckingham. It was one of the times when Rewi felt most keenly his exile from family and home. The woman who loved 'ducks, bees, roses, cats, tramps and all kids', who donated her pension to keep Rewi's school open when funds dried up, left behind a gap no one else could fill. 'She was a part of me,' Rewi wrote in his memoir. 'I would have told her anything she asked.'

CHAPTER FOUR

Beijing, 9 April 2017

WE are in Beijing, the 'northern capital' of China: 北 (*bei*) meaning northern and 京 (*jing*) meaning capital. I'm standing by the open window of my hotel, bleary from lack of sleep, looking down on the city where Rewi spent the last three and a half decades of his life, a city shaped and re-shaped by history, ringed by crescent hills (not that I can see them from my window), protected in the late Qing period by a castellated wall with four imposing gatehouses rising from its ramparts. A city of emperors. A city of rebels. A city that knows how it feels to be abandoned to its fate. Beijing was always Peking to Rewi. A fluent Mandarin speaker (albeit with a strong Shanghai accent), he never adjusted to the 'modern' Pinyin system of spelling and pronunciation, preferring the system that was operating when he arrived in China in 1927.

'After a while all big cities seem the same,' a friend once said to me. I must remember to ask him if he ever came to Beijing! An alien, high-pitched music reaches me through the open window. I can distinguish the tooting of car horns – I'd been expecting bicycles, not bumper-to-bumper vehicles – but that broken syncopation is the only sound that's familiar. The air, to my sleep-deprived eyes, seems alive. From my eighteenth-storey room I feel as if I'm watching the spinning of a giant washing machine far below me. Shapes are tossed into view, only to vanish a second later. Now I look more closely there are bicycles, lots of them, many of them battery powered, but they are confined to the wide cycle-lane bordering the expressway. As for the smell, that too is unique. It's like a complex chord in music, composed of numerous 'notes' – petrol, cooking, plants, trees, dogs, fish, sewage, rubbish, the press of human bodies …

We are to meet in the foyer of the hotel at noon. A Sichuan lunch has been planned. I should be getting dressed, but I'm mesmerised by the scene outside my window, a scene I could, if I'd made different decisions, have been part of, for a time at least. I was a student at the University of Otago in 1960 when Rewi wrote inviting me to do a postgraduate degree at Peking University. He made it sound easy, but I wasn't having a bar of it. The Cold War was raging, but that wasn't the reason I wrote back saying no. I was engaged to be married. There was no room for China in my dream of the future. 'No one will stop you expressing your views here,' Rewi wrote in answer to my pious concerns about free speech – my feeble excuse for rejecting his invitation. 'You just won't be able to practise what you preach. When I come to New Zealand I can say what I like – though maybe not to the press, given their spineless adherence to the American view of things – but I have to live according to your system of government. It would be the same for you if you came to China.' (My memory may be faulty but I'm sure about that phrase 'spineless adherence to the American view'!)

I didn't want to disbelieve my cousin, but there were competing voices in my head and they spoke louder. In 1956 two people I was close to – Tom, a Presbyterian minister, a cousin on my father's side of the family, and Angus Ross, who would, three years later, be teaching me history at university – had travelled to China, along with nine others, including old China hand James Bertram (the only one of the group who, as a person of interest to the SIS, had trouble getting a visa). They were part of a New Zealand cultural group, invited by the Chinese People's Committee for Cultural Relations with Foreign Countries. The invitation, the first of its kind post-Liberation, had been made at Rewi's prompting. The civil war was over. Rewi's passion now was to further the cause, led by the USSR and China, of international peace, in the course of which he hoped to bring New Zealand and China, the two countries he called home, closer together.

I don't recall specific conversations about what Tom and Angus learned on their 20-day journey through China, but I remember head-shaking and concerned looks whenever Rewi's name was mentioned. My beloved father had died two years earlier. As a consequence of my mother's mental ill-health I was living at home only intermittently. One of the homes I would live in was Angus Ross's. Was that where I heard the words that lodged in my brain? Or was it at the manse in Hillsborough when visiting my cousin Tom? 'Rewi has been brainwashed.' 'He has a gun to his head. If he speaks out he'll be shot.' 'Chinese Christians are persecuted.' 'The Communist Party is a dictatorship. It will never permit opposition …'

Recently I have been able to read Tom's journal written during his time in China. He doesn't mention brainwashing but he does talk about the Chinese insistence on 'correct thinking'. Mistakes will always be made, the Chinese tell Tom, but once 'correct thinking' has been achieved mistakes will be kept to a minimum.

Tom's journal records several meetings with Rewi, whom he describes as 'portly' and looking 'none too well'. I can't help wondering if what Tom was seeing was depression. The visit of the New Zealand cultural group took place four years after Rewi had been relieved of his post as headmaster of the Gung Ho movement's training school in Shandan. The life he was living in Beijing in 1956 was a pale shadow of the one he'd lived in China's remote northwest. When I read Tom's words describing how Rewi, after each meeting with the New Zealand group, insisted on walking them back to their hotel, the figure I see in my imagination is not a portly man in his sixtieth year but Doody, the lonely boy, camouflaged in the walnut tree.

What is clear from Tom's journal is Rewi's eagerness to see as much of his visitors as possible. In one memorable meeting, attended by Premier Zhou Enlai, Tom records James Bertram asking Zhou if he would send Rewi to New Zealand. Zhou, whose humanity and warmth charmed even his critics, smiled. 'Oh we won't send him,' he answered. 'He's free to go.' (But Rewi, worried, Tom assumes, about his reception in his homeland and the very real possibility that his passport would be revoked, doesn't go.) At that same meeting there is talk of New Zealand's refusal to recognise the People's Republic – a recognition Rewi has been fighting for behind the scenes. India and Ceylon have both established embassies. When, Zhou asks, is New Zealand going to follow suit? The embarrassed Kiwis rush to explain. The present government is right wing. If Labour wins the next election maybe … 'China can wait,' Zhou responds, smiling again.[1]

Rewi's deep, warmly reciprocated affection for the Paris-educated Zhou Enlai was rooted in a shared humanitarianism and love of art. So many people who came into contact with China's deputy leader remarked on his humanity and his humility. Ronald Hall, the Anglican Bishop of Hong Kong and one of the few missionaries Rewi respected, made no secret of the fact that he believed any government with Zhou Enlai in it had to be a good government.

A fluent English speaker, Zhou first met Rewi in 1937. Like Rewi he opposed imperialism not out of personal anger – though anger, particularly where cruelty to children was concerned, was never far away with Rewi – but of 'historical necessity'. 'The backbone of the Party is not the Comintern – the international organisation working to achieve world communism – but the Chinese people,' novelist Han Suyin quotes Zhou as saying.[2] Describing him as a shy man with a natural wit, 'slim, thin-faced, and very handsome', she goes on to record that he was also a brilliant strategic thinker, a quality that helped save the Red Army from annihilation during the Long March.[3] His exploits in the civil war as a commander – there were no ranked officers in the Red Army, just commanders and men in the field – left no one in doubt about his courage, his tactical skill and his resolution.

On one occasion in 1970 – high point of the Cultural Revolution – at an event in the sports stadium in Beijing, Zhou left his seat in the praesidium and came down to the lower benches where Rewi was sitting by himself. To the astonishment of the 400,000-strong crowd, the Chinese Premier remained with Rewi for the rest of the afternoon. 'That's the kind of thing he would do,' Rewi wrote in his memoir, a statement – given the role Zhou played in protecting him – charged with the electricity of the unsaid. Had Rewi ever given vent to his emotions, as he gave vent so exhaustively to his enthusiasm for the New China, what words of love and gratitude and connection might we have had to bring us closer to the inner man? But that was not Rewi's way. Unable to believe that his emotions would be of any interest to anyone, he kept them hidden in the cave he had built to house his heart.

When Zhou died in January 1976, Rewi's grief, shared by China's millions, spilled out in verse. Zhou, known throughout China as 'the well beloved' – a reference the Reverend Tom would have easily identified, suggesting as it does the deep bond that existed between Jesus and the 'beloved disciple' John – was quite simply irreplaceable, both as a friend and as the human face of the revolution.

Hills over which he marched
bend their heads in grief; rivers
he crossed cry as they flow;
peoples of hill and grassland,
on commune grain fields, in city
factories, fishermen at sea, oil
workers at their rigs and miners
underground, feel tears start
to their eyes … He who
was loved by the many has gone on …[4]

*

'Rewi is employed as a writer by the Chinese to describe some of their achievements,' Tom writes in his journal. 'A job he does very well.' Having read my way through Rewi's written work, some of which can only be described as state propaganda, I was shocked to learn that in Beijing in the 1950s he was paid a salary by the government. I had imagined him dependent on some kind of state pension, a reward for his wartime service and the nationwide success of his co-operatives. Discovering that he was, in effect, a government employee, tasked with selling the New China to the world, threw me off balance. When I tried to put myself in his position, a chilling sense of hopelessness crept over me. No wonder there's so little trace of the inner man in his work. How could he write freely with the Communist Party breathing down his neck?

'Rewi Alley is undoubtedly one of New Zealand's most famous sons,' James Bertram wrote in that 1972 Victoria University citation. When he first broached the subject of an honorary degree with Rewi the answer was a resounding 'no'. It took several letters from Bertram before Rewi reluctantly agreed.[5] Bertram had wanted Rewi to be honoured for his humanitarian work, but Rewi preferred to be recognised for his literary achievements. The ironies behind this are heartbreaking. A man whose very existence depended, at least during the Cultural Revolution, on writing to order, would rather New Zealanders forgot him altogether if they couldn't remember him as a literary man.

So was Rewi 'brainwashed'? I ask myself as the streets below my window begin to blur, and what I see is my young self, wearing a 'Mao suit' (first worn by Father of the Republic, Sun Yatsen, and his followers) and headscarf, hurrying along the pavement to meet my cousin. Like most people of my generation I would have said, until recently, that I knew what the word brainwashing signified – a Machiavellian practice performed by the 'other side' in the Cold War. That may well be true, but the 'other side' didn't coin the word: that was the CIA's doing. Needing an explanation as to why so many American prisoners cracked under interrogation during the Korean War, they came up with the notion that the communists had devised a technique that not even American heroes could withstand. Brainwashing, they declared, was the work of an evil regime hell-bent on converting its enemies to their 'correct thinking'.

By 1960, the year I received Rewi's first invitation to visit, the word was lodged in my consciousness. Brainwashing, communism, Red China – fear clung to those words like sweat to skin. No wonder my instincts screamed No! Say no!

Do I regret that decision? Since the trip I am currently describing has turned my thinking about China on its head, perhaps I do, or at least should.

Studying in Beijing, living close to 'Uncle Rewi', would have made me a different person. But then, three years after that invitation, I found myself at the American embassy in London applying for a visa to travel to America, and was given a taste of what might have happened to me had I said yes. My visa was refused on the grounds of my close relationship with 'the communist Rewi Alley'. Did the Americans know of our correspondence over the years? Surely my visa would not have been turned down because of a bunch of family letters? Eventually, after several attempts, the Americans relented. I could travel to the States on condition I signed a document undertaking to refrain from any political activity while on American soil. I duly signed. Then I told the young crew-cut official behind the desk that he had just politicised me. The days of happily following my husband's lead in matters political were over.

*

It's hot in the hotel room. My enquiry as to how to turn off the heaters is met with the statement that they will all go off on the first of May. Until then the temperature – it's hovering around 32°C – is fixed. 'If Madame wants cool she must open window.' I smile and point out that I have already done that. The young man smiles back and scuttles out of the room.

I wonder for a moment if the smell that's hitting my nostrils and climbing up into my sinuses is coming from blossom. The air is full of it. As I watch the gentle descent to earth of this perfumed confetti – the Chinese call it 'snow in April' – I'm reminded of Rewi's description in his memoir of being taken as a young child by his mother to admire the beauty of apple blossom. But I don't think it's blossom I'm smelling. There are too many other odours competing for attention …

A steady flow of pedestrians, many of them wearing masks, seem indifferent to the drifts falling about their feet. Later I will learn that the air is also filled with clouds of seedpods from the willows and poplars planted by the British and the French. There are reckoned to be two million poplars and 1.5 million willows in Beijing, creating a springtime hazard for asthma and sinusitis sufferers. I assume the people I'm looking at are headed to work, until I realise it's Sunday. Is Sunday a holiday in China? I discover it is, more or less, though not for religious reasons. In the course of two and a half weeks, travelling far and wide, I will see only a dozen or so Buddhist temples (many of them doubling as tourist attractions), the occasional mosque and one Christian church. For the next three days, during which we visit the Great Wall, the Forbidden City, Tiananmen Square, the 'Bird's Nest' (site of the 2008 Olympic Games), the Beijing Bailie University (founded in recognition of Rewi's educational work) and the New Zealand embassy, I grapple with the mystery of this 3000-year-old city that has gone from being capital of the ancient, pre-unification northern states of Ji and Yan, to a mere provincial city during the first thousand years of imperial rule over a united China, to being called capital again after Kubla Khan established the Mongol-led Yuan dynasty. Changes of name, changes of dynasty, invasions and occupations, Beijing/Peking/Peiping/Beiping/Yanjing/Dadu/Youzhou/ Zhongdu/Fanyang/Jicheng/Guanyang has seen it all.

Today the city is home to 21 million people. I'm already primed to experience the sheer weight of those numbers once we move out into the streets, but in fact it's not till the end of our journey, when we find ourselves stranded along with thousands of others on the main platform of Beijing Railway Station, that the numbers translate into an actual pushing, shouting, sweating crowd. 'Don't leave a gap,' our guide warns. 'If Chinese people see a gap they will fill it.' By this time we all know each other well. No one complains. We are Alleys after all, and those of us who aren't seem to have decided, at whatever cost to their personal comfort, to become, temporarily, Alleys too.

There's a knock on my door. The same young man who answered my query about the heating has been sent to remind me it's time to come down to the foyer. This too will be a regular feature of our travel. The timetable must be adhered to. We are guests of the government. I'm curious as to who would have given this man his orders. He isn't a hotel employee. So does he work for the government? The explanation our guide gives is that orders normally originate at provincial level and are passed down first to the county, then to the village. But in Beijing, as in other cities, there is no village level. Trying to discover who authorises what here is like trying to find the proverbial needle in the haystack.

'Total democracy would never work in China,' I will be told more than once in the course of our travels. The explanation is that that there are simply too many people. But I'm assured democracy does exist at grassroots level. It even has a name – Bottom-up Democracy – used to describe the elections held at village, county and provincial level. When I ask if you have to be a Party member to stand as an official I'm told that membership is not mandatory, though it *is* an advantage. What I am not told, but will later learn, is that at the higher levels of government, being a member of the Communist Party is essential if you want to advance. It doesn't guarantee your success, but there will be no success without it.

Over the next 15 days, as I slowly piece together the snippets of information I'm being given, the image of an octopus takes shape in my mind. Sixty-eight years of communist rule has seen the development of a highly sophisticated bureaucracy, its tentacles reaching into every corner of the land, controlling not just the various forms of local government but the media, schools, universities, business, publishing and sport.

I dress hastily and hurry down to the foyer. The first person I see is my cousin Ross from London. We greet each other warmly. He and his two friends, Peter and Irene, have already been here nearly 24 hours. 'A warning,' Ross whispers in my ear. 'Peter and Irene are lifelong members of the Tory Party, so don't talk politics.'

I raise an eyebrow. 'You must be joking,' I answer him. 'This is a Rewi Alley tour. How can we not talk politics?'

CHAPTER FIVE

ACCORDING to the New Zealand writer and publisher Dan Davin, just as marriage cannot truly be written about by a spinster or a bachelor, so war cannot truly be written about by someone who has not experienced it.[1] Like Rewi, Davin left New Zealand – in his case in the late 1930s – and returned thereafter only as a visitor. Rewi neither experienced nor wrote, except in general terms, about marriage, but he did experience war, several times over. On his return from World War I, like so many others of his generation he had little to say about it. But when he left New Zealand in 1926 to travel to China, the explanation he gave his family was that he wanted to 'take a look at the Chinese revolution'. The implication behind this throwaway remark was that, having had a look, he would return and resume his interrupted farming career. War was something he knew about. He might, he told himself, even be able to 'help a bit'.[2]

Yet Rewi hated war. He hated the hideous intimacy of it. When he wrote about it years later, his anger at the waste and suffering was as fierce as ever:

> … and there was the apprentice from the bookshop
> who sold me treasures in High School days – and
> he lay beside and died
> with torn intestines and a calm face; and the
> policeman who once had
> warned me for riding bicycles on footpaths – his
> arm was torn off …[3]

So why did Rewi tell his family he wanted to 'take a look' at the Chinese revolution? To answer this question we have to go back to 1916, to the day Rewi, determined to emulate his war-hero brother, enlisted in the New Zealand Expeditionary Force. (True to his resolution he had tried to enlist earlier, lying about his age and changing his name to Buckingham – his mother's maiden name – doubtless in the hope of escaping his father's wrath. The army turned him down.)

'As a boy I had the idea of the army as a career,' he writes in his memoir. (Did he know, I wonder, that soldiering was in his genes? That his great-grandfather fought the French and his great-uncles fought in Lincoln's army?) The accepted version is that this ambition went out the window after his experiences at Ypres and Bapaume. But the record, as well as Rewi's own words, tell a different story. Private (later Corporal, then Lieutenant) Rewi Alley, service number 55386, awarded the Military Medal for bravery, will call himself a soldier all his life. (In her revisionist book *Friend of China: The myth of Rewi Alley*, Anne-Marie Brady even goes so far as to claim that Rewi went to China as a mercenary. This, while untrue, is not completely wide of the mark. Rewi would keep up his connection with the New Zealand Army till 1933.)

So here is Rewi, aged 19, kit bag on his shoulder, boarding the converted passenger ship *Ulimaroa*, bound for England. He is a private in C Company, 28th Reinforcements, Canterbury Infantry Regiment. Though he will later claim to have little in common with the officer class, he had in fact applied to join them. At the age of 17 he'd sat the entrance examination for the Duntroon Royal Military College in Australia, requesting that he be examined in French and chemistry. He failed. The explanation for his failure – provided both by Clara and by Rewi himself – was that he realised that if he was accepted for the college he would probably miss the war. So did he fail deliberately? The record doesn't say.

The ship calls at several ports on the way, but the place that prints itself on Rewi's memory is Cape Town. By the time the *Ulimaroa* berths there, Rewi has already demonstrated his ability to fall foul of the authorities. A broken arm, the result of a tumble from his third-tier bunk, is seen by his superiors, alert to the practice of soldiers faking injuries to avoid the battlefield, as evidence of malingering. A court of enquiry is convened. Private Atkinson, who witnessed the accident, told the court that he was woken by Rewi 'calling loudly as if in a nightmare and on looking around it appeared as if he were about to jump out of bed'. Another witness heard him call out 'away' three times, 'as if dreaming heavily'.[4] (Away from what? I ask myself.)

Luckily for Rewi the verdict of the court was that he 'fell out of bed while asleep'. I can see Rewi, his uniform incorrectly buttoned – this is a man who will travel all over the world with a battered suitcase stuffed with unfolded shirts and shorts – standing insolently to attention while the verdict is read out, muttering to himself, 'I don't care, I don't care.'

He will not be so lucky second time round. Determined, despite his broken arm, to make the most of his shore leave, Rewi's mood changes when he discovers that his Māori comrades are not allowed to travel on Cape

Town's trams. He is not alone in his outrage. Before the morning is over all the trams in the main street have been tipped over. 'We were not political,' Rewi writes in his memoir, 'just ordinary healthy lads. It was unthinkable that our friends should be publicly shamed because the sun had tanned their skins a richer brown than ours.' This time a court of enquiry rules there will be no more shore leave for the culprits.

Rewi's reluctance to talk about his wartime experiences lasted a lifetime. 'I don't know why you always think there's more to a thing than there is,' he snapped when biographer Geoff Chapple tried to push him on the subject. Chapple knew that Rewi still carried a piece of shrapnel in his shoulder, the result of a wound received during the fighting at Ypres. Rewi had admitted it still 'moved around a bit' and sometimes 'got a bit sore', but question him about psychological or emotional damage, and down came the shutters.[5]

But there was one incident Rewi was happy to talk about, not because it provided a window into the soul – he would scoff at those words – but because it taught him a valuable lesson: 'the value of each and every human life'.[6]

We are at the Ypres Salient in Belgium, March 1918. Rewi and a fellow soldier have been ordered to move up to the front line. As they near their destination they see a man, one of their own, lying apparently dead in a ditch. Rewi is all for marching on – dead bodies are two a penny in this hellhole – but his mate insists they stop to check. The man is alive. They hoist him up and carry him along the plank road built over the mud to the first-aid dugout. Rewi asks the orderly, 'What are his chances?' The orderly, after a brief examination, says, 'He'll live.'

With only minor editing, Rewi could have told this story to demonstrate how he had saved a man's life. Instead he told it to show how hardened he had become – a hazard of long exposure to warfare – and how essential it was to remain human even in the worst conditions. Thirty years later he would sing the praises of his mate – the illegitimate son of a watersider and a hotel servant – who'd insisted they stop and check on a fellow soldier. Temperamentally unable to blow his own trumpet, Rewi could be fulsome in his praise of others. That soldier, he maintained, had 'more guts than any man I have ever met'.[7]

Rewi's shrapnel wound may have been the one he was reminded of every day, but it was a later, more serious wound that I – along with others in the family – now believe affected his life more profoundly.

This time we are on the outskirts of Bapaume, a German-held town in northern France. Built on a hill, it has an apparently impregnable advantage, but Rewi's Canterbury Battalion, along with other New Zealand and British forces, have the town surrounded. The Germans are in retreat. Not that the fighting is over. Rewi can see and hear the shells whizzing overhead from the new front line beyond the town boundary.

An order comes through to Rewi's platoon. They are to be part of an attack designed to knock out snipers and machine-gun nests. Rewi, by now a corporal, is among the first to start the ascent. He is almost at the top when the Germans open fire. Rewi is the first to be hit. His companions, intending to apply a dressing, pull off his trousers, but are stopped in their tracks by a second round of gunfire. Forced to take cover from the hail of bullets, they lower Rewi into a manure pit (the 'shitty slitty'), figuring that at least he will be out of the line of fire there. For the next 20 hours Rewi, presumably in great pain, lies alone in the foul-smelling, fly-infested trough. Next morning he is rescued by his platoon commander and taken to a first-aid post. Told by the padre to prepare himself for 'a long journey', he mutters, 'All I need is a piss and I'll be okay.'[8]

And he was. But when, on his return to New Zealand, he was met by his sister Gwen, she described a man – he was still only 22 – who 'looked much thinner and older' than the kid brother she had farewelled three years earlier. Gwen never doubted that Rewi's bachelorhood was a direct consequence of this particular war injury. As an Alley she would not have been thinking of psychological damage – something she would in any case have expected her brother to shrug off – but of something far easier to describe. She believed Rewi's wounds had left him impotent.

(Of all the explanations given for Rewi's lifelong bachelorhood, this was the one his immediate family latched on to. The bullet went in through the thigh and hip and came out near the backbone, so the assumption is not in any way fanciful. But as I got to know Rewi better, and to learn more about him, I realised there was another explanation for his bachelorhood – that he was gay. For a long time I, like many others, believed this to be the case, but I no longer do. What I have never accepted were the accusations made against him of misogyny. He was too warm and encouraging a correspondent; he had too many women friends. 'One of the most truly civilised and tender-hearted of the men who walk this spinning ball of mud,' according to the American journalist Agnes Smedley, one of several women rumoured to be in love with him.[9] He himself prophesied, in *The People Have Strength*, that 'When China's women get going mountains will move.' None of which, of course, establishes one way or the other whether he was gay. But I have to say, after examining the available evidence, I believe his siblings were right. A throwaway remark in the last decade of his life supports their claim that he was impotent.)

*

Citation: 25 August 1918: Bapaume: Rewi Alley: Recommended for the Military Medal. 'For courage and devotion to duty. During the period of consolidation he went forward several times under heavy fire in charge of patrols, and by his courage and initiative gained and brought back valuable information. His coolness and courage were a fine example to the rest of his men.'[10]

'I am a slow learner,' Rewi writes in his memoir, 'so cause and effect, who made wars and why, did not come home to me until years later, though the actual events of the war years were and still are startlingly clear in my mind, as are its beastliness and its degradation, as well as the courage and dedication of fighters on both sides. It was a lesson to be pondered.'

There are two postscripts to Rewi's wartime experience, the first anecdotal, the second vividly described in Geoff Chapple's biography.

The anecdote first. Invalided to England after being wounded at Bapaume, Rewi finds himself in the very hospital where, two years earlier, his brother Eric had been treated. The matron, then as now, is his childhood champion, Pen. Needless to say he receives special attention.

As soon as he's well enough to be moved, he's shifted to a convalescent hospital in a converted stately home near Lucknow Barracks in Wiltshire. There he finds himself in a room that shows signs of its former glory. Lined with fine Regency wallpaper, boasting a marble fireplace (Italian is Rewi's guess) and a chandelier that on the occasional sunny day throws sparks of light onto walls and ceiling, it reminds Rewi of the pictures he used to pore over in his parents' art magazines. From his bed he can reach out and touch the discoloration marks where once paintings were hung. He can almost touch the tracery of autumn leaves tapping against the window, a sound, combined with the muted songs of thrush and blackbird, that sends his thoughts racing back to the family home in Amberley.

At least once a week the men – there are no officers in this ward – are visited by the medical CO and whoever of rank happens to be around. It's meant to cheer the men up, boost morale, but what it usually does is inspire a fresh batch of lewd jokes. This morning is no different. 'Hands where they can be seen,' the soldier in the bed next to Rewi warns, flashing a buck-toothed grin. 'Here come the pooh-bahs.'

Medals dangling, shoes polished to within an inch of their lives, vowels as crisp as Pen's hospital corners, the top brass – five today, one up on last week – march down the ward, pausing for just the right number of seconds at each bed. Rewi, second to last in the row, has time to take in the scene. One bloke has so many medals across his chest Rewi assumes his ruler-straight posture is necessary to prevent himself tipping over.

'And who have we here?' the be-medalled bloke says, stopping by Rewi's bed.

The accompanying officer – a mere subaltern – answers the question, while Rewi braces himself for the usual, 'Good lad. Well done. Carry on'. But it doesn't happen. The bloke plonks himself down on the end of the bed and starts to chat.

A barely audible titter runs around the room. Rewi Alley of all people. Not known for his deference. Calls a spade a spade.

Anecdotal evidence being what it is, there's no record of what the officer and Rewi talked about. What is recorded is that the conversation went on for quite a while – long enough for the other officers to become restless. Not that they did anything about it. If there was any deference in the room that morning it was theirs towards the man sitting on Rewi's bed.

'Well, thank you,' the officer says, when the unscheduled chat comes to an end. 'Most enlightening. Where did you say you came from?'

'New Zealand.'

'Ah …'

'You've been there?'

'1901. Before …' He clears his throat. 'Beautiful country.' He holds out his hand. 'Take care of yourself, Mr Alley.'

'May one ask your name?' Rewi says as they shake hands.

The officer smiles. 'I'm King George,' he says, over his retreating shoulder.

Imagining Rewi's face – blue eyes widening in astonishment, laughter threatening to disrupt the orderly departure of the King and his entourage – I find myself wanting this anecdote, more than any other I've been told, to be true.

'Where the hell've you been hiding, mate?' I hear the man in the bed next to him exclaim. 'Don't ya know the king when ya see him?'

'Today I am elated, joyful, happy etc etc,' Rewi writes to Pen a few weeks after this putative encounter with royalty. 'I can see my stay at this most interesting place drawing to a conclusion. I went up for classification this morning and got the MO quite bluffed by showing him the nice-healed cut and camouflaging the other one. He marked me off B6, gave me fatigues. Physical drill and route march with B3 so that I will only have to work it next Friday to get out … [maybe I'll] eat my Christmas dinner in Etaples like I did last year …'[11]

The second postscript, as told to Geoff Chapple, features Rewi the scamp, intent on disobeying orders.

We are in France, soon after Rewi's arrival. He has yet to see battle. Along with other soldiers he has been quarantined, quite possibly for dysentery, from which he at one point almost died. Bored with so much inactivity, he and a mate slip under the wire one night and go in search of entertainment. They meet up – to their considerable surprise – with two tall Chinese soldiers wearing distinctive fur hats. 'We're from the British Labour Corps,' the Chinese tell the Kiwis. Rewi invites them to join forces for a feed of fish and chips at a local café. Wine is purchased. The evening becomes merry. At the end there's an argument over who is to pay, the Chinese insisting it is their shout, Rewi and his friend insisting the opposite. Chapple doesn't record who paid in the end, but he quotes Rewi as saying, 'They were the first Chinese in our lives that we had been able to meet on the level ground of mutual respect.'

'It's not colour that makes the difference between men,' Rewi wrote 30 years later in *Yo Banfa!*. 'It's their thinking.'

There are some who see this chance meeting with two Chinese conscripts as the birth of Rewi's interest in China. I don't agree. What was birthed in that casual encounter was Rewi's acknowledgment of the racism of his homeland. It would not be long before his outpourings on the cancer of racism would find their way into print. He called himself a 'slow learner', so it's entirely possible that prior to that meeting, despite what happened in Cape Town, he hadn't given much thought to the issue.[12] Racism was commonplace in early twentieth-century New Zealand, where newspapers regularly referred to the Chinese as 'coolies'. Other insults – 'slit-eyed chink', 'yellow belly' – may not have been printed, but from one end of the country to the other they were part of the vernacular.

Ching chong Chinaman sitting on the grass
Along came a bumblebee and stung him on his …
Ask no questions, tell no lies
I saw a policeman doing up his …
Flies are a nuisance, bugs are even worse
And this is the end of my silly little verse.

A playground chant that Rewi was bound to have heard. I certainly did, decades later, reciting it with glee, unaware of any offence, enthralled by the hovering presence of rude words.

Given his family background, with its emphasis on education and socialism, Rewi must have known that Chinese immigrants arriving in New Zealand in the late nineteenth century were subject to a law – the Chinese Immigration Act, 1881 – obliging them to pay a poll tax of £10 a head (roughly $1650 in today's money). Many of these men – there were almost no women – were refugees from the Opium Wars and the suppression of the Taiping Rebellion (1850–64). Nor was tax the only burden they had to shoulder. Organisations such as the Anti-Chinese Association, the Anti-Asiatic League and the White New Zealand League kept up a constant campaign of harassment directed at anyone who looked even vaguely 'oriental'. The poll tax – increased in 1896 to £100 – was finally waived in 1934, following Japan's invasion of Manchuria. But the law itself was not repealed until 10 years later.

Yet in this green and fragrant land
that is my homeland
the old contradictions …
still stand …[13]

Rewi's fear that 'the folk of [his] homeland still sleep through their days' recurs in both his poetry and his prose, often as a caveat to his celebration of the beauties of a country he never, in his mind and heart, left. He had nothing but disgust for the land that classified the Chinese as second-class citizens, but he could celebrate what he believed it would become once the virus of racism had been eradicated – a 'new Polynesian centre', 'part of a new Pacific and Asia to be'.[14] Even if he'd never gone to China, that meeting in 1916 on the battlefields of France would have had a profound effect on him.

CHAPTER SIX
Beijing, 9 April 2017

THIS journey is happening back to front. We're following in Rewi's footsteps but he didn't start here. As in the joke about asking an Irishman for directions and being told he can't give them because he wouldn't set out from where you are, our starting point shouldn't be Beijing, it should be Shanghai, where Rewi spent the first 10 years of his China life. But logic is not the guiding principle of this adventure. Our travels will spin us around a country that has seen the best that human beings are capable of, and the worst. At each stop we will be shadowed by the history Rewi lived through and even helped to shape, but we will not find easy answers to our questions. Rewi and the country he loved are as hard to separate as a long-married couple.

We've had our first authentic Chinese meal – a Sichuan feast washed down with Chinese beer. It almost didn't happen. Arriving at the popular Beijing restaurant we were told the room that had been set aside for us had been double booked. Just for a moment there was the threat of chaos as other diners pushed past us, and our guide and the waiters engaged in a shouting match. 'No hard feelings,' our guide assured us, after the argument was resolved. 'The Chinese "shout to live"!' – a sentiment colourfully endorsed by New Zealander Robin Hyde in *Dragon Rampant*, the story of her travels in China during the turbulent year of 1938. 'In English hens cluck, sheep bleat, a kitten mews, a dog barks, a cow moos, but in China everything yells. A chicken yells, a cow yells, a bird yells …'

In the days ahead we would often find ourselves caught up in apparent chaos only to have order suddenly, and seemingly without agency, restored. According to the popular conception, China is a land that imposes chaos on order. Both visitors and citizens can often feel as if it is about to descend into full-scale anarchy, but behind all the yelling and shoving a cast-iron system is in operation. Everyone has his or her orders. As James Bertram put it in his China memoir, *Capes of China Slide Away*, 'Nothing [in China] is what it seems to be on the surface.'

As we ate our way through course after course of the delicious peppery food for which Sichuan is famous, I practised putting names to faces. Ross and his friends from England are not the only new additions. We were joined this morning by Dave Bromwich, president of the New Zealand–

China Friendship Society, who is coming with us as tour leader (along with cousin Jocelyn). I feel I already know Dave. He comes with a glowing recommendation from my daughter, who's had contact with him through her work. An old China hand, with an excellent grasp of Mandarin and years of experience of how things work on the ground, Dave will be our greatest asset as we move into the remote northwest where Rewi's happiest years were spent. Looking around the table, I can't help wondering if 16 days will be enough for me to get to know all my fellow travellers: there are 22 of us now, counting Dave. And we have a packed programme. So far conversations have been limited to 'Are we where we're supposed to be?' 'Did you have time to eat breakfast?' 'Did you manage to turn the heating down?' and 'Have you tried the coffee?' (Answers unprintable.)

The moment the meal is over we're bustled back onto the bus to take us to the next place on our schedule. We're not yet used to the Chinese way of control, herding us on and off buses, making sure there's no wandering away on our own, so there are a few feet-draggers. But we will learn. By the end of our three days in Beijing the ALLEY WHANAU – the words displayed across the front window of our bus – will be more or less under control.

We are being taken to the Olympic stadium, the Bird's Nest as it is popularly called. Our Chinese guide wonders out loud if we can be trusted to wander about unsupervised. 'Do you promise to be back on the bus on time?' she asks, frowning. We chorus yes, and head out to the freedom of the wide open space fronting the stadium. I'm still trying to digest the information we've just been given about the vast acreage of farmland taken over by the state to build the stadium. It's a story, with different settings, that we will hear again and again. Once China's population was 80 per cent rural; today it's less than 50 per cent. Paddy fields, orchards, pastoral land, fields of wheat, potatoes and sorghum, plots producing green vegetables (the basis of most Chinese meals) have been dug up to make room for the high-rise towers mushrooming all over the country. Some of these towers are deserted. Developers have gone bust, or lost their money in one of China's many Ponzi schemes. What is sure is that China is rapidly becoming an urban country. Everyone wants to come to the city. No one wants to be *luohou*, backward. Strolling around the stadium forecourt I don't yet have an image in my head of the mile upon mile of tower blocks, devoid of any architectural merit, rising out of the grey dirt like the chimneys of some bleak underground city, but by the end of the week my head will be full of them.

We're running late. Watching my fellow travellers amble towards the bus like reluctant school children I feel sorry for our guide, who is trying to inject some urgency into the situation. Our next appointment is at Beijing Bailie University. There is to be a ceremony. Plaques will be unveiled. Speeches will be given in Mandarin and English. We will meet Michael Crook, current chair of the revived International Committee for the Promotion of Chinese Industrial Co-operatives (ICCIC), who will accompany us on parts of our journey. The schedule is tight. 'This way, Alley family … Please … This way …'

*

From the window of the bus, shops, signs, banners, cars, bicycles, a constant blur of people race past. New Beijing – expensive cars, skyscrapers, Western-style advertising – jostles alongside the Old – tricycles loaded with folded cardboard and vegetables; street sweepers with old-fashioned straw brooms; an alley, glimpsed in a break between tall, featureless buildings, where three old men play mahjong beneath a line of washing. I peer at the Chinese characters displayed above shop fronts and in advertisements, and for the first time I'm struck by how beautiful they are. If it weren't for the delicate calligraphy, Beijing's advertising hoardings would be like others all over the world – beautiful young men and women enticing customers to spend money. But the (to me) incomprehensible characters set these images apart. They are maps of a world I cannot enter. Back in New Zealand I will read that they operate as bridges linking time and space, something that could be said, surely, of any language. But there is a difference. Chinese characters also operate as bridges linking Mandarin (the official language) and the other main Chinese dialects – Cantonese, Hokkien and Teochew. As in all languages, meaning is fluid and subject to change, but in Chinese this process is even more elusive because of the ways in which meaning changes according to what goes before and after each particular character. When Confucius was writing 500 years before the birth of Christ, he had 6544 characters to choose from. Now there are more than 50,000 (though the dictionary lists only 20,000 as being in use). I think of my embarrassment as a poor speaker of French and know there's no point in my resolving to learn this fascinating new language. I am doomed to remain an outsider.

When Rewi was learning Mandarin he used to pin new characters around his mirror every day so he could memorise them while he was shaving. He became fluent enough to translate works from China's ancient dynasties, particularly the Tang (618–907) when Europe was lost in the Dark Ages and China was the most civilised country in the world. The only woman ever to rule China in her own name – the Tang Empress Wu Zetian – invented her own characters, which Rewi, determined to bring the poetry and art of that vanished golden age into the twentieth century, had also to learn. That he was so drawn to this period, when poets wrote in a classical style that bore little resemblance to spoken Chinese, is one of the many ironies of his life and work. When he came to write his own poetry he declared himself firmly on the side of the demotic. The classical rules of the Tang dynasty poets were not for him, though the world they described was.

'WELCOME HOME TO CHINA', 'WALK ALONG REWI ALLEY ROAD AGAIN' the posters at the Bailie University proclaim. Rewi may as well have saved his breath when he insisted that the university not be named after him, as was planned, but after his mentor, Joseph Bailie, the man he credited with putting him on the road that led to Gung Ho. Rewi's name is everywhere, as is his photo. There's a Rewi Alley International Exchange Centre and a Rewi Alley Building displaying another poster with the words 'WARM WELCOME TO ALLEY FAMILY' emblazoned across it. There are photos of Rewi from his revolutionary days with American friends Agnes Smedley and Evans Carlson. Another photo records the day Zhou Enlai came to sit with him in the Beijing sports stadium, an action (one of several) freighted with significance that kept Rewi safe during the dark years of the Cultural Revolution. And here he is with Soong Chingling, one of the three beautiful Soong sisters who played starring roles (though ultimately on different sides) in China's story, and in Rewi's. Joseph Bailie's name is almost nowhere to be seen. Yet he, as will be shown, really was the start of it all.

Our guides lead us into a large auditorium where we are ushered in individually, rounds of applause greeting each of us as our names are called. Seated on the dais is a double row of officials and teachers, with cousins Jocelyn and Maurice, our first scheduled speakers, positioned at the centre front. Behind us sit row upon row of students, all, judging by the smiles on their faces, delighted to see us. 'Overwhelming' is the word I will hear in the post-event bus chatter. None of us was prepared for such a display of warmth and enthusiasm.

I have the impression photos of Rewi are following us. The ones inside this hall are life-size and larger. Later in our journey we will encounter statues:

Rewi with his co-worker George Hogg; Rewi with the Shandan children; Rewi with President Xi Jinping's father, Xi Zhongxun, whom he met in the northwest during the war years. 'There are more statues of Rewi Alley in China than there are of Mao Zedong,' I'm told by one person I meet. Not true, but indicative of both the Chinese desire to please and the veneration in which our cousin is held.

What would Rewi's reaction have been had that preposterous claim been made in his hearing? He would have been horrified, surely. But then I remember the bust of him by Francis Shurrock – making him look 'like a Western variant of Peking Man' in the opinion of one critic – exhibited at London's Royal Academy in 1939.[1] Rewi must have agreed to sit for that, raising the question of whether he was a modest man with occasional flashes of vanity, or a vain man concealing his pride behind a cloak of modesty.

Shortly before this book went to print I was provided with a decisive answer to that question. Writing in response to reading the above paragraph, lifetime NZCFS member Eric Livingstone emailed these words to me: 'The only reason Rewi agreed to have his bust made was because he was visiting his mother at the time it was suggested and she persuaded him to agree to sit for it, and because he would do anything she asked him, so it came about.'[2]

We will get used to the photos and statues, as we will to the long speeches praising Rewi's work. What we will find less easy to swallow is the sometimes reverent approach to the man who was, for most of us, a family member – one we are proud of, but not a saint. The irony of the situation would not be lost on Rewi. His work, about which we will hear so much on this trip, was abruptly terminated by Mao in 1951. For a long time he was anything but venerated, his former association with the Kuomintang being cited as evidence of his lack of commitment to the communist cause. Had he died during either the Japanese or the civil war he might, like the Canadian doctor Norman Bethune (who will come into this story later), have been seen by Mao as a martyr. But he lived on, embroiled in the often subterranean politics of the day. Several decades would pass before, with Mao gone and Chairman Deng Xiaoping in power, Rewi Alley was reinstated as a Liberation hero.

'If I hear one more speech beginning "In 1927… [the year Rewi arrived in China]" I'll scream,' Judy will complain as Rewi's praises are sung in speech after speech, in city after city, across China. Those of us who didn't know the facts of Rewi's life before we came on this trip will know them by heart at the end.

The Bailie University event ends with the unveiling of two plaques: the first celebrating the 'Rewi Alley International Exchange Centre'; the second the 'Site for Education in Internationalism'. (After several such ceremonies Dave will confirm what we had begun to suspect – that the Chinese have a love affair with plaques.) This is followed by a group photo. (Another love affair – dozens will be taken over the next two weeks.) Then we are sent off on a tour of the university accompanied by students – one to every two or three of us – as our guides. Out of the corner of my eye I see my cousin Ross, the best-looking male in our group, surrounded by female students all eager to show him around the campus. This too will become a feature of our tour. 'You're outrageous,' I tease him towards the end of our journey. 'You're breaking hearts all over China.' Ross grins. An openly and happily gay man, he is delighted by all this female attention. 'Are you sure you're gay?' I can't resist asking.

At last the Bailie tour comes to an end and it's time for us to board the bus again. 'I will miss you,' my student says to me, holding my hand tight, asking for my email address. Others have the same experience. 'I will miss you.' 'I love you.' 'Please come again to our university.'

CHAPTER SEVEN

'I was glad that the killing had ceased,' Rewi writes in his memoir, describing his reaction on hearing that the Armistice had been signed and the Great War had ended, 'but scared too that the comradeship which had seemed more important than life would soon cease.' Losing himself in the shared life of the common soldier, 'helping each other in every way possible', Doody had found a way not to be lonely. Now he faced an uncertain future. He'd gone straight from school to war. He knew nothing about so-called 'normal' civilian life. He was acutely conscious of the success of his siblings – Eric a war hero; Gwen a trained teacher; Geoff, Clara's 'gorgeous boy', a star in the classroom; even Pip, whose childhood had been plagued by illness, exhibiting enough Alley grit to get to university – and couldn't help but see himself through his father's eyes as the 'dumbbell', the one who hadn't 'amounted to anything' and probably never would. 'I was the cuckoo in the nest. The unsuccessful one of the family,' he wrote.

Despite being welcomed back warmly by his mother and siblings – how much warmth came his way from Fred is not recorded – he was aware from day one that he didn't fit in. Only Gwen had met him at Addington Station. Fred was busy at school and Clara was home nursing Kath – like Pip, a sickly child. I imagine an awkward hug, Gwen trying to disguise her shock at the change in her kid brother, Rewi coming to the rescue with a teasing remark before hoisting his kit bag onto her bicycle and starting out on the five-kilometre walk home. 'One felt like something from another world, apart,' was his wry commentary on his homecoming.[1]

He was 22. The rest of his life cast a long shadow. The army, his original career choice, had become, in the wake of the 'war to end all wars', less attractive to him, but it was the only thing he knew, the one place where he might make his mark. He was a decorated soldier – that should count for something. But there was a problem. He'd been discharged in April 1919 on the grounds that he was no longer 'physically fit for war service on account of wounds received in action'. His ability to 'earn a livelihood in the general market' was reckoned at 30 per cent. A pension had been awarded. Would the army take him back, given he was no longer considered battle-worthy?

The answer was no. His application to re-sit the Duntroon entrance examination was declined. At 22 years of age he was considered too old to become an officer cadet. Also declined was his request to be sent to Quetta in India where British troops were stationed. 'No further commissions in the Indian Army are being granted,' he was told. 'With the signing of the Armistice the issuing of these commissions has ceased.'[2] Peace, apparently, was here to stay.

Enter Jack Stevens, an old school friend who'd been an air force pilot in Egypt during the war. Turning up on the doorstep for what Rewi no doubt imagined would be an evening of yarns told over a few beers, Jack surprised him by wanting to talk about something else altogether – the Returned Soldiers' Settlement Scheme. As Jack explains how the scheme – designed to help returning soldiers purchase land – works, the normally reserved ex-airman becomes positively animated. He's already got his eye on some land in Taranaki. Sheep country. He wants Rewi to join him. As a partner.

Rewi looks at him in astonishment. Farming is the last thing on his mind. His experience on his father's Southland farm, where he was bullied by a sadistic farm manager, has put him off for life.

'Eight hundred acres,' Jack announces. 'Hilly. Lots of it still in bush. But enough cleared for us to make a start. Not saying it'll be a picnic.'

'Neither was the war.'

'My point exactly.'

For the next couple of hours the conversation resembles a tennis match – a defensive Rewi returning the balls lobbed at him by a determined Jack. For every point Rewi scores Jack scores two – the depressed state of the job market, Rewi's lack of qualifications, his rejection by the army, his meagre army pension. In the end Rewi admits defeat. What choice do I have? he's said to himself. Who knows, maybe we'll make a go of it. But what really seals matters for him is the realisation that if he moves to Taranaki he'll be a long way from his father. He can run his own ship, not be answerable to a man who compares him at every turn to his siblings.

'How do you know I'll be up to it?' he asks in a last-ditch attempt to forestall the inevitable. 'I'm damaged goods, remember.'

'Look pretty fit to me.'

'Tell me where this place is again?'

'Taranaki. And it's not really a place, just a smudge on the map. It starts with an M and goes on for 10 minutes. Moe … awa … tea. Means daylight sleep.'

Rewi grins. 'A holiday then.'

*

So once again Rewi packs his kit bag, says goodbye to his family, and walks the five kilometres to Addington Station. There he boards a train that will take him to the inter-island ferry and an overnight sailing to Wellington, from where he will catch another train for the 10-hour journey to New Plymouth. By the time he meets up with Jack in the South Taranaki town of Waverley, he will have been travelling for two and a half days.

Rewi has poured all his savings into this venture. He has also poured Eric's. Six thousand pounds. So much for government help to returned servicemen. Jack has already spent money on a truck, an essential piece of equipment for anyone living nearly 50 kilometres from the nearest town. The two friends spend a day in Waverley, loading the truck with tools, tucker, and a dog apiece to help with the mustering. Setting off in high spirits they've barely started their journey when the road turns into a mud track. For the rest of the journey they will slip, slide and bump over land that seems determined to send human beings back where they came from.

I try to imagine what Rewi is thinking as he takes his turn driving, graunching the gears as they crawl up yet another hillside, pumping the brakes to dry them after fording a creek. He's seen the destruction war can cause, but what he's seeing now, through the misted window of the truck, is the destruction nature can cause. The hills are covered with dense native forest. Every few miles an ugly blue-grey stripe, evidence of a recent landslip, cuts a swathe through the dark green. Twice they have to stop, once to move rocks off the road, the second time to manhandle a fallen tree. 'What in God's name were the Māoris doing up here?' Rewi asks. '"Sleep in the daytime"? Whoever dreamed that one up must have had a good laugh. Look at it! It's a fortress.'

Jack reminds Rewi that this particular fortress is home to more wild rabbits and pigs, not to mention possums, than the two of them could ever hope to eat, but Rewi, who's beginning to suspect this is a war zone he's entering, just shrugs.

A few minutes later the forest clears, revealing a rough patch of farmland in the middle of which stands a makeshift wooden cottage. 'Home Sweet Home,' Jack says. To which Rewi answers, 'Sweet? Can think of other words.'

As he lowers the truck gate to let the dogs out, Rewi starts to laugh. An image of his baby sister Joy throwing her toys out of the pram has jumped into his mind. That's exactly what the cottage looks like. As if it's been dropped into the valley by a bad-tempered baby. A makeshift veranda with a sloping roof is the one and only architectural 'feature'. Unless you count the chimney. 'I'll huff and I'll puff and I'll blow your house down …' No need to wait for the Big Bad Wolf, a simple earthquake will do it.

But the cottage, which Rewi will call a whare, the Māori word for a dwelling, doesn't hold his attention for long. There's too much else to take in. Razorback ridges rise on both sides of the valley, so steep even horses – as the two novice farmers will discover – can't scale them. Where the forest has been cut down there are tree stumps and scrawny re-growth – rough pasture, torn from the bush, that to Rewi's eyes is as far from the tidy fields of Canterbury as New Zealand was from the trenches of France. Somewhere out in the wilderness are the sheep that will, so Jack has assured him, provide them with an income. Wool prices are good. All they have to do, a cheery Jack asserts, is break in more land, increase their stock, and Bob's their uncle.

For the next six years the only music Rewi will hear is the sound of running water, the bleating of sheep and yapping of dogs, the sweet song of the bellbird in duet with the throaty tūī, the raucous cries of magpies, and the occasional rumble – reminding him of the earthquakes he experienced as a child in Amberley – as another hillside comes tumbling to the ground. 'Loneliness and struggle.' Those are the words he uses in his memoir to describe those six years. He and Jack work together, but when Jack has to take the wool to the market in Waverley, or travel to New Plymouth for supplies, there are long nights when the only voice to be heard is the mournful cry of the morepork and the screech of the kiwi, backed by those ominous rumbles. Rewi will read, by candlelight, anything he can lay his hands on: romantic novels that have become cemeteries for desiccated insects; the Bible, its pages so flimsy they threaten to disintegrate in his fingers; dog-eared thrillers left behind by possum hunters; a dusty pile of *Reader's Digests*; old copies of *Truth* and the *Auckland Weekly*. Well, that's it, I don't care, he mutters to himself, when the thought that this might be it for the rest of his life overwhelms him.

> The game is played, the interest due
> too high to make it further ado
> so out he rides along the track
> all he owns light on his back;
> stops by the river and tethers his horse
> drops his duds and swims across
> then up through the bush the mossy vines

lightly caressing his body at times
as he pushes through, then coming out

on a sunny clearing, sheep grazing about
looks long at the valley he loves so well.
'They take your dough, your sweat, then say
go to Hell', he shouted as he balanced on a fallen tree
so lithe, so young, limbs clear and free
'They think they've got the goods on me!'
Then swiftly he turned, ducked down the road
Heart a bit lighter of some of its load
With a stubborn idea coming into his mind
Of things to be done for him and his kind.[3]

Rewi called this poem, written many decades after he'd turned his back on Moeawatea, 'Foreclosure'. He'd written it, he told Geoff Chapple, for 'someone like myself at that time'. Perhaps, hiding behind a third-person persona, he thought he was safe to express some of the emotion he felt about that failed six-year experiment. Reading it, it's impossible not to hear an echo of the famous poem of New Zealand's Depression years, written 40 years later – Denis Glover's 'The Magpies'. With its repeated refrain mimicking the cries of magpies, the setting could as easily be the empty, bush-choked hills and echoing valleys of Moeawatea as the anonymous wilderness Glover describes. Glover's tale of the (mis)fortunes of farmer Tom and his wife Elizabeth, as their farm first prospers then slowly falls into debt, is Rewi's story too.

Moeawatea is still there, though no one lives in the whare (no one would want to: the road is cut off in winter) and no one tries to cultivate the land. Twenty-five years later Rewi would reference his life as a Taranaki farmer in a letter urging New Zealand not to follow America's lead in foreign policy. Do that, he warns, and you will be 'like the fool sheep leading a flock over a precipice', a disaster he witnessed in his 'sheep cockey' days.[4] He might have escaped New Zealand, but he couldn't escape his past.

*

… where horses could not pull, we pulled: sweating up cliff faces,
The last garment, tattered shorts, put on shoulders to keep fencing posts
From chaffing: shearing sheep, building houses, cooking, reading, swimming
Flooded rivers after timber, swapping lies about pig hunts …

The Alley Family at Amberley in 1901. From left: Gwen, Pip (the baby), Eric, Clara, Fred, Rewi.

From *At 90: Memoirs of my China years* by Rewi Alley

Rewi on his return from war, 1919.

From *At 90: Memoirs of my China years* by Rewi Alley

The farm at Moeawatea, 1987.

From *Rewi Alley of China* by Geoff Chapple

Rewi at Moeawatea, 1924.

From *At 90: Memoirs of my China years* by Rewi Alley

Rewi (left) with Edgar Snow and an unknown friend (probably Anna Wang, secretary to the China Welfare Institute), about 1936.

From *Rewi Alley of China* by Geoff Chapple

Joseph Bailie, the American missionary who inspired Rewi with his educational ideas.

From *At 90: Memoirs of my China years* by Rewi Alley

The Soong Sisters: Chingling on right, Ailing wearing a hat, Meiling in front.

From *At 90: Memoirs of my China years* by Rewi Alley

ABOVE: George Hogg, Rewi's close friend and fellow teacher, at Shandan.

RIGHT: Rewi with his sons Alan (middle) and Mike.

From *Rewi Alley of China* by Geoff Chapple

At a birthday banquet for Mao Zedong. Edgar Snow is on Mao's right and Rewi is on Mao's left. From *Rewi Alley of China* by Geoff Chapple

Inside the cave house, home to Rewi and George Hogg at the Bailie School, Shuangshipu.

Photo by Ken Watkin

Like 'Foreclosure' these lines, part of a longer sequence titled 'Autobiography', were written several decades after his failed experiment in farming – further evidence of how those six years continued to haunt him. He'd started writing poems in Shanghai, sending them to his mother 'for her amusement'. ('Meant to write you all the news but my fingers strayed in idle verse ... A bunch of Mongols here watching me write ...'[5]) But it was while travelling through northwest China for Gung Ho that he began writing poetry in earnest, scribbling the words on whatever scrap of paper was to hand, often while waiting on a roadside to hitch an illegal ride in a truck – an activity, common in pre-Liberation China, known as 'yellow-fishing'. '[The poems] were completely marginal, scribbled because I had nothing to read,' Rewi told his niece Philippa, daughter of Pip. Many of them were written on bamboo paper or on the backs of envelopes. 'I did not care to keep them,' he said, adding, with a laugh, that many of them ended up being used as toilet paper. 'My habit of writing verse is really a release mechanism,' he insisted. 'They're blow-offs. Not worth much. The ragged lines come as gusts or outbursts as my fingers stray over the typewriter.'[6]

Fortunately, most of the people Rewi sent his poems to held onto them. Because eventually he would stop hiding behind the smokescreen of modesty and allow them to be published. Rough-hewn they may be, but they are also a form of record, a diary written in haste when there was no time, and frequently not enough paper, for prose. Calling them 'blow-offs' was not so much a joke as an accurate description of how the poems came into being. He made no claim to profundity or felicity of style. From the start he placed himself firmly in the Chinese tradition of writing poetry in the midst of the difficulties and dangers of life. 'First they'll live poetry, then they'll write it,' he said of the *xiao gui*, young devils – children, sometimes as young as 10, who joined the Red Army:

Little Red Devils of the Red Army
What a name they have;
They are the Red Army ears
the Red Army lips and on
their sturdy legs go
the messages the Red Army sends ...[7]

The best of Rewi's poetry, like so much of the poetry he translated from China's past, grew out of his empathy for the suffering of the Chinese people – the horrors he witnessed, the kindness he experienced, the courage he was determined to emulate. Forced to witness an execution in Wuxi, a 'Road to Damascus' experience that changed his life, he wrote:

A thing that tears at the heart
of any real lover of this land
to see a patriot going to execution
… with a little smile
as he strides to his end …[8]

I see my cousin wearing his trademark shorts, squatting in the dirt and dust, waiting for that elusive truck, sweat pouring down the back of his shirt, flapping the flies away with his hand as he briefly forgets his worries and allows Moeawatea to flood back into memory:

… and there was the loveliness after rain, the bell birds
In crimson rata trees, sheep stringing out on the ridge …[9]

*

Rewi turned his back on Moeawatea at the end of 1926. Jack, who'd declared a wish to marry, stayed on. Rewi knew there was no way the already failing farm could support three people, so he gave his share to Jack and took himself off. Twelve years later Jack too walked away from the farm. The whare was abandoned, of interest only to pig and possum hunters. That changed in the 1980s thanks in part to Geoff Chapple's book, but also to pressure from the family, particularly Maurice Alley and Dorothy Waymouth, as well as Rewi's friend Dave Harré, who raised the necessary funds. Freshly painted and restored, the cottage gives a visitor, on a good day, a somewhat rosy impression of the life Rewi lived there. But a glance at those forbidding hills, frequently wreathed in mist even in summer, is enough to evoke those long, lonely, back-breaking days. Rewi and Jack planted vegetables and lemon trees and clover for animal feed. They cleared bush, sheared sheep, introduced cattle. When cash was short they worked on the roads. Sixteen hours a day on average they toiled, returning to the whare when the light failed to cook their own supper and read or tell yarns. Rewi became expert at baking damper bread. He made butter and jam. But the anticipated profits never arrived. Wool that had been 29 pence a pound in 1920 had dropped to two pence by 1926.

'Better that we had tilled the flats and let the hills stay in forest' was Rewi's wry comment on those 'wasted' years in 'Autobiography'. Elsewhere, with typical understatement, he described an accident – one of several – that almost ended his life.

> I was going to meet some sheep Jack had brought back from Waverley. I saddled up Hamud, a horse we'd bought cheap as he'd only been half broken. The morning was beautiful as I went out of the valley – the mist lying low, rata trees in flower, fantails laughing at me … I passed a blue papa [mudstone] cliff, when some earth and stones, loosened by rain the night before, suddenly fell in front of Hamud who reared up … I was thrown off, as I was just dreaming along, and not expecting anything … With one foot in the stirrup I was dragged some miles until the stirrup iron cut through the leather and left me lying in the road …[10]

It took Rewi three months to recover. Moeawatea 'gave me the ability to face up to cold wind for days and smile,' he wrote in his memoir. 'It cleared away a lot of war dreams and brought me down to earth, teaching me anew the value of simplicity.'

What it didn't do was tell him where to go next.

CHAPTER EIGHT

FAILURE. That is how it will look to Fred. However Rewi spins those six years of farming, he knows how his father will see things. Acting the pioneer, claiming he could turn bush into farmland in a part of the country even Māori had turned their backs on, has set him up for ridicule. Returning home is out of the question.

Though he never voices the thought aloud, it must be lodged somewhere in Rewi's mind – he fought for King and Country and was rewarded with banishment to a place unfit for human habitation. Add to that the catastrophic drop in wool prices and here he is, like so many other returned soldiers, left without the means to live. How is that just?

But he doesn't blame the army, he blames the government. Armies do what governments tell them to. Okay then, I'll try the army again, he says to himself. Agreeing to go into partnership with Jack hadn't meant he'd said goodbye to any hope of an army career. In fact he'd kept up his credentials by joining the Legion of Frontiersmen, a paramilitary group formed in Britain in the wake of the Boer War to protect the empire. Later, when his military past became an embarrassment to him, Rewi would claim he'd joined because of the free ammunition needed to shoot all those possums and rabbits, but there was clearly a great deal more going on for him than this, since by the time he left Moeawatea he was on the staff of the legion's headquarters.

Rewi had sensed long before Jack which way the wind was blowing. He knew their days on the land were numbered. When, in late 1925, he applied to join the First Battalion, Wellington West Coast Infantry Regiment as a territorial, it was with an eye to his future, post-Moeawatea. Having sat for a commission he was gazetted in January 1926 as a second lieutenant. (It's as far up the ranks as he will go. Captain Eric Alley will always be his superior.) He still had to fulfil his obligation to attend camps and undertake an 18-day training course, but he was encouraged enough to believe that, having settled things with Jack, the army might take him back. Given the drastically reduced peacetime numbers, his best hope, as medically-unfit-for-service, was that they would accept him into the Staff Corps.

'From my earliest days soldiering has been my passion,' his letter of application begins, moving on to describe his war experiences, his winning of the Military Medal and his involvement with the Legion of Frontiersmen.

'While farming I was too far away from any centre to take up Territorial work,' he offers, explaining his six-year absence from the army. Then he gets straight to the nitty gritty. 'I am aware that the only openings at present in the Defence Department are as staff sergeants on the permanent staff but perhaps it is possible that an opening on the Staff Corps might be made.' He ends the letter with these words: 'I do not think I should ever be as good a soldier as my brother Eric was. He, in the opinion of Generals Russell, Braithwaite and Brown, was a born soldier, but I do think that I would make good at it.'

Across the bottom of the letter the Minister of Defence, clearly impressed by Rewi's determination, has scribbled, 'Is there any opening for this young fellow in the direction he wishes?'[1]

There isn't. The application is declined on the grounds of age.

What Rewi felt when that particular door was slammed in his face is not difficult to imagine. Soldiering was the one thing he'd always wanted to do. Suddenly he was in limbo again, a state in which he might have thrown in his lot with any number of hare-brained schemes. Instead, what caught his attention was China. He'd first read about the upheavals in that country in an old copy of the *Auckland Weekly*, squinting over the magazine at the whare, deciphering words in the feeble light from a candle. Now China is in the news again. Momentous things seem to be happening there. The 1911 revolution – led by a man called Sun Yatsen – that brought centuries of imperial rule to an end, is in peril. Forced into exile by the usurper Yuan Shikai, who tried to have himself declared emperor, Sun was restored to power four years later when Yuan died. Now Sun himself is dead. Trying to find out what's going on in the wake of Sun's death is like trying to find a lost sheep in the Moeawatea bush. But Rewi is hooked. This is some story! From what he can gather, an army officer called Chiang Kaishek is calling the shots, but there's another bunch known as communists whom Chiang seems to have it in for …

Maybe I'll go and have a look, Rewi thinks. That Sun Yatsen sounds as if he was a pretty decent sort of bloke. Be a crying shame if his revolution were to be betrayed. Who knows? I might be able to help a bit …

*

Rewi's decision to 'take a look' at the Chinese revolution could have been the end of his relationship with the New Zealand Army, but it isn't. He's still a territorial. He may be headed out of the country but he doesn't offer his resignation. What he does do is apply for a year's leave of absence, requesting that he be transferred to the supernumerary list. Like his family, he seems to believe he'll return to New Zealand once his wanderlust has been satisfied, and take up farming again.

Two years later he's not so sure.

'I have the honour to request that my period of leave be extended by still one more year,' he writes from the Yangtze Hotel in Nanking, in a letter dated February 1929. It's his fourth application for an extension. He gives as his reasons:

- That I am serving with a force run on British Army lines so that I am keeping in training. [He is referring to his work as a fireman and factory inspector, in the employ of the Shanghai Municipal Council.]
- That this force is an integral part of the Shanghai Defence Force commanded by Major General Woodford. [The Shanghai Defence Force was a tri-service organisation – army, navy, air force – established to protect European nationals and their property.]
- That the knowledge I am gaining of Eastern subjects may possibly be of use to the NZMC [New Zealand Military Command].[2]

The NZMC must have valued him, because his request is granted. Most soldiers would have been discharged at the third request. Nevertheless, time is running out. By 1933, when Rewi still hasn't returned to New Zealand, the army recommends he be retired. No record exists of this order, or of Rewi's reaction. Nor is there any record, in Rewi's autobiographical writings, of his long involvement with the New Zealand Army. No doubt he brushed over this part of his story – inadvertently giving credence to Anne-Marie Brady's claim that he went to China as a mercenary – because he'd thrown in his lot with the communists. Whatever the reason, knowing that the army was, for so many years, his 'passion', that he clung to the dream of being a soldier again long after there was any real hope of that dream being realised, both colours and re-shapes the story he tells about his early years in China.

'No good man can become a soldier.' As Rewi's ability to speak the language improves, he will encounter this old Chinese saying. It troubles him. Why do you say this? he asks his Chinese friends. The answer – that tax collectors, the most hated people in China, are always accompanied by soldiers – sets him thinking. He hasn't lost his love of soldiering, but the thought that he, as a soldier, could be put to such use disgusts him. As he says more than once in his memoir, it's a 'lesson to be pondered'.

CHAPTER NINE
10 April 2017

TODAY we are to visit the Great Wall, the *Wanli Chang-cheng* (Ten Thousand Mile Wall). I'm feeling mildly irritable. We're not tourists. The Wall may be one of the wonders of the world, but what has it to do with Rewi? 'I don't suppose any American comes to the Great Wall without wanting to run an automobile on it,' Rewi wrote in *Human China*. 'It would make a cracker-jack highway!' he added sourly.

A week later, when we reach Gansu province, and Rewi's lived life is all around us, I will change my tune. Remnants of the Wall which, according to the latest archaeological evidence, stretched more than 16,000 kilometres across northern China, emerge out of the landscape like hibernating animals. These crumbling piles of yellow earth are all that remains, in the non-tourist northwest, of the original 8-metre structure, first built in the seventh century BC to stop Mongol horsemen stealing the harvest. (Months later, reading Edgar Snow's pictorial record of his time in China, I will come across a photo of Chinese soldiers stationed on the Wall, firing at the Japanese on the other side. Suddenly the Wall acquires a personal relevance. Had the Japanese succeeded in subduing the whole of China it's highly likely their progress down into the Pacific, and eventually to New Zealand, would have been unstoppable.)

Meanwhile, having arrived at the Beijing section of the Wall, I have to admit that in its restored form it's magnificent. My fellow travellers take photos, while I stroll over the battlements, trying to overcome the symptoms of vertigo – a serious handicap to my late middle-age passion for mountain climbing. Forced finally to sit down, I hope people will assume I'm lost in thought. Which I am! But not about this Wall, about the one Donald Trump wants to build to stop Mexicans crossing the border into what used to be their land. At least the Han Chinese were keeping out genuine invaders, people who would ultimately conquer China and establish their own dynasty. I don't imagine even President Trump believes that the Mexicans who cross the border into the US are planning to lay siege to the White House.

Wanli Chang-cheng. The Wall that failed, ultimately, to keep the Han Chinese safe. I can't get my head around the span of centuries. The China of 770 BC is as great a mystery to me as the moon. Originally built in sections, the Wall became a nationwide barrier only in the second century BC, when Emperor Qin, credited with the creation of the Terracotta Army (verification of this awaits the excavation of Qin's tomb), managed for a brief time to rule over a united China.

Emperor Qin was a paranoid megalomaniac. The jury is still out on whether President Trump is 'mad, bad' or merely 'dangerous to know', but I can't help but see parallels.[1] Knowing that Trump is at this moment hosting China's current president, I conjure up a scene in which, over drinks at his Florida mansion, Trump asks President Xi how the Great Wall came to be built.

'Thinking of building one myself,' he confesses modestly.

'So I've heard,' his guest answers.

'Not on such a scale, of course. But close.'

'You want to know how the Great Wall of China was built?' China's paramount leader asks, his voice, like his expression, neutral. 'I will tell you, Mr President. It was built by the sacrifices of the people. A million workers died in the course of its construction.'

'So? What's the problem? Population control. You people need to deal with that. Right?'

President Xi smiles. 'The longest cemetery on Earth. Is that what you want to build, Mr President?'

✳

Back on the bus the conversations are real and noisy. We're getting to know one another. Carol and Christine are busy knitting. Seldom seen without their knitting bags, the sisters will, over the next two weeks, finish the garments – gifts for Carol's grandchildren – started on the flight from New Zealand. Their friends Helen and Betty sit opposite them. Sarah has joined her Aunt Dorothy. Maurice, Dorothy's husband, sits with the other Maurice, not a relative but a keen supporter of Rewi's co-operative movement. Later in our journey I will learn how this other Maurice came to be involved in Rewi's story. He was a young shepherd working in the Mackenzie Country when he heard about a North Canterbury farmer sending sheep to some Kiwi bloke in northern China. He was intrigued. So he started making enquiries …

Zeke and Judy sit together. Ross, Zeke's brother, sits behind his friends Irene and Peter. I sit with Ken, Jocelyn's husband. A former professional photographer, Ken copes with my requests for specific photographs – I've never owned a camera – with good-humoured patience. Alison and David sit together. Later in the journey couples will feel more comfortable about splitting up, but it's early days. Till we know each other better, most of us are opting for the familiar.

Jocelyn and Dave, our joint tour leaders, sit, as is their right, at the front. The young ones, Rachel and Stewart, have made a beeline for the back. Their energy and good humour soon lifts us out of any exhaustion we might be feeling after our wanderings over the Wall. This will become a feature of the days ahead. However tired the rest of us might be, Rachel and Stewart, along with Sarah, the other 'young one' on the trip, will make sure we keep up. Their enthusiastic embracing of each new challenge is infectious.

On the way to the Wall our guide, Ben, told us about his experiences during the Cultural Revolution. Accustomed to hearing tales of hardship and suffering, we were, to put it mildly, taken aback by his story All of us had some idea of what went on in those violent years from 1966 to 1976: the teachers and artists – anyone, in fact, who'd fallen foul of Mao – being made to parade the streets with placards around their necks proclaiming their crimes; the Red Guards marching those same 'criminals' out of the cities and into the countryside for re-education. I'd read Jung Chang's *Wild Swans*. I knew about the forced labour and the compulsory study meetings where the works of Chairman Mao were discussed ad nauseam. I knew what Mao's attack on his own officials had done to people unaccustomed to physical labour. What I didn't know (if indeed what we are being told is the truth) is that for some people, notably our affable guide, the Cultural Revolution was a blast.

Listening to Ben's cheerful tale while Beijing's dreary suburbs, pockmarked by ugly high-rises, sped past our window, was a surreal experience. He must have told his story many times, yet he was clearly enjoying himself as he burst the bubble of our notions of what went on during the Cultural Revolution. The catch-cry of that time was 'Smash the Four Olds' – the Ideas, Customs, Culture and Habits of the past. But the only smashing Ben seems to have done in that dark decade was his record as a mahjong player.

'I was a student,' he told us, 'so I was caught up in it from the beginning. "Too much learning makes a counter-revolutionary" – Mao's words. And when Mao speaks …' He laughed. 'So off we went, the whole class, to the countryside, to learn from the peasants.'

At some point in Ben's story we reached the countryside ourselves, but because it was only marginally less depressing than the suburbs we didn't take much notice. Wisps of mist – this was a good day, you could see the sun – drifted across the distant mountains, reminding us that more often than not mist becomes smog, smearing its dirty hand across Beijing's windows. Village after village of grey, mud-built houses, surrounded by grey fields and a few mis-shapen trees, slid past our window. Men lay sleeping in the dirt, not homeless men but workers employed to turn farmland into suburbs. Soon mud houses, trees and fields will be gone, replaced by ugly high-rises standing sentinel over a barren landscape.

Despite being in full flow, Ben did pause occasionally to answer questions. Asked to explain the strange, beehive-shaped protuberances dotted across the land, he informed us they were burial mounds. For thousands of years Chinese have buried their dead according to ancient rites and practices, but that, he informed us approvingly, is changing. In the future burial mounds will be relics of a forgotten past. Following the instructions laid down by the first communist leaders, people today are choosing to be cremated. It was the choice Rewi made when his time came. The one exception among party leaders was Mao, who was embalmed, apparently against his own wishes.[2]

A further interruption to Ben's tale occurred when the photographers among us demanded the bus stop so that they could photograph a Buddhist temple rising out of the dirt like a mirage. It was an impressive sight, the golden *paifang* (symbolic gateway) glowing defiantly in the weak sunlight. While the photographers positioned themselves on the roadside like a ragged corps de ballet, Dave informed those of us left on the bus that the temple was built by a wealthy businessman, one of China's new 'coal bosses' (a term applied to the new rich, regardless of how they made their money).

I was curious. I'd thought religion was frowned on by the government. 'It is,' Dave confirmed. 'The official position is atheist. But allowances are made …' What he went on to say, once we were mobile again, left me in no doubt about the scale of change in China since the country was opened up to capitalism in the 1980s. The mass migrations from country to city have not just re-drawn the population map, they've altered the fabric of Chinese society. The millions who moved to the cities in search of a better life left behind more than their villages; they left a way of living – the sense of community and co-operation that had been the modus operandi of village life for centuries. As a result, in every major city in China, the government was faced with an avalanche of social problems. Its solution was to encourage Buddhism – not to endorse it (atheism was still the official policy), but to promote its values, particularly its emphasis on co-operation, among China's new city dwellers. One in every five Chinese is reckoned to be Buddhist, so the policy was well received. 'And unlike the Falun Gong,' Dave concluded, 'the Buddhists don't agitate for democracy. So everyone is happy.'

My mind was full of questions – about the Falun Gong; about religious freedom – but they would have to wait. Ben had the microphone again. Flashing his trademark grin, he told us he hadn't wanted to leave the city. It was his home after all. But being sent to the countryside to work with the peasants wasn't the worst thing that had happened to him. 'Might even have been the best,' he quipped, explaining that he was a bit adrift at the time, unmotivated. He paused for a moment as if testing the temperature of his audience. Then he went on, more soberly than before, to admit that he was lucky; others had a much harder time. 'Mao wanted us to learn from the peasants how to be a good person,' he said. 'He thought students and intellectuals had become too soft and needed to be reminded whose revolution this was.'

I tried to picture Ben, clutching Mao's book, chanting 'Long Live Chairman Mao', as he marched out of Beijing and headed for the countryside. Was it really as much of a Sunday school picnic as he wanted us to believe? 'We went to have our "wrong thinking" corrected,' he told us, 'and it worked, but maybe not in the way Mao intended!'

Clearly enjoying himself, Ben went on to describe how the People's Communes operated. The hard worker and the lazy worker got the same pay, so where was the incentive to work hard? At the end of the day everyone had the same amount to eat. And drink. Work for 40 minutes, then sit under the trees for a couple of hours, smoking, talking, playing mahjong – that was the daily routine. 'Not quite the re-education Mao had in mind,' a giggling Ben observed. 'At the end of my time in the countryside, I'd learned how to smoke, drink and gamble. And I was a champion mahjong player. That's what the good peasants taught me.'

I found myself wondering what China's current president, Xi Jinping, would make of Ben's story. At age 15 he too was sent to the countryside. For seven years he lived in a cave in remote Shaanxi province, working by day as a peasant farmer, studying the works of Mao by night. His parents, far away in Beijing, were in prison. Xi's father, a founder member of the Chinese Communist Party (the *Gongchandang*, Share Property Party), was celebrated after Liberation as one of the 'immortals', but he'd fallen out with Mao over the Party's re-writing of history, particularly in relation to the disaster of the Great Leap Forward. What the teenage Xi felt as he watched his parents being led away, then set out himself for one of the most backward provinces in China, is hard to imagine. He also made light of the experience, though not in the same way as Ben. There was no drinking and gambling, no midday naps under trees or drawn-out games of mahjong in his story. 'Nothing taught me as much as those years in the countryside. I was useless, afraid of the cattle we cared for, and exhausted after even a few hours of work in the field. But I learnt some humility, and how resourceful, generous and kind the poorest people often are.'[3]

My preconceived ideas about China were being blown away like snow in April. I had assumed that discussion of the Cultural Revolution, like discussion of the Tiananmen Square protest, would be off-limits. But here was Ben prepared to answer questions on both subjects, though his analysis of the Tiananmen massacre turned out to be something of an apologia. 'China is evolving,' he insisted. 'We have to be patient. Mistakes have been made, but we are moving in the right direction. Evolution, not revolution. That's the way to look at China.'

Clearly he hoped that would be the end of the matter, but this was a busload of Alleys he was dealing with. We wanted answers, not excuses. So we pushed him harder, reminding him that hundreds of people were killed on that infamous day in June 1989 (368 is the official figure, but the reality is almost certainly higher).

'What was the government to do?' Ben shot back. 'The students had been occupying the square for two months. They were demanding democracy, Western-style. Deng Xiaoping was never going to allow that.' Reminding us of the scale of Deng's reforms – chief of which was the breaking up of the communes, allowing farmers to sell directly to the markets instead of only to the government – Ben clearly felt he'd won the argument. Millions had been lifted out of poverty. Many concessions had been made in response to the students' demands. Why were they asking for more?

'Freedom of speech? Isn't that what they were asking for? Freedom of the press?' Questions from the back of the bus, which Ben dismissed with a cheerful wave of his hand.

'"To get rich is glorious,"' he said, quoting Deng's words (which many insist he never actually said). 'Once everyone is rich there'll be no need for freedoms.'

'So are you rich, Ben?'

He laughed and shook his head. But he admitted he wasn't poor either. 'Forget what happened at Tiananmen Square,' he urged. 'It's history. China has moved on.'

Deftly steering the conversation away from the minefield of politics, Ben, after a short break, took up the microphone again and launched into a description of how marriages are arranged in China. '"Women hold up half the sky,"' he began, an old Chinese proverb quoted by Mao. Since Liberation women have been treated, in law and in practice, as the equal of men. No more selling of young girls to be brides of elderly husbands or mistresses of warlords, or to work in city brothels. No more lily feet … Ben peered at us, doubtless wondering if we knew what he was talking about. 'Foot binding,' he explained, in case we didn't. From 1949, men who wanted to get married had to have something to give their bride, not the other way round. At first the prospective husband had to find only one thing to give, but it had to be big – a sewing machine or a bicycle. No self-respecting girl would have him otherwise. After Deng came to power, two things had to be produced – a washing machine and a fridge-freezer, or a large TV and a computer. Today a man would be lucky to find a bride if he didn't have a car to offer, or an apartment, or both. 'See what I mean about moving on?' he concluded, grinning.

I couldn't help admiring Ben. He'd succeeded in de-clawing us. Nothing we asked seemed to faze him. He had an answer for everything.

Fielding another question, Ben admitted he'd got off lightly in the marriage stakes. He came back from the countryside knowing how to make oil for lamps – a skill which greatly impressed his future wife. Added to that, he'd learned how to make alcohol, 120 proof. 'Which meant,' he told us, 'that we would never be in darkness and we would always be happy. My wife considered me a great catch.'

*

Our day visiting *Wanli Chang-cheng* ends with a reception at the New Zealand embassy. More photos of Rewi. More speeches. But the only one in Mandarin is from the ambassador, John McKinnon. His Mandarin is fluent, his English eloquent. Jocelyn replies on behalf of the whānau, after which we tuck into a meal of New Zealand lamb washed down by the country's best pinot noir.

Ambassador McKinnon's view of Mao is that he was fatally restless. The Cultural Revolution, which even the Chinese now admit was a disaster, was born of that restlessness. Zhou Enlai, Mao's closest comrade from the 1920s onward, almost became a victim. As did Soong Chingling, the 'Mother of the Revolution'. By the time Deng Xiaoping had established himself as leader in 1978, it was possible to criticise both what had happened and the man who'd made it happen.

'It doesn't matter whether a cat is black or white, so long as it catches mice,' Deng famously said – though not, as I'd assumed, after he came to power, but back in 1962, in a speech to the Communist Youth League in Beijing. Everyone who heard him would have known what he meant. You don't have to be a revolutionary (or Party member) to get on. So long as you support the socialist economy, work hard and get results ('catch mice') you will prosper. No wonder he fell foul of Mao, who had him purged twice during the Cultural Revolution.

Deng's declaration that Mao was 'seven parts good, three parts bad' was meant to reassure the nation that the man who'd led them to Liberation could still be their hero. Rewi is on record as blaming the 'ultra-leftists' for the worst excesses of the Great Leap Forward and the Cultural Revolution – 'The ultra-left extravagances … cost China dearly,' he wrote in his memoir. But he is also on record as saying, in a conversation reported to New Zealander David Mahon, one of Rewi's regular Beijing visitors in the last decade of his life, 'There is only one person I hate in China, and that's Mao Tse-tung. He led a revolution to end feudalism, then he established his own.'[4] Another report, quoted in Anne-Marie Brady's book, has him describing Mao (to Tom Newnham) as a 'prick' for what he did to Rewi's comrades during the Cultural Revolution. A third, told to me by New Zealander Dave Harré, who visited Rewi in his Beijing home in 1986, is similarly unambiguous. 'Mao,' Rewi declared, 'was a bad man.'[5]

'It's a shame you're not visiting Mao's mausoleum,' Ben had said to us, as our bus journey came to an end. 'Everyone who goes there is asked to keep their voices down. It's meant to show respect. But the real reason you have to whisper is that nobody wants Mao to hear what people are saying about China. He wouldn't like it!'

CHAPTER TEN

'IT is always the unexpected that happens in China,' Rewi's first biographer, Willis Airey, records him as saying. For a man who's come to 'take a look' at a revolution, Rewi is more than ready to face the unexpected. Ypres and Bapaume, not to mention the lonely years at Moeawatea, have primed him to cope with whatever life throws at him.

I'm picturing Rewi standing on the deck of the ship that has brought him to Shanghai from Hong Kong – a place he will come to refer to, dismissively, as 'Treasure Island'.[1] It's 21 April 1927. He's been travelling, on and off, for five months. Having left New Zealand with only a few pounds – all that remained of his Moeawatea money – he had no choice but to stop off in Sydney to earn enough for the rest of the journey. For two months he worked in a fertiliser factory in Botany Bay, studying at night to gain a wireless operator's certificate so he could get free passage on an Australian ship.

He's had adventures. He's been in a fight. One of his co-workers at Botany Bay accused him of being the boss's man. Rewi gave him a bloody nose. He's made friends in the Philippines where the ship stopped for a week. In 1940 he will return to that country to raise money for Gung Ho, but that task is well in the future. He has come to China on not much more than a whim. He knows what he's getting away from. What he's getting into is anyone's guess.

He's aware, of course, that there's some kind of revolution going on – it's why he's come. What he doesn't know is that in the past two weeks the city he will soon be calling home has seen arrests and executions on an unprecedented scale even for China. Sun Yatsen's decision to form a United Front with the fledgling Communist Party has been revoked by his successor, Chiang Kaishek, whose rise has ended the power vacuum that followed the death of Sun. Hundreds of workers identified as communists, often wrongly, have been rounded up and shot. There has been a strike organised in part by a young communist called Zhou Enlai, recently returned from study in France. The strike has been called off, but that hasn't stopped Chiang ordering the arrest of Zhou and the wholesale massacre of what Chiang disparagingly refers to as *gong fei*, red bandits. Anyone seen wearing red, the bandits' chosen colour, is liable to be shot on the spot.

Rewi, the 'slow learner', will take a while to work out what is going on. ('I am not the type which develops fast,' he wrote to Isabel Airey, wife of his biographer. 'Truths penetrate but slowly, and sometimes quite painfully.'[2]) He will hear the words 'White Terror' and wonder what they mean and how worried he should be. At first he sees little of the violence. He's a European, after all. Europeans don't live as the Chinese do. They live in 'international concessions', areas scattered along China's eastern seaboard, conceded to foreign governments by the dying Qing (Manchu) dynasty in the wake of the Opium Wars. Britain, France, Germany, the United States, Belgium, Russia, Japan all hold concessions governed and policed not by Chinese law but by their own rules and regulations. In the British-run International Concession, where Rewi will spend his first few nights in China, most of the police are Sikhs.

So what does Rewi see from the deck of his ship as it steams up the mighty Huangpu River (Rewi will spell it Whangpoo) so slowly as to be almost stalled? Everywhere he looks he sees boats – sampans rearing up like Spanish galleons; junks with dark red sails, packed with coal and bales of cotton and silk; ferries like the one that will take him from the ship to the jetty at Nanjing Road; barges carrying fruit and vegetables, iron girders and machinery; a couple of Japanese gunboats lurking menacingly. He's done his reading. He knows that this river, the last tributary of the Yangtze before it flows into the East China Sea, is vital to China's trade, most of which is conducted for the benefit of the foreign powers that control the concessions. But there is a world of difference between knowing something and seeing it in action.

Ten years later Christopher Isherwood will describe the view over the city side of the river as a collection of 'semi-skyscrapers … dumped on an unhealthy river bank.'[3] Rewi could have said much the same. Even in 1927 Shanghai was a city growing skywards. Despite the havoc wrecked by Japanese bombs, this view won't change much in the following decades. What will change, once China is opened up to the West, and capitalism takes hold, is the view over the opposite bank. Instead of paddy fields stretching all the way to the horizon there will be houses, schools, industrial complexes, universities – the fruits of Shanghai's insatiable appetite for expansion.

By the time the ship docks at Nanjing Road, Rewi is suffering from sensory overload. The sights, sounds and smells of Shanghai are like nothing he's ever experienced before. He's used to chaos, the default condition of warfare, but this deafening, technicolor, highly pungent bedlam is something else.

He disembarks carrying his battered suitcase containing all he owns in the world – a few books, some writing materials, shirts, socks and three pairs of his ubiquitous shorts. (No one else in Shanghai wears shorts, but that doesn't deter Rewi. For the rest of his life, wherever he is in the world, he will prefer

Kiwi mufti: shorts, shirt – he wears a tie only when compelled to – socks pulled up to the knee, sandals.) He looks around for signs to Immigration and Customs. Surely he has to register his arrival, declare what he is bringing into the country? But there's nothing. Just groups of Chinese shouting at one another, darting this way and that as if in response to the calls of a drunken dancemaster. Rewi has made a start on learning Mandarin, but nothing he hears makes sense to him today. Soon he will learn that speaking Chinese is frowned upon by Europeans. 'Why are you bothering with that monkey language?' is the question put to him, in various different ways, soon after his arrival. 'Not a good idea to "go native", old boy. You know what they say. Mix with the Chinese and you'll get typhus!'[4]

Well, I don't care, Rewi says to himself, having concluded this country doesn't give a hoot who comes and who goes, I'm pressing on.

He is about to leave the wharf when a Chinese man – a worker, judging by his clothes – appears in front of him, stares at him a moment, then spits in his face. Rewi reels back, more in astonishment than outrage. What an extraordinary thing, he says to himself, wiping away the spittle. What an extraordinary country.

He swaps his suitcase to the other hand and heads towards the city. He doesn't record whether anyone spat in his face again but spitting, he writes years later in his memoir, is endemic. 'Ninety-five percent of the population seemed to have chronic catarrh.'

It's April, there's blossom on the trees, but that's not what he smells. Like me in my Beijing hotel room, he's assaulted by a mixture of other smells: petrol fumes, cooking, the fishy smells from the river, the stench of rubbish, human sweat … Later he will identify something else, the distinctive battlefield odour of sewage and rotting flesh. Even in peaceful times – which these are not – people living in the Chinese part of Shanghai die every day on the streets from famine, from overcrowding, from industrial accidents and appalling working conditions. Their bodies are tossed in the river, or gathered up, doused with gasoline and burned. No one talks about it. It's commonplace. The smell is not supposed to reach the international settlements, but when the wind blows from that part of the city not even the most privileged inhabitants can claim to be ignorant of what's happening beyond their borders.

Rewi stops to blow his nose. Something other than the smell is irritating his nostrils. He looks up. The air is full of thistledown. Of course, he thinks. Pollen from plane trees. Two out of every three trees in Shanghai, he will learn, is a plane tree.

He's about to move on when he hears the unmistakable sound of rifle fire. A brisk rat-a-tat-tat, followed by silence. He freezes. Old instincts pulse through his body. He doesn't have a rifle but he knows how to take cover. Strange, he thinks, as his eyes scan the seemingly indifferent crowd, how gunfire, like the crying of babies, sounds the same wherever in the world you are.

Right, he says to himself as he starts walking again, I get the picture. It may be out of sight but there really is a revolution going on. For a moment back there he'd thought he was in France, shouldering his rifle, a merry-go-round of sensations making him dizzy with fear, his feet stuck in mud as thick and wet as pea soup. There were plane trees in France too. He remembers stopping to listen to a thrush singing its heart out from a tree miraculously untouched by the destruction around it. A single bird singing through the whistling of shells and the pounding of guns. 'The slaughterhouse of history'. Whoever said that – was it Hegel? – knew about mud and death and the miracle of birdsong.

He steps aside to avoid a rickshaw. It's being pulled by a stick-thin coolie – the word comes from the Chinese word for bitterness – dressed in ragged trousers and sandals made from straw. The passenger is a fat European gent, wearing a white panama hat and sweating copiously. As the rickshaw passes, Rewi meets the man's eye. A flicker of acknowledgement. 'Did I tell you to slow down?' the man shouts at the coolie. He glances back at Rewi. There's more than acknowledgment now. It's as if they're in league. 'Got to show the natives who's boss,' he yells, grinning. 'Don't pay them to dawdle.'

Rewi, his temper flaring, drops his suitcase. The frightened coolie is running now. Rewi makes as if to follow, then changes his mind. Punching that fat bastard's nose would give him great satisfaction, but what would it do to the coolie? Earn him a whipping probably, or worse.

Sobered by the experience Rewi walks on. That man had recognised something in him that he would rather not think about. You and I are the same, he'd signalled. We're the ruling elite. Well, I may be a supporter of empire, Rewi silently answers him, but that doesn't mean I'm going to sit back and watch men like you lord it over people with far more right to be in this country than we have.

He pushes his way through the press of people, anxious now to find the boarding house in Sichuan Road where he's arranged to stay. He's been in big cities before but nothing has prepared him for this maelstrom. It's not just the shoving, shouting, spitting crowd he has to navigate, it's the streams of bicycles, rickshaws, wheelbarrows, carts pulled by mangey mules. It's the swerving cars and trucks, the children shouldering yokes from which buckets carrying God knows what swing precariously. The noise is frightening, a clamour that reminds him of a Brueghel painting – *The Fall of the Rebel Angels* – that had caught his attention when leafing through his parents' art magazines. What he heard when he looked at that crowded, terrifying canvas was the clash of swords, the shrieks of the condemned, the blaring of trumpets. What he's hearing now – shouting, tooting, banging, braying, the screech of brakes – is not so different.

As a foreigner he attracts the attention of street sellers: a man with a wispy beard and a *queue* (pigtail) tries to sell him cigarettes; a woman with a child tied to her leg offers fried turnip cakes and basket buns (Shanghai specialties); other women proffer dumplings, pancakes, sugar cane. He passes children sitting on the pavement making briquettes; a beggar playing a bamboo flute … He sees first one pawnshop – 'The Venue of Mercy', spelled out in English under the Chinese characters – then another, 'The Compassionate Place'. At one point he passes a curtained doorway with the signs of the zodiac carved into the wall above. He watches as one man enters and another leaves. Might as well throw your money down the dunny, he thinks.

Now he's in a tiny alley which he will mistakenly call a *hutong* (the Mongolian word for well), the name given to the maze of alleys and lanes, home to poor and working Chinese in Beijing. Here in Shanghai, he will learn, they're called *longtangs*. As he threads his way from one to the other, like Theseus seeking the Minotaur, he becomes increasingly disoriented. Pointless to consult his map. These muddy thoroughfares don't even warrant a mention. (In his 1935 diary he will describe these human rabbit warrens as 'crowded alleyways teeming with life which offer so much less than life'.[5])

For some time now he's been followed by a gang of kids wearing split pants. Some are carrying straw bags filled with cigarette butts. When they crowd close, he reaches into his pocket for coins, explaining – pointlessly, they don't understand him any more than he understands them – that this is all he has. In one particularly odorous *longtang* he stops to watch a woman shake bamboo sticks out into a fan on the baked mud outside her straw hut. What is she doing? He will learn soon enough. Like the customers coming and going in the zodiac house, she's in search of information about her future.

Eventually he finds his way out of the maze and steps with relief onto a wide, tree-lined avenue. The presence of Europeans is reassuring, though most of them are whisking past in cars and rickshaws. One elegant woman, her face half hidden under a parasol, is being carried in a rickshaw decorated with fans and butterflies.

Everywhere he looks he sees men in uniform – Japanese and British mainly, but there are others as well. Some are on horseback. They're there to protect the international settlements – this much he knows already. What he will learn is that Chiang Kaishek, whose name means 'boundary stone' (something Rewi will find significant, as China, thanks to the government's anti-communist policies, is split in two), has little interest in disturbing the existing arrangements with foreign powers. Chiang views the concessions, and the revenue they raise, as necessary to China's future. The nationalist government, or Kuomintang (KMT), might claim to be the modernising force in China, but nothing has been done to change the archaic and inefficient methods of tax collecting. So the concessions stay … until in 1949, the year of the communist victory, their foreign inhabitants turn and run.

Confident that he is now walking in the right direction, Rewi quickens his pace. His brain is racing. How can he hope to make sense of this rowdy, kaleidoscopic world? The non-political soldier who went to the defence of his Māori mates in Cape Town may have developed some new ideas but he's still not a political animal. For all he knows, Chiang's distrust of the communists is justified. As a member of the National Revolutionary Army, China's new leader fought bravely to end the rule of emperors in China. But the close alliance with Russia formed by Chiang's predecessor, Sun Yatsen – his overtures to the West having been rejected – seems to be coming apart at the seams. Chiang, Rewi has read, is now looking to the West again. Who's to say the West won't reject him as they rejected Sun? Dependent as China is on foreign loans, how will it manage if no one is willing to keep it afloat?

Trams clatter past, the jerky syncopation of their progress and the clang of their bells reminding Rewi of his school days in Christchurch. Banners flutter above his head but he can't decipher the signs. He passes a whole wall covered with painted dragons. He side-steps around a table where men are playing mahjong. They glance at him but unlike the crowds in the *longtangs* they seem as indifferent to his presence as they are to the soldiers nervously fingering their guns. One of the men bends sideways and aims a gob of spit into the pavement spittoon. Rewi smiles. He has just spotted an old man in a long silk gown, sitting in a doorway, calmly smoking his pipe.

Well, what d'ya know? he says to himself. I'm in China.

CHAPTER ELEVEN

NOT one to sit around waiting for things to happen, Rewi, after only a few days in Shanghai, has found both a place to live and the job he will keep for the next 18 months, working with other Europeans – Chinese are employed only in a menial capacity – at the Hongkou Fire Station. (Later, as a factory inspector, he will be based at the Shanghai Municipal Council.) That he found a job so quickly was no doubt down to his army connections. The fire service was an arm of British imperial power in Shanghai. Rewi, as a decorated soldier, on extended leave from the New Zealand Army, would have been taken on, no questions asked.

His new home is in the French Concession, not far from the girls' boarding school where 28-year-old Mao Zedong held a secret meeting in July 1921 to plan the founding of the Communist Party. Designed along the same lines as the Paris arrondissements, the concession, with its gracious, tree-lined boulevards, is a welcome change from the bush-tangled hills of Moeawatea and the monotony of sea travel. Plane trees are everywhere. The locals call them *faguo wutong*, the French phoenix tree. Their familiarity is comforting.

'I was struck by the contrast of wealth and poverty,' Rewi wrote four decades later in his memoir, describing the Shanghai he encountered in 1927. 'Away from the main streets, with their palatial buildings, you were soon in a maze of narrow, stinking, congested lanes.' Families were crowded into flimsy straw huts with no sanitation and no protection against either summer's 'tiger heat' or winter's ferocious cold. Beggars were everywhere, many of them refugees from the fighting in the north and the industrial upheavals in Shanghai and Canton.

The year before Rewi's arrival Chiang Kaishek had launched his 'Northern Expedition', with the aim of overthrowing the warlords who controlled large areas of China and unifying the country. He was supported in this aim by the fledgling Chinese Communist Party (CCP). Together they succeeded in bringing large areas of China under the central control of the nationalist government. His desire to defeat the warlords and unify China was genuine, but he had another agenda, one he intended to put into operation as soon as the Northern Expedition was completed. His allies, the communists, were to be re-branded as enemies.

Chiang's hatred for the communists, shared by many but by no means all in the KMT, stemmed as much from what united the two parties as what divided them. The bitter struggle that began in the wake of that first Northern Expedition was a struggle between brothers. 'It was the similarity of the Nationalists to the Communists in so many areas that made their mutual hatred so much more intense,' historian Rana Mitter writes in *A Bitter Revolution: China's struggle with the modern world*.[1] An old and inevitably tragic story: Cain fighting Abel; Catholic fighting Protestant; Sunni fighting Shia …

From the end of 1926 Chiang's determination to rid the country of the *gong fei*, the red bandits, was the motivating force behind every policy decision he made. When the strike organised by Zhou Enlai at a Japanese factory in Shanghai threatened to spread to other factories, he ordered the police to fire on the strikers, unleashing what would become known as the White Terror. Eventually, infuriated by the communists' challenge to his authority, Chiang ordered Shanghai's notorious Green Gang to round up and massacre as many CCP members as they could find. Thousands, most of them workers with no connection to the communists, were killed. Thousands more, like Zhou, were forced to flee.

Rewi, struggling with a welter of information, sensory and otherwise, knows it's going to take him months if not years to make sense of things. But he's not a man to turn a blind eye. Some truths are all too evident. 'The Shanghai of luxurious clubs, sleek cars and well-trained servants was the Shanghai in which one slept and ate one's food,' he wrote in *Yo Banfa!.* 'But one's working and emotional life was spent up and down the alleyways where the vast majority of Chinese lived – where every tiny room held a family, and where rows of night pots lined the streets.' Rows of washing too, hanging on bamboo poles, a common enough sight. Only later will Rewi learn that those humble garments flapping in the breeze were not always as innocent as they seemed. If you were a member of the communist underground you could arrange your washing in such a way as to signal to the *gong fei* that your house was safe to enter.

Rewi the soldier has seen and experienced terrible things. Now, in Shanghai, he will see worse and come to understand, like Orwell writing a few years later, that when human beings are reduced to the level of survival, moral judgements are superfluous. The horrors of child labour, of the buying and selling of peasant children, of poverty so extreme it forces people to live like rats, renders so-called civilised values redundant. What Rewi sees as he goes about his work is a society reduced to the level of psychopathy. Who is he to blame the people he encounters for behaving as if human nature were purely animal?

It's not an observation that goes down well with his fellow Europeans. In their eyes the coolie is a sub-human creature bereft of both decency and morals. In this sought-after, fought-over, gangster-controlled city, the European is king. In the British and French concessions, where officials share club membership and drink imported wines and spirits with local Chinese warlords and gangsters, life is a giddy whirl of dances, receptions, race meetings, polo matches and garden parties. 'Do business big or don't do it at all' is the rule of thumb for both investor and gambler in this fabled 'Paris of the East'. Jazz clubs, dance shows, musical shows, brothels and opium dens compete with the latest craze – martial arts movies – for the dollars and pounds floating around like paper boats on a lake.

Officially China is ruled by the nationalists, but in Shanghai power is in the hands of gangsters, led by the notorious Sun Chuan-fang, in association with the triads (secret societies) who control the city's opium trade. Crime, drug trafficking and prostitution flourish. There are rumoured to be close on 150,000 prostitutes – the legendary 'singsong girls' – working in Shanghai. Having escaped the floods and famines in the interior, and the fierce fighting in the north, these hapless young women are picked off the streets by gangsters, forced into brothels and made to dress as schoolgirls, the look favoured by the clientele in 1927. Adventurers of all types and stripes crowd the bars and restaurants, drawn by the prospect of easy money, lax law enforcement and the lure of luxury. White Russians, Jews, Sikhs, Indian revolutionaries, Japanese spies, gangsters who interpret the KMT's order to 'follow and obey' as a licence to kill, British and American journalists, tourists looking for a good time, poets and novelists looking for inspiration – all rub shoulders in this heaving, multi-lingual metropolis.

This is the city that will be Rewi's home for the next 11 years – a city that, according to Han Suyin, made the Chicago of Al Capone look positively staid. The apartment Rewi eventually lives in, after lodging for a period in a house owned by White Russians, will see him metamorphose from a disappointed ex-bush farmer and wannabe soldier to, in the words of one Kiwi visitor, 'a New Zealander of the recognisable missionary type', before reaching his final incarnation, the one that will stick – as a revolutionary.[2] Meetings will be held at No. 4 Lane 1315, Yuyuan Road, with other like-minded ex-pats. The first plans for the Gung Ho movement, devised by Rewi and his American friends Edgar and Peg Snow, will be drawn up there. Communists on the run will take refuge within its walls. A radio transmitter will be set up on its roof to send messages to the Eighth Route Army. Eventually Rewi will resign from his job as factory inspector and leave Shanghai to work full-time for Gung Ho. There will be no going back. The blue-eyed, golden-haired boy, who rebelled against his father's punitive regime, will find in China a rebellion that will define the rest of his life.

CHAPTER TWELVE

11 April 2017

WE are to be tourists again: Tiananmen Square; the Forbidden City; the Temple of Heaven; followed by a tour through the surviving *hutongs*, inaccessible to cars, that are all that remain of the old Peking way of life. Not that Rewi is forgotten. Coming with us on the bus is Rewi's only surviving foster son, Lao San, the third of four brothers whom Rewi took care of after their adoptive father, George Hogg, headmaster of the Shandan School, died of tetanus.

Dave leads Lao San – a slight, grey-haired man with smiling eyes, looking at least 10 years younger than the 80 he claims to be – across the hotel foyer to meet me. I am suddenly choked with emotion. I had no idea any of the children Rewi regarded as sons were still alive. Lao San shakes my hand. His smile is impish. I don't know whether it's all right to hug him, but it's what I do. And it is all right. He says something I can't understand – the English Rewi taught him has mostly been forgotten – but his smile makes words unnecessary. I'm introduced to his wife who has no English at all, and a friendship begins.

Over the next day and a half, then later when we return to Beijing at the end of our journey, I will talk to Lao San whenever I can. And he will talk to all of us while travelling on the bus, at one point bursting into song, one of many Rewi taught him:

The more we are together, together, together,
the more we are together, the happier we'll be.
For your friends are my friends and my friends are your friends …

As Lao San's story unfolds, a picture prints itself on my brain: Rewi in Shandan, seated on the *leitai* – a raised platform, known as the Thunder God Platform, built during the Ming dynasty to stage wrestling matches – with nine-year-old Lao San seated beside him. This little urchin, who'd arrived covered in lice, his body wasted by dysentery and beri beri, one eye closed by infection and trachoma, loved nothing more than singing. While George Hogg, an enthusiastic singer, was alive, Lao San always had someone to sing with. But with George gone, Rewi had to fill the gap.

It takes me a while to stitch together the threads of Lao San's tale. He may have forgotten most of his English, but after singing his way through 'The More We Are Together' he launches into 'Three Blind Mice'. We sing along with him, while outside the bus window the North China Plain rolls past, its dirt-grey fields and mud villages repeating themselves like the notes of a stuck tune.

The story Lao San tells is a personal one. He's not concerned with the historical record, nor with politics or dates. I will hear other similar stories on this extraordinary journey, with sometimes confusing results. A lot of nodding and smiling from both sides accompanies these exchanges, though what is being agreed to is likely to be mere guesswork. What this tells me is not that I'm being lied to, but that facts and figures sometimes get lost in translation. The personal and the historical don't always match. When more awkward questions are asked – for instance, about the Tiananmen Square massacre – the resulting confusion, despite the smiling, doesn't feel quite so benign. What we are being told doesn't tally with the facts.

Happily no such difficulty arises with Lao San. His story belongs with the spirit of openness associated with the May 4th Movement – the cultural and political upheaval that followed the publication of the Treaty of Versailles in 1919 – when, with Chiang's anti-communist crackdowns still some years in the future, discussion and story-telling flourished.

Lao San – the name given to him by George Hogg – means Number Three Son. His family name is Nie (or Nieh), his given name Guangtao (or Guangpei). This practice of naming children by their position in the family – First Daughter, Second Daughter, and so on – was common in Old China. Since the one-child policy it has fallen into disuse, but family members are still sometimes addressed as 'Elder Brother' or 'Number One Uncle'. So Nie Guangtao, the third son, became Lao San. His brothers became Lao Da (Number One), Lao Er (Number Two) and Lao Si (Number Four).

All four Nie boys were born in Manchuria. Their father was a revolutionary, a member of the communist underground. Arrested by the KMT during one of Chiang's 'bandit extermination' drives – the Northern Expedition was only the beginning: four more followed, the focus shifting from ridding China of warlords to ridding it of communists – the father on his release moved the family to Baoji, where he found work as a teacher. But the KMT had kept him in their sights. He was arrested again and badly beaten. Then he disappeared. When he failed to return, his wife assumed he was dead.

Life from then on was a desperate struggle to survive, but at least she and her sons were together. That is, until a second blow struck. The mother, who had been supporting her boys by spinning yarn, became seriously ill and was admitted to hospital. Had they remained in Manchuria she would have had family to help, but Baoji was hundreds of miles from her home village. Besides, Manchuria was by this time in Japanese hands. To go back there would be suicide.

Having no other choice, the mother sent her four boys to an orphanage outside the town. There George Hogg, on a mission for Rewi's school, based at that time in Shuangshipu (the name means Twin Rock Village), decided to take the two older ones back with him so they could get an education. Seven-year-old Lao San was heartbroken. Without Elder Brothers One and Two, the loss of his mother became unbearable. He made up his mind to find her. He had no food, no boots, no winter coat. He walked without stopping for a day and a night. When he got to the hospital in Baoji he was told his mother had 'gone'. No one thought to tell him she had died. He would learn that a year later.

'How did you survive?' I can't remember now whether someone asked this question or whether he just went on to give us the answer. 'I sang songs,' he tells us. 'That's how I stayed alive. I sang the guerrilla songs my father taught me before he went away, then I sang the old Chinese songs – "The Crescent Moon Rises", "Jasmine Flower", "The Rain Prayer." I was always singing.'

Before long news of Lao San's amazing journey reached George Hogg in Shuangshipu. He didn't hesitate. The two younger Nie boys must be brought to the school to join their brothers. Rewi agreed. Two days later George knocked on the orphanage door and the process of adoption began. But there was a problem: Lao San was too ill to travel. So George arranged for him to be admitted to the Baoji clinic to be treated for his various ailments. After a few weeks all signs of dysentery, beri beri and trachoma had gone. Rewi, who had business to attend to in Baoji, undertook to fetch him and his younger brother. 'I left the clinic fat and happy,' Lao San tell us. 'And with no lice. I had no idea you could live without lice. I thought everyone had them. They were just part of the body ...'

'I am now, officially and legally, a father of four,' George Hogg wrote home to his parents. 'They [the two youngest] were a bit weedy at first and needed rubber sheets.' In a later letter he described the boys as 'growing up to be very tough and will, no doubt, be a credit to me in my old age'.[1]

For four years the Nie brothers lived under George's protection. Then in July 1945 George died and Rewi stepped up to the plate. From then on the boys were his responsibility. 'Rewi wasn't like other foreigners,' Lao San tells us. 'He washed our sheets himself when we peed on them, and he was happy to use our toilets.' (Chinese squat toilets will become a regular topic of conversation as we move out of the cities into the remote northwest.) 'He could be strict,' Lao San adds, grinning. 'I was often naughty, so I got hidings. But he loved us. He was our father.'

> ... thin wisp of a seven year old,
> walked ten miles back to the village alone
> to find her ...
> then how you came with me
> to Shuangshipu; malaria, dysentery
> and a bad red eye ...
> ... then how you lifted
> your voice and sang a guerrilla song,
> high notes filled with courage
> and defiance, so that the eyes
> of folk began to shine like your good one ...
> ... and I thinking
> how good it was to have lived those years
> along with you, Lao San.[2]

In fits and starts, helped along by our guide who is acting as translator, Lao San brings Rewi alive for us. We see him wearing grass sandals like everyone else; sharing the *kang* – a heated platform made of mud bricks on which whole families slept – like everyone else; using the pit privy like everyone else. We see him as a father, giving his sons haircuts, scrubbing their backs in the bath tub, carrying them on his shoulders, telling them bedtime stories – Jack and the Beanstalk, Hansel and Gretel, Snow White and the Seven Dwarfs ... 'I had a very happy childhood,' Lao San says, as his story comes to an end. 'We lived happily like father and sons.'

Did my mother tell me about Lao San? Is that why I have another false memory of playing with Rewi when I was just a toddler? This particular memory is so vivid I have difficulty accepting that it's not true. I see Rewi sitting cross-legged, like my little fat daddy Buddha, with me bouncing off him as if he were some kind of human trampoline. I would have gone on swearing this was true had I not seen the dates proving it could never have happened. Either my mother's stories about her adored first cousin were so vivid I simply commandeered them as my own, or the Rewi of the letters and photos so infected my childish imagination that I put myself into the stories about him, and stayed there.

After the war Lao San and his brothers were miraculously reunited with their father. This is how Lao San, in a translation from his spoken words, described the parting from Rewi: 'In 1950, one year after Liberation, Rewi sent the four of us to the northeast to reunite with our father. In so doing he lost the children who had lived with him for so many years. Loneliness often haunted him.' There were visits over the years, but during the decade of the Cultural Revolution, when Chinese were forbidden to associate with foreigners, no contact was possible. For Lao San this was 'an unspeakable pain in my heart'.[3]

*

I'm a distracted tourist. The vastness of Tiananmen Square (*an* = peace, *men* = gate) is impressive but I can't silence the voices in my head. 'Evolution not revolution,' Ben had said. 'We have to be patient.' Less than a hundred years ago Chinese in their millions died every year from famine and flood, from execution and political massacres (Chiang Kaishek referred to the KMT's massacres of communists and their sympathisers as 'the holy work of extermination'[4]). Nothing like that is happening today. So I will take Ben's advice and withhold judgement …

In 1860, during the Second Opium War, Tiananmen Square was occupied by British and French troops. Camped by the Gate of Heavenly Peace, where I'm standing now, they planned on burning down the entire Forbidden City, but settled instead for setting fire to the Old Summer Palace, the *Yuanmingyuan*. Later, during the brutal suppression of the Boxer Rebellion in 1900, troops of the Eight Nation Alliance – formed to protect foreign interests in China – quartered themselves here, turning the political and cultural heart of China into a parade ground for enemy troops. From them on, until the revolution of 1911, this square, as iconic to the Chinese as Trafalgar Square is to the English and Times Square to the Americans, was home to foreign armies and diplomatic missions.

For the last three decades of his life Rewi lived in an apartment to the east of the square in what is still known as the Old Legation Area. I turn in that direction. Look around you, I hear Rewi say. What do you see? People from all over the world. Families enjoying the spring weather. No soldiers. No foreign troops. No armed police. What does that tell you?

Then another voice starts up in my head, that of a young Chinese student taught by a friend of mine in New Zealand. Asked what he thought about the Tiananmen Square massacre of 1989, he expressed surprise. He'd never heard of it!

I remember thinking at the time of that 1989 rebellion it was a good thing Rewi didn't live to see it play out. One of the themes of his now lost letters to me was the importance of listening to the young. I don't recall his exact words, but the message was clear. The young know what's right. They are the true revolutionaries. Older generations get tired. Stuck in their ways. They start to build little empires with themselves at the centre. Mao had the same thoughts when he kick-started the Cultural Revolution.

'A revolution upsets people,' Rewi told a group of international students who visited him in 1967, one year into the Cultural Revolution. 'When you have a revolutionary situation, everything is upset. People's lives are upset. Everybody is touched by it. People who thought they were doing well, everything was going alright … suddenly find there is questioning about that … The history of China is really a history of revolutions. Change has always come in China through revolutions …'[5]

So what would Rewi have made of the events in Tiananmen Square in 1989? I try to put myself in his shoes, then realise it's entirely possible he would not have known what was going on. He would have been aware of the protest, since it was happening on his doorstep, but I doubt very much that the image, broadcast around the world, of the lone figure clutching plastic bags full of groceries, standing defiantly in front of the advancing tanks, would have been seen by him or anyone else in China. 'Tank Man' – the name he will forever be known by – was not a student but a passer-by who decided, on the spur of the moment, to stage his own protest by standing in front of the advancing column. What happened to him after he was bundled away by police is not known. There have been rumours covering everything from execution to a quiet release back into society, but the truth remains hidden.

Rewi had welcomed the reforms, initiated by Deng Xiaoping in the late 1970s and early 80s, opening China up to investment, breaking the stranglehold of the commune system, but would he have continued to support Deng in the wake of the Tiananmen Square massacre? As the reforms started to bite, he privately expressed dismay at the direction China was taking, but no hint of disapproval appears in his public statements. Deng was his friend. He'd hosted Rewi's eightieth birthday celebrations in The Great Hall of the People. Years of keeping his mouth shut, toeing the line, had changed Rewi. 'I don't care' no longer worked. Something – a residual innocence perhaps – had been lost.

I've listened to the answers he gave those eager young students who wanted to believe the best of him and of China in 1967. I've heard the hesitations, the awkward convoluted answers which tell so much about the confusion he was feeling and, no doubt, the fear. Many of his friends had been gaoled. Israel Epstein, editor of *China Today*, the paper Rewi wrote for under a pseudonym, spent five years in prison. British-born David Crook, father of Michael, who'd fought in Spain before going to China to support the communists, was placed in solitary confinement. His wife Isabel, daughter of missionaries, whom our party will meet on our return to Beijing, was gaoled for two years. Rewi would almost certainly have shared their fate had it not been for the protection of Zhou Enlai and Soong Chingling, widow of the revered Sun Yatsen.

In the decade from 1966 to 1976, no one dared criticise the Red Guards or challenge the 'Thoughts of Chairman Mao'. Not even the traditional vehicles of protest, the *Dazibao* (Big Character Posters), were safe. The Red Guards were using them to denounce members of the Party whom they had targeted as revisionist. Anyone posting an alternative message risked being shot on the spot. 'What can I write about?' Rewi asked his friend Zhou as the attacks increased, and more and more of the people he knew were locked up. Zhou thought for a while before answering: 'People abroad know very little about the good things while the bad things spread far and wide ... write about some of the good things.'[6]

So Rewi did, or tried to, referring again and again in his poems of this time to 'Mao Tse-tung Thought'. 'To fit into the new society I must correct many organisational faults,' he wrote in *Travels in China*, a long (overlong) book published in 1973. Like a Red Guard emerging from a self-criticism – aka 'struggle' – meeting, he insists that 'The fundamental question has been, and always will be, whether the correct line is being followed or not.' I think of my cousin Tom, full of admiration for what the Chinese government was doing for the people in 1956 but disturbed by the insistence on 'correct thinking'. Now here is Rewi, my cousin on the other side of my family, claiming that

Mao, the Great Helmsman, had led 'whole people … to forge a revolutionary base of immense value to the whole of struggling mankind'. I look at that sentence, with its clumsy construction and repetition of the word whole, and have a sense of the muddle in Rewi's brain at that time.

Surely none
will listen if
your admonitions
are too many,
your pontifications
too heavy … [7]

There is a contradiction here – the poet-to-order at odds with the truth-teller – but not a lie. Rewi's every instinct was to speak plainly whatever the circumstances, but speaking plainly during that turbulent decade would have seen him silenced, possibly forever. Besides he was not, initially, against the Cultural Revolution. He understood why Mao felt he had to break up the power cliques that had formed in every department of government. Keeping the spirit of the revolution alive made sense to Rewi. It was only later, when reports of the destruction taking place all over China started to trickle back to him, that doubt set in.

Underlying this speculation as to what was going on for Rewi at this time was the stark fact that he couldn't return to New Zealand. That door had been closed when the government, in the wake of the Korean War, refused to renew his passport. For the next 20 years he would travel on a special document issued by the Chinese government – the Peking Citizen's Certificate. That would change in 1976 following the visit of New Zealand Prime Minister Robert Muldoon. Enquiring of Chairman Mao what he could do for him, Muldoon was told, 'Give Alley his passport back.'[8]

From 1960 on, Rewi would be shadowed by the Security Intelligence Service (NZSIS) whenever he visited New Zealand. Even the New Zealand Broadcasting Service, following the official line, issued a directive ordering that his name never be mentioned on air (the ban was lifted a few years later). Had information about what was going on in China been available, it's possible Rewi would have been seen more as victim than willing apparatchik. But, as I can testify, not even his family knew what was happening.

In 1973 I'm living in England with my husband and two young children. A letter arrives from Rewi. He wants me to visit. There's talk of my writing his biography. 'Elspeth … has produced her first novel and made a name for herself in the literary world,' he writes to his sister Gwen, generously exaggerating my very quiet arrival on the British 'literary scene'.[9] Conscious that I had turned his last invitation down, my instinct is to accept. As it happens, we had been planning to return to New Zealand. Our careers – mine as a writer, my husband's as an actor – were not producing enough income to support a family.

I phone the Chinese embassy. I explain the situation and enquire about applying for a visa. The official on the other end of the line tells me to phone another number. I do this, only to be told the same thing again. Finally I get someone who is prepared to speak to me. 'Why you want to visit China?' this person asks. I explain, for the fourth time, that I've been invited by my uncle. 'What your uncle name?' is the next question. 'Rewi Alley,' I answer. A short, and in retrospect rather ominous, silence comes to an end with the words, 'One moment, please.' During the long wait that follows I become aware of excited chatter in the background. Then the official comes back on the line. 'You find China all full up,' he says. And the phone goes dead.

Words 'stiffen under [the] touch,' George Orwell wrote, describing the plight of writers living under totalitarian regimes, obliged either to tell lies or deny their feelings. Rewi didn't write lies during those dark years but he didn't write the truth either. And what he did write was mostly 'stiff', tethered to the Party line, devoid of any but officially approved thoughts and feelings. 'To present negative things along with the good, people in China seize on that,' he explained to Geoff Chapple. '[They] say that's what you're talking about … [yet] to present only positive things is a bit self-destructive … How do you solve a contradiction like that? I don't think you can.'

*

Back in the present I do what Rewi's voice in my head has told me to do – I take a long slow look around this famous square. We're not the only tourists, of course. Buses disgorge visitors from all over the world, though I don't hear any American voices. What I do see are hawkers selling their wares and smiling policemen dressed in smart green uniforms with spotless white gloves. The voice was right. The police are not armed. Over the following days, travelling by train, bus and plane, visiting densely populated cities and remote villages, I never see a gun. The contrast with the US, where

I recently spent a month, is, to say the least, surprising. Guns in Trump's America are everywhere.

What am I looking at? The present is occluded by the past. This vast square has really only been in existence since 1958 when the open area in front of the famous Tiananmen Gate was transformed into what we see now. Designed to both copy and surpass Red Square in Moscow, it's one of the largest public squares in the world. But long before it could lay claim to that status it was a place of symbolic and real significance in China's history. Along with its surrounding buildings and courtyards it has witnessed death, demolition, reconstruction, battles, occupations, punishments, proclamations, rebellions, displays of imperial then communist power, ancient Chinese festivals and seasonal celebrations. Despite the tourists, it looks half empty. But if I close my eyes the ghosts come – the generals, emperors, rebels, students, soldiers – filling up the spaces so that all I can see are people, China's millions, shoulder to shoulder, each with his or her own story.

CHAPTER THIRTEEN

REWI is finding his feet. He knows his way to the Hongkou Fire Station where he has already started work. He's mastered enough Chinese vernacular, thanks to conversations with his driver – his new job comes with a car – to handle transactions with stall owners and street sellers ('Please excuse my "worker's Chinese",' is how he begins his conversations.[1]) He no longer needs to use his fingers to indicate how many steamed buns he wants. He is greeted by name – Mr Ai-Li – by the woman who sells him his evening pancake. Soon he will have his own apartment and a houseboy to cook for him, but for now he is in a boarding house run by exiles from Lenin's revolution in the international settlement.

One of his tricks to help him learn Mandarin – he's having lessons with a 'kindly old Manchu' – is to memorise the names of the streets as he walks or bikes around the city, then match them to the Chinese characters when he gets back to the boarding house. Not that he can do this in the international settlement, because the names are all in European script. He wishes there were Chinese people he could talk to socially. He wonders what they would have to say about the recent mass executions. So far the only people he's managed to engage in conversation have been European, all of them seemingly grateful for the presence of troops in the streets. 'Chiang's right,' he's been told. 'We need the barricades and the barbed wire. Those communists are nothing but trouble.' Like everyone else Rewi has heard the stories of Pat Givens, the Irish chief of police, who's ability to flush out 'red bandits' is being lauded in bars and clubs the length and breadth of the city. 'By the time Givens is done there won't be a bandit left alive in Shanghai,' his supporters boast.

Rewi, the new boy on the block, keeps his own counsel. But he can smell the fear, taste the paranoia. The international settlements are like luxurious rafts, packed with nervous survivors determined to hang on to what they have. As for conditions outside the settlements – the horrors Rewi sees every day in the course of his work – no one wants to hear about those. Chinese peasants have always lived that way, he's told. It's what they're used to. When he asks his new boss, the fire chief, to explain why communists are being liquidated when all they're doing is trying to organise workers into unions, he's told not to ask such 'bloody fool' questions.[2]

Bankers, merchants, teachers, military and naval personnel, diplomats, government officials, tourists, missionaries, writers, musicians – at one time or another, as a European living in an international settlement, Rewi will come into contact with them all. Almost without exception they share a collective blindness to the conditions under which the Chinese employed in the factories and institutions of the international settlements are forced to live. This Rewi cannot understand. Even if they feel nothing for the wretched humans packed like pennies in a jar into flimsy, bug-infested straw hovels, surely they can see what a fire hazard they're nurturing on their doorstep? There are days when Rewi is called out to as many as 30 fires. Nor is that the only hazard he faces. Disease, spread by the rats, lice and mosquitoes that feed off the raw sewage running down the muddy borders of the *longtangs*, is rampant. The first time Rewi saw bed bugs clinging to the ceiling waiting to pounce, he thought his eyes were deceiving him. At least in the trenches, where rats and lice were commonplace, bed bugs, if they existed at all, had the decency to remain hidden from sight. Something, he is beginning to suspect, is desperately wrong with this country …

'China's not a nation' is the kind of remark he hears every day. 'It's a market, a geographical entity. Think of it like that and you'll stop worrying about the bloody Chinks. They're used to bed bugs. And lice. And they eat the rats.'

When Rewi is on call, he sleeps at the fire station. As an officer he has his own room. When we finally reach Shanghai at the end of our tour we will visit the Hongkou Fire Station, to be told that the room Rewi occupied is now a dormitory housing six. The days when Europeans were granted privileges as of right have been consigned to history.

Park Lane, Barrier Road, Rue Chevalier, Route Garnier, Avenue Joffre – these were the names Rewi saw on signposts as he moved around the international concessions. Today there are still streets with English names but they are translations from the original Chinese: Rich People Road, Peaceful Happiness Road, Famous People Road, Lucky Gold Road, Bubbling Well Road. The Racecourse, a favourite haunt of the British, has become the People's Square. The exclusive Shanghai Club ('No Chinese Allowed') has metamorphosed into the Seamen's Club. The Public Gardens, reserved in 1927 for the sole use of foreigners, is now Huangpu Park, open to everyone. The Palace Hotel, site of the famous piano bar, a mecca for jazz musicians and film stars from all over the world (Noël Coward wrote part of *Private Lives* while staying in its penthouse suite), is now the Peace Hotel, a popular tourist destination. After Mao came to power the Palace Hotel fell into disrepute.

Jazz, Mao declared, was the music of the enemy. But Mao is no more. In today's China, where money rules, tourists with dollars in their pockets are welcome, and no one complains when jazz is played.

'I did not enjoy fire department life very much,' Rewi writes in his memoir, admitting he found it difficult 'to acclimatise ... to the usual conversation in the officers' mess'. The companionship he cherished – that of the serving soldier – was born of an entirely different set of circumstances from those he was encountering in this city of a million souls. He began his China life believing that the Shanghai Defence Force, of which he was a part (a fact not mentioned in his memoir), was doing the right thing, protecting the empire and its citizens. But all that was about to change.

He doesn't describe himself as lonely at this time – he's too anxious to get to the period in his life when what he is doing will make a difference – but the person I see in those first two years, working as both a fire officer and a factory inspector, is Doody, the lonely boy, perched at the top of the walnut tree. He is not a club man. Even had he wanted to socialise with Europeans, he will never be able to keep his mouth shut. He's an Alley, after all. He can't help raising hackles.

'I remember going to one place,' he writes, recalling his work as a factory inspector. 'A white Russian lady had a boarding house, and she wanted a licence for it, she had filled up all the exits with bathrooms. "Wait a minute," she said and went into her bedroom ... She came out without anything on except for a wrap over her shoulders ... "Come in, darling," she said, and I said, "Oh I better go."'

History doesn't record whether the lady got her licence.

*

By early 1929 Rewi has stopped being a firefighter and is working solely as a factory inspector. He examines factories producing silk, rubber, paint, enamel goods, chromium, steel, lead, torches, bottle tops ... He visits brass foundries and tobacco-cutting factories. When accidents happen he's told they're caused by 'worker carelessness'. 'It's just a coolie with his hand torn,' he's reminded when he shows concern. 'The list of industrial accidents does not stand too much thinking about,' he writes in his diary. 'One becomes convinced that we are after all very crude savages.'[3]

Writing in his memoir over four decades later, he has this to say about his visits to the notorious silk factories:

In my work as a factory inspector one of the most miserable experiences was to see the incredible torture of the young children working in silk filatures … Many not more than eight or nine years old stood for twelve hours over boiling vats of cocoons, with swollen red fingers, inflamed eyes, and sagging eye muscles. Many would be crying from the beating of the foreman who would walk up and down … with a piece of Number Eight gauge wire as a whip. Their tiny arms were often scalded in punishment if they passed a thread incorrectly … the heat was unbearable …

Other factories were no better:

Antimony poisoning in the enamel works and lead poisoning in places where battery plates were made were vicious industrial hazards. I recall small boys who stood wearily, day and night over buffing wheels, their pitiful limbs encrusted with the grime of emery powder, sweat and metal dust. They worked over open chromium vats without exhausts for the poisonous fumes around them, sores ate into their flesh, and their hands and feet were pitted with 'chrome holes' …

As his fellow Europeans while away their leisure time in bars and nightclubs, Rewi reports these terrible facts to employers, urging them to take action. 'You are all potential murderers,' I imagine him telling the British, French and Japanese owners of these hell-holes. The argument that the children employed in the foreign-owned factories are refugees and would otherwise be left to starve cuts no ice with him. The more he sees of these child workers and the miserable conditions in which they live and die, the more insistent he becomes. At the same time he questions himself. I'm a soldier pledged to protect foreign interests. How can I justify that when I see what suffering those 'foreign interests' have caused?

In the end some, though not all, of the businessmen he confronts agree to implement the changes he's asking for. This should have brought satisfaction but it didn't. Nothing did. There's not just something wrong with China, he's beginning to tell himself, there's something wrong with the whole damn set-up. A system that allows foreigners to treat China's children as if they were no better than cattle is slavery by another name.

Ultimately it will be children, his own and the thousands of others – factory slaves, orphans of war and famine – who give him the courage to leave the comfort of his well-paid job and follow the dream of Gung Ho.

'You're mad!' his fellow officers tell him when he announces at the end of 1938 that he's quitting. 'You're throwing your life away!' They remind him that China is a mess, that no one will protect him if he moves outside the settlements. 'Don't you read the papers?' they shout. 'Fall into the hands of the communists and you'll wish you'd never been born …'

Rewi is deaf to it all. The only argument that gives him pause is the one that forces him to acknowledge how much more could be achieved if he stayed on. At his insistence the vats in the silk filatures have been replaced by central boiling systems. Children will no longer be horribly burned in the course of their work, or fall ill from breathing in the poisonous fumes. At the same time he's demanded that guards be placed on machines where children routinely suffer finger amputations. Nor has he limited himself to conditions on the factory floor. Wherever possible he's established canteens to provide meals for the factory children, insisting that only fresh food be served – fruit, vegetables, and unpolished rice, an invaluable preventative against beri beri. There's even a chance, if he stays on, that he'll be the one to announce a cure for chrome poisoning, having co-opted his Lebanese-American friend George Hatem (known as Ma Haide, the name given to him when he went to work with the Red Army), whose studies in the field of industrial poisoning are gaining nationwide recognition, to work on the problem.

Accepting the challenge to head the fledgling Gung Ho, Rewi turns his back on the whole stinking Shanghai mess. Along with others who feel the same way, he has set himself the herculean task of bringing to an end the abject poverty and its attendant suffering that he has witnessed every day since his arrival in China. Gung Ho will unleash a force unlike anything that has been seen in China before. By the end of the 1940s, more than 400,000 co-operatives will be operating throughout the country. Inevitably words such as 'missionary in disguise', 'a man whose churches are the workshops of China' will be used to describe Rewi – an insult in his book, given his dislike of most missionaries.[4] 'If I'm a missionary what is it I'm supposed to be preaching?' I imagine him saying in a fit of Alley temper. 'I don't have a religion. Work is the only worship I engage in. And I don't belong to a political party. I just want to get the job done.'

CHAPTER FOURTEEN

'THIS way, Lady, please, hurry now.'

I've been lagging behind. Our Tiananmen Square guide is cross. The others have all moved on to the Forbidden City while I've been dawdling, conjuring up the ghosts of China's past.

Beijing has not always been China's capital – during the tumultuous first half of the twentieth century the capital was sometimes moved twice in one year – but it is the city where history happens. And this square is at its heart. The 1911 uprising that dealt the fatal blow to imperial power in China may not have started here – it began in Wuhan, in Hubei province – but the movement that did start here, the May 4th Movement, already mentioned, ultimately ensured the survival of the new republic. 'The world is ours, the nation is ours, society is ours,' a young Mao Zedong wrote in a student editorial of July 1919. 'If we do not speak, who will speak? If we do not act, who will act?'[1]

Mao, employed at the time as an assistant librarian at Peking University, was writing in response to the Treaty of Versailles, the terms of which had just been published in China. Mao was not yet a communist, but he had studied the works of Marx and Lenin, and joined in discussions with other radical students about the way ahead for China. Marx's works were not widely available – Li Dazhao, director of the Peking University Library, was one of the first to translate Marx into Chinese – but every student knew about Lenin and the revolution in Russia. Lenin was the Man of the Hour. His writings were studied, often clandestinely (not everyone at the university was radical), fuelling the discontent that had followed the overthrow in 1913 of China's own Man of the Hour, Sun Yatsen.

Yuan Shikai, the man responsible for ousting Sun Yatsen, had lost no time in declaring himself emperor. Had he succeeded in his daring usurpation, the republic might have ended up as little more than a blip on the screen of history. But Yuan died, and in the ensuing chaos China's powerful warlords established control. That was the signal for the exiled Sun to return. His call for China to unite led to the revival of the Kuomintang, the Nationalist Party of China. It would be many years before the warlords were vanquished, but China was a republic again, free to plan its future. Or so it thought. China, an ally of Britain and France for the last two years of the Great War, had been promised that the territories formerly held by Germany would be returned to her when the war was over. Instead, under the terms of the Versailles treaty, those lands were ceded to Japan. As the news spread, so did the unrest.

On the afternoon of 4 May 1919, 3000 students from Peking and other universities (Mao almost certainly among them) marched to Tiananmen Square to voice their protest. The Armistice had been signed the previous November. The job of the Peace Conference was to punish the defeated, reward the victors and divide the spoils. China, still more or less at the mercy of its warlords, could, so the Western powers had concluded, be safely ignored. The students thought otherwise. 'Don't sign the Treaty of Versailles!' they chanted as they breasted Tiananmen Gate. 'Shandong belongs to China!'

The protest ended in disaster. Not only did it fail to change the terms of the treaty, it led to the arrest and imprisonment of hundreds of students. But it did achieve something: it unleashed a desire for change that would, over the next months and years, sweep across China, gathering support at all levels of society. Strikes, demonstrations and protests would lead, eventually, to pitched battles between those who wanted wholesale change (the communists with their rejection of Confucianism) and those who wanted to preserve Confucian hierachies in the new republic (the nationalists). For a time the New Culture Movement, as the May 4th Movement came to be known, was described by both nationalists and communists as the inspiration behind their own increasingly divergent notions of revolution. But with Chiang Kaishek's expulsion of the communists from Sun Yatsen's United Front, lines were drawn in the sand. From then on only the communists could truthfully claim to be the heirs of that history-changing demonstration.

In 1932, when Chiang Kaishek advocated a policy of appeasement towards the advancing Japanese who had invaded Manchuria in September 1931, insisting that China must first be united – he meant freed from communist influence – before Japan could be resisted, it had the opposite effect to the one he'd intended. Instead of persuading moderate Chinese to get behind his extermination campaigns, it revived their enthusiasm for the principles and values of the May the 4th Movement. Chiang's catch-cry – 'First Reunification then Resistance' – fell, for the most part, on deaf ears. Communist enthusiasm for fighting the Japanese mirrored the mood of the country. Only when the Japanese advance threatened Beijing did Chiang agree, under pressure from his American advisers, to make common cause with the hated *gong fei*. The fragile coalition, known as the Second United Front, didn't last long, but for a time, with Red Army and KMT soldiers fighting together, significant victories were won.

'When China wakes she will shake the world,' the emperor Napoleon is reported to have predicted (though many believe what he really said was, 'China is a sleeping giant. Let it sleep'). No one would dispute the fact that the giant is now well and truly awake. And few would quarrel with the assessment that it all began on that warm spring afternoon, eight years after the overthrow of the Manchu dynasty, here, in Tiananmen Square.

'Coming, I'm coming,' I say to the impatient guide, adding, because she looks genuinely distressed, 'Sorry.'

*

The Forbidden City. 'Forbidden to whom?' I ask our guide. She gives me a kindly look. How ignorant these foreigners are. 'To the common people,' she answers. 'No one could enter or leave without the emperor's permission.'

I look around at the school parties, the tourists, the hawkers, milling about in a 'city' that was once forbidden to them, and smile to myself. We are all emperors here.

'The emperor received his powers as a mandate from heaven,' the guide tells us. 'He was no ordinary mortal. He was a Celestial Being. And his home, everything you see around you now, was no ordinary collection of palaces, but the earthly expression of the power of heaven.'

Today the Forbidden City is a museum, housing what survived from the Japanese invasion, the civil war, and the flight to Taiwan of Chiang and his defeated army, taking with them as much as they could carry of China's priceless art (as well as US$450 million worth of bullion). It's a bewildering place: 999 rooms – that sacred number nine again – designed for 24 different Ming and Qing dynasty emperors. The Hall of Union, The Palace of Earthly Tranquillity, The Hall of Mental Cultivation, The Palace of Heavenly Purity, The Hall of Supreme Harmony – the names ring out like the pealing of a bell.

'I can't stop humming Puccini,' my musical cousin Ross whispers in my ear. '*Turandot*,' he says, catching my frown. 'It was filmed here.'

'The roof tiles were made from the yellow clay of the Yangtze River,' the guide explains, gesturing around the whole complex. 'Yellow being the imperial colour, no one else was allowed to use it.'

I'm swallowing information like a hungry bird. Facts – the ones I've remembered from my reading, the ones I'm being told – clog my brain like undigested food. Where is Rewi in all of this? How often did he come here? Did he bring his visitors here? What would they have talked about?

I want to ask about Pu Yi, the last emperor to sit on the Dragon Throne. After his forced abdication in 1911 he was allowed to stay on in the northern half of the Forbidden City. He was six years old. That comfortable incarceration came to an end when the Japanese decided to install him as a puppet emperor in Manchukuo (Manchuria) in 1934. Then, at the end of the war, that too came to an end. The communists arrested him and imprisoned him as a war criminal. But they didn't kill him. He didn't share the fate of the Romanovs. On his release, 10 years later, he became a gardener, and – if his testimony is to be believed – a happy man. He was even allowed to become a member of the People's Congress.

'Alley whānau, this way please! Follow my flag! Your bus is on other side of Gate of Divine Prowess. Please to make sure you get on right bus.'

I haven't been concentrating. I've missed most of what was said about the emperor's concubines, the many 'mothers' of the child Emperor Pu Yi. And I was miles away when we were shown the eunuchs' quarters. The building we're passing now is called The Palace of Tranquil Longevity. Our attention is being drawn to the Nine Dragons Screen that fronts the palace. To be born in the Year of the Dragon is considered lucky. This year, 2017, is the Year of the Rooster. The fiction writer in me, on the lookout for parallels, can't help noting that the Chinese Communist Party came into being in Shanghai in another Year of the Rooster, 1921. 'Restless, aggressively frank, likes to be noticed, conservative' are the qualities attributed to people born in such a year. All of which, including the last, can be attributed to the CCP at one time or another.

We follow the moving flag across the crowded carpark, but what I'm seeing are not the streams of people heading to and from the buses but those Peking University students shouting their protests against the Treaty of Versailles. Under the terms of the treaty, German Samoa was handed to New Zealand, the occupying power having invaded it, on Britain's instructions, in 1914. The island would stay in New Zealand hands until its independence in 1962. No broken promises there (though that may not be the way the Samoans see things in the light of Black Saturday, 28 December 1929, when New Zealand police fired on demonstrators). Nor were promises to Canada, Australia or

South Africa broken. So why was China treated so badly? The answer I'm coming up with is not pretty. 'Ching chong Chinaman …'

The bus is full of chatter. I close my eyes and see Mao, standing on top of the Gate of Heavenly Peace – from where, in imperial times, the emperor's edicts were lowered to officials waiting on bended knee – proclaiming the People's Republic and the victory of the Liberation Army. The date is 1 October 1949. '*Zhongguo renmin yijing zhan qilaile*,' he declares in his high, Hunan-accented voice. 'The Chinese people have stood up!' The words are enshrined now in legend. Only trouble is, he didn't say them – at least not on that momentous day. He said them a month earlier in a speech to the Chinese Congress. But it scarcely matters what he said. The excitement, the pageantry, the relief that the fighting is over, the heady faith in the future, shared by China's millions, is as palpable as the planes flying overhead and the soldiers, men and women, marching past the wildly cheering crowd. Mao is 56 years old. His hair is thinning, his voice unimpressive, but he stands six feet tall, the undisputed leader of a quarter of the Earth's population, looking out over the square that had once been the exclusive property of emperors but is now filled to bursting with the 'common people'. Everywhere he looks there are red flags, shimmering as if in response to the excitement on the ground. Bands play, guns sound the salute, planes dip their wings in tribute. No one on that day, least of all Mao himself, doubts that history is in their hands.

*

I should have paid attention when the guide was telling us about the eunuchs, because Rewi wrote a poem about them. It seems there was almost nothing he didn't know about China's 4000-year dynastic history and the achievements and failures of the various imperial courts. Were the poems he wrote about those lost worlds a form of escapism, or was he using the past to explain the present? It's true his prose work never strays far from the contemporary, but every so often the man who might have been an artist, had he been born in a different time, shows through. Like his favourite Tang dynasty poet, Tu Fu (Du Fu), known in China as the Sage of Poetry, Rewi might have been a 'writer of poems whose lines will last as long as time'.[2] Instead, in the midst of his busy life, he wrote 'blow-offs'.

My foot turns up a broken shard,
looking I see it is part
of a porcelain dog buried with
a neuter who had poured affection
on a Peking poodle! Forgotten now
in the tragedy of making boys into
eunuchs, ripping out bloody testicles
drying them, hanging them under
roof beams until there came the time
they could be buried with their owners …[3]

CHAPTER FIFTEEN

'I BECAME determined not to be one of the big greedy people,' Rewi wrote in his memoir, looking back on his Shanghai days. After a year living in the French Concession, surrounded on all sides by 'big greedy people', he's still not certain where his life is headed, but he is sure of one thing: what he's against. To the Chinese he is *yang guizi*, foreign devil, but he doesn't take that as an insult. 'Foreign' is the same as 'ocean', because the ocean is the place foreigners come from. So rickshaws, introduced by Europeans to replace wheelbarrows, are 'ocean rickshaws'; bicycles 'ocean donkeys'; imported paraffin wax candles 'ocean candles', and foreigners of all stripes 'ocean devils'.

Yang guizi, gao bizi (high nose) – Rewi knows enough Mandarin now to be able to see himself through Chinese eyes. He knows it's his 'great ugly western nose' that has earned him the second title.[1] Not that he's the only European to be addressed this way. To the Chinese the nose is what distinguishes Europeans from other races. No offence is intended.

Meantime the language Rewi speaks with his Chinese friends and acquaintances – a strange hybrid of Han Chinese, from his study of the classics, and Shanghai dialect, from his conversations with his driver – while not exactly fluent, is good enough to get by on. The Europeans he works with or meets socially are frankly perplexed as to why he's bothering to learn the 'monkey' language at all. What on earth does he need it for?

'Everyone thinks I'm Russian,' Rewi records in his diary. Like him, Russians are both *yang guizi* and *gao bizi*, with alarming amounts of white hair on their legs and ugly brown-red hair on their heads. A common enough sight in the big cities, where they are referred to, not always affectionately, as 'the old hairy people', they are either White Russians – refugees from the 1917 revolution – or Soviets, come to help the fledgling CCP. Rewi doesn't mind being mistaken for a Russian at this time. Later, when the Soviet Union inexplicably (to him) decides to back Chiang and not Mao, he will change his tune. Having started out as an elder brother to China, Russia will end up acting like a bullying father.

By the end of that first year in Shanghai Rewi has a third title: *lao touzi*, old rascal. It's the name the Chinese workers at the fire station have given him. He likes it. Accustomed to the teasing of his siblings, it makes him feel he belongs. 'Funny thing about this country,' he writes in a letter home in 1928, 'it sort of grows on me. Everyone hates it at first. I am liking these cranky Chinese people more and more.'[2] He particularly likes their sense of humour. It chimes with his own. He likes the way it mocks pretension and stops self-pity in its tracks. He's not thinking politically. In fact I would make a case for Rewi becoming 'political' only when what was happening in China left him no choice. But he is not, and never has been, neutral. He has put himself on a collision path with the exploiters – factory owners, bankers, businessmen with no other aim than to make money. He didn't come to Shanghai to make his fortune, as so many of the 6000 or more British nationals living there did. He – the 'slow learner' – came to learn.

'There is a warmth in the comradeship of ordinary people in China,' Rewi will write in *Yo Banfa!* two and a half decades later, 'a warmth that one has hungered for – a warmth that makes every hardship a trifle of no account.' Those few words make it possible, for the briefest of moments, to see behind my cousin's customary mask. Though capable of passion, even fury, on behalf of others, what he felt on his own behalf remains veiled. Those emotions have to be deduced from what he doesn't say, rather than from what he does.

*

Of all the people Rewi met in those early years in Shanghai, the one who influenced him most profoundly was Dr Joseph Bailie. Bailie was an American and a missionary. After little more than two years in the country – the two men met in Shanghai in 1928 – Rewi had formed a low opinion of missionaries, that 'pack of mongrels'. (His opinion of Americans at this time was mostly positive.) 'Jesus was a carpenter, not a capitalist,' he would remind people whenever the subject of China's missionaries came up. 'He didn't live in a luxurious compound with a large staff and cars to drive Him around.'[3]

Granted access to China in the wake of the Opium Wars of the 1830s and 50s, Catholic and Protestant missionaries had arrived in their thousands. By 1928 there were more than 8000 preaching throughout China. To Rewi they were no more nor less than an arm of the imperial powers that had been humiliating China for the last hundred and more years. He liked to tell a story – I can see what his childhood champion Pen would have called his 'scallywag' grin as he tells it – about missionaries handing out tracts to apparently grateful Chinese women. The women would bow their heads politely, wait till the missionaries had gone, then stuff the tracts in their shoes to keep out the cold.

It would not have been surprising, then, if Rewi's first meeting with missionary Joseph Bailie was prickly, but if that was the case the prickliness didn't last. 'Bailie seems a pretty sound sort of old chappie,' he wrote in a letter home soon after their meeting. 'Born in 1860 but can still think and act in a fresh and original manner … His yarns of early days in China, especially of the Relief of Peking (at the end of the Boxer Rebellion) in 1900, are priceless.'[4]

It was an unlikely friendship. There wasn't just Rewi's distrust of missionaries to overcome, there was the age gap as well (Bailie was more than 30 years Rewi's senior). But in the end neither of those things mattered. When Bailie told Rewi he considered it blasphemy to preach when people didn't have enough to eat, he was talking Rewi's language. Bailie understood why the common Chinese greeting before Liberation was not 'How are you?' but 'Have you eaten?' (Today, for the millions of migrants from the countryside trying to survive in China's cities, the greeting is, 'Have you found a place to live?') Starvation was commonplace, famine as predictable as the floods that caused it. Officials in a position to do something about the suffering were mostly indifferent. Not so Joseph Bailie. Every fresh flood and its attendant famine saw him working with the survivors, repairing dykes, building canals, determined to bring what relief he could. When he succeeded in resettling the survivors of a flood in Manchuria, the Japanese who controlled the territory sent bandits to beat him up. He almost died of his injuries. He was undeterred. Back in Shanghai he set up a technical school for factory apprentices, arranging for the most promising students to be sent to the US for further study. 'We have to develop industry from the ground up,' he insisted in his conversations with Rewi. 'Chinese industry for the Chinese people. That's what's needed. Forget the foreign concessions.'

With that aim in mind, Bailie went to Nanjing (he would have spelt it Nanking) to establish a forestry school. Deforestation was one of the main causes of the constant flooding. Rewi gave his full support to the scheme. As an ex-farmer, schooled in the vagaries of the New Zealand weather, he knew all about erosion. The school flourished until mission politics forced its closure. But the mission couldn't close down Bailie's ideas. One of Rewi's many practical legacies was his passionate commitment to reforestation in the northwest, a scheme with a direct link to Bailie's Nanjing school. Like Bailie, Rewi knew the only way to stop the Gobi Desert reclaiming the farmlands of the North China Plain was to cover the hillsides with trees. No wonder the two men got on. 'Go out into the villages,' Bailie advised his new friend soon after they met. 'To understand China you have to understand the people who till the land.'

I picture Rewi and Bailie sitting in Rewi's Shanghai apartment, nutting out the best way to prevent the catastrophic yearly flooding, the conversation turning, as the night wears on, to the relationship between faith and works. Rewi's antagonism to missionaries, symptomatic both of his father's teaching and of his observations of the general run of foreign priests in China, does not, as yet, extend to the religion they ostensibly follow. Confirmed as a Christian in Salisbury Cathedral before sailing to France in 1917, he still occasionally attends services in Shanghai Cathedral, to the delight, no doubt, of his Anglican mother. Perhaps it was at one of those services that he heard about the Christian pacifist group, the Fellowship of the Reconciliation. He starts attending their meetings with a view to joining. But then his interest wanes. Pacifism is not for this old soldier. And neither, eventually, is Christianity. 'You have to care for your fellow man and not get all locked up in that religious rubbish,' he told David Mahon near the end of his life. 'It's been the cause of too much suffering.'[5]

I imagine Bailie, unwilling to come between a man and his conscience, nodding sadly when Rewi tells him Christianity is not providing answers to the questions he's been asking. 'I love the language,' Rewi concedes. 'The poetry, the wisdom. But as a blueprint for living in China it doesn't do the trick for me.'

'Man shall not live by bread alone.' 'Peace on earth, goodwill to men.' 'Love thy neighbour as thyself.' 'Blessed are the meek for they shall inherit the earth' ... The texts Rewi memorised as a boy have, like childhood songs, lost their potency.

*

Joseph Bailie's life ended in tragedy. Writing about it nearly 20 years later, Rewi gave little of his own feelings away. '[In 1935] Old Man Bailie took his last voyage to America, penniless after 40 years struggle to reform the old system. He was given enough money for an operation for cancer of the prostate gland, but the operation failed. He took a gun and shot himself ... Always impatient, always somewhat fanatical, always young in mind, he battered his head against a thousand walls and did not bend much ... A great soul ... a humble man ... who loved the people he worked amongst.'[6]

So far as I know there are no statues of Joseph Bailie anywhere in China. But he has left a legacy that will last as long as China exists. Every tree that is planted, whether it be to prevent erosion, or to combat the pollution affecting so many cities, has, to my mind, got Bailie's name on it. As we travel around the country I will see evidence in almost every city of Bailie's influence. Tree-planting programmes have become de rigueur. I think of my mother – a member of the National Society of the Friends of the Trees – who shared Rewi's passion for re-afforestation not because she saw it as a solution to erosion, but because she preferred trees to people.

Determined to know the names of the local flora – an obsession planted by my gardening father – I will become something of a pest as our journey progresses, constantly asking our guides to identify trees. By the end I will be able to reel off names – plum, peach, jujube, persimmon, dragonfruit, pear, apple, banyan, gingko, pagoda – but there is one I keep seeing, almost as common as the poplars, planes and willows, that no one, not even our guides, can put a name to.

I decide to call it the Bailie Tree.

CHAPTER SIXTEEN
11 April 2017

UNTIL this moment I would not have described Beijing as beautiful but, suddenly, here we are, climbing out of our bus on the side of a lake, its surface broken by tiny ripples moving as if in response to music I can't hear. While we have been eating a sumptuous lunch, the sky has been washed clean. It is now the colour of the birds' eggs my brother and I used to steal as kids. Not the stabbing blue of our New Zealand skies but something altogether softer and more mysterious. The trailing branches of the willows bordering the lake look as if they have been freshly painted.

'What's that tree?' I ask Dave, pointing to what I will end up calling the Bailie Tree growing in a clump of earth beside the bus.

Dave shrugs. 'Blossom tree,' he answers.

'Beijing tree,' the guide corrects, laughing. 'Very special. Only grows in Beijing.'

We are being taken on a tour of the *hutongs*, travelling by rickshaw. Our destination is the home of Soong Chingling, the 'Mother of the Chinese Nation' and Rewi's beloved friend. As we hurtle along the narrow alleys, caught up in the rickshaw drivers' undoubtedly rehearsed games of Chicken, the sights, smells and sounds act as my passport to the pre-Liberation China Rewi knew. This is what Beijing would have looked like, only dirtier and smellier, and teeming with human life, when it was Peking or Peiping or Yanjing. This is where factory workers and street sweepers, old people and children, beggars and soldiers too broken in body to fight lived when emperors sat on the throne. When Mao Zedong was working as an assistant librarian at Peking University in 1919 he stayed in a *hutong* called Three Eyes Well. Seven people shared the *kang* he slept on. When he became leader of the Red Army, one of his Eight Principles of military behaviour was that any soldier bedding down in a peasant's house must, in addition to paying for his food, make sure the door was put back in place in the morning. The door, in poor peasant homes, often acted as the *kang* at night.

1919 was a crucial year in China's emergence from its feudal past. It saw both the birth of the May 4th Movement and the arrival in Beijing, from the southern province of Hunan, of 26-year-old Mao Zedong. By this time Mao had already seen service as a revolutionary soldier, fighting in Hunan in support of the 1911 revolution. He hadn't yet formulated his belief that 'political power grows out of the barrel of a gun.'¹ But he had formed his own student organisation – the New People's Study Society – to discuss ways in which China's seemingly intractable problems might be solved. China in the years following the 1919 protests was awash with societies dedicated to finding a way out of the country's miseries. Most were left-leaning; many were associated with Peking University. There was the Heaven and Earth Society, the United League (*Tongmenghui*), the New Culture Movement (May 4th Movement), the Revive China Society, the National Salvation Movement, the Awakening Society …

When Chiang Kaishek, not to be outdone, formed his own New Life Movement in 1934, he claimed it enshrined not only Confucian principles but the tenets of the Methodist faith he'd adopted on his marriage to Soong Meiling. On his orders, blanket-sized flags and banners proclaiming the aims of the movement were hung from telegraph poles and plastered across the walls of public buildings all over China. 'Don't Smoke.' 'Don't Spit.' 'Be Modest, Button Up Your Tunics.' 'Men and Women to Walk Separately.' Rewi, by 1934 no longer a greenhorn, was not the only one to be outraged by the hypocrisy of a movement advocating honesty, cleanliness, righteousness and propriety, while turning a blind eye to the extermination policies of its leader. As for the movement's claim to be following the teachings of the Methodist Church, that too earned Rewi's contempt. The man who orchestrated the White Terror of 1927 was no Christian.

Mao was an avid reader, a poet, and a prolific writer of political tracts and articles. The latter were published under a pseudonym, as all such political writing was. Rewi, writing in the late 1930s for *The Voice of China* (a Moscow-funded English-language magazine that gave voice to the liberation movement because it operated outside Chinese law), used a variety of pen-names: 'Kate Dawson'; 'Richard', 'Howard'; 'Chao Da Chi'; 'Ming Fu'; 'Han Su Mei'. (I imagine Rewi, the boy who was always dreaming, having fun with all these changes of identity.) But Mao stuck to the one pseudonym: 'Twenty-eight Strokes Gentleman'. In that disguise he wrote passionately about the revolution begun in 1911, recognising from the start that its unfolding would be fundamentally different from the Russian experience.

It's not the cities that are important now it's the countryside … The rural forces of democracy will overthrow the rural forces of feudalism … Several hundred million peasants will rise like a mighty storm, like a hurricane, a force so swift and violent that no power, however great, will be able to hold it back. They will smash all the trammels that bind them and rush forward along the road to liberation. They will sweep all the imperialists, warlords, corrupt officials, local tyrants and evil gentry into their graves.[2]

As the son of a peasant, Mao knew what he was talking about. His seemingly outrageous predictions – at its inception in 1921 the CCP had a mere 57 members – were based on first-hand experience. Where he differed from other peasants was in his education. His father, wealthier than most as a consequence of his dealings as a usurer, had paid for his son to be educated. Well versed in the teachings of both Confucius and the Tao, Mao could interpret and explain the old China and the China he saw coming. He understood what lesson was being taught when Confucius told the story of his meeting with a woman weeping piteously at a graveside. 'Woman, what is the cause of your sorrow?' the great philosopher asks. 'I weep because the tiger took my father, then he took my husband, then he took my son,' the woman replies. 'So why do you live here where there are so many tigers?' 'Because there are no harsh taxes,' the woman answers.

Taxation: the subject no one concerned with China's problems could avoid. It was the stone around the neck of the peasants, condemning them to perpetual poverty and recurring cycles of famine. There were poll taxes, property taxes, road, dyke and highway taxes. You had to pay a tax to send your children to school or to have them released from military service. There were taxes on grain, salt, seed, bedding, wheelbarrows, windows, carts, carriages. You paid a slaughter tax to have your pig butchered. There was even a 'happy tax' designed to 'promote happiness'. If you couldn't pay, there were pawnshops, like the ones Rewi passed on his first day in Shanghai, where you could sell your few remaining possessions. Once you had nothing left to sell and you were faced with a new round of taxes, there was only one outcome – starvation. All this Mao understood, and resolved to change.

When new areas of China came under Red Army control, the first thing Mao did was abolish all taxes imposed by landlords and KMT officials. He also abolished foot binding, child slavery, prostitution, infanticide and forced marriage (a personal issue for him, as he had been forced to marry at age 14). No wonder he was popular. His rejection of his usurer father, symbolised when he cut off his *queue* – symbol of Manchu imperial power – and refused to consummate that teenage marriage, would metamorphose into rejection of the entire corrupt landlord system.

*

Rewi will meet Mao a number of times, although he will never refer to him as a friend. Unlike his fellow countryman James Bertram, he makes no attempt to bring Mao alive for us. Bertram met and interviewed Mao in October 1937 and painted a vivid pen-portrait of the 43-year-old army commander, describing him as tall, with 'long hair parted in the centre and hanging down over his ears', looking 'more like an absent-minded scholar than a political commander'.[3] A chain-smoker of British-made Pirate cigarettes with a habit of dropping his trousers to pluck the lice from his pubic hair, Mao made a deep impression on the young New Zealander. His ability to stay up all night talking, smoking, reading reports, writing instructions and responding to the steady flow of radio and telegraph messages, left Bertram in no doubt that he was the right man to lead China in the war already being fought against the Japanese.

The contrast between Bertram's enthusiasm and Rewi's reticence raises an interesting question. Were the seeds of what Rewi would later feel about China's charismatic leader – expressed verbally but never committed to paper – sown in the wake of that initial meeting? His friend Agnes Smedley – never one to keep her opinions to herself – described Mao as 'arrogant, effeminate and shifty', and believed he wasn't to be trusted. I imagine her sharing those opinions with Rewi; and Rewi, aware that what he was hearing was blasphemy, saying little beyond his usual words of caution.

'I met [Mao] the first time in what had been an old Swedish mission,' Rewi told Geoff Chapple. 'I was sitting with Chu Teh (commander-in-chief of the Eighth Route Army) and the place was filled with army commanders – suddenly he came in ... I talked a lot to him in mixed-up Shanghai and southern Chinese. He was a good listener ... The second time I was there at a birthday party of the old revolutionary government ... The third time ... was in his cave.'

This was the man Rewi persuaded himself he believed in for so long: the good listener, the general who shared the same conditions as his soldiers, the man who dressed like everyone else and liked to share a joke. Like Mao, Rewi knew that 'a revolution is not a dinner party or writing an essay or painting a picture or doing embroidery'.[4] But the Cultural Revolution, which Rewi initially supported, would first challenge, then crush his faith in China's paramount leader. He saved his main criticisms for the Gang of Four, describing them in 1976 in a letter to Gwen as 'a horrid wicked gang'.[5] But heaping the blame on the discredited Gang failed to stem the slow drip of a much wider disillusionment. By the end of the 1970s Rewi's faith in Mao has gone the way of his faith in the Anglican church: 'There is only one person I hate in China ...'

CHAPTER SEVENTEEN

11 April 2017

WE have arrived at an enchanted place. Soong Chingling's mansion, now a museum, is not grand, though it is large, as befits the former residence of Qing dynasty nobles (the last emperor's father lived here). The house itself – two-storeyed, painted soft grey with red pillars and doors (red, the Chinese 'lucky colour', denotes happiness) – seems oddly familiar. Then I realise this is the China of my father's treasures. I see my mother, grey head bent over the latest issue of *China Reconstructs*, trophies of my father's travels displayed around her, and for a moment I'm a curious child again.

'We go inside now,' the guide instructs. 'Follow, please.'

We are led into rooms with names that sound as if they've been dreamed up for a fairy tale: The Hall for Gazing at Flowers; The Pavilion for Listening to Orioles; The Room for Listening to Rain; The Waves of Kindness Pavilion. The whānau are busy photographing. It's hard, amid so much loveliness, to know what to focus on. We step out of one room, and there in front of us is a pond with a rockery border, its surface tickled by weeping willows; from another we find ourselves moving over the arched 'Happiness on the Hao River' bridge. Peach, plum and Chingling's favourite lilac trees fill the air with sweetness. Roses and peonies – China's national flower – along with others I can't identify line the pathways. Red lanterns flutter in the breeze. A statue of Chingling, agelessly beautiful, rises out of a bed of red flowers. A flag – the national flag of China, bright gold stars shining in a sea of red – flies from a tall pole. When Chingling lived here there would have been doves cooing in the branches of the camphor trees. Today there are swallows and other birds I can't identify. Beijing, with its nostril-teasing smells, redolent of drains and coal smoke and human sweat, belongs to another continent.

I move back inside. Rewi's friendship with Chingling is one of the more intriguing mysteries of his life. She called him 'Bill'; he called her 'Susie'. But almost no record remains of their association. At Chingling's request, their letters to one another were destroyed during the Cultural Revolution. As for Rewi, his answer to questions about the relationship invariably drew a blank. Till the end of his life he would honour her request to keep her private life private.

I observe the to and fro of people moving through the rooms of Chingling's home, but the picture in my head is of Rewi sitting with his friend, sharing a meal, as they so often did, discussing the issues of the day. Discovering, at the height of the Cultural Revolution, that her parents' grave had been vandalised – a clear sign that her own life was in danger – Chingling turned to Rewi, the man she trusted more than any other. Would he store her most precious personal belongings in his apartment? Rewi didn't hesitate. Earlier the roles had been reversed. Rewi, whose own life had been threatened so many times both by the Japanese and by Chiang's gangsters, had attracted the attention of the Red Guards. Had it not been for the intervention of Zhou Enlai and Chingling, both of whom were, in 1968, regarded as untouchable, he would almost certainly have been gaoled.

'I have known Rewi Alley since 1933,' Chingling wrote in her submission on Rewi's behalf. 'Devoting his efforts to China, he helped us in defence of our country. When Japanese Imperialists invaded China it was he who organized Chinese Industrial Co-operatives in the interior and helped us train a younger generation. For this work he even gave up his good job. When the White Terror reigned in Shanghai, and secret agents, both Chinese and foreign, hunted down communists, it was he who made his home their sanctuary …'[1]

Rewi had no doubt that this letter, written in Chingling's own hand, was instrumental in saving him from further persecution. It seems unthinkable now that these two faithful revolutionaries, one of them the widow of the revered Sun Yatsen, the other a man who would two decades later be declared one of the 'Top Ten Foreign Friends of China', should have come under attack at all.

I don't want to leave this house. I feel as if I could solve the enigma of Rewi here, that this is where the poet, the lover of art and the dreamer came together. 'I have tried to give up personal life … and put all into making this one idea [a socialist China] come true,' Rewi wrote in a letter to his adopted son Alan.[2] 'No one is important and everyone is important. What is important is the Chinese people,' Willis Airey records Chingling as saying.[3] Is it fanciful to see here Shakespeare's 'marriage of true minds'? Chingling believed passionately that children were the future and China's most 'valuable asset'. So did Rewi. 'Children more than doves rank as the symbol of peace, because it is for their future that we fight to make and keep the peace,' he wrote in *The People Have Strength.*

It was in this house that Chingling hosted a party for Rewi's eighty-third birthday on 2 December 1980. Who would have been there? Not many of the old gang of idealists and revolutionaries (in James Bertram's opinion, the only true socialists left in China) were still around. Death had claimed Rewi's journalist friends Edgar Snow, Anna Louise Strong and Agnes Smedley. Kathleen Hall, the missionary nurse who smuggled medical supplies to the Red Army during the War of Liberation, had died of exhaustion back in New Zealand. Joseph Bailie was dead, as was Rewi's friend and fellow-teacher, George Hogg. The American soldier-diplomats, Evans Carlson and Joe Stilwell, both of whom had championed Gung Ho, had died in the States, their China work discredited. Ida Pruitt, star of INDUSCO and one of the women believed to have been in love with Rewi, had returned to America. Joseph Needham, whose journey to Gansu province with Rewi led to the founding of the school at Shandan, was back in Britain. Shirley Barton, Corso's liaison officer in China 1947–49 and Rewi's amanuensis (she edited many of his books), was now living permanently in New Zealand.[4] As was James Bertram.

One person who would have been there with his Chinese wife and family was Dr Ma Haide, whose adventures with the Red Army during the Japanese war, treating, among many others, Mao Zedong, ensured his place in China's revolutionary story. Isabel Crook would almost certainly have been there, as would her son Michael. Chingling's close friend Israel Epstein, whom she had appointed editor of *China Today*, the successor to *China Reconstructs*, was bound to have been invited, along with his Chinese wife and daughter. Likewise Rewi's other Jewish friend, journalist Sid Shapiro, whom Chingling knew well.

But my spotlight is on the two old friends, survivors of the Japanese occupation, of Chiang's anti-communist purges and the Cultural Revolution. They alone knew the secrets of each other's hearts. The widow of Sun Yatsen never remarried. Her duty was to her husband's memory and the ideals he represented. 'The only way to keep me silent is jailing or killing me,' she wrote at the time of her final break with the KMT.[5] From that time on she was committed, heart and soul, to the communists.

Rewi, as we know, never married. 'I like children, comfort, pleasant company, and I would have loved a wife and home,' Willis Airey quotes him as saying in 1961. What he had instead was an ad hoc family, acquired not so much to fill the gap in his life as to do what he could for China's suffering children. By 1933 he had two legal sons. Later he would take on five more through fostering. In this he was enthusiastically supported by his New Zealand family, especially his mother Clara and his brother Pip, both of whom wrote regularly, sending vital material help when conditions became difficult. (On learning that Rewi had skin cancer, Pip sent over a special ointment to treat the condition. Clara went further. Having seen in a photo the state of Rewi's bicycle, she arranged for a new one to be delivered.)

'After coming to China and getting into revolution, it was either revolution or family life. Not both,' Rewi confided in a letter to Pip. 'Serving the revolution took the place of a family,' the poet Chen Yi wrote in 1936, a line Rewi could have written himself.[6] Wounded and expecting to die, Chen spent three weeks hiding from the advancing KMT army, writing poems on the lining of his jacket while he waited for death. He survived. Four decades later Rewi, recognising a kindred soul, set about translating his poetry. He and Chen Yi had made the same choice – to renounce family life and serve the revolution – just as Soong Chingling had.

Rewi the poet, the writer of China's stories, had no time for the language of romantic love. But occasionally the longing shows through. 'Kiangsi', one of the poems in his collection *Beyond the Withered Oak Ten Thousand Saplings Grow*, describes how he sat on a hill watching a family, 'stealing a little of their joy', absorbed by the sight of 'a grandfather with bent old legs chopping wood'; 'a mother nursing a baby'; a 'father striding home, leaning a carrying pole against a cottage'; 'three little boys … playing around a hillock … laughter reaching up through the pines …' His longing to be part of this scene is palpable.

In the same collection, in a poem titled 'Sinkiang', he describes a visit to the Thousand Buddha Caves in the Uyghur Autonomous Region: '… on walls and ceilings lovers embrace as they have embraced these sixteen hundred years … Why did the old monk-artists put such great feeling into those embraces they denied themselves?' he asks. I can't help wondering what he was feeling as he wrote that line.

When I lift my hands from hauling stone,
Run them down bare, sweating legs …
When I lie on warm ground after a midday meal
… of what do I think? …
Children with soft greasy skins in all the lure
Of summer nakedness, clasping my legs and laughing

... a wife with food enough
To cook; salt and sauce; fuel to burn, and cloth
To make winter clothing; clever fingers and a welcoming
Smile; a clean swept kang where she will lie beside me ...
These would be perfect things ...[7]

The unnamed, longed-for woman in this poem is not Chingling. For Rewi, whom Willis Airey reports sometimes referred to himself as an 'obstinate Pig Islander', the only possible wife was a peasant like himself. Susie, the 'irrepressible spirit', the 'everlasting flower', 'the greatest woman of our day' whose 'wit and humour' were destined to become a 'fragrant memory', was not for him. She died a few months after that eighty-third birthday celebration. Summoned to her bedside, he knelt down and whispered, 'It's Rewi.'[8]

... her house so
Quiet that morning when just before
Dawn one left it, the great red doors
Swinging open, the gateway framing
Weeping willows bending over the lake ...[9]

*

So who was Soong Chingling, this woman, celebrated for her beauty, who was appointed one of six vice-presidents of the republic after Liberation, and was made honorary president of the People's Republic of China in 1981? What was it about her that inspired adoration on both sides of the political divide? James Bertram was one of many who fell under her spell. 'Madame Sun *is* China,' he declared, citing her 'inner serenity and fineness of spirit ... her steadfastness and loyalty not only to her dead husband's memory but to his revolutionary ideas'. In *Capes of China Slide Away* he wrote, 'For her I would have crossed the world.' (He did. When Madame Sun asked him to return to China to work with her Defence League he didn't hesitate.) To Edgar Snow, Bertram's American counterpart, Soong Chingling was 'the conscience of a still unfinished revolution'. In dedicating his book *Living China* to her, he described her as one 'whose incorruptible integrity, courage, loyalty, and beauty of spirit are burning symbols of the best in living China'.

Even my own father, the staunch anti-communist, succumbed to her charms. I have a memory – I believe a true one – of him showing me a photograph of the 'three famous Soong sisters', wearing sarongs and Western-style hats, being rowed down one of China's rivers. (It's Shanghai so it must have been the Huangpu.) I was already at school so I would have been about six. In a voice full of admiration he points out Madame Sun Yatsen, then her sister Madame Kung, then – saving his highest praise for last – Madame Chiang Kaishek. 'A wonderful woman,' he enthuses. 'A great friend to China's orphans.'

I wanted to know more. My father was the chairman of our local orphanage. I'd recently spent a fortnight living there while my parents were travelling. I think I was meant to learn a lesson about humility – we were not always kind to the orphans at school – but the opposite happened. I decided I wanted to *be* an orphan. Sleeping in a dormitory full of girls appealed to me far more than sleeping in a freezing room at the end of a long corridor, with only the distant hum of the wireless to tell me there was anyone else in the house. 'Perhaps I could go and stay in her orphanage,' I pouted, pointing to the doll-like woman in the boat, 'since you won't let me stay in yours.' I don't recall what my father said in reply.

Rewi would have been astounded if anyone had told him, during his first days in Shanghai, that he would over the next decade have close dealings with the three celebrated Soong sisters. And not just with them but with the powerful husbands of two of the sisters. Ailing, the eldest, married H.H. Kung, a descendant of Confucius and the richest man in China. Paunchy and bespectacled, Kung, as finance minister in the nationalist government, wielded enormous power, not only in official circles but also in Rewi's co-operative movement. Much of the overseas funding that was the lifeblood of Gung Ho was funnelled through Kung's bank. Rewi's opinion of him – he called him 'Fat old Kung' behind his back – was anything but flattering.[10] He described him as vain, venal, and interested in the co-operatives only because his wife (for a time) supported them.

Meiling, the youngest, did even better in the marriage stakes. She married the Generalissimo himself, making her the most powerful woman in China. I have another memory, again I believe a true one, of being shown a photo of Rewi with Madame Chiang, and my mother telling me what good friends they were. There was even a rumour, circulating at the time the photo was taken, that Meiling had referred to our cousin as 'darling Rewi'. True or not, there was no doubting the warmth on both sides in those early years when co-operation between the communists and the KMT was a going, albeit frequently threatened, concern. All that would change when full-scale civil war broke out in 1946. By 1949, when the defeated Chiangs and Kungs fled to Formosa, the friendship was not just over, it had become a millstone around Rewi's neck.

Even as children the Soong sisters stood out. They were beautiful, smart, strong-willed. All three would, like their businessman-missionary father, be educated in the US. All three would become fluent in English. All three, for a time, would follow their parents' lead in working for the New China. But there the similarities ended.

'One loved money, one loved power, and one loved her country.' No one knows who said it first – my money is on James Bertram – but the description caught on.

The eldest married money and it grew,
The youngest married power and liked that too,
But the third sister, different from these, married a dream.[11]

When Chingling, at the age of 22, announced her intention to marry Dr Sun Yatsen, her parents were outraged. Politics was not the issue. Chingling's father, Soong Chiashu (Charlie), and his high-born wife, Ni Kwei-Tseng, who traced her ancestry back to the Ming dynasty, were friends of Sun's. They supported the new republic. But that didn't mean they wanted their daughter to marry a man 26 years her senior, who was, as it happened, already married. But Chingling was determined. She was in love with Sun, and she was in love with his revolution, describing it in the *Wesleyan*, the magazine of the American college where she and her sisters had studied, as 'the greatest event of the twentieth century'. So she broke off the engagement her parents had arranged for her and eloped with Sun. 'No girl of a family such as mine had ever broken a betrothal,' she told Rewi's friend Anna Louise Strong.[12] She and Sun were married in Japan on 25 October 1915.

Chingling would never be reconciled with her father, who died three years later, but she would, for a time, stay close to her sisters. Then that too came to an end. In 1927, in protest at Chiang's expulsion of the communists from the KMT, Chingling resigned her position as a member of the KMT's executive committee. Sun, who had died two years earlier, was adamant that the only way forward for the Chinese people was for the nationalists and the communists to work together. Now here was Chingling's brother-in-law not only throwing the communists out of government but actively launching a campaign against them. 'I will finish off this bandit Mao,' Han Suyin, married at the time to a high-ranking KMT officer, reports him as saying. 'My head upon it if I fail.'[13]

For Chingling, who had hoped to influence her brother-in-law and keep the troubled alliance between the KMT and the communists alive, there was no alternative but to go into exile. The revolution her husband had led was committed to defeating the warlords, uniting China and ridding it of imperialism. Now Chiang was making deals with those same warlords, using them and their gangster associates to fight the communists. China was no longer safe for her. It wasn't safe for anyone who defied the KMT.

Chingling's analysis was right. Chiang's anti-communist crusade would tear the country apart. In 1927, the year of Rewi's arrival and Chingling's flight, some 20,000 people were executed in Changsha alone. Thousands more would die in subsequent extermination campaigns. Street shootings were commonplace, but it was the staged executions that marked a new low of savagery. Many people were beheaded, a particularly cruel form of execution for Chinese, since a headless body cannot be admitted to the spirit kingdom. Displaying heads in baskets hung from traffic signs and street posts was meant as a warning not just of what could happen to you in this world but of the agony that awaited you in the next. Others who fell foul of Chiang's thugs – the notorius 'Blue Shirts' – were buried alive, the traditional Chinese punishment for sedition. (Rewi, in Yo Banfa!, refers to the Blue Shirts as 'Nanjing's Gestapo'.) Little wonder Chingling's brother-in-law came to be known as the 'General Franco of the Orient'.[14]

Four years after fleeing China, Chingling returned. Her husband's body was being moved from Beijing to a sacred imperial burial site on the slopes of Purple Mountain in Nanjing, where the first Ming emperor is buried. Chiang, who would have had his sister-in-law killed had his wife not restrained him, didn't dare sully the memory of the man who was and always would be the Father of the Republic.

As it happened, Rewi was in Nanjing on the day the ceremony took place. 'I stood on the sidelines … watching her walking quietly abreast of her brother-in-law, but keeping her distance,' he wrote in his memoir. 'To me she was very much the central figure of the piece.' They didn't meet then but their paths would cross four years later when Agnes Smedley took him to Chingling's Shanghai home. From that day on they would be friends.

After the ceremony in Nanjing, Chingling went back into exile. She returned, finally, in 1931 and took up residence in Shanghai. Chiang, busy with his extermination campaigns, ignored her, a decision he may well have come to regret since, in the wake of the Japanese 'terror bombing' of Shanghai in 1932, she would come to be seen as the leader of the resistance to his appeasement policy. 'First Reunification then Resistance' cut no ice with Chingling. Japan's excursions into Chinese territory outraged her. Like Rewi, living in Shanghai, she would witness the death and destruction caused by Japanese bombs, the indignities of occupation, and the ever-present threat of assassination by the KMT. But she would never seek sanctuary again.

Rewi and Chingling – the down-to-earth Kiwi and the sophisticated beauty – would seem, on the face of it, to have little in common. But when it came to China, its future and its freedom, their hearts were as one. Chingling became a passionate supporter of Gung Ho, as Rewi did of her Defence League, founded in 1938 to ensure that vital supplies of food and weapons got through to the Red Army. But perhaps what united them most was their love of literature and their belief in the power of art to transform lives. Filling their homes with artefacts from the past – an activity that would get them both into trouble in the Cultural Revolution – they made no secret of their shared fascination with China's dynastic history. Almost alone among their group of revolutionaries, they fought for the New China while preserving the best of the Old. But they never lost sight of what needed to be done to end the cycles of suffering that had been China's story for thousands of years. *China Reconstructs*, to which they both regularly contributed, writing under pseudonyms, was published by Chingling's China Welfare Institute. The stories it told would bring the struggles and triumphs of the New China into living rooms around the world.

'Let's walk as sticky rice.' There's no way of knowing whether the two friends ever said those words to each other, but they would have known what they meant – everyone did. And they would have agreed that walking together was the only way ahead for China, as it was for the two committed revolutionaries who had turned their backs on personal happiness.

With the strength and grace
of the blue and white porcelain
she loves so well: a life
that has taken steeled courage to live,

steadfastly serving those she has
so great a faith in …

a woman who can set a flower
so that it speaks a message,
write so that hearts are stirred,
encourage so that some
of her daring spirit is shared …
her very name a tocsin –
Soong Ching Ling.[15]

ABOVE: Rewi's bicycle on display in the Shandan Museum.

Photo by Ken Watkin

Long March hero General Zhu De with American marine (later Brigadier General) Evans Carlson.

Photo by Ken Watkin

Rewi typing at Shunagshipu 1941.

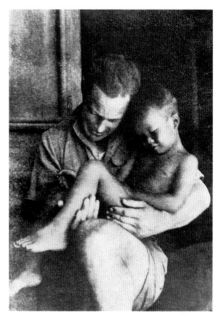

Agnes Smedley, American author of the autobiographical *Daughter of Earth*, one of a handful of journalists reporting on what was happening in China in the 1930s.

From *Rewi Alley of China* by Geoff Chapple

George Hogg with a sick child.

From *Fruition: The story of George Alwin Hogg* by Rewi Alley

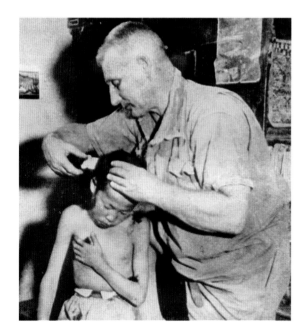

Rewi cutting a student's hair at Shandan.

From *A Learner in China: A life of Rewi Alley* by Willis Airey

On the lei tai at Shandan: Lao San on the right, Lao Si on Rewi's knee.
From *At 90: Memoirs of my China years* by Rewi Alley

Rewi's close friend Soong Chingling, widow of the Father of the Republic, Sun Yatsen, revered throughout China as the Mother of the Revolution.

Photo by Ken Watkin

The Eurasian novelist Han Suyin, author of *A Many-Splendoured Thing*, a close friend of Rewi's who often turned to him for advice.

South China Morning Post

CHAPTER EIGHTEEN

In northern mountain valleys
I saw children
standing numbly, naked in the snow;
the people forced to grow opium, to pay as
taxes; encouraged to smoke it
for solace; prostitutes, some with
as many as seven diseases, living
short miserable lives; illiteracy
rampant. And all this along with
too much more, I had seen with my
own eyes ...[1]

BY the spring of 1929 Rewi is a changed man. The things he has been seeing every day in his work as a fire officer and factory inspector have shaken his belief in the essential decency of the British Empire. Chiang's bandit extermination campaign, initially concentrated in the northwest, has now reached the Chinese sections of Shanghai. Bodies keep turning up in the tree-lined avenues of the French Concession. As do refugees, thousands of them, fleeing war and famine. Not even the most determined 'look-the-other-way' citizen can ignore what's happening.

Rewi has no clear idea who the red bandits are, or what they stand for, but he's impressed by their courage, organising strikes and labour unions when so much is pitted against them. He admires their skill too, slipping away under cover of night when things get too hot, regrouping in another city and starting again. He knows what his fellow Europeans think. Communism is 'a disease of the skin'. Its disciples 'wear long beards and make noises with their soup and carry homemade bombs in their briefcases'.[2] With Chiang's men armed and ready to shoot anyone they suspect has even the most casual connection to the reds, the city is as jumpy as a flea.

'Hunan people eat peppers. That's why they're so fiery' – a truism put to use by Chiang and his followers to disparage the 'number one bandit', Mao Zedong, a native of the pepper-growing province of Hunan. Chiang has put a price on Mao's head – US$250,000, a king's ransom. He's boasted he will 'mow the grass of red revolt', conveniently forgetting it was he who broke

Sun's agreement with the communists and drove them underground. 'Fight the Communists. Leave Japan to the League of Nations' is his mantra now.[3]

I picture Rewi weighing all this information, balancing one story against another, wondering what to make of it …

Rewi won't meet Zhou Enlai until 1937, but he will hear his name during this bloody time when upwards of 100,000 workers and students die at the hands of the KMT. Chiang has put a price on Zhou's head as well. The escape from Shanghai of the young Paris-educated revolutionary, mastermind of the failed strike of 1927, marked the start of a decade of constant moving and many disguises, not just for him but for his wife. Ten years later, following the Japanese capture of Beijing in August, Zhou's wife Deng Yingchao, trapped in the city, will approach James Bertram and Edgar Snow to ask for their help. The Japanese are not yet at war with the West, so Bertram and Snow are still safe. But Yingchao is not. The Japanese are arresting anyone whose face, in the words of James McNeish, 'suggests the possibility of political thought.'[4] The two 'ocean devils' lose no time. Disguising Yinghchao as their servant, they board a train and get her safely to the unoccupied part of China.

'Anything is possible in Shanghai' – words an increasingly angry Rewi hears on all sides, as if the chaos and contradictions, the cruelty and indifference he encounters every day on the streets is no one's fault, just a fact of nature.[5] He watches with disgust as a parade of missionary children carrying banners promoting the Society for the Prevention of Cruelty to Animals lead a pet spaniel coddled in a yellow blanket past emaciated beggars, some of them as young as five. Then, exhibiting the same cheerful indifference, a troop of well-fed Boy Scouts passes by. He turns away in disgust. How can people not see what's in front of their eyes? Is their blindness wilful? 'The greatest thing a human soul ever does in this world is to see.' John Ruskin's words, read years ago in the *Graphic*, toll in his mind like a warning.

At a Christian meeting he attended around this time, Rewi hears a speech deriding the Soviet system as bound to fail because it is 'founded on hate'. But the regime he is living under, founded, it seems to him, for the sole purpose of generating profit, is unleashing 'hates so bitter that only a Soviet system can possibly remove them. I fear anarchy will take place if something is not done.'[6]

Never particularly strong, Rewi's Christian beliefs are beginning to crumble, not, as has often been assumed, because he preferred to see justice done in this life rather than wait for the next, but because his interest in religion has from the start been intellectual and philosophical rather than spiritual. In the last decade of his life he will describe himself to David Mahon as not a spiritual person. But this doesn't mean he didn't ask the big questions. A man who calls himself a 'learner' is always going to be open to new ideas. So for a time Rewi turns to Buddhism, a religion with many followers in China, then and now. There are numerous references to Buddhism in his writing, but we have to wait till the autumn of 1938 to get a sense of where his study of Buddhist teachings took him.

Rewi is travelling in the northwest of China on business for the fledgling Gung Ho movement. One of the places he has to visit is the Buddhist stronghold of Tibet, where he is to supervise the setting up of a wool-producing co-operative. Transporting, with the help of two Gung Ho workers, the spinning wheels and other equipment needed for the co-op, Rewi is making heavy weather of the journey. Whenever possible they ride horses, but mostly the terrain is so rugged they can only proceed on foot, clambering up steep mountainsides with the spinning wheels balanced precariously on their backs.

After several mostly sleepless days and nights, sheltering in caves, eating rice and whatever they can find, the three travellers arrive in Lhasa, where Rewi is immediately declared a Living Buddha. The attendant adulation embarrasses and alarms him. A European claiming to be a Living Buddha could easily be mistaken for an agent of British imperialism – the last thing Rewi, busily distancing himself from his imperial connections, would have wanted.

He goes along with the charade, waiting for the moment when, having instructed the local people in how to set up their co-op, he can beat a hasty retreat. 'If I'm a living Buddha I can get any kind of message,' Geoff Chapple quotes him as saying. So he invents a message summoning him back on urgent business to the Chinese wartime capital, Chongqing.

Clearly he has not become a follower. A follower would have stayed to enjoy his unexpected elevation.

As for Confucianism, the philosophy that has shaped the lives of rich and poor in China for millennia, I imagine Rewi studying its strict rules for living (known as *li*) and feeling an immediate empathy with poor Chinese peasants raised under a strict authoritarian regime. 'In old China custom not law fixed the framework of existence,' he will write 30 years later in *Fruition: The story of George Alwyn Hogg*. 'Ethics not theology or political interest gave life its meaning.' Aware of its universality – Confucianism in 1929 was as much a part of China as Christianity was a part of the New Zealand of Rewi's youth – he would have looked on it as a given, not something he could do anything about.

But as Rewi's knowledge of Confucian teachings grew – its veneration of ancestors, respect for elders, subjugation of women (his friend Han Suyin described the women of China as 'having Confucius upon their backs'), upholding of a class system based on family and education – he began to seriously question the philosophy that had dominated Chinese thinking for so long.[7] In this he was, consciously or not, following the lead of Mao, a Confucian scholar who declared the teachings of the fifth century BC philosopher to be the enemy of progress. Free the peasant from the shackles of Confucian thinking, Mao argued, and he will answer the call of revolution. Chiang Kaishek thought otherwise. He saw in Confucianism a useful weapon to keep the peasant in his place. 'The rich man in his castle, the poor man at his gate', the popular hymn of both Rewi's and my own Christian childhood, would have been sung with enthusiasm by Chiang and his followers.

One philosophy that did hold Rewi's interest was Taoism, a philosophy based on a close study of nature. Tao means 'the way'. 'The real Taoist of the village solves people's problems,' he wrote in his memoir. 'He lives close to nature, maintains a sense of humour.' Almost as old as Confucianism, Taoism does not lay down strict rules for living. It's not rule-based at all, but a system – a relationship to the world that enables the individual to live in harmony with the 'source of life', the 'cosmic force'. The dreamer in Rewi, the boy who had spent so many hours 'just finking', the man who found in the art of the past a way to live with the stresses and contradictions of the present, was always going to respond more warmly to this than to a set of rules that reminded him of his father.

> Oh! Open your eyes, the Tao lies clear,
> Lift them from the glitter of the trivial.
> Lift them, and take man into your arms,
> Stand with him, and look at the stars.[8]

Rewi will never stop looking for answers to the fundamental questions of existence, but after two years in China there are more immediate things on his mind. How can he go on living in the comparative comfort of the French

Concession when all around him is suffering and misery? How can he go on thinking of himself as a soldier in the service of empire when the very people he's tasked with protecting are, as often as not, the exploiters, responsible for the suffering?

Answers will come but not all at once, and only after an experience even he might have described as his 'Road to Damascus' moment.

CHAPTER NINETEEN

DESPITE Rewi's growing uncertainty about the future, some things, by the spring of 1929, have become part of a pattern. Taking his mentor Joseph Bailie's advice – 'Go out into the villages. To understand China you have to understand the people who till the land' – he has, for the past year, been spending his weekends exploring the countryside around Shanghai. On this particular weekend he's headed with a Belgian friend, whom I will call Jan, for Wuxi, north of Shanghai, not a village but an ancient city bordered by both river (the Yangtze) and lake (Lake Tai).

Rewi has fallen in love with China in springtime: the deluge of blossom from peach, plum and lilac trees; the distant mountains wreathed in early morning mist; the emerald-green paddy fields; the temples rising out of the land like mirages; the valleys where azaleas grow in such profusion they cover the land as water covers the sea. In his bag are melon seeds and walnuts to chew as he walks. If he's lucky he'll be able to pick up fresh apples from the market. He knows, from past experience, that at some stage he will almost certainly be ambushed by homesickness, brought on by the crunch of an apple or the squirt of juice when he bites into a gooseberry, but he's happy away from the stink and misery of Shanghai. For a few precious hours he'll forget the bodies floating in the river; the beggars shouting 'Have a kind heart', 'Have pity on baby she is dying'; the flies that settle on food before you can get it to your mouth; the children with swollen bellies and 'pinky' eyes; the stories full of pathos written on the pavements by refugees too proud to ask for money. Only yesterday he passed a girl, no more than six or seven, abandoned by her no doubt starving parents, sitting on the pavement with a placard around her neck. 'Chen Feng-ying a Girl for Sale' it read. He'd seen such sights before, but the shock was as great as ever. Just the thought of children being sold filled him with stomach-churning rage.

'China is finished. This is the end. There is no hope for China.' Every day he hears these words from people who shake their heads and look away. 'What can be done?' they say when he challenges them. Rewi doesn't as yet have an answer.

He starts to walk. To his right is the mighty Yangtze, the dragon river of golden sands. He can't see it yet, but the dormant poet in him can imagine it. Fabled for its beauty, feared for its destructive power, the river he will describe years later as the 'heart of China' will play a vital part in shaping the direction of his life. Two years after this visit to Wuxi he will experience for himself the primal power coiled beneath the Yangtze's muddy waters. 'On its surging waves rolls the history of this ancient land,' he will write in 'Song of the Yangtze.'[1] He could have added that his own history will 'roll' there too. What he will experience in Wuhan, working on flood relief, will cement his decision to stay in China.

As Rewi walks – or rather strides – towards his destination he thinks about his last conversation with Joseph Bailie. That man is a walking encyclopedia of ideas and theories. It's not just his vision of forests springing up all over the North China Plain, but his conviction that only with education will the cycle of famine and flood be broken. 'China's rivers have to be tamed,' he insisted last time they met, striding up and down the narrow room in which he lived like a caged lion. 'Dykes, canals, dams – they have to be built now! Trees have to be planted! A dam cannot stand without the forest to support it. So we have to train workers, not just to use their hands but to use their minds. Cause and effect. Once they understand that they will know what to do. And you and I will be superfluous.'

'Minds and hands'. Rewi thinks about this as he pushes on towards the lake. There's the usual melee of rickshaws, carts, donkeys, bicycles, people of all ages carrying goods tied to the end of a pole – but he no longer looks at these things with the eyes of a visitor. He's grown used to the crush of people, to the spitting and the shouting. He's even gone in for a bit of shouting himself when his temper's been roused. China may not yet feel like home but it has stopped feeling foreign. 'Minds and hands ...' His teacher-father had similar ideas about education – the practical and the theoretical working in harmony.

Markets should be around here somewhere, he tells himself, as the city disappears behind him and the lake comes into view. The excitement he is feeling is familiar. It happens every time he approaches a market he hasn't visited before. It's not the prospect of fresh apples that's making his heart race, it's the prospect of finding a treasure from China's past. Already he has a sizable collection of scrolls, amulets and figurines, picked up for a few yuan in Shanghai's antique markets. He suspects the bone knife he stumbled on when out on one of his walks might be Neolithic. He loves the feel of old things, the way they make past eras come alive. On lonely nights in Shanghai, when the misery he sees every day threatens to trigger either tears or temper, he will pick up one of his new treasures, the *hutong* dancing girl perhaps, or the portrait painted on silk of a Tang dynasty princess, and dream his way back into a different, possibly kinder time.

Rewi has been reading all he can about China's many dynasties, hoping to be able to put a date on the bits and pieces he's collected. So far the dynasty he's most drawn to is the Tang – by all accounts a golden age when peasants were treated justly and art was encouraged. To become a government official during the Tang you had first to be a poet, a requirement Rewi feels certain is unique in history. The celebrated Tu Fu, whose poems Rewi has begun committing to memory, worked for most of his life as a government official. He hated it! 'I am about to scream madly in the office,' he complained, 'especially when they bring more papers to pile higher on my desk.'[2] I imagine Rewi laughing out loud when he read that. Twelve hundred years and nothing's changed, he would have thought, as he contemplated the piles of factory reports and submissions on his own desk.

What I wouldn't give to get my hands on one of the famous Tang pottery horses, Rewi thinks, quickening his pace. Designed to celebrate the prowess in battle and on the polo field of the legendary 'horses who sweated blood', it would sit well beneath his Tang dynasty scroll … He smiles as lines from one of Tu Fu's poems spring into his head. It's typical of the Sage of China that the title is as much a part of the poem as the lines themselves: 'Written on the Wall Beside the Horses Painted by Wei Yan'. Plain, clear, vivid. One day, Rewi has resolved, when his Mandarin is good enough he will translate Tu Fu's peerless poetry into English.

Rewi's passion for collecting began soon after his arrival in China. Though, like Chingling, he enjoyed having these treasures to hand, his main objective was to preserve them from destruction. Whenever possible he would arrange for them to be transported to Canterbury Museum. Family and friends, visiting from New Zealand, would suddenly find themselves co-opted as couriers. (I can't help wondering if that was the motivation behind his 1973 invitation to me.) It wasn't illegal in 1929 to take art works out of China, but this would change post-Liberation. Not that this stopped my cousin! Export licences, as hard to come by as travel visas, continued to be made available to him thanks to his friendship with Zhou Enlai, a firm believer in cultural diplomacy. The more people who knew about China, past and present, the better. So Zhou didn't just turn a blind eye to his friend's traffic in art, he facilitated it.

By the end of his life Rewi, the dedicated forager, who never had much money of his own, will have amassed artworks worth millions. Under the terms of his will, what hadn't already gone to the Canterbury Museum or to museums in China was gifted to the revived school in Shandan. No doubt he would have been astonished to learn that a special museum has had to be built to house the collection.[3]

Rewi's not writing poetry yet, but lines keep forming in his head. Walking by the lake, watching the slow progress of the junks and sampans, their colourful sails barely moving on this calm spring day, words – his own and Tu Fu's – start to run together and a new, hybrid poem takes shape, one that links the world he is moving through, the world he has left behind, and the increasingly familiar world in which Tu Fu lived and worked.

Six hours later, clutching a pair of pottery scissors bought for a song in the market, which he suspects may be as old as the Han, Rewi is on his way back to the railway station. Busy keeping a lookout for Jan, he's distracted by a commotion breaking out behind him. He turns. A squad of what he describes in his memoir as 'tough-looking soldiers with blaring trumpets and bugles', accompanied by officers on horseback, are striding down the road, heading, apparently, for the same place he is – the railway station. Staggering behind them are six half-naked young men 'hung from carrying poles like pigs'. Rewi watches in horror as a crowd gathers to witness what he quickly realises is going to be an execution. The officers dismount. The soldiers hand over pistols. The six men, not one of whom shows the least sign of fear, are made to kneel. Then, one by one, they are shot in the back of the head.

What had they done? No one in the enthusiastic crowd seems to know. Learning later that their crime was organising silk workers into a union, an activity that defined them as communists in the eyes of the local KMT officials, Rewi is stunned. He knows, of course, that executions occur – he's seen the baskets of severed heads suspended from street lamps in Shanghai – but there is all the difference in the world between being made aware of an atrocity and witnessing it for yourself.

He looks round for Jan, wondering if he's among the slowly dispersing crowd. On the way here they'd talked about Longhua, the execution ground on the outskirts of Shanghai, a conversation seeded a few weeks earlier when they met by chance in a tea house. Jan, a native of Ghent in Belgium, had come to China to work as a mid-level manager in a textile company. His revulsion at the KMT-authorised killings had persuaded Rewi they were singing from the same hymn sheet. Now, suddenly, he's not so sure. What if he's a spy? There are plenty of them around, men in the pay of the KMT or the Russians, not to mention the British and the Japanese. He'll be more circumspect in future.

As it turns out Jan didn't witness the execution but he heard the commotion and knows what's happened. On the journey back to Shanghai, Rewi is careful to steer the conversation away from the shootings, talking instead about what he saw in the markets. On reaching Shanghai the two men part company. Neither of them suggests meeting again.

Over the following weeks and months Rewi will play that scene at the Wuxi railway station over and over in his mind. What he remembers most vividly are the smiles on the faces of the condemned men. He'd seen that same serene smile on the face of a young man being led off to execution in Shanghai the year he arrived, but he hadn't understood what it signified. Now, two years on, he's beginning to believe that the mantra he'd thought applied only to soldiers – 'Being killed is just like going to sleep' – may be universal.[4] The children he encounters in the course of his work, condemned by disease and ill-treatment to die young, smile in the same way as those men being led to their deaths. What he will describe in his poetry as 'reckless gaiety' – a total lack of fear in the face of death – is starting to seem like the very heart and soul of China.

'I did not have any strong political ideas at that time, just goody-goody ones – that you had to do your best wherever you are,' he writes in his memoir. Wuxi changes all that. An English friend, one he has known long enough to trust, gives him a copy of Karl Marx's *Das Kapital*. He will go on to read Lenin and Stalin. 'You need to keep on learning,' he will insist in a letter to his parents. 'One doesn't change from one old system to another in one dramatic act,' he explained to Geoff Chapple. 'One little thing happens and you begin to look at it, then another … [Finally you conclude] nothing will do but a revolution.'

CHAPTER TWENTY

REWI'S *annus mutabilitatis*, 1929, will finally push this 'slow learner' out of the comfort of received ideas – he voted conservative in the 1925 New Zealand election – to a place where the idea of revolution begins to play an increasingly significant part in his thinking. He receives an invitation, the kind he can't refuse, from Joseph Bailie. A flood has devastated Inner Mongolia. News of the disaster has reached Shanghai but, like the rumour of red bandits and their acts of derring-do, it's easy to dismiss as just that – a rumour. Bailie knows better. He's seen the destruction caused by lack of rain and the consequent spread of sand and dust across once-fertile plains. Like Edgar Snow, who will compare the drought-ravaged hinterland of China with the Oklahoma dust bowl, 'only worse, much worse', Bailie knows what drought means for the Chinese peasant. In 1929 over five million will die. By 1931 that figure will have risen to more than 10 million.

There was only one way to prevent the region's devastating annual flooding and that was to build a canal linking the Yellow River with the Heihe. If the flooding of the Yellow River could be prevented, farmers would only have to deal with the consequences of drought, a situation they at least had some hope of managing. It was the double catastrophe of flood followed by drought that killed so many millions.

Over a meal of vegetables and rice Bailie spells out his plan, reminding Rewi he has an annual leave coming up. Surely he can spare part of it to lend a hand? Rewi protests that he knows nothing about canals. His host brushes his words aside. 'Do I have to spell it out?' he growls. 'People have nothing to eat. They're existing on bark and weeds. Or straw, which kills them anyway.'

Rewi doesn't doubt what he's hearing. What he doubts is his ability to do the job Bailie seems to have already assigned him. Stalling for time, he asks what's being done by the International Famine Relief agencies. That unleashes another diatribe. 'They're under government control,' Bailie seethes. 'Every little trumped-up official is demanding his cut. Official unction equals official suction! That's what's being done.'

But what seals it for Rewi is his friend's reminder about the number of times he's complained about how little he feels he's achieving in his current job. Over the course of their many discussions they've agreed that if things don't change soon the country will spiral into revolution. They've also agreed that the communists have the right ideas when it comes to the peasants. Co-operation, the lodestar of communist thought is, in Bailie's view, the only hope for China. Revolution would be a disaster. 'This is your chance to show how co-operation can work,' he concludes, clinching his argument.

Two weeks later, on a blazingly hot summer's day, Rewi boards the famous Peking 'Blue Express' bound for Suiyuan province in Inner Mongolia. The year doesn't have a name yet, but it soon will. In pre-Liberation China years were named according to the catastrophes that occurred in them: Year of the Long Drought; Year of the Warlords; Year of the Locusts. With one disaster following another, the old astrological signs almost fell into disuse. What connection did flood, famine and war have with the Year of the Rooster, or the Dragon or the Rat? For millions of Chinese the only reality was the one nature, aided by a rapacious government, threw at them. The year 1929 is no different. It will come to be known as the Long Punishment of the Rain God.

Rewi takes three days to reach his destination. Squashed into the open goods van with dozens of others, many of them refugees, he marvels at the stoicism of his fellow travellers, exposed to sun and sandstorms, plagued by lice and mosquitoes, surrounded by the stench of unwashed bodies. At every opportunity he gets out to stretch his legs. Sometimes there's a fiddler playing on the station platform, a welcome break from the clattering monotony of travel. At others, with nothing by way of distraction, the train stays put for hours. If there is a timetable it's clearly not being adhered to. (We will have similar experiences in 2017.)

On the third day, when the train pulls up at a remote country station, Rewi, his eyes red from exposure to dust and sand, his khaki shirt and shorts crumpled and sweat-stained, climbs down from the van and lets out a gasp of surprise. Standing amid the crowd of Chinese refugees and farm folk is a tall European wearing an immaculate white shirt, shorts and long white socks. Rewi approaches him warily. He's not about to make the mistake he made with Jan.

The man introduces himself. 'Edgar Snow, journalist,' he says. 'American.' He laughs. 'Obviously.'

Rewi holds out his hand. His strident anti-Americanism is still a decade and a half away. He's happy to shake this man's hand. 'I'm a New Zealander,' he corrects, when Snow assumes he's English. 'Least you didn't take me for a Russian!'

'A New Zealander?' Snow grins. 'Never met one of those before.'

Rewi doesn't know it yet, but this will prove to be one of the most important meetings of his life. Snow, an idealistic young American, has come to China in much the same spirit as Rewi himself – seeking adventure, curious to find out what's going on in this land of mystery and mayhem. Like Agnes Smedley, another American journalist whose life will have a similar impact on Rewi's, Snow was born in Missouri. But there the similarities end. Where Smedley, part Cherokee, raised in rural poverty, will have to fight her way into newspaper offices and government departments, doors will be opened for the handsome, charming, middle-class Missouri boy. Not that his life will be plain sailing. The man who will go on to write the book that introduced Mao Zedong to the West, *Red Star Over China* (one of many books Snow will publish based on his China experience), will find himself out of favour and out of work in the Cold War McCarthy years.

When the whistle blows for the passengers to re-board, Snow, who is travelling courtesy of the vice-minister of railways on what is officially a railway inspection tour, suggests Rewi join him in the VIP carriage. Rewi is tempted. It's been a long hot journey. But when Vice-Minister Hu sees the state of him – Snow later described him as 'strangely out of place in that dark sickly crowd, his sunburned face covered with dust beneath a fiery bush of upstanding hair' – it's obvious his presence is going to cause embarrassment.[1] Rewi waves goodbye and makes his way back to the goods van and the company of the refugees. Rewi will see Snow again, in Salaqi, site of the canal-building project, but it is not until they are both in Shanghai – by which time Snow, employed as a journalist by the *China Weekly Review*, has caught the 'China bug' – that their friendship really begins.

Arriving in Salaqi, Rewi is immediately assigned the job of erecting telephone poles to connect the canal-side villages. At the end of each day's work he shows up at the local mission-run soup kitchen to help out. Handing over the miserable portions of sorghum and millet, under the watchful eyes of the local warlords, Rewi curses under his breath, aware that the thousands queuing up for their one meal a day are only a fraction of the millions displaced and starving across China's northwest. 'Refugees would sit around for a few days to try to get strength enough to work,' he writes in his memoir. 'Villages were ransacked of timber, animals stolen or killed, women sold to dealers who would ship them south while the men, old women and boys existed on the charity of the soup kitchen until most died and were thrown into the city moat ...'

No wonder the Huang He, the Yellow River, is called 'China's sorrow'.

*

Returning to Shanghai, Rewi can't get what he's seen in Salaqi out of his head. He knows nature is not alone in causing the devastation; warlords and greedy government officials have to take their share of the blame. The warlords have been forcing farmers to tear up their food crops and grow opium, a valuable cash crop, in their place. The government has been demanding taxes of the peasants even when famine has devastated the harvest. Money to repair dykes and canals has been diverted to the nationalist army. Chiang's extermination campaigns don't come cheap.

Rewi is in turmoil. His Shanghai life has lost whatever lustre it had. He's angry and lonely and, despite his work as a factory inspector, at a loose end. He can't stop thinking about the children orphaned by the famine in Salaqi: pathetic, lice-infected youngsters with protruding ribs and bellies swollen from beri beri. When he hears that the Red Cross is bringing several thousand of these waifs to Shanghai, he makes up his mind. There's room in his apartment for a child. His salary is more than enough to cover expenses. At least one child can be spared famine's relentless destiny.

He doesn't discuss his plan with anyone. He knows what would be said. You're out of your mind! If you must adopt, find one of your own kind.

It turns out to be surprisingly easy. He'd expected checks and counter-checks, documents to be signed, money to be paid. But all he's had to do, once the adoption papers were in his hands and he's paid the required US$60, is take himself down to the refugee centre and choose a child. Two boys are produced for him to inspect. One is a tall, well-fed, handsome lad, son of a deceased Manchu official; the other is a farm boy with a strong peasant face. He selects the farm boy. Duan Rumei (later changed to Duan Simu) is 14 years old. Rewi will call him Alan, not, he claimed, because he wants to give him a European name but because Suiyuan province was once the country of the Alans. I wonder about this. Rewi, who chose not to take a Chinese name when almost all his European friends were doing so, will call his second son Mike. So far as I know there isn't a country of the Mikes in China.

Father … I'm a father, I imagine Rewi saying to himself, as he ushers his son into his apartment. He's surprised how comfortable the word sounds. It will take a while for father and son to adjust to their new life, but Rewi has no second thoughts. He knows what Alan's existence has been. He's braced for defiance, nightmares, sullen withdrawal. His hope is that in time Alan will start to remember his life before the famine, when he had a family and a future. Weekend excursions to the countryside help, as does Rewi's patience in teaching his son the routines and rituals of his hybrid European–Chinese life. (Watching Alan struggling to use a knife and fork prompts Rewi to describe his own early attempts at using chopsticks.) Eventually they 'grow to love each other very much.'[2] Alan's words. And Rewi's loneliness is eased.

Rewi now has a personal stake in the future of China, a fact that will influence his thinking more profoundly than anything else. 'The Family Alley became a kind of legend,' Edgar Snow will report after Rewi adopts a second son. 'In Municipal Council circles few white sahibs would dream of sitting down with a coolie at the table.'[3] But there's Rewi, who likes to refer to himself as 'China's Number One Coolie', telling stories to his son, singing the songs his English mother sang to him, bringing the worlds of New Zealand and England and China together:

The more we are together, together, together,
the more we are together, the happier we'll be.
For your friends are my friends and my friends are your friends …

CHAPTER TWENTY-ONE
12 April 2017

OUR last day in Beijing, for now. We will be back in just over a week for a special function in the Great Hall of the People. By that time we will have had our heads filled with words of praise for Rewi and his work. He is a 'Sky-high Tree', gifted with 'personality glamour', who has lived a 'miracle life'. His 'glorious life' will inspire us to do better. The 'faithful devotion' and 'immortal performance' of this 'Great Fighter for Internationalism', 'Old Comrade and Loyal Friend of China', will, so we have been assured, last till the end of Time.

We have even been invited – in Baoji, former headquarters of the co-operative movement – to kowtow (bow) three times to his statue. I will discover later that this is not quite the obeisance I thought it was. Bowing to a statue or grave is commonplace in China. Initially, I felt indignant on Rewi's behalf. 'Why the devil do we bow anyway?' he complained in his poem 'Hsing Lung Shan' when asked to do so before the mortal remains of Genghis Khan.[1] 'He slaughtered millions ...'

Rewi, the man who once responded to a speech in his honour with a cheerful, 'Up yours too, Squire', would have had plenty to say about the veneration in which he is held in China today.[2] He may have told Willis Airey he was glad he never grew up, but he did, or rather his ghost did – in the legacy he left behind. In this version of his life the Rewi who pushed over the tram in Cape Town, who absconded from barracks in France for a night on the town, who muttered 'I don't care' from his perch in the walnut tree, has grown so tall he has become a Sky-high Tree. Who is to say which Rewi is the true one? He never took himself seriously. The fact that others did, and continue to do so, might have earned a sigh, but would more likely have triggered the Alley temper.

But bowing to Rewi's statue is still ahead of us. For the moment we are tourists, whisking in our ALLEY WHANAU bus from one temple to another, marvelling at the 18-metre-high gold Buddha we have been brought to see in the Yonghegong Lamasery. Some of us, the sinus sufferers, are coughing and spluttering into our tissues, afflicted by the spiralling clouds of incense pouring out of the burners placed at dismayingly close intervals in the courtyard. So many Buddhas: happy; sad; angry; thoughtful; small; large; in warrior pose; in peace-maker pose. I am about to leave – there are only so many Buddhas a person can take in one day – when I spot a medium-sized Buddha with a fat tummy and a contented smile on his face. My little fat daddy! I blow a kiss in its direction and move out into the courtyard.

'Alley whānau! Attention please. Follow my flag. This way ...'

We will see more temples in the afternoon but by then we will have visited Rewi's Beijing home, the place he lived in for over 30 years, and I will have little appetite left for temple gazing. The Temple of Heaven, where Ming and Qing dynasty emperors came to pray, is a three-kilometre square complex encompassing the Hall of Prayer for Good Harvests, the Imperial Vault of Heaven, the Earthly Mound, the Circular Mound Altar and the Seven Star Stone Group. Fortunately I can place Rewi here, otherwise my temple fatigue would have won the day. He didn't, like the emperors, come to pray, he came – often in the company of Anna Louise Strong, who lived until her death in the apartment below his – to walk along the lilac-scented paths.

What did he and Anna Louise talk about? Presumably not the buildings, whose beauty they would have taken for granted and whose function, as source and symbol of the emperor's power, they would have dismissed as superstition. I suspect these two old revolutionaries-turned-authors would have been at their happiest when discussing the work they'd done that day, Anna Louise complaining about the noise of his typewriter, Rewi complaining about his addiction to poetry – and the fact that he's run out of marmalade.

Anna Louise Strong was a remarkable woman. An American pacifist and writer, her work as a foreign correspondent for the International News Service took her first to Poland, then to the USSR, where she became an enthusiastic supporter of Russian socialism. She would finally get to China in the late 1920s, but another 10 years would pass before she met Rewi. By then, distressed by the Stalinist purges, she made no secret of her preference for the Chinese revolution over the Russian. This shift in loyalty would be cemented when, in 1949, she was gaoled in Moscow on a charge of espionage. Her crime? Supporting the Chinese communists when it was Stalin's policy to support the KMT.

That Stalin was at the time supporting Chiang Kaishek is not as extraordinary as it sounds. The Leninist view of revolution was that it had first to go through a bourgeois phase – a necessary softening up in preparation for the Real Thing. Stalin, like Lenin before him, regarded China as too backward, not sufficiently industrialised, for revolution to stick. So he supported the 'bourgeois' KMT, biding his time until, with Russian guidance, a lasting proletarian revolution could take place.

Anna Louise was eventually freed, on condition she left the USSR and never returned. Later that order was rescinded and she was invited back, but by that time she'd decided to make China her home. Rewi never did hear her whole story. No one did. When she embarked on writing a memoir she got as far as her imprisonment, and stopped.

After Anna Louise's death, Rewi continued coming to the Temple of Heaven to walk, either on his own or with his friend George Hatem (Ma Haide). He missed Anna, the 'big strong American woman' from Nebraska who gave her life to the communist cause.[3] He missed her pugnacious nature and her refusal to be intimidated. In his mind the walk that had become part of his weekly routine would always be the 'Anna Louise Walk'.

The day of our visit the complex is packed with tourists. I try to imagine how it must have looked during the Cultural Revolution when there were no visitors at all, but the crowds and the noise get in the way. Had it not been for Zhou Enlai, who declared it a military base and ordered guards to be placed at the gates, the temples would almost certainly have been destroyed. As would the Forbidden City, for so many centuries the Celestial Kingdom's centre of power, and today a magnet for tourists on a par with the Temple of Heaven. Hearing of the Red Guard plan to attack it, Zhou acted quickly, moving troops into the area and declaring it, too, a military base. China has a lot to thank Zhou Enlai for, as does the Alley family.

On the way to Rewi's Beijing home I found myself thinking about Rewi's great love for the Chinese people – what David Mahon describes as 'a rare kind of love … nurtured in the heart but really an intellectual love for humankind'.[4] I wonder what he would think about today's China, and where his empathy with the poor and the rejected might take him. Would he be an aid worker, a champion of refugees, a warrior in the fight against racism? I can't see him as a politician. And I can't see him as a preacher. 'I don't have the "good works" complex,' he insisted whenever anyone tried to praise him as a humanitarian.[5] In his mind he did what anyone else would have done in his place.

'Rewi has taken Chinese liberation as his own endeavour,' Mao Zedong is said to have declared.[6] Mao's insistence on the supremacy of moral over material incentives, of working for your country not for yourself – an ironic foreshadowing of President Kennedy's challenge to his Peace Corps volunteers – chimed perfectly with Rewi's code of conduct. Long before he encountered communism he'd demonstrated his lack of personal greed, his distrust of wealth and his empathy for the downtrodden of the world. 'How does one become a big man?' he said in answer to a question, from students who visited him in 1967, about China's revolutionary leaders. 'Not by political trickery nor trying to make friends in high places but by … learning to work with others, retaining the humility of Zhou Enlai, in the face of immense tasks.'[7]

*

Arriving at No. 1 Tai Ji Chang, Rewi's home for over 30 years, I'm ambushed by a sense of regret so powerful it brings tears to my eyes. This is where I would have stayed had I accepted his first invitation, or been allowed to accept his second. Once part of the Italian embassy, the 'Compound for Foreign Friends of China', as the entire complex was referred to in Rewi's day, is now a museum. There's a pomegranate tree, planted by Rewi in memory of Anna Louise, and a walnut tree planted in the 1980s. The gardens are lovely but the mosaic-fronted house where Rewi and Anna Louise lived – an embassy add-on built by the Italians – is unremarkable. Rewi described it in a 1978 letter to Shirley Barton as a 'poem factory', his choice of the word 'factory' pinpointing, perhaps unconsciously, the functional appearance of the place he called home.[8] Suddenly I understand why people feel the need to scrawl their names on ancient monuments. How else can you speak to the dead? Making your mark physically is a way of holding hands with your ancestors. But there is no need to scrawl anything here because I know where I am, and I know whose hand I'm holding.

Rewi moved here in 1953 and stayed for the rest of his life. The garden in which I'm standing would have stretched as far as the eye could see in pre-revolutionary days. No traffic noise would have disturbed its privileged European inhabitants. Most of the buildings we can see now were built while Rewi and Anna Louise lived here. The din of construction would have been constant. But it was Rewi's two-fingered bashing of the typewriter keys that got on Anna Louise's nerves. Her constant complaint – that he sounded as if he was drilling holes in the paper – would be followed by a stern warning that if he wanted to go on being her friend he had better learn to type properly.

Directly opposite the house is a building known in Rewi's day as the Peking Party Headquarters. It was a favourite meeting place for Red Guards during the Cultural Revolution. I imagine Rewi, moving tentatively around the garden, glancing in the direction of that sinister building, wondering what was being plotted for him and his friends.

Reports of what happened to him in those dark years are contradictory. One report, printed in April 1968 by *New Zealand Truth*, describes him as under arrest – 'the latest and perhaps most surprising victim of the national lunacy that is the Cultural Revolution'.[9] Dismissed as 'opium-addled fiction' by the *People's Voice*, the New Zealand communist newspaper, this was in fact partly true.[10] When Zhou Enlai, in the wake of a Red Guard attack on Rewi, ordered a sentry to be stationed at the gate of the compound it was, in effect, a form of 'protective custody'. Later, when things had quietened down – Mao, recognising that the revolution had got out of hand, sent troops into the countryside to discipline the Red Guards – the sentry was removed and Rewi was allowed to travel. He was even allowed to visit New Zealand. But there was a price to pay. *Travels in China*, the book he wrote following the nationwide commune inspection Zhou sent him on, is, like his book about the Great Leap Forward (*China's Hinterland in the Leap Forward*), almost unreadable. When my Alley cousin Merryl, visiting him near the end of his life, told him she'd seen the book in a market and planned to buy it, his response was, 'Don't! It was written in a bad time.'

The conclusion reached by the SIS was that Rewi, whatever his own views, was under pressure throughout the Cultural Revolution to toe the Party line.[11] He was spared imprisonment, but he was not spared suffering. His sons were gaoled; his phone tapped; his letters censored; his books pulped;[12] his life, despite Zhou's protection, under constant threat. 'How could Mao let this happen?' Anna Louise complained angrily to Rewi when news reached them that Liu Shaoqi, the third most powerful man in China, had been denounced as a traitor.[13] What Rewi said in reply is not recorded, though in a letter written in June 1980 to Shirley Barton he confessed that the poem he subsequently published about Liu was composed 'in penance for believing in the frame-up, with no real knowledge of what was going on'.[14]

Out of concern for his friends, especially Soong Chingling and Ma Haide, neither of whom it was safe to visit, Rewi burned their letters to him, asking that they in turn burn his to them. He also asked Pip to burn the letters he had written to the family (fortunately Pip disobeyed the order). When in mid-1970 Pip wrote to ask what was going on, Rewi replied, 'I have no knowledge whatsoever … There has been a complete stop to publishing my books here. But I am all for the Cultural Revolution. It is important …'[15] Five years later in a letter to Gwen he would write, 'I am … subdued, overawed by all I do not know.'[16] What he never acknowledged, even in his diary, was that it had become a criminal offence to associate with foreigners or to have relatives abroad.

Even back in 1952, more than a decade before the Cultural Revolution, Rewi was aware of the danger of committing certain words to paper. In a letter to Hugh Elliott, a Shandan colleague, he warned, 'The man who would write about things in China today has to think of every kind of twist that every kind of person can give … the sheer distortion of the foreign press … One can hardly say anything except sheer fact or progress …'[17] 'You're here at an interesting time,' Rewi said to Pip when he visited in the spring of 1976, just as the revolution was coming to an end. 'Things are changing, I think for the better. Keep your eyes and ears open. Watch the notices going up.'[18] Five months later, following the arrest of the Gang of Four in October, he could be more open. In a letter to his brother he wrote, 'It [the Cultural Revolution] was nearly the end of Alan and Mike, and would have been for your elder brother too if they [the Gang of Four] had won out.'[19]

*

So what was Rewi's life like when it wasn't under threat from Red Guards? What did he do in the three decades he lived here? The answer is he wrote – 13 books in the first eight years, 66 in total. He wrote the story of Gung Ho; he wrote books explaining the New China to the West; he wrote poems, his own and the translated works of Chinese poets, ancient and modern; he wrote travelogues and reports of the peace conferences he attended; he wrote and wrote and wrote. 'I don't think of myself as a natural writer,' he told David Mahon. 'Writing is hard … one of the hardest things I've had to do.'[20] Given the sheer volume of his output and the rushed, uneven quality of much of his work, his claim that he often laboured all day over a few lines is hard to believe. Perhaps he wanted people to see him as a poet who sweated blood trying to find the right line, the right word. Perhaps he really did labour as he said, driven by his own inner demons. By the end of his life the words were literally falling off the edge of the typewritten page …

I look around the garden with its peach and cherry blossoms, its beautifully tended flowerbeds, and try to place Rewi in its ordered loveliness, but even though we haven't yet been to Shandan, that is the place I see. No. 1

Tai Ji Chang was his home for most of his Chinese life but it wasn't where his heart was. That was 3000 kilometres away in the remote northwest. People around me are saying how peaceful it is here, but what I'm seeing, plastered across the door, is the Big Character Poster (*Dazibao*) identifying Rewi as a 'Bourgeois Rightest', 'Imperialist with Ulterior Motives', 'Capitalist Roader' that could have ended his life.

'This way please! First Rewi Alley house, then lunch.'

*

Four of our group have been in this house before: Maurice (Pip's son), his wife Dorothy, Dave Bromwich and Zeke. As we walk through the door, Zeke goes straight to the chair Rewi always sat in. 'I can see him now,' he says, looking for a moment as if he is Rewi (though we all agree the one who really looks like Rewi is Ross). 'He was wearing an embroidered cap on his head.' That would be his Uyghur cap. Bright green with silver threads. Worn to remind him of his beloved northwest. Zeke goes on to describe the room as it was in 1985 – the books, papers, artefacts, paintings, the thermos of coffee on the table. 'There was artwork everywhere,' he tells us. 'Place was stuffed with it.'

The thermos was legendary. It would have been filled with Nescafé. That was what visitors were asked to bring with them from the West – Nescafé and Oxford marmalade. By the end of the tour I will know why. Congee (Chinese porridge) and steam buns – the typical Chinese breakfast – can never replace toast and marmalade. 'I remain a New Zealander but I have become Chinese too,' Rewi writes in the preface to *Beyond the Withered Oak*. Perhaps he woke up a New Zealander but became Chinese as the day wore on …

We move from the front room to Rewi's office, which doubled as a dining room. There is his typewriter and a few of his published books, as well as what remains of his personal library, the bulk of it, like his art works, having been bequeathed to Shandan.

So what we are seeing is a stripped-down version of the Aladdin's cave that was Rewi's home. In this room he and Anna Louise took their meals, decamping to the veranda when Beijing's 'tiger heat' got too much for them. They shared a cook and a driver. And what else? Did Anna Louise open up to Rewi about her famous meeting with Mao in Yan'an in 1946? It was she who sent his words, 'All reactionaries are paper tigers', spinning around the world.[21] We know she talked about her love for America, despite the fact that her passport had been confiscated and she couldn't go back. She died in 1970, at the height of the Cultural Revolution, without seeing her homeland again. 'She gave a shout and her heart stopped,' Rewi wrote in a letter to Shirley Barton.[22] There was no need to say more. Shirley would know how much he was going to miss his cantankerous housemate. In his poem dedicated to Anna Louise in *73 Man to Be* he predicted that her name would be remembered. He was right. Despite her pariah status as a foreigner she was buried in Beijing's Babaoshan Revolutionary Cemetery, an honour reserved for China's heroes.

I block my ears, metaphorically speaking, and see Rewi sitting at his desk in the quiet of the evening, writing one of his thousands of letters to his New Zealand family. Somehow he managed to keep track of us all, congratulating us on achievements, commiserating on disappointments and losses, constantly telling his siblings and cousins how wonderful they were and how dear to him. 'My dear and beautiful sister,' a letter to his 'darling Gwen' began.[23] Was it from here he wrote to tell me about shooting the sparrows in Beijing? A direct order from Mao, part of his 1958 Four Pests Campaign designed to eradicate flies, sparrows, rats and mosquitoes. First the sparrows were killed – either shot, or starved as a result of people banging pot lids and beating drums to stop them feeding. Then it was the turn of the flies. People were paid according to how many they killed, so when the supply ran out so did the wages. 'Bring back the flies,' they begged. 'We never minded them before.' As for the attack on the sparrows, this had even more dire consequences. The year after the successful campaign China's harvest was destroyed by a plague of locusts – something Rewi neglected to tell me about.

Living for decades in Beijing was not what Rewi chose. He'd never wanted to leave Shandan. His diary for his last weeks as headmaster is crammed with lists of things to be done, things achieved and materials to be ordered, suggesting that his dismissal, when it came, was a bolt from the blue. More blows follow until, by the end of 1952, he is gone for good. Exiled to Beijing, he is overwhelmed by a sense of helplessness. What is he supposed to do? But he believes in China and its government. Likening himself to a bolting horse – no doubt thinking of Hamud and his close shave with death in Moeawatea – he reminds himself that horses are eventually caught and managed.

Despite the presence of friends, Rewi is often lonely. But he is not a man to sit around and bemoan his fate, so he starts writing. He writes fast and furiously. He has so much to say there's no time to sort the wheat from the chaff. When the government eventually finds a job for him as a peace envoy on the international stage, he tackles it with the passion of a man who's experienced the very worst aspects of war, civil and international. He's not a pacifist – his dalliance with that movement lasted only a few months – but he's more than willing to use his skill with words and his power as a speaker in the cause of world peace.

For the next 14 years, until the outbreak of the Cultural Revolution when his works are labelled 'poisonous weeds', Rewi will keep up a steady flow of books and pamphlets.[24] The one book that is published in China during this dark time, *Travels in China*, is written to order.

With the overthrow of the Gang of Four, the ban on Rewi's books is lifted and he's able to publish freely again. But the Red Guard decade has taken a toll. The fire in Rewi's belly has been doused. He still believes in the revolution, but he sees it now as vulnerable, liable to run amok if leadership fails. He can pick up the old life, displaying his treasures without fear of armed youths bursting into his house and destroying them, but he can't summon the words that once blistered the pages falling from his typewriter. He can't even lose himself in translations from the poets of China's past, having forgotten many of the old dynastic characters, banned under the policy of 'Smash the Four Olds'. He's free to move around the city, visit the markets, see friends, practise tai-chi and breathe in the smell of lilac on the Anna Louise Walk, but he's a shadow of the Rewi who launched Gung Ho on the world.

CHAPTER TWENTY-TWO

REWI, by 1932, has become so used to being a father he finds it hard to imagine a time when there weren't teenage boys to fill his head with their chatter – and sometimes their squabbles – at the end of a day's work. Alan, having at first stood aloof from the new arrival, is now a loving brother to Mike, helping him with his English, teaching him how to use a knife and fork, speculating with him as to what their father is up to when he disappears for a few nights. They know better than to ask. Rewi is a loving father, given to impulsive hugging and competitive game-playing, but he is also strict. Both boys have been beaten when they've failed to live up to his high standards. Not that this bothers them. They would have considered it strange had they not been punished.

Alan and Mike don't of course know that their father was himself regularly, and often unjustly, beaten as a child. What effect these punishments had on Rewi can only be guessed at, but there can be no doubt they played a part in shaping his character. Had it not been for his mother Clara, whose gentle nature hid a steely resolve to do the very best for her children, he may well have grown up to emulate his father. But he didn't. He beat his sons rarely and only after repeated provocation. Later when he found himself in charge of a school, corporal punishment was part of the regime, as it was in the school I attended in 1950s New Zealand. (Like Rewi, who was once strapped five times in one day, I held the record for being strapped – for talking in class – more often than any other pupil.) But punishment is not what Rewi's students remember him for. They remember his warmth, his love of play and his empathy with suffering. Like Mike and Alan they tell tales of sorties into the countryside to forage for treasure and hear lessons on the need for sustainable farming and tree planting. The man they describe loved opera and theatre and listening to music. He loved to dance. And when, as happened too often, an orphan child brought to the school could not be saved, he wept.

One of the many stories told about Rewi, in confusingly different versions, gives a new slant to his use of corporal punishment.

It's 1970. The 'Great Proletarian Cultural Revolution' is raging. Rewi, who was for part of that decade under virtual house arrest, receives a visit from a band of Red Guards (the notorious *hongweibing*) intent on smashing up his collection of Chinese artefacts. Recognising one of the group as his own grandson, he threatens to take down the boy's trousers and 'tan his hide'. The guards slink away without touching a thing.

Clearly Rewi believed in a limited form of corporal punishment as a necessary tool for disciplining the young. 'This will hurt me more than you,' he was said to have muttered to his son Mike, before delivering a smacking. I don't remember when I heard this – it can only have been from my mother – but I do remember the indignation I felt. How could it hurt Rewi? He wasn't the one being whacked!

'Most modern educators in the West say it's not necessary to spank kids any more,' Rewi quotes himself saying to the old Chinese doctor who was his travelling companion on one of his many wartime journeys through the Chinese hinterland. 'Big people bullying the small ones, sadistic teachers, all that kind of thing ...'

'Yes, I've heard about that from some of the mission people in Nanking,' was the doctor's answer. 'But I never saw so many unspanked ruffians as that family of American mission children ... They gave their own parents a terrible time and terrorised the whole neighbourhood.'[1]

I can see Rewi smiling as he types those words. 'Spare the rod and spoil the child.' A mantra he would, like me, have grown up with.

*

In March 1932 Rewi took Alan back to New Zealand to introduce him to his family. It was his first visit home since his departure in December 1926.

A video is playing in my head: Rewi and Alan walking up the gangway of the liner due to sail from Shanghai that afternoon; Alan, like his father, wearing shorts, shirt and a sleeveless pullover; like him too, carrying a battered suitcase containing a change of clothes, a pack of cards, and some books in Chinese and English. Rewi's case is bigger and heavier. It's stuffed with presents for the family, and artefacts, as many as he's been able to pack safely, for the Canterbury Museum.

Alan is 17 years old. His English has progressed since he came to live with Rewi but it's not fluent. Rewi, while anxious to improve his son's language skills, has no wish to turn him into a parody of an Oxford-educated Englishman. When they are on their own, they mostly speak Mandarin.

Rewi is exhausted. The weeks spent repairing dykes as part of the flood-relief work in Wuhan have knocked the stuffing out of him. If all he'd had to do was labour with his hands, then a good night's sleep would have restored him, but he'd had to do far more than flex his muscles. Most of the dyke workers were refugees dependent on the miserable meal handed out to them at the end of a day's work. Trouble was, local KMT officials were doing everything in their power to divert food supplies away from Wuhan. Battling to get the precious cargoes of wheat and millet through the army blockades, Rewi was shouted at, threatened and, in at least one instance, shot at. Even when he succeeded in unloading the barges, greedy officials would be waiting to syphon off their portion, which they would then sell on for profit, a practice known as squeezing. As a result, millions who could have been saved died of starvation.

But food was not the only problem Rewi faced. The officials overseeing the repair of the dykes gave orders for him not to bother with full-scale repair work, but to simply place a layer of stamped earth on top so that the dykes looked as if they'd been properly repaired. That was it as far as Rewi was concerned. The Alley temper could be contained no longer. 'The foolish man built his house upon the sand ...' I imagine the old Bible song pounding in his head as he struggled to find Chinese words to express his disgust. He'd seen whole families clinging to the top branches of trees to escape the flood waters. He would not be party to a programme that guaranteed those sights would appear again.

Disobeying instructions came naturally to the man who'd cheerfully overturned a tram in protest at the treatment of his Māori mates. So when he learned that a whole bunch of refugees had been targeted by the KMT as communists and were in line to be shot, he acted quickly and without permission to move them out of harm's way. A subsequent League of Nations report claimed that by this action alone he had saved thousands of lives. Rewi, insisting that anyone would have done the same, dismissed the claim as nonsense.

Executions were a daily event. Either the Japanese were killing refugees who, with nothing to lose, had stormed their military posts, or the KMT were killing workers suspected of being communists. Rewi, unlike most of his contemporaries, was constitutionally unable to look away. Cruelty was everywhere. In these extreme circumstances it wasn't confined only to the haves. Rewi understood this. He didn't judge. He knew that he was witnessing what Geoff Chapple would call in his biography the 'psychopathy of a broken-down society'.

Alan loves every minute of the month-long journey to New Zealand. He especially loves the ocean. When he becomes a father himself all six of his children will have the character for ocean 海, pronounced *hai*, as part of their names. Four will be named after seabirds. It's Alan's way of keeping alive his delight at encountering the ocean for the first time.[2] Unlike his father, Alan doesn't complain when he is a target of the casual and not-so-casual racism of Australia during their brief stopover there. He's on an adventure, the greatest of his life. What do a few insults matter?

But for Rewi the journey seems interminable. He's impatient to see his mother, to reconnect with his siblings and to take a look at Westcote, the new family home about which he's heard so much. The one positive aspect to the journey is the chance it's giving him to spend time with Alan. When they get back, Mike's adoption will be legal and he will be a father of two. As yet Alan isn't too keen on the idea. He likes his 'only son' status. But he'll come round. Especially once Mike starts calling him 'Elder Brother'.

Father and son arrive in New Zealand at the end of April. Rewi takes one look at Westcote and falls in love with it, as I will two decades later:

> … quiet talks around the fire, apples and nuts, books and kids; the Good Friends who come, and the fragrance of a great spirit …[3]

But Westcote, and the joy of seeing his mother again, are only part of the experience. He takes Alan to Moeawatea, riding along the mud road, the horses slipping and sliding like the hillsides on either side of them, and the nostalgia he had anticipated turns to anger. China, someone said to him once, is not a country for old men. Well, neither, he thinks, in a moment of bitter clarity, is this wilderness. It's good to see Jack again, but he can't help wondering how much longer his friend can go on scraping a living for himself and his wife. God knows why he's hung on so long. He should have let the whole shooting match go back to the bush years ago.

Over afternoon tea Rewi asks about the neighbours. They're still there, Jack tells him, but they don't want to see you. When Rewi asks why, Jack nods in Alan's direction. Rewi shakes his head in disgust. He can hear the words. He heard them in Sydney when Alan was refused entry to the public swimming baths. He heard them when they travelled on the express from Auckland to Wellington. 'Fuckin' Chink! What's he doing on the train?'

'It's a country of ghosts,' I imagine him confiding to his mother when he and Alan get back to Westcote. 'Deserted farms, empty houses, hopeless, despairing men ...' What he might not have told her was that it is also a country of bigots.

*

'This is the Christchurch police,' the voice on the end of the line says. 'Do you have a young Chinese living at your place?'

'Yes,' Rewi answers. 'My son. Is something wrong?'

'He's been seen driving a car. An old Rover.'

'That's right. I've taught him to drive.'

The policeman clears his throat. 'I see ... Well, would you mind telling your son that a red light means he has to stop.'

Rewi chokes back a laugh. 'Yes. Yes of course. Thank you. I'll make it crystal clear to him.'

'I assume he has a licence,' the policeman says.

'All in order,' Rewi answers.

'You haven't changed,' Clara scolds when Rewi relays the conversation to her. 'What were you thinking? That policeman was very nice, considering. Imagine what would have happened if your father had answered the phone ...'[4]

*

The day comes for Rewi and Alan to leave. Rewi tries to make light of it but he can see the tears in his mother's eyes. There'd been an argument last night. His fault. And now there's no time to put things right. His father had started it, seizing on a throwaway remark of Rewi's to sound forth about the evils of drink. 'Want to change the licensing laws, do you?' he'd snapped, jumping at the chance to lecture his son about the demon drink and the devastation it causes. 'That what they do in China? Stay up all night drinking?'

He should have let it go. When had he ever won an argument with his father? But the old man's habit of deliberately misunderstanding riled him. His mild protest about the law requiring pubs to close at six o'clock – won after a long battle by the New Zealand Temperance Movement – was nothing to do with the demon drink, it was the loss of communal time he was objecting to. Watching men tip as much beer down their throats as they could in the time available was not a pretty sight. Nor were the drunks, thrown out at closing time, lying in the gutter in full view of passers-by. No wonder people called it the 'six o'clock swill'.

Inevitably his father had had the last word. 'Know what your trouble is, Rewi? You talk too much. You assume everyone wants to hear what you have to say.'

'Goodbye Father,' Rewi says now, holding out his hand.

'Goodbye Son.'

'Goodbye Mother.'

Clara lets go of Alan, whose hand she's been holding, and pulls her son close. 'More poems please,' she whispers. 'I like them.'

CHAPTER TWENTY-THREE

THE Shanghai Rewi and Alan return to is even more on edge than the city they left seven months earlier. There were gunboats moored in the river then, but now there is an armada, some lining the banks, others anchored in the centre from where they have a 180-degree view over the city. The locals, used to such sights, have re-named this section of the river Battleship Row.

Four times the taxi taking Rewi and Alan to Yuyuan Road is stopped by Japanese sentries. They grow tired of showing their passports, explaining where they've been, opening their suitcases to prove they are not carrying weapons. Buildings, those still standing after the bombing, are sandbagged. (Historian Barbara W. Tuchman will describe this first bombing of a civilian population as an act that will 'change the face of modern warfare.'[1] From 1932 on, dropping bombs on civilian populations will become an accepted part of military strategy.)

Rewi comes to a decision. As soon as Mike has joined them he's going to arrange for both boys to go to a boarding school outside the city. Shanghai isn't safe any more. A miasma of fear, infinitely more sinister than the familiar cloud of pollution, hangs over the city. The boys will protest, of course they will, but he'll soften the blow by promising they can come home at weekends.

What he won't tell his sons is that since the Japanese attack on Shanghai there have been major defections from the KMT army – officers and men, convinced that China is finished. Over half a million, including 42 generals and 70 high-ranking officers have, so he's been told, thrown in their lot with the Japanese. Which isn't to say the majority aren't still loyal. The 19th Route Army put up a heroic defense in the face of the Japanese bombardment, but in the end they were forced to retreat, leaving Shanghai in the hands of the enemy. Even the capital has had to be moved, from Nanjing – considered now to be too close to Shanghai – to Luoyang.

Rewi is an optimist. He wants to believe that China will come through this. But he has to admit the future looks grim. The further his boys are from the action the better.

*

Rewi goes back to work. He doesn't like the way he's feeling. He's missing the boys; missing his mother; missing his siblings, especially Gwen to whom he's closest. Gwen is married now, to a splendid chap, Crawford Somerset. The discussions he had with them about early childhood education and the value of play are among his happiest memories of his time back home. But this is home now, he reminds himself. Every week 4000 corpses are collected from the streets of this city. Is it any wonder he feels low?

He looks up at the sky, what he can see of it. Crows sway over the tops of buildings, waiting for their chance to eat the carrion this city so thoughtfully provides. Yesterday, forced to get out of his car by a surly Japanese soldier, whose one word in English seemed to be pig, stripped half naked and searched, he was about to climb back into the car when he spotted a parcel lying on the pavement. Something about its shape made him want to look to see what was inside. He wished he hadn't. A baby girl, so starved it was impossible to tell her age, stared sightlessly back at him. Fighting back tears he carried the bundle to the car. He would bury her later when no one was around to ask questions.[2]

*

The year 1933 arrives with the usual fanfare in the clubs and bars of Shanghai. The difference is most of the clientele is now Japanese. Despite his best efforts – redoubling his pressure on factory owners, throwing his weight behind the canteens – Rewi's melancholy lingers. He's given the boys his copy of *Das Kapital* to read. They agree with him that it makes a lot of sense.

A few days into the new year he bumps into Agnes Smedley, whom his friend Maud Russel, secretary of the Shanghai YWCA, an organisation held in high regard both by Rewi and by the Chinese, had introduced him to the previous year. They find a place to have tea. At last, Rewi thinks, as their conversation ranges over China's wars and China's miseries, someone who understands. Agnes hasn't been in China as long as Rewi but she's way ahead of him when it comes to moving on from analysis to action. She hasn't got time for frustration. Or hand-wringing. Her harsh upbringing has more than equipped her for life in China. Already famous as the author of the biographical novel *Daughter of Earth*, she's busy writing as much as she can, as fast as she can, about China.

By the end of this tea-drinking session the two have become friends. Agnes will introduce Rewi to her friend George Bernard Shaw when he arrives in Shanghai in April. (I like picturing those two old rascals together. They had much in common: Anglo-Irish ancestry; red hair; a habit of plain-speaking;

the courage to speak truth to power.) She will also introduce him to China's most famous living writer, Lu Xun (Zhou Shuren). Lu's unsentimental, profoundly humanitarian stories and poems, with their repeated rejections of China's Confucian past, chime exactly with Rewi's thinking. For the next 10 years he will carry Lu's photo in his wallet, parting with it only when his wallet is stolen.

But it's not so much Agnes the writer Rewi is drawn to, as Agnes the activist. She is part of a network of people helping the communists to survive Chiang's relentless extermination campaigns. She hides fugitives in her Shanghai apartment. She arranges for medical supplies to be spirited past the Japanese sentries so they can be transported to the Red Army. She carries a pistol in her handbag, assuring Rewi she wouldn't hesitate to use it if she had to. Rewi believes her. Despite knowing that anyone wearing red is likely to be arrested as a communist she persists in wearing red every day: a red jersey under her jacket; a red feather in her hat; a red carnation in her buttonhole. Rewi remonstrates with her but to no avail. When he visits her in her apartment he takes the precaution of climbing over the roof of the neighbouring building and entering through the stairwell. She finds his caution amusing. 'You'll break your neck one of these days,' she teases.

Writing under the pen-name of R.K. Nailes, Agnes publishes regular articles in the *China Weekly Review* attacking the KMT. (Like the later *Voice of China*, the *Weekly Review* was able to operate freely because it was not subject to Chinese law.) 'Why R.K. Nailes?' Rewi asks her. 'Because my friends call me Rusty Nails,' she answers. 'You'll see why soon enough. I'm a big mouth. And I've got a rotten temper. My mother blamed it on my Cherokee blood.'

As the friendship develops, Rewi learns that Agnes is being followed, not by the KMT but by the British. 'They want to deport me,' Agnes scoffs. 'They can't. I'm American. But you know the British. Think they rule the whole goddamn world!'

Rewi is in awe of her fearlessness. People are disappearing all the time – not just Chinese, but Europeans suspected of being sympathetic to the communists. His English friend, Henry Baring, the man who gave him *Das Kapital* to read, has committed suicide. There have been several of these 'suicides' lately. No one believes the official verdicts.

*

Agnes does more than just lift Rewi's spirits. She extends his circle of friends. He meets her fellow Americans Manny Granich and his wife Grace. He meets Tabitha Gerlach who works with Maud Russel at the YWCA. (Gerlach will be one of several old China hands denounced during the Cold War years as a communist – something she never was. Unable to return to her homeland, she died in Shanghai in 1995 at the age of 99.) He meets Polish-born Israel Epstein, one of a growing number of Jewish refugees finding sanctuary in China. He meets the Viennese journalist Ruth Weiss, who fled to Shanghai in 1933 to escape the Nazis. But the most significant introduction happens the day Agnes takes him to Rue Molière to meet Soong Chingling. She is even more beautiful than he'd remembered from his glimpse of her in Nanjing. And now she is his friend.

By the time of the Qingming (Tomb Sweeping) Festival in April, Rewi has become part of the regular meetings Agnes organises to discuss the future of China. The works of Lenin and Marx are pulled apart and discussed well into the night. Articles in the *China Weekly Review* are pored over for signs that others think as they do. At first they meet in Chingling's apartment, moving, when it becomes clear she is being watched, to Agnes's home in the Berne Apartments. When that too becomes dangerous, they hold their meetings in Rewi's home in Yuyuan Road.

Through 1935 and 1936 the number of people attending the meetings grows. By the end of 1936 what was at first spontaneous and irregular has become an organised study group (Rewi refers to it as the 'Marx-Lenin' study group). Rewi's fellow countryman, James Bertram, travelling in China on a Rhodes fellowship, starts turning up. Edgar Snow, busy working on the book that will make him famous, becomes a regular. Bringing along his new wife, the elegant and fearless Helen Foster (pen-name Nym Wales), whom everyone calls Peg (and Rewi, when he knows her better, will call Spark-plug), the Snows, like Bertram, add a touch of glamour to this otherwise homely group of would-be revolutionaries. The Snows are based in Beijing where they teach journalism part-time at Yenching University, but they come and go in Shanghai (and will eventually move there in September 1937), covering stories for the *Daily Herald* and the *Saturday Evening Post*. Then there's Ma Haide, based with the Eighth Route Army, whose fleeting visits back to Shanghai are greeted with barely concealed excitement by everyone connected with this growing underground. George – as Rewi calls him – has been part of Agnes Smedley's circle from the beginning. When Rewi learns that the perennially cheerful American, with his fluent Arabic and easy rapport with Moslems, is a specialist in skin conditions, it's the start not just of a friendship but a working relationship – finding a cure for chromium poisoning.

There is Chinese membership of the group too. Liang Shishun, one of the boys sent by Bailie to the US to study at the Ford School of Technology, is a regular attender, as is Lu Guangmian, a student at Yenching University.

By the end of 1938, as a direct result of these underground meetings, Gung Ho has come into being, and more names – Chinese as well as European – have been added to the list. The new movement's chief fundraiser, Ida Pruitt, Chinese-born daughter of American missionaries, will become one of Rewi's closest friends. He is full of praise for what she is doing, calling her a 'gallant little woman' and a 'good comrade'.[3] 'All my life I have hoped to find a man big enough to follow or a cause big enough to work for wholly,' Ida is recorded as saying about Rewi. 'To find both in one is marvellous.'[4] Finally in 1940 Rewi will meet Anna Louise Strong, fresh from her ordeal in Russia, and another lifelong friendship will begin.

*

At last Rewi can see ways to help beyond his work as a factory inspector. Initially he confines himself to writing for the *Weekly Review*, a job he takes on after Agnes Smedley introduces him to the American editor, Bill Powell. Already impressed with Agnes's courage and conviction, Rewi's admiration will reach new heights when he learns about her work with the Chinese Soviets, smuggling reports of their success through Japanese lines, past suspicious KMT officials, to the safety of Bill Powell's office in the American Concession.

Does Powell know the risks you're taking? Rewi wants to know. Agnes dismisses his concern with an irritable flutter of fingers. The reports are written on silk handkerchiefs and stitched into the padded jackets of the couriers. Nothing could be safer. When Rewi refuses to be reassured, she lets out a hoot of laughter and reminds him she's an American. If she's caught she'll plead the Fifth![5]

Once started on writing articles, Rewi can't stop. From 1936 on he will publish under a variety of invented names, not just in the *Weekly Review* but in *China Today* and the *Voice of China*, the latter now edited by Manny Granich. ('You and I, Manny, can say things to each other,' he writes 40 years later in his poem 'For Manny' in *Snow Over the Pines*.) Rewi's article 'Visitors from Naziland', published under the pseudonym 'Han Su Mei' in the February 1937 issue of the *Voice of China*, causes a sensation. A more subtle writer might have pulled his punches but Rewi is not known for his subtlety. His attack on the KMT for its connections to Nazi Germany is withering.

'Please do not be too peeved if I bring a certain amount of opprobrium on the family as a result of my political opinion,' he writes in a letter to his mother. 'It is not the faintest use worrying and I would never be happy anywhere but in China.'[6]

His diary makes things even plainer. 'Roll on the revolution,' he writes.[7]

Top of the agenda at the now regular meetings of the group is the news that reaches them via the letters of Ma Haide from Yan'an, where the Eighth Route Army is based. When Jim Bertram announces he's planning a second trip to the communist stronghold, Rewi feels a pang of envy. Ed Snow gives Bertram a Mauser pistol to deliver to Mao. (When he returns, confessing he had to throw the pistol away when it looked as if he was going to be arrested, no one, least of all Rewi, is surprised. China, outside the concessions, is a minefield. The Japanese might hesitate to arrest a foreign citizen, but the roaming gangs of conscripts taking orders from Chiang's Blue Shirts have no such qualms.)

Jim Bertram is not the only person Rewi envies. Every time he encounters Ma Haide, he envies him his role with the Red Army. Recently married to fellow revolutionary Su Fei – another cause of envy – he boasted, on one of his brief visits back to Shanghai, that he was the luckiest man alive. 'Look at me,' he crowed. 'What do you see? An Arab brigand, with tangled black wire on his head and skin like old leather. And I'm even shorter than you!'

'So how on earth did you persuade Su Fei to marry you?' Rewi wants to know.

'My high-powered American salesmanship of course. What else?'[8]

Occasionally there are parties. Particularly when Agnes Smedley is around. Her habit of leaping up to put a record on the gramophone, then demanding that everyone join in singing the chorus, drives serious discussion out the window. She knows all the old cowboy songs – 'She'll be Coming Round the Mountain', 'On Top of Old Smokey', 'Tumbling Tumbleweeds'. She heard them as a teenager hanging out in Missouri bars and speakeasys. What she lacks in musical skill she makes up for in enthusiasm.

Sometimes the compulsive foot-tapping leads to dancing. Rewi, no slouch on the dance floor, is more than happy to whirl around the room with Agnes. When they're joined by the Snows, as they often are, he experiences another of those pangs. Watching them demonstrably happy to be in each other's arms causes him to question, briefly, what he's doing with his life.

The day Jim Bertram turns up, full of his interview with Mao (and the loss of the pistol), there's not just singing and dancing, there's a haka. Bertram, in so many ways the perfect gentleman – tall, handsome, Oxford-educated, the kind of man who manages to look well groomed when everyone else is covered in dust and sweat – throws out his arms, pokes out his tongue, and lets out a bloodcurdling yell.

'Ka mate, ka mate! Ka ora! Ka ora!

Ka mate! Ka mate! Ka ora! Ka ora!'

Rewi, a grin on his face – he loves watching the effect of the haka on non-Kiwis – is quick to join in.

'Ā, upane! Ka upane!

Ā, upane, ka upane, whiti te ra!'

'I think we've just won the war,' a smiling Chingling declares.

CHAPTER TWENTY-FOUR
12 April 2017

FOR the last hour and a half we've been sitting in a plane going nowhere. We're on the runway of Beijing airport awaiting permission to join the dense traffic in the skies and fly to Xi'an. A meal has been served – the first tasteless meal we've had since we arrived in China. By now we know one another well enough to be able to fall easily into conversations. We're all tired – it's been a hectic three days – but Dave has warned us that what we feel now is nothing to what we'll feel once we hit the northwest. 'Beijing was just the beginning,' he's reminded us cheerfully.

So far cousins Jocelyn and Maurice have delivered the required speeches, Jocelyn at the New Zealand embassy, and Maurice at the banquet hosted by the Chinese People's Association for Friendship with Foreign Countries (Youxie) whose headquarters are in the same complex as Rewi's apartment. Maurice is an old hand at this. He's visited China eight times. Jocelyn has been before, but in her role as a tai-chi instructor, not an Alley family member. The rest of us, apart from Zeke and the other Maurice, are in China for the first time, but we know our turns will come. Non-family members are exempt, but relatives are expected to make at least one speech.

Rewi had little time for banqueting and speech-making. His experiences, first in Salaqi helping with canal-building, then in Wuhan working on the dykes, cemented his distrust of official partying. As a matter of course, funds raised to help with relief work were syphoned off by local KMT officials to pay for champagne banquets, ostensibly to discuss the 'situation' but really just to fill bellies and massage egos.

By the spring of 1932 Rewi still hasn't formed any definite political ideas, but he's read *Das Kapital*, he's experienced at first hand the tragedy that is China, he's seen for himself the corruption at the heart of the KMT government. 'Governments exist to serve the people'. Rewi had held this to be true long before he read Marx. He'd learned it at his father's knee. So what happens when a government fails to serve its people? Trying to answer that question, in the light of what he's experiencing in China, will bring him closer every day to the idea of revolution. 'One's earliest ideals do not always hold water,' he will tell Willis Airey in 1961, explaining the slow but steady change in his thinking. 'The Chinese people are actually infinitely more heroic, in quite an ordinary sort of way, than I or anyone else could have made them out to be,' he asserts in *Fruition: The story of George Alwyn Hogg* published in 1967. 'I suppose someone will come along some day,' he writes in a letter to Pip, 'for the Good Lord cannot and will not neglect the best of his children, tempted as one may be to think otherwise.'[1]

Sitting on the plane, chatting with my neighbours, I wonder what direction our lives would have taken had we lived through what Rewi lived through. Canadian journalist John Fraser, who visited China and met Rewi, dismissed him as 'a fantasist who sees only what he wants to see.'[2] But the truth is Rewi saw a great deal of what he never wanted to see, and could never forget.

One day, the coldest of the winter, with a light fall of snow on the ground and a bitter wind blowing down the street, I stood in my greatcoat watching a procession advancing. In the centre of the road the convicted, with their hands tied behind their backs; flanking them on each side of the road, heavily armed guards ... The convicted were all political, men and women, school kids, peasants and workers. At the rear of the group came a man whose face and eyes are as clear to me today as they were then. He was tall, clothed in a single thickness of faded army uniform, too big for him, that the wind pressed against his thin body. His head was erect, his eyes calm, and he was smiling ... The look and the smile struck me with the impact of a bullet. The moment his eyes met mine, and then looked on over the crowd – the fat shopkeepers, the curious street people, the guards, the sordid scene – in that moment I felt like doing one thing, throwing off my warm coat and joining him in the march to the great sullen Yangtze, where his life would be torn from him. But I only fell back against the shopfront, retreated inside my warm coat and stayed in a daze ...[3]

The scene Rewi is describing took place in Wuhan at the beginning of 1932. This time he'd needed no prompting from Joseph Bailie to cut short his annual leave and travel to the scene of China's latest disaster – a catastrophic flood in Hubei province. In his memoir he describes the task of reconstruction of the dykes, essential to prevent further flooding, as 'rather a big job for me, the biggest I had attempted so far'.

But repairing dykes is not all Rewi does. His actions in moving thousands of refugees – conveniently targeted as communists – away from the machine-guns will bring him to the admiring attention of the British government, with consequences he could never have imagined. He will also adopt 11-year-old Mike, whose father had been executed for taking part in an uprising against local landlords. (Rewi tells Mike's story in 'Buffalo Boy', published in *Children of the Dawn*.) 'It's dangerous for Honghu boys here,' the official in charge of the orphanage where Mike was living told him. 'They are sometimes picked out and shot as communists.' Rewi, looking at the 'thin eager face that showed so much warmth, character and hope', didn't hesitate.[4] A brother for Alan, he told himself, as he paid Mike's fare to Shanghai, where he would stay till Rewi returned from his delayed trip to New Zealand. *Now I really am a family man.*

Rewi would never forget what he witnessed in Wuhan:

> It looked grim and sordid
> to me in 1932.
> Bloated bodies of dead
> babies floating in backwaters;
> four hundred thousand
> refugees of a vast
> Yangtze flood, driven
> on freezing winter days
> into the mud of the Han River
> by the bayonets of soldiery
> of a rotten establishment
> that thieved relief wheat
> mercilessly, leaving
> a starving people to build
> the broken dyke system
> as best they could …[5]

*

I've been trying to find time to talk with the cousins I don't know or know only slightly, but our bus journeys have been filled with lectures from our friendly guides, while conversation at meals is mostly about the food, exotic to many of us, delicious, so far as I can tell, to all of us. I've made a tentative arrangement to sit next to Alison, the cousin who's related on both sides of Rewi's family, next time we travel by bus. And with Sarah, Maurice's niece. No one is suggesting a conversation on the plane. It's nearly midnight. All we want to do is sleep.

Finding out what's happening beyond China's borders – I'm something of a news junkie – has been proving difficult, thanks to China's firewall. But with Trump in the White House the world feels as if it's resting on dangerously unstable tectonic plates. The only paper I've been able to lay my hands on is the *Global Times*, the official government newspaper. There's a photo of Theresa May on the front page, and a long article about the Chinese Belt and Road initiative, designed to increase trade between China and its immediate neighbours, with the long-term aim of negotiating free trade agreements around the world. In January of this year a train named 'East Wind' ('The East wind will prevail over the West wind', Mao famously predicted[6]), packed with goods for export to Europe, made the marathon journey from the Chinese city of Yiwu to Barking in East London. Where once carts and camels loaded with opium and gemstones covered the long dusty trade routes of the Old Silk Road, today's train carried household goods and clothing. It will return packed with pharmaceuticals and spirits.

Over the next week and a half I will think a lot about this ambitious move of China's, launched by President Xi in 2013. Underpinning this vision of a vast trading empire, with China at its heart, is the universal desire of the Chinese people for peace. When in 1952 Rewi was given the role of peace envoy he was representing a movement, spearheaded by China, that was unique in the world at that time. In poem after poem, both his own and those he translated, he gives voice to this universal longing for peace. 'Jaw jaw not war war', was Winston Churchill's advice to the nations. 'Trade not bombs' would seem to be Xi Jinping's.

It's easy to be cynical about the peace work Rewi undertook after his role in Gung Ho was abruptly terminated. His appointment as a peace envoy came at the height of the Korean War, hardly an auspicious moment to begin lobbying for peace on the international stage. In the years that followed, his many appearances at peace conferences did nothing to stem the outbreaks of violence in Indo-China and Malaysia, not to mention the on-going armed conflict on the India/Pakistan border. But he did succeed in bringing the two countries he loved into closer relationship. New Zealand didn't acknowledge the People's Republic of China until 1972, but a great deal went on behind the scenes – diplomatic meetings, moves to facilitate trade – before that time. The New Zealand–China Friendship Society, founded in 1952, was largely inspired by Rewi. He was also, as Prime Minister David Lange acknowledged when the Queen's Service Order was conferred on Rewi in 1985, instrumental in bringing officials of both governments together long before New Zealand's formal recognition of China. 'I was aware that I had met someone out of the ordinary,' Lange wrote after his meeting with Rewi in 1986, 'who yet retained all the qualities of a down-to-earth caring New Zealander.'[7]

So how genuine is China's desire for peace today? Should countries like New Zealand and Australia be worried about Chinese buying up of land and property? Does China's growing influence in the Pacific pose a threat? And what of her incursions by way of aid and loans into so many of the emerging nations of Africa? Do all these things add up to a desire to take over the world? If the answer is yes, is it so very different from America's post-war drive to spread its trade and culture throughout the globe? What China does *not* want is to destroy the world. Unlike President Trump, Xi Jinping has renewed China's commitment to the Paris Climate Change Agreement. If there is a desire to dominate, it's commercial rather than military. Money rules in China. It's taken the place of the old Confucian system of values whereby a person earns respect because of his or her education, family background or place in society. The Confucian idea of the 'good man' no longer holds. Money is the gauge of where you stand and how much power you have. 'Teach people to fish much better than to give them fish' – an old Chinese proverb that has taken on new meaning in the China of Belt and Road.

*

Belt and Road isn't the only thing that catches my eye in the *Global Times*. The headline 'Rumours debunked that China uses cult practitioner prisoners' organs' jumps out at me, both for what it is signalling and for the clumsiness of the wording. Is this what Orwell meant when he said that words 'stiffen under [the] touch' when lies are told? Or is it just an example of the difficulties of translation? The article refers to the Falun Gong, the semi-religious organisation I'd wanted to question our Beijing guide about. Owing its origins to both Buddhism and Taoism, Falun Gong is, in essence, a blueprint for daily life, involving meditation and a routine of exercises, widely practised in China, known as *qigong*. Through the cultivation of virtue and the practice of meditation, it aims to help the individual achieve enlightenment.

So why has the government labelled it an 'anti-society cult leading its followers to suicide, self-mutilation and murder'? In my home town of

Wellington there is a constant presence outside the Chinese Embassy protesting the persecution of Falun Gong members. If the reports are to be believed, people have been arrested, jailed and in some cases killed simply for belonging to Falun Gong. The *Global Times* is vehement in its denunciation of the organ-harvesting claims. So what, I wonder, would Rewi tell me if he were here? I've no doubt he would have agreed with the government that the group's emphasis on individual enlightenment is not 'correct thinking'. The highest achievement for the individual, in Rewi's book, was to work co-operatively with others. He believed that was the Chinese way. Yet you only have to look around the cities of China today to see that this is a country as dedicated to the ideas of individual enterprise and entrepreneurship as any in the West.

At Rewi's eighty-fifth birthday celebration, Ma Haide paid tribute to his old friend's ability to be 'flexible', to know 'when to lie low'.[8] I suspect it's what Rewi would have done – lain low – if I'd asked him about Falun Gong.

'We should guide and educate the religious circle and their followers with the socialist core values,' Xi Jinping said in a speech to the 2016 conference on religion, which he convened. 'Believers must dig deep into doctrines and canons that are in line with social harmony and progress … [interpreting] religious doctrines in a way that is conducive to modern China's progress, and in line with our excellent traditional culture.'[9] In other words, little has changed since my cousin Tom visited in 1956. The state still exercises control over religious content and practice. On these terms, Christianity, Taoism and Buddhism are more or less tolerated, particularly Buddhism. So why have the Falun Gong fallen foul of the state? Their values can hardly be described as seditious.

I have to wait till Michael Crook joins us again in Baoji to get even a partial answer to this question. But at least I know I can ask it. No one would deny that censorship exists in China, as it does in one form or another in every country, but we've been able to talk openly about the Cultural Revolution and even the Tiananmen Square protest, so perhaps the clampdown on freedom of speech is not as severe as I'd imagined.

As part of my preparation for this journey I read a selection of modern Chinese novels, hoping they would give me a feel for the country I was about to visit. What struck me was the obsession (one, by Liu Heng, is even called *The Obsessed*) with money, sex and martial arts. The most popular novelist in China today is Jin Yong (Louis Cha Leung-yung) whose books, set in the thirteenth century, widely adapted for TV and film, chronicle the lives of kung fu heroes. Politics barely feature in the novels I read; religion not at all. The exceptions – *Soul Mountain*, a brilliant, difficult book, a spiritual as well as a physical quest, by Nobel Prize winner Gao Xingjian, and *The Day the Sun Died* by current Nobel Prize contender Yan Lianke – fell foul of the censorship laws and had to be published outside China.

'So,' I say to Michael Crook when we get to Baoji, 'what's the story with the Falun Gong? Why are they being persecuted?' His answer – that the government believes the Falun Gong are plotting not just in China but in countries throughout the world to overthrow it – troubles me. As with so much else I have read (and will read subsequently), deciding what is true is like trying to find your way out of a maze. 'It's a movement that openly espouses democracy,' Michael reminds me, grinning to show there are no hard feelings. 'Not a good idea in China.'

It's hard to feel there's anything 'rotten in the state of China' when you're with Michael. Born in the country – for the first six years of his life he spoke only Chinese – he moves between the two cultures, Chinese and Western, with the lightness of a dancer. His 100-year-old mother, the indomitable Isabel, is as passionate a revolutionary now as she was when, heavily pregnant, she travelled into Beijing on the back of a truck on that momentous day in October 1949 when China was liberated. Isabel, one of only a handful of European woman to witness these historic events, spent the next six hours watching the reviewing of the troops at Tiananmen Gate. I'll learn more about China from these two amazing people, mother and son, than I do from all the statistics and facts offered up in speeches.

*

We land in Xi'an in a thunderstorm. As we walk towards our bus the sky bursts into flames, dissolving the darkness into boiling lakes of blue, red, gold and silver. None of us has seen a sky like this before. It's as if the world is being born again. I look around at my cousins, and a phrase Jocelyn used once in relation to the Alley family comes to mind – 'integrated misfits'. The words aren't hers but they strike me at this moment as apposite. If I'm going to be struck by lightning I can't think of anyone I'd rather go up in flames with than this bunch of exhausted, uncomplaining, persistently hopeful 'integrated misfits'.

CHAPTER TWENTY-FIVE
Xi'an, 13 April 2017

I'M sitting next to Cousin Ross. We're in Xi'an, on our way to see the famous Terracotta Army. As far as I know, apart from a brief reference in a poem, Rewi never mentions it. So why are we making this journey? The answer of course is that we have become tourists again.

We've already had a tour of Xi'an's ancient city wall, the largest civic defence system in the world, according to our guide. Some of us hired bicycles to ride the ramparts. Some, under Jocelyn's expert eye, practised tai-chi, otherwise known as 'Chinese boxing' – a system of body movements developed during the reign of the first Ming emperor, Hong Wu. (Rewi always gave it its full name, *tai-chi-chuan*, describing it as 'an excellent tonic for the middle aged'.[1]) Some of us were content just to stroll, stopping to take pictures of the Drum Tower or the Gate of Long Happiness or the colourful market on the street below. I tried to imagine this city as it was when Rewi came here in 1936, but what he saw, and what we were seeing from our vantage point on the city wall, are two different places. Modern Xi'an, said to be the most polluted city in China, was largely rebuilt in the 1950s. All that remains of the ancient Han dynasty capital is the wall, the towers, some restored temples and a mosque.

'Xi'an matters more than you think,' Dave told us on the plane. 'You'll find out when you get there.'

Ross and I know each other well. We met while I was living in England and have kept in touch ever since. What we have in common, apart from the Alley connection, are a love of music and the experience of living precariously, he as a pianist and lecturer on opera, me as a writer. But there is something else, something we don't discuss directly on this trip but which is implicit in much that we do talk about. Both of us fled New Zealand in part because of its sexual puritanism. Ross's father, my Uncle Digger, would (like many others in the family) have struggled to come to terms with his youngest son's sexual orientation. My own flight was prompted by a court case which labelled me an adulteress, even though the so-called 'adultery' happened after my marriage had ended. The difference between us is that I returned to New Zealand. Ross did not.

Eventually, inevitably perhaps, we fall to discussing whether Rewi was gay. I make the point that a person's sexual orientation shouldn't matter, but

Ross counters with a reminder that it *did*, back then. He's right, of course. I tell him about the theory put forward by, among others, Anne-Marie Brady, that Rewi, while still living in Shanghai, entered into a Faustian pact, choosing to stay rather than return to New Zealand because it was easier to be homosexual in China. Ross finds this notion highly dubious. As do I. The Homosexual Law Reform Act was passed in New Zealand 10 years before its equivalent in China, so the theory doesn't even stand up to the test of fact.

We lapse into a companionable silence. The guide has started his talk but I'm only half listening. I'm remembering something Rewi wrote in one of those lost letters. It was about the cold in Shandan and how in winter when the temperatures hit minus 30 and more he would often wake to find several small boys snuggled beside him in bed. At the time I couldn't picture it. How could *several* boys fit into even a double bed? Now that I know about the *kang*, built for a whole family to sleep on, the story has taken on its proper shape.

'I did notice the gays in Beijing,' Ross says. 'They made themselves pretty conspicuous.'

I admit I'd noticed the same thing, but since same-sex relationships have been legal in China since 1997 the only surprise to me was the fact that, as Ross put it, they were so conspicuous. The official position of the Communist Party has always been anti-gay – reflected in the fact that gays are still not allowed to marry or father a child – but so far as I know there has not been open persecution. When I tell Ross that gay men in pre-revolutionary days, far from not being allowed to father a child, were expected to do so anyway, since to fail to produce a child was to dishonour your ancestors, he lets out a guffaw. 'Good thing I wasn't born in China then,' he says.

'Why? Wouldn't you have liked a child?'

'No thank you. There are enough Alleys rattling around in this world without me adding to the number.'

I look at him and wonder for a moment if, like Rewi for so much of his life, he is lonely. 'I'm no good at love,' Ross told me once. 'I can be affectionate, but I don't seem able to feel the big stuff.'

Somewhat reluctantly – I like talking with Ross – I tune in to our guide. He's telling the story of the Terracotta Army. It's a tale worth telling, but I can't seem to share my fellow travellers' excitement. I don't like armies of any kind. Why should I spend time looking at a clay army, created (if the record proves true) on the order of an emperor whose vanity and unbridled narcissism rival that of the current occupant of the White House?

Emperor Qin Shi-huang, the first ruler to govern a united China, was a man obsessed with mortality. Much of his ill-fated reign was spent trying to find the elixir of life – the guarantor of immortality and victory over death. While he waited for his scholars and officials to find the magic potion, he decided – so the story goes – to hedge his bets. He ordered a clay army to be built, modelled on the real human one. Just as in life, no two soldiers were to look the same. If, despite all his efforts, he did die, he was going to make damn sure his troops were with him to protect him in the afterlife.

I listen dutifully, but the story I want to hear stars Rewi, who came to Xi'an as a money-launderer for the communists. Is this what Dave was referring to when he said Xi'an matters more than we think? I know this ancient city played a crucial part in the war against Japan, but I'm hazy about the details.

We've arrived. We pile out of the bus and follow our guide into a building the size of several football fields. And there it is. The Terracotta Army. Hundreds, no, thousands, standing in rows, ready to escort a vain and silly man through the afterlife. Emperor Qin would have been better off paying attention to what was going on in this life. Feared and despised for his cruelty, he survived three assassination attempts and died after drinking mercury, having convinced himself it was the longed-for elixir.

We spend more than an hour circling the silent army standing in serried ranks awaiting Qin's summons to the afterlife. I try to print the images on my mind but I find myself thinking about Shandan and what those winters must have been like. The *kang* Rewi slept on was heated by burning manure. It would have stunk to high heaven … Is what Ross said about himself, about not being able to feel the 'big stuff', true of the Alleys in general? I'm sure it was true of my grandfather. He only knew how to love horses! As for Rewi's father, he was by all accounts an unloving father, at least to Rewi and Pip, but I hope he loved Aunt Clara. Everyone else did. As for Rewi, I don't think his son would have written those words about him – 'We grew to love each other very much' – if he hadn't felt, and lived, the 'big stuff'.

Love makes a man dare to fight –
Love for the many looted of so much love …
A queer thing this love!
Love for the good woman who is
all good things brought together.
Love for a whole world of lovely things:

white seagulls over blue seas, children
under apple trees, or swimming
in the river.
The love of the close-knit family living as part of one another –
the perfect mother, the understanding friend.
All these are loved as part of living …[2]

*

When we gather again at the bus one of our party is missing. There are murmurings of anxiety – cellphone coverage is dodgy at the best of times – while we resign ourselves to waiting patiently in the heat. We tell ourselves not to worry, that no one stays lost, not even in China, but as the minutes pass and our minders become increasingly uneasy, I can see some of us are beginning to think the unthinkable.

Eventually the lost sheep is found and we clamber onto the bus. That night we are taken to a Tang dynasty dine-and-dance show. I've been looking forward to it. Something of Rewi's love of that period in history has rubbed off on me. But the show is uninspiring. 'A triumph of costume over content,' is Ross's opinion. Tourism at its most lifeless.

Rewi the two-fingered typist.

From pictorial book titled
Rewi Alley, published in
Gansu province, 2016

Rewi on a commune
inspection tour,
c. 1972.

From *Rewi Alley of China*
by Geoff Chapple

Rewi with his great-grandsons in 1982. From *At 90: Memoirs of my China years* by Rewi Alley

Anna Louise Strong, an American radical, widow of a Russian revolutionary, who had an apartment in the same building as Rewi in Beijing.
From *Rewi Alley of China* by Geoff Chapple

Rewi's return to Shandan in 1982.
From pictorial book titled *Rewi Alley*, published in Gansu province, 2016

Rewi's 80th birthday party in 1977, hosted by Chairman Deng Xiaoping.
From pictorial book titled *Rewi Alley*, published in Gansu province, 2016

Rewi's 83rd birthday. Soong Chingling (the host) is on the right.
From pictorial book titled *Rewi Alley*, published in Gansu province, 2016

Rewi's meeting with Prime Minister David Lange, Beijing, March 1986.

From pictorial book titled *Rewi Alley*, published in Gansu province, 2016

Rewi lying in state (in defiance of his instructions!), 1987.

From pictorial book titled *Rewi Alley*, published in Gansu province, 2016

CHAPTER TWENTY-SIX
14 April 2017

'NO,' Dave is saying, as we're herded on to our bus next morning. 'I haven't forgotten. I've been saving the Xi'an story for today. We've a long ride ahead of us.'

We are on our way to Shuangshipu in Fengxian county, site of Rewi's first Bailie School. Ahead of us is a four-hour journey through the Qinling mountains. Predictably, things don't go according to plan and the four hours stretches to 11. An accident on the hazardous bends on the Qinling mountain crossing is blamed. But we are in such a state of bemusement we'd have believed it if we'd been told the delay was caused by marauding tigers! Rewi would not have been pleased. Visitors who complained about the unpredictability of China were simply reflecting their 'western failure to get to the root of things Chinese'.[1]

'I want you to try and imagine Xi'an in 1936,' Dave begins, once everyone is settled, water bottles stowed, knitting needles clicking, talk muted to a murmur. I peer out the window trying to replace what I see – the jumbled skyline of modern Xi'an, ancient pagodas nestling in the shade of skyscrapers, the fabled wall, hung with red lanterns – with the town that was here 80 years ago. Xi'an was once the most populous city in the world, the creative and political centre of three dynasties – Qin, Han and Tang. Known as the 'Place of Eternal Peace', it was the terminus for goods from all over Asia, a trade centred on the Old Silk Road and the river Wei, the largest tributary of the Yangtze. Now the city is part of a new trading initiative, based around that same Silk Road. History is repeating itself. China, as Napoleon may or may not have foreseen, has 'woken up'.

'What you need to know,' Dave is saying, 'is that the future of China was decided in Xi'an. The future of the world, come to that. If things had panned out differently you wouldn't be sitting there speaking English, you'd be speaking Japanese.'

I'm all ears. But Dave, whose timing, I'm beginning to realise, is that of a true master of suspense, makes us wait. First he's going to tell Rewi's story.

Dave has asked us to imagine how Xi'an would have looked in 1936. September, to be exact. Autumn. But how can we do that when so much has been rebuilt? I put myself back on the ramparts of the wall we visited yesterday and do my best to shut out the skyscrapers and the jets roaring overhead. Gradually a different city emerges – a dusty market town, its streets littered with the rubble of 2000 years of human occupation. By concentrating hard I manage to conjure up the famous thousand-year-old Wild Goose Pagoda, with the ruins of a Ming-dynasty mosque nudging the clouds in the distance. With a little more effort I see the Drum Tower, covered with the anti-Japanese slogans Rewi describes in his memoir. This Xi'an, still called by its ancient name Chang'an, is smelly, dirty, noisy, full of beggars and refugees, donkey-drawn carts and bicycles, farmers pushing wheelbarrows and soldiers on horseback. I hear the shouts of people haggling in the markets; the *ai-ya, ai-ya* of the crowd watching the snake charmer draw a python from his basket. I hear the same cries from men in grubby silk robes, urging on the participants in a street wrestling match. Beyond the market, I spy a group of ill-clad citizens, gathered to watch a drama being enacted by two half-naked men, their prominent ribs and enormous eyes evidence of starvation. I see a man with a long queue hanging down his back, ignoring the drama, his attention fixed on the cage he is carrying in which sit three chirruping grey birds with tiny red heads. I see skinny kids, toes poking out of ragged straw sandals, flitting in and out of the crowds, scavenging …

And then I see the hero of the story Dave is telling – Rewi, dressed in his 'uniform' of shirt and shorts, but looking unusually well groomed. He's striding along in the shadow of the wall, heading for the train station. He has only the haziest notion of why he's been sent here. The summons he received said no more than that he was to meet Liu Ding, a young communist whom he's been hiding in his Shanghai apartment for the last year. He's hoping people will take him to be a typical Westerner, confident, arrogant, not someone to be stopped and questioned. If he was here purely on his own account, he'd be stopping to look at the broken bricks and shards of pottery – the lucky-dip rubble of the past – at his feet. He knows enough about Chang'an to appreciate what a treasure trove he's marching through. But he's not here for himself, he's here for China.

He reaches the station. Stops to pull up his socks. Normally he wouldn't bother but today is different. He's acting a part.

Someone taps him on his shoulder. He turns. It's Liu Ding, clutching a white canvas bag.

'Don't open it now,' Ding instructs, pushing the bag into Rewi's chest. 'Wait till you get to your hotel.'

'Am I allowed to know what's in it?'

Glancing round to check they're not being observed, Ding explains that the bag contains bank notes captured by the Red Army. Rewi 's job is to take the bag to Taiyuan, where's he's to remove any evidence of where the notes came from, before getting them changed into Central Bank notes, the only currency valid throughout China. 'Don't take them all to the same money-changer,' Ding instructs. 'That's important. There are three in Taiyuan. It's essential you divide the notes among the three.' Rewi doesn't have to ask why. A foreigner changing such a large sum in one place would be bound to attract attention. 'Soon as the job's done, head back to Shanghai and wire the new notes from there.'

'Why not wire them from Taiyuan?'

'Too easy to trace.'

As Ding dissolves into the crowd Rewi, doing his best to look nonchalant, strolls up to the office and buys a ticket to travel hard class to Taiyuan (an experience we too will have when we travel from Baoji to Shandan). Clutching the precious bag, he boards his train, makes himself as comfortable as he can on the unpadded wooden seat, and settles down for a journey involving two changes that will not only rattle his nerves but ratchet up the ache in his shoulder. Why couldn't they have cut the bloody shrapnel out? he says to himself, not for the first time. Isn't as if it's lodged in my heart.

Arriving in Taiyuan, he books himself into the first hotel he comes to – the French Railway Hotel. He waits till he's sure he won't be disturbed, then he tips the contents of the canvas bag out onto his bed. One-yuan notes scatter like giant confetti all over the room. Thousands of them, Rewi calculates, as the scale of what he's been asked to do begins to dawn on him. He takes a closer look. A few 10-yuan notes stand out among the sea of singles, but it's not that that's making his heart race – it's the blood. Clumps of notes are stuck together with dried blood. Others are badly stained. Some even have bullet holes. What did I expect? he says to himself. There's a war on.

He orders tea and sets to work. It's going to take all night to clean the notes. And it'll be a race against time to get them to the three money lenders before someone catches on and spills the beans. By the time the sun is up, the job of cleaning and sorting is all but done. A few of the worst-affected notes will have to wait to be cleaned back in Shanghai, but the rest, divided into three piles, are ready for delivery.

Three hours later, Rewi is hot-footing it back to the station. His luck has held. No one seems to have realised the Westerner doing business in three different places is not three different people but the same man. He clambers onto the train and breathes an audible sigh of relief. 'I have never been so glad to leave a place as I was that one,' he writes in his memoir. 'It was a dangerous time.'

CHAPTER TWENTY-SEVEN

THE future of China, if not the world, was decided in Xi'an. Over the long hours of our delayed journey Dave will explain why this claim is not as fanciful as it sounds and Xi'an matters more than we think. As I listen I feel, not for the first time, how skewed our cultural narratives can be. I would have said what mattered in the story of World War II were the Battle of Britain, Dunkirk, Guadalcanal, El Alamein … I will have to wait till I get back to New Zealand to fill in the gaps, but by the time Dave's story is ended I'm left in no doubt as to Xi'an's right to be on that list. What happened there in December 1936 did indeed change the course of the war.

By the end of 1936, three years before World War II breaks out, fighting has been going on in different parts of China for more than four years – a fact too often overlooked in Western narratives. Over half the country is in Japanese hands. What began in 1932 with the bombing of Shanghai, and the setting up of the puppet state of Manchukuo in Manchuria, is now a full-scale campaign designed to turn China into a client state of Japan. The Japanese decision in 1934 to install Pu Yi as emperor of Manchukuo – a ploy to win over those Chinese still hankering for the old imperial regime – may have fooled the young Pu Yi, comfortably imprisoned in the Forbidden City, but it didn't fool the movers and shakers of China's destiny at the time. Chiang Kaishek knew as well as Mao Zedong that emperors were never going to be allowed to rule China again.

Japan had justified its invasion by claiming to want to free China from the double curse of warlords and communists. This was music to the ears of many in the US (though not President Roosevelt, who took a more nuanced view) anxious to preserve their favourable trading relationship with the Empire of the Sun. Those who suspected that Japan's real motive was not to 'free' China, but to keep America – busy supplying it with iron ore and weapons – onside, were largely ignored. The US went on supplying arms to Japan right up to the bombing of Pearl Harbour. Even the League of Nations was hoodwinked, accepting at face value Japanese assurances that it would not expand any further into China. By 1933 Japanese troops were within 100 kilometres of Beijing.

Far from ridding the country of warlords, Japan, once its control was established, took a leaf out of Chiang's book and made alliances with them.

Having already implemented a similar policy in Shanghai in relation to the city's ruling triads, the Japanese turned their attention to the opium trade. Ply the peasants with opium, they reasoned, just as the warlords had before them, and resistance will crumble. Japanese and KMT secret agents were everywhere, on trains and buses, spending money in bars and restaurants, lurking in the shadows of banks and post offices and universities. Just to speak of resisting the Japanese was to be labelled a communist. Appeasement was not what everyone in the KMT wanted, but it's what was happening in 1936. By turning a blind eye to Japanese domination of northern China, the KMT, under Chiang's obsessively anti-communist leadership, had effectively agreed to the partitioning of the country.

'The Red Goose is cooked,' Chiang boasted in the wake of his fifth bandit extermination campaign in 1934.[1] His total-war, no-mercy rules of engagement – which the Japanese would carry to even more violent extremes when full-scale war broke out – had decimated the communists, forcing them to abandon their base in Jiangxi province in the southeast and set out on what would come to be known as the Long March. Thousands died on what was really a series of marches, zig-zagging across China to escape the pursuing nationalist army. Chiang's confidence never wavered. Victory was in his sights. He had the numbers. Taking the crushing of the Taiping peasant revolt of the 1850s and 60s as his model, he waged a campaign of encirclement, building blockades to cut off supplies, surrounding the enemy so that nothing, not even salt, could get through. With more communists dying from starvation than in battle, how could he not triumph?

The God Worshippers Society, instigators of the doomed Taiping Rebellion, had advocated, among other things, abolition of punitive taxes (peasants unable to pay their rent were punished by being locked in bamboo cages), the establishment of communal ownership of land and an end to child slavery. Now, 80 years later, the communists were advocating the same things. Anathema, not just to Chiang but to his German military advisers sent, along with weapons and military supplies, by Hitler. It took the Manchu dynasty 14 years to defeat the Taiping rebels, at a cost of over 50 million lives; Chiang had no intention of taking so long. The human cost didn't bother him – when a peasant was killed there was always another to step into his shoes – it was the cost in time and money that enraged him. Once, when receiving unwelcome news, he hurled his spittoon and its contents at the unfortunate messenger.[2] A regular occurrence, I imagine, as events outside his control forced him to do the unthinkable – revive Sun Yatsen's partnership with the hated *gong fei*.

*

By 1936 the Long March has ended. The communists have established themselves in Yan'an, an ancient garrison town in the northern province of Shaanxi. The war with the KMT isn't over, nor is the blockade, but the Red Army has survived. The soldiers wear hemp sandals and fight, when they have to, on empty stomachs. When there are no guns, they use bamboo spears and pitchforks. The army, which numbered 80,000 (though some put it as high as a 130,000) when it left Jiangxi, was reduced to 8000 by the time it reached Yan'an (again the numbers vary depending on who's telling the tale). But no one disputes that many thousands died on that 9000-kilometre trek across China. 'You could have assembled the whole Red Army on a football field,' Ma Haide, who was there, will tell Rewi.[3]

As news spreads that the communists are not *bing* – the common word for soldier with its connotations of banditry and brutality – they are *zhanshi*, warriors, who kill warlords and rapacious landowners, more and more young men begin to leave their villages to join the Red Army. Many of them are teenagers; some – the famous *xiao gui* – not even 13. No records were kept, but Edgar Snow, whose interview with Mao in 1936 would catapult both him and his subject onto the world stage, calculated that the average age of the Red Army soldier was 19. 'I often had the queer feeling among the Reds that I was in the midst of a host of schoolboys engaged in a life of violence because some strange design of history had made this seem infinitely more important to them than football, games, love etc,' he wrote in *Red Star Over China*.

*

In speaking to the Taipings, how
could one ever forget their kindness
and care for the people …
always eating along with their own men
at the same table, and as they lie
sleeping on one floor no one can tell
which are officers, which men …[4]

Every peasant knew the story of the Taiping Rebellion. The songs from that time, celebrating the courage of the long-haired, red-turbaned soldiers who took on the might of the Manchu (Qing) dynasty, were still being sung 80 years later by men and women working in the fields. Now at village meetings there's a new peasant rebellion to discuss, one led by the Hunan fighter Mao Zedong. The guerrilla tactics he and his commanders have devised, avoiding fixed battles, working behind the lines to undermine the enemy, breaking up into separate units to confuse the advancing forces, are analysed at length as hope grows that this rebellion might succeed.

Holed up in his cave-house in Yan'an, Mao knows what he's up against. He's lived alongside his soldiers for the best part of a decade. He's suffered with them the terrible deprivations caused by the KMT's encirclement campaigns. He's seen the bodies of people lying in the fields, killed not by gunfire but by Chiang's Three All policy, which Japan will emulate – Kill All, Burn All, Destroy All.[5] He's become expert at cooking his favourite dish of red peppers with nothing but the peppers themselves and sometimes not even that. 'Down with Capitalism and Eat Squash' is one of the many catchphrases he coined as he and his rag-and-bone army struggled up mountainsides, waded through swamps, built makeshift pontoon bridges to cross rivers, coughed the red dust of the Gobi Desert from their lungs, and warded off attacks not just from Chiang's army and fighters loyal to local warlords, but nature's own assassins – jackals, tigers, wolves, lions, bears.[6] To avoid Chiang's bombs the Eighth Route Army and its subsidiaries travelled mostly at night, sheltering during the day in caves, ruined temples, and the homes of peasants willing to give them all they had. Many died from the diseases endemic to China – typhoid, cholera, malaria, typhus, bubonic plague, beri beri. Many more died of starvation. But still they kept on.

'The enemy advances, we retreat; the enemy halts, we harass; the enemy slackens, we attack; the enemy retreats, we pursue' – Mao's mantra, known to every man and and woman who fought with him.[7] 'Whoever wins the peasant war will win China. Whoever solves the land question will win the peasants' – Mao's words again, passed from one village to another, one county to another, one province to another.[8] Chiang may have the military numbers, but Mao has the population. China in 1936 is 80 per cent rural. Which means 80 per cent of its 260 million citizens are peasants. The communist revolution, as Mao never tires of reminding people, is an agrarian peasant revolution. How can it fail? Feudalism, which has held sway for so long, is coming apart at the seams.

Mao, whose grasp of events both inside and outside of China will win the admiration of Edgar Snow, is a forward thinker, not one to dwell on the past. But every so often, now he has reached the comparative safety of Yan'an, he likes to think back on that epic march across China. He has no doubt it will go down in history as a great military exploit, turning what began as a retreat into a victory. Not even the Mongols managed such a feat. Singing songs all the way from Yudu to Yan'an, songs of the Taiping rebellion, of home, of harvest and family, they were, Mao likes to think, an army of poets and artists. When they ran out of songs they wrote their own. They wrote plays too, with the help of the drama troupe travelling with them. Mao knows the value of art. He knows it can lift spirits and instil courage. His own poetry, scribbled on bark or torn pieces of cloth, grew out of experiences shared with the peasant soldiers:

The Red Army, never fearing the challenging Long March,
Looked lightly on the many peaks and rivers.
Wu Liang's Range rose, lowered, rippled,
And green-tiered were the rounded steps of Wu Meng.
Warm-beating the Gold Sand River's waves against rocks,
And cold the iron-chain spans of Tatu's bridge.
A thousand joyous li of freshening snow on Min Shan,
And then, the last pass vanquished, Three Armies smiled![9]

I will hear these words of Mao's, set to music, at an Alley family gathering in Christchurch in December 2017. Travelling in the bus to attend a ceremony at Rewi's birth place, my Chinese cousins suddenly burst into song, pumping the air as they sing, their voices raised so that it seemed to me the words would be heard all over Canterbury. Mao's reputation may have taken a nose-dive after the Cultural Revolution but, like Lenin in Russia, he's the man who made the revolution happen. His name will live on.

When first Mao's sister, then his wife Yang Kaihui, mother of his three children, were executed by the KMT, Mao refused to grieve in public (though he did, in private, writing a poem in memory of his wife). Similarly, when he had to leave his two youngest children behind with a peasant family (he would never see them again) he said nothing. Only China mattered. That was the message he was sending. China and the Revolution.

CHAPTER TWENTY-EIGHT

MAO paces up and down the room that serves as living room, study and bedroom in his Yan'an cave-house. It's evening, 14 December 1936. The candles are lit. He's eaten well, a meal of rice, his favourite Hunan peppers and *youtiao* – fritters fried in linseed oil – with a pot of chrysanthemum tea to wash everything down. Normally he would be sitting at his makeshift desk, working with his secretary on plans and directives, possibly even tossing out a poem. Most nights he works through till dawn, chiding his secretary when he yawns, unable to understand why grown men need more than a couple of hours sleep. But on this particular night he can't settle. There's too much at stake.

He lights a cigarette. He has given orders not to be disturbed. The only message he wants is the one from Xi'an telling him that the coup he's been orchestrating for months now has been successful and Chiang Kaishek is dead.

Pausing for a moment he thinks back to the night in July 1921 when the Chinese Communist Party came into being: a small room in an undistinguished house on Wang Chih Road in Shanghai's French Concession. Fifty-seven names on the roll. By 1927 this had grown to 57,000. Now it's in the millions.

'I believe that someday it will be found that peasants are people and I believe that someday they will find this out too – and then! Well then I think they will rise up and demand to be regarded as part of the race, and by that consequence there will be trouble.'[1] Mark Twain's words, remembered from Mao's reading marathon when he was assistant librarian at Peking University. So not every American is an imperialist, Mao had thought at the time. But most are, he answers his younger self now, thinking of the American weapons confiscated from Chiang's army, needing no reminder of the damage they could inflict.

'We are the fish and the people are the waters through which we swim.'[2] Mao has quoted these words – spoken by Peng Dehuai, one of the generals who fought alongside him on the Long March – so many times he's come to believe they're his own. He likes the image of the Red Army as a fish swimming through the waters of the people. Fish and water belong together in the same way as earth and sky. It's what he's been saying to the Russians who persist in seeing Chiang, that son of a turtle, as necessary to the revolution. Wrong! Wrong on all counts. Chiang is the face of the West, of capitalism and imperialism.Why can't the Russians see that?

He finishes his cigarette, lights another. At least it keeps the mosquitoes away. Not even winter finishes off those disease-carrying pests.

He goes to the cave entrance, pushes back the padded drape, and looks out over the fudge-coloured loess hills, shrouded now in darkness. Flickering pools of light tell him there are others keeping watch. Zhou Enlai, his closest ally in the Party, will be one of them, poised and ready to travel to Xi'an when the signal comes. If it comes. With the KMT blockading the city, it's a miracle they get any news at all. The previous day's flimsies (wireless messages) confirming that the first part of the plan had been executed, and Chiang was now in custody, was encouraging, but it was only the start.

He moves back inside. His spies have done a good job. They'd assured him Chiang would be at the Huaqingchi guesthouse in the hot-spring resort of Lintong on the day in question, and he was. (Rewi, the amateur money launderer, had stayed at that same guesthouse, chosen for its proximity to Xi'an, three months earlier.) The arrest was carried out by a man who had once been an ally of the KMT – the northern warlord, Zhang Xueliang Zhang, known throughout China as the Young Marshall. Mao doesn't trust him. He doesn't trust anyone associated with the KMT, conveniently forgetting that he was associated with it himself before Chiang's expulsion order. But the arrest could never have taken place without the Young Marshall's help, so for now he is being treated as not just an ally, but a friend.

Mao smiles as he pictures the scene at Lintong: the curved roof of the Lady Spring, where the fabled beauty Yang Guifei, mistress of the Tang Emperor Xuanzong, took her daily bath; the ornamental gardens; the statue of Yang Guifei emerging from her bath; the Lianhua pool, the Guifei pool, the Huaqing pool; Mt Li, with its cloak of cypresses and pines … Famous for centuries for the story of an emperor's love for his mistress, Lintong will be famous for something else now – the capture and summary execution of the hated Generalissimo.

Over the next 24 hours a drama will play out in Xi'an that will, as Dave has told us, change the course of history. Tired of waiting for news of Chiang's execution, Mao dispatches Zhou to make sure the deed is done. By the time Zhou reaches Xi'an, drama has turned to black comedy. The Generalissimo, escaping his captors, has fled from the guesthouse in his nightshirt and without his false teeth. With the Young Marshall in hot pursuit, Chiang takes refuge in a cave in the hills. His freedom is short-lived. 'If you are my comrade, shoot me,' he says, when his pursuers catch up with him. 'We will not shoot,' the Young Marshall replies. 'We only ask that you lead our country against the Japanese.'[3]

'*Cao ni zuzong shiba dai!*' Mao is said to have screamed when he heard the news (literally, 'Fuck your ancestors to the eighteenth generation!') His orders were clear. Why didn't that dog Zhang shoot? He was right not to trust him. Once a warlord always a warlord … What galls him most is the thought that the Young Marshall, in flouting his orders, was – whether he knew it or not – obeying a directive from the Soviets. Russia's desire to keep Chiang in power is something Mao will never understand, or accept. He'd planned to pass off the assassination as an act of an ill-disciplined former warlord; now he's going to have to do what Russia, and most of his generals, want – make peace with the hated Chiang!

When Zhou Enlai returns, Mao's temper flares up again. But Zhou holds his ground. He agrees with the decision to negotiate. 'You want a United Front to fight the Japanese,' he reminds Mao quietly. 'Well, you won't get it if you kill Chiang. You'll just get more civil war. And a serious rap over the knuckles from the Russians. We don't have to trust him, but we do have to make our peace with him. For now. Once we've rid China of the Japanese …' He leaves the thought unspoken. He can see his words have had an effect.

'Save the country, then save the Party,' Mao concedes. 'Hmmm …'

'Look at it this way,' Zhou encourages. 'Chiang has been well and truly humiliated. You should have seen him on the way back to Xi'an, half naked, shivering, no teeth. Not even his wife would have recognised him.'

Mao allows himself a brief smile. A humiliated Chiang is no substitute for a dead one, but the picture Zhou has painted is pleasing. His mind races ahead, grasping at ways to turn this new situation to his advantage in the future. 'Chinese Don't Fight Against Chinese.'[4] A new catchphrase. He can see it now, plastered across buildings the length and breadth of China. Throw out the Japanese, then throw out the nationalists. He likes it. Likes the symmetry of it.

'Perfect,' Zhou says when Mao tries the new slogan out on him. 'Brilliant. As always.'

*

Eleven days later New Zealander James Bertram rides into Xi'an. It's taken him more than a week to get there from Beijing. He quickly makes contact with Agnes Smedley, the only other Western journalist in town. Despite the KMT blockade, these two manage to broadcast reports of Chiang's capture to the rest of world. Without them it could have been months before the news got out.

Back in Shanghai, Rewi will hear his friends' reports on his shortwave radio. Agnes's enthusiasm is infectious. Even when her voice starts to fail – turns out she has the flu – there is no disguising her excitement about the events she is describing. Wish I'd been there, Rewi thinks. Since I seem to be a communist now.

CHAPTER TWENTY-NINE

AT last I've managed to sit next to Alison, one of the cousins I'm meeting for the first time on this trip. We're winding our way up a steep mountain road with hairpin bends that remind me of our occasionally lethal mountain roads back home. As we climb higher I feel twinges of vertigo. I'm relieved that it's Alison sitting next to the window, not me. One look at the yawning chasm below and I'd be in meltdown.

Alison is an artist. Formerly a nurse, she has dedicated her life since retirement to painting and environmental activism, working with the Nelson City Council to protect her local river, the Maitai. Alison reminds me of Aunt Clara. She has the same statuesque beauty, the same calm presence. As we talk I have a sense of that strange disconnect I've encountered before in the family. Rewi's books were on her aunts' shelves, Alison tells me, but he was never talked about. 'He's a communist!' was the answer she got when, in all innocence, she asked about their author. His name was never mentioned again.

Alison and her partner David will take more than 900 photos on this trip. Some will no doubt end up in this book. But it's Alison's evolution from distant cousin to proud promoter of Rewi's life and work that interests me. 'My thoughts changed from not knowing very much about Rewi to feelings of great admiration for a man who had the ear of the mighty and powerful but remained humble to the end,' she wrote in answer to my post-journey question as to how China had affected her. 'I would put him up there with Mother Teresa, Nelson Mandela and Gandhi.'

On their return to New Zealand, Alison and whānau friend Betty Gray will start a campaign to get Rewi's image put on a banknote or stamp. Alison writes to Eric Livingstone, chairman of the Rewi Alley 120th Anniversary Commemoration Committee. This is his reply: 'Rewi did not support our Government over the wars in Korea and Vietnam so he was soundly rubbished by officials and there are many people still believing that action is right …'[1]

Clearly we will not be seeing Rewi's image on a banknote any time soon. The virus of anti-communism – and its country cousin, racism – still infects the land. 'New Zealand has had many great sons, but you, Sir, are our greatest Son,' Prime Minister David Lange declared when he met Rewi in Beijing in March 1986.² A few months earlier, at an intimate ceremony at the New Zealand embassy in Beijing, Rewi had been presented with the medal of the Queen's Service Order – an exclusively New Zealand honour instituted in 1975, only 30 of which are granted in any one year. It could have been a knighthood! Back in New Zealand, Don Brash, who would become leader of the National Party in 2003 but was at the time working in business, had written to the minister of science and technology suggesting that Rewi be offered a knighthood (Sinophiles are to be found on both sides of the political divide). The fact that the offer was never made was down to Rewi himself. Everyone who knew him was adamant he would refuse. But an award for 'community service' – that was something he could live with. 'This is just a piece of metal,' he said in his speech of thanks, 'but if it helps relations between the two countries then I am pleased.'³

'Rewi has not only built a bridge between his two countries,' Ma Haide declared at that investiture. 'He stands successfully at both ends.'⁴

Don Brash was not the first person to lobby for a knighthood for Rewi. Back in 1948, on, I assume, the recommendation of the British ambassador to China, Sir Archibald Clark-Kerr, a keen supporter of Gung Ho, Rewi was offered a knighthood by the British government. He turned it down. George Wood, the Foreign Office official tasked with delivering the offer in person, travelled from London to Hong Kong by sea, then across war-torn China to Shandan by truck, only to be turned down. 'A ridiculous thing!' Rewi called it, when the subject came up in conversation with Geoff Chapple. 'A hopeless idea … I was trying to work with people. What on earth would I want with a knighthood in China?'

Nearly four decades after that exchange with George Wood, Rewi meets the Queen on her first state visit to China in 1986. Wearing his QSO, with its eye-catching ribbon decorated with the poutama – 'stairway to heaven' – pattern, 89-year-old Rewi is asked why he turned down a knighthood in 1948 when he seems perfectly happy to wear the Queen's medal now. 'Because the offer was made by the New Zealand government, Ma'am,' he answers, 'not the British.' History doesn't record whether the Queen was offended or not.⁵

By the time of his death in 1987 Rewi's reputation has been restored both in China and in New Zealand. But then in 2003 Anne-Marie Brady's book is published. *Friend of China: The myth of Rewi Alley* was, according to Tom Newnham, author of *Interesting Times*, written with the intention of 'crucifying' Rewi and destroying the myth that had grown up around him.

But though the book states as fact that Rewi was homosexual (something he never admitted to), and even hints at possible pederasty, it cannot deny the evidence of his achievements. Unfortunately, what also cannot be denied is that Brady's book, like Christopher Hitchens' attack on Mother Teresa in *The Missionary Position: Mother Teresa in theory and practice*, left a bad taste. Not that this seemed to affect New Zealand's recently retired ambassador to China, John McKinnon. He credited Brady's book for 'prompting public debate about many aspects of Alley's life, including the extent to which the New Zealand Government, having shunned Alley as a communist fellow traveller before 1972, embraced him thereafter as a means to invigorate our new relationship with the People's Republic'.[6]

'Good is a complex thing and conducive to pompous language,' Russian writer Andrei Makine claims in his novel *The Woman Who Waited*. To solve the problem he decides to give up the attempt to capture his character's goodness in words and rely instead on simply recording 'the impulsive simplicity with which [she] acted'. Rewi would have approved, not only because it's how he would have wanted to be judged himself, but because actions, not beliefs or allegiances, formed the basis of his own judgements. He had plenty of faults – he could be ruthless, particularly in his determination to see Gung Ho succeed. His temper was legendary, as was his impatience. He made enemies, falling out with the publicity secretary of INDUSCO, the international fundraising arm of Gung Ho, over the allotment of funds. But his faults, like his virtues, were never in the service of his own advancement. Love of the 'common man' was what drove him ('I have never lent myself to anything but the cause of the common man,' he wrote in response to an attack on him published in the *Dominion Post* in June 1952. 'I wanted … to express the truth.'[7]). The instruction, instilled in him as a boy, to 'open wide your hand to your brother, to the needy and to the poor', was one he had taken to heart.[8]

> … A commune
> schoolboy, short clothes a light brown
> coloured by some forest dye, bag
> of books on back, hoe over one shoulder
> carrying-basket at the other end
> a broad palm leaf hat thrown back,
> halts a moment or two to look across
> downs lying in their afternoon warmth;

bare legs tanned by the suns of
a summer gone by, beautifully-formed
bare feet, and big toe that etches
a design on the sandy path; then
a smile that includes the whole
wide world of folk like himself;
never realizing how near the centre
of things he stands, in his quiet
casual magnificence.[9]

'How we ever came to look on him as a traitor beats me,' a member of the
consulate staff in Beijing was reported as saying shortly after Rewi's death. 'He
was never any kind of threat to New Zealand. But they tried a few things back
in those Cold War days. Accusations of this and that. All in the past thank
God. There's absolutely no doubt in my mind that New Zealand wouldn't be
where it is today if Rewi Alley hadn't opened doors for us.'[10] Lindsay Watt,
New Zealand's ambassador to China in 1992, went further. 'There can be
no doubt that Rewi Alley put New Zealand and New Zealanders on China's
map.'[11]

So why, given his fame in China, is Rewi's name not widely known in
his home country? Had he been a rugby star or the man who 'knocked off'
Everest, Alison would have had little trouble getting his image on a postage
stamp. The answer, I suspect, lies in that word *communist*, a label that
continues to blind people to the man or woman it is attached to.

*

Having risen to the top of yet another mountain pass we are now making our
way down into a wooded valley. Power pylons march across the valley floor
like soldiers from another narcissistic emperor's eternal army. Daring, now
we're descending, to look out the window, I see a river, light flashing from
its surface, reminding me of the braided rivers in Rewi's home province of
Canterbury. A cluster of houses surrounded by blossom-laden trees perch
on the river bank. This is where we'll have our lunch, in a cafe beside that
silver river.

Tumbling out of the bus, clutching our bags with their discreet contents
– toilet paper, tissues, hand sanitiser, masks, cough lozenges, inhalers – we
make our way across the courtyard to the restaurant. I wonder if it will be

called The Co-operative Restaurant, as so many were post-Liberation, but it doesn't appear to have a name. The signage, though, is hopeful. 'Women's Toilet', it says in English. Minutes later that hope is dashed when a voice calls out, 'It's a squat. No paper, no soap.'

Well, I don't care, I say to myself, mimicking my cousin. The sun is shining, the birds are singing and I'm certain I can hear the river. 'It's going to be a brave new world,' Rewi told Willis Airey, 'with lots of kids, lots of trees and flowers.' He didn't mention birds. Perhaps by the time he made those comments Mao's order to kill the sparrows had already been carried out.

Lunch is eaten outside to the sound of water flowing over stones and the muted midday chorus of birdsong. No one can tell me what the birds are. Or what the river is called. Snatches of Schubert's *Trout Quintet* play over in my head. Schubert wrote it while staying in the countryside where the only sounds, apart from human voices, were made by water, wind and bird. After the din of Beijing and Xi'an this place feels like a slice of Schubert heaven. Lizards dart among the stones. Flies hover, but not so many as to spoil the mood. When Dave tells us there are musk deer in the woods on the hills around us, I move from Schubert's Austrian paradise to one of my own: the village I lived in for 10 years, nestling under the ancient Wychwood Forest in England's Cotswolds. The muntjac deer that had lived in the forest since the crusades kept escaping onto the roads, with sometimes fatal consequences. I can still see the animal I so nearly hit one day, more like a dog than a deer, huge eyes staring back at me as I screeched to a halt …

The tree under which we are sitting is a walnut. I see the schoolboy Rewi hiding in its top branches, aiming walnut shells onto our tables. 'Don't care,' he's say when he's caught and punished. 'It was fun.'

For a few magical moments everything in my life seems connected.

'Okay, Alley whānau, this is where we get to rehearse our waiata. It's the perfect place.' Jocelyn's attempts to get us to practise the Māori waiata we're supposed to be singing at each official function have so far failed. But we're a captive audience on this river bank. Not even the non-singers among us can come up with an excuse.

Tūtira mai ngā iwi
Tātou tātou e … ('Line up together people, All of us, all of us …')

Our voices float uncertainly over the sparkling river. None of us speaks te reo Māori, though many Pākehā Kiwis have a good ear for the language. Peter and Irene, the only non-New Zealanders among us, listen to Jocelyn's lesson in pronunciation, managing in the end to sound as Kiwi as the rest of us. The incongruity of a bunch of Pākehā standing on a river bank 'somewhere in China', stumbling through a song in te reo Māori, is not lost on any of us. By the time the rehearsal is finished, to Jocelyn's satisfaction, we are all feeling rather pleased with ourselves.

We're reluctant to get back on the bus. No one has complained of sickness but several of us had queasy moments on the way here. Still, the worst is over, we're told. Wrong! We've been driving only a few minutes when we grind to a halt. Ahead of us a trail of paralysed cars and trucks snakes up the mountainside. Somewhere, several kilometres further on, there's been an accident.

For the next three hours we will sit in the overheating bus, drinking water from our bottles, talking (in my case to cousin Zeke) to the click of Carol and Christine's knitting needles. Eventually even those distractions pall, and we close our eyes.

Like me, Zeke remembers copies of *China Reconstructs* arriving in the house when he was a boy. Intrigued with the pictures and stories, and the strange smell of the paper, he started cutting out items to put in a scrapbook. Years later, living in Sydney, he met Rewi travelling with his old friend Ma Haide. Zeke remembers the encounter fondly. A decade later they met again in Beijing. Zeke was there on business. What struck him was the number of people who greeted Rewi in the street. People over 35 mostly, he tells me. The younger people didn't seem to know who he was. Airbrushed out of history during the Cultural Revolution, is Zeke's guess.

Now that I have Zeke's ear I decide to ask him if he knows anything about my grandfather's death. (If I've learned one thing on this trip it's that family stories are not to be trusted.) The story I was told as a child was that Grandpa Alley drove his horse over a cliff. It had always troubled me, not because I couldn't believe this cold, judgmental man wouldn't kill himself, particularly after he'd been thrown out of the house by his sons, but because I couldn't believe he'd kill his horse! 'He didn't,' Zeke informs me. 'He was hit by a truck during a blackout.' So now there are two completely different versions of the same event. Perhaps I should take a leaf out of Michael Ondaatje's book. His answer to criticisms from his family that he hadn't told the truth in his brilliant memoir, *Running in the Family*, was that he simply selected, out of all the stories on offer, the ones he liked best!

Talk comes easily to Zeke, so I ask about another family story, one I grew up with, source of my lifelong reluctance to visit Japan. Our mutual uncle, a missionary in the Solomons during World War II was, so I'd been told, beheaded by the Japanese. Wrong again. He died when the ship he was travelling in was sunk by a torpedo … Suicides, executions – I didn't invent these stories, so is there a tendency in this Irish diaspora family to embroider the facts, add a bit of sensationalism? Is that what's made me a writer?

At last we are on our way. Nose to bumper we crawl up the hill, graunching through the gears as we stop/start, stop/start. I move to sit up the front where there is a row of viewing seats. I talk first with Ken about photography and the difference between the photos being snapped on cellphones and the professional photos he's taking. Then I talk with Irene and Peter, whose good nature in the face of our sometimes gruelling schedule has impressed me. 'Your cousin was an amazing man,' Peter says. 'You must be very proud.'

I feel a rush of gratitude. So politics doesn't explain everything. 'I had human principles and I made choices based on these,' Rewi told David Mahon during one of their regular Sunday afternoon conversations in the mid-80s. They'd been talking about Mao's disastrous Great Leap Forward, instigated in 1958, and the even more disastrous Cultural Revolution a decade later. 'After the war and the revolution, I knew I had a choice,' Rewi went on. 'I could have joined the critics of China, but China had become like my family and as in all families, even though you might have been arguing with each other, when the guests come you present a loyal unified face to the world … It was like a marriage and I wrote what I wrote and said what I said out of loyalty to that marriage.'[12]

> Even if you try to sit
> on top of the fence
> you have to get down on one
> side or the other eventually …[13]

It's dark by the time we reach Shuangshipu. We're given an hour to shower and change before showing our faces at yet another banquet. Is it an illusion, or are we all drinking more than usual? The toasts seem to go on forever.

Back at our hotel we are treated to a dance from a minority group known as the Man, from whose numbers the ruling elite of the Qing dynasty were chosen. One of the largest of China's 55 official minorities, the Man – sometimes referred to as 'red-tasselled Manchus' because of the ornamentation on their hats – look, even to my grit-filled eyes, distinct from the Han people we have been meeting and travelling with. When I ask one of the hotel staff about this I'm told that the Man people are more handsome than the Han, that is the difference. Clearly my informant belongs to this once elite Manchu minority!

Back in Beijing we'd been taken to see the Minority Cultural Park, celebrating China's ethnic diversity. I'd been impressed. Included among those minorities were the Tibetans. Surely, if they were being celebrated they couldn't also be being persecuted? Then I would learn that minorities make up only seven per cent of China's population. In other words, 93 per cent are Han Chinese. And the official policy is to move whole populations of Han into the minority areas, particular the Xinjiang Uyghur Autonomous Region where there has been so much unrest. I wonder what Rewi, who celebrated the presence of Mongols, Uyghurs, Tibetans, Manchus and Japanese in his school, and recorded with his camera the smiling faces of China's ethnic minority children, would make of the current policy? Wonder too if he would be as surprised as I have been to find that Chinese people no longer address each other as *Tongzhi*, Comrade.

'Rewi Alley was foolish for believing in something that Chinese people have long given up believing in,' one of the students we talked to in Beijing said, possibly in a sudden fit of truth-telling.

'What was that?'

'The ideals of the communist revolution.'

CHAPTER THIRTY

'I want you to take in another refugee,' Agnes says to Rewi. It's just the two of them, sharing a meal in a restaurant overlooking Soochow Creek. Though they stand out among the Chinese clientele it's safer than meeting in a restaurant favoured by Europeans. Agnes with her blunt-cut hair and loud American voice, not to mention her political notoriety, attracts altogether too much attention in that world.

It's the autumn of 1937. Rewi is not long back from New Zealand. The country he's returned to is facing up to the prospect of total warfare. The capture of Chiang at Xi'an and the consequent signing of the Second United Front, had goaded the Japanese, on the flimsiest of pretexts, into launching a full-scale invasion. For the second time in a decade Shanghai was bombed to within an inch of its life. Alan and Mike, schoolboys no longer, were living at home, awaiting their father's return when the attack happened. They were lucky to escape with their lives. Fleeing the bombs, they were knocked off their bikes, Alan suffering a shrapnel wound to the arm.

Rewi's delight at being reunited with his sons is tempered by the knowledge of the danger they were in. He'd left for New Zealand comforted by the thought that both boys were headed for university: Alan to medical school; Mike, having graduated with top honours from school, to study mathematics. But all that was about to change.

'Only be for a few days,' Agnes says.

That's what you say about all of them, Rewi thinks. Liu Ding stayed a year.

'It's not safe to keep him at my place any longer.'

Rewi raises his eyebrows. It's never been safe for Agnes to hide anyone in her apartment. It's not just the British watching her, it's the KMT and, for all he knows, the Japanese as well. But reminding her of that fact will only bring on another tirade. He tells himself the KMT, the most likely bunch to arrest her, would probably stop short of killing her. It would hardly be in their interests to offend the country that is bankrolling their army. In addition to which, Henry Luce's *Time* magazine has just declared Generalissimo Chiang Kaishek and his wife 'International Man and Woman of the Year', a clear sign that American support for the KMT now has the seal of public approval. As for the Japanese, it's not in *their* interests to provoke the US either (Pearl Harbour is still over three years away), though they're bound to know, from their network of spies, that Agnes has recently been keeping company with the Eighth Route Army, gathering information on the progress of the war. They may not be able to silence her, but they're bound to be watching her.

'The boys have made up their minds,' Rewi announces bluntly, dropping his chopsticks onto his plate as if suddenly offended by them. 'They're not going to university. They're going to Yan'an. To fight. I've tried to stop them but …'

Agnes reaches across the table and takes his hand. 'Good for them,' she says softly.

Rewi rubs his eyes. The United Front is coming apart at the seams. KMT officers loyal to Chiang have turned away from the fight against the Japanese to train their weapons on soldiers of the Red Army. 'Chinese don't fight against Chinese,' Mao Tse-tung has proclaimed, but they do – they are – and Rewi's boys are walking right into it. He blames himself. At Agnes's instigation he'd installed a radio – part of a network of communications with the Red Army – on the roof of his apartment. He should have told the boys about it. Just as he should have told them about the food – dumplings and *mian bing* (flat bread) wrapped in rice paper – he and Ed Snow have been tossing to the starving Chinese in the *longtangs*. He'd thought that, by keeping silent, he was keeping his sons safe. Wrong! The day Mike discovered the radio all hell broke loose.

At least the boys don't know about his gun-running. He doubts if even Agnes knows. It was George (Ma Haide) who got him into that. 'You're perfect for the job,' he'd insisted. 'Jap sentries are never going to stop a middle-aged European gent in a rickshaw.' Rewi had kept his thoughts to himself. He'd been stopped too many times to be anything like as sanguine. So far there's been no trouble. Using his faithful Kiwi woollen blanket as cover, he's succeeded in getting several caches safely out of the city on the first stage of their journey to Yan'an.

'So … You going to tell me the name of my new houseguest?' Rewi asks, picking up his chopsticks again.

'You can call him Chen.'

'And is he a general, like the last one you sent?'

Agnes grins. She likes stringing Rewi along. Zhou Jianping, the last man to seek refuge in Rewi's apartment, is with Mao now. She told Rewi he was a general only after he was well clear of Shanghai.

Someone should patent you, Rewi thinks, responding to his friend's grin with an exasperated sigh. Not even Mao Tse-tung could stand up to you!

So don't tell me my new house guest isn't a general because I won't believe you. You didn't even warn me when you asked me to escort that short-sighted professor and his wife to the Nanjing Road jetty. Disguising him as a rich Shanghailander off to farewell a friend on an overseas cruise was all very well, but you didn't have to shepherd him through the crowded streets where every loose stone threatened to blow his cover. Without his trademark spectacles he was blind as a bat. I'd assumed he was a communist, but you told me later he was merely a liberal who happened to be friends with Enlai – more than enough to get anyone on a KMT death list. Well, they're safe now. Ferried to freedom on the very ship they were meant to be farewelling. If you'd escorted them yourself, as I know you wanted to, I hate to think what would have happened. You may be able to disguise a blind professor and his wife, but no one could disguise you. Everything about you attracts attention. You should hear what Jim Bertram says about you: 'You don't talk, you shout, you don't walk, you stride. You're a one-woman Red Army.'[1]

Rewi smiles. He knows what Agnes would say to that. She'd take it as a compliment. He watches as she drains her glass of *mao tai*. Distilled from sorghum and wildly intoxicating, the stuff never seems to have any effect on her.

'Good,' Agnes says, banging her glass down on the table. 'You've stopped scowling. So what's your answer? Can I send Chen to you?'

CHAPTER THIRTY-ONE

... where stands he,
barefooted, worn, there most truly stand I.[1]

'NOW look here, Rewi,' Peg Snow blurts out in the middle of yet another
evening of talk. 'You say you're frustrated nothing's being done. You accuse us
of tinkering away at the edges. So ditch your job of making Shanghai a better
place for the Japanese to exploit and get out and make this thing happen.'

Rewi, for once, is lost for words. The 'thing' Peg wants him to 'make
happen' – the subject of tonight's study group discussion – is moving China's
industry away from the eastern seaboard and out of Japanese territory. Might
as well ask me to move Mt Cook and plonk it down in the middle of China,
he thinks.

We are in Rewi's apartment in Yuyuan Street. February 1938. The Japanese
have attacked the old Chinese capital Nanjing. The scale of the destruction is
only just being made clear. People are calling it a massacre. As for Shanghai,
it's a desert of bombed-out buildings and smouldering *longtangs*. Only the
foreign concessions have been spared. Some 60,000 factory workers, their
livelihoods destroyed, have been forced out of the city or left to die. Nothing
and no one can get in or out of Shanghai without Japanese permission.

So why me, Rewi asks himself. The annihilation of so much of industrial
Shanghai has doubled his workload. Factories in the foreign concessions are
working overtime to keep up with demand, which means he's working round
the clock. Ma Haide is at the Front. Jim Bertram is in the US raising funds
for Chingling's newly formed China Defence League. Chingling herself is in
Hong Kong where the League is based ... He looks round the table, aware
that all eyes are on him. All very well for you to ask me to give up my job,
he thinks sourly, how about one of you giving up yours? Not that that's ever
likely to happen. Ed Snow, whose *Red Star Over China* has sold over 12,000
copies worldwide, is up to his eyes with the attendant publicity. Peg is flat out
teaching at Yenching University. Agnes barely stops for breath in her pursuit
of stories about the exploits of the Red Army. Israel Epstein and Ruth Weiss
are working day and night to get what's happening in China reported in the
foreign press. So is Manny Granich, sitting with his wife Grace at the far end
of the table ... Trouble is, Rewi scolds himself, I've complained too often

about how little we're achieving. Writing articles, moving a handful of guns from A to B, housing the occasional refugee, tossing loaves and fishes from the roof of my apartment – what has it achieved? About as much good as bunging a sticking plaster on a broken leg.

'You're the man to do it, Rewi,' Manny is saying. 'No doubt about it.'

'Unoccupied China,' Peg enthuses. 'Away from the bombardment. Think of it, Rewi. The hinterland. It's vast enough.'

Rewi rubs his hand over his unshaven chin. He'd come straight to the meeting from his factory inspection work. He hadn't expected to have the spotlight turned on him.

'Rewi?' Agnes prompts.

'Let me get this straight. You're asking me to spearhead the removal of what remains of Shanghai's industries to the interior. Where I roll up my sleeves and get them all going again. Correct me if I'm wrong.'

A chorus of voices answers him. He raises his hand for silence. 'You seem to have forgotten I already have a job.'

Peg fixes her luminous eyes on him. Sheer bloody flattery, he thinks, as she throws adjectives at him, praising him for his ability to understand the Chinese, to fit in as if he's always lived here … He drops his head onto his hands. While we sit here and talk, China is being carved up. That's the reality. His sons know the score. It's why they've thrown in their lot with the communists. He tells himself his job is important, but at the end of the day he knows where the profits from the factories go. Straight into the pockets of the foreign owners … So is Peg right? Is he the only man who can do this lunatic thing? So many people have died already. If he agrees, he'll almost certainly die himself. Either the Japanese will kill him, or Chiang will …

Now it's Ed talking. You're as bad as your wife, Rewi thinks, buttering me up with all this stuff about Wuhan and the dykes. Calling me a pied piper leading people to safety. Wrong! The pied piper led children to their deaths …

'Co-operation. The Chinese have a gift for it. Your words, Rewi.'

He raises his head. Wrong again! Joseph Bailie's words. His mantra, in fact.

'There was a song. You wrote down the words. The people were starving, yet they sang.'

'It's what they do,' Rewi mutters. 'The Chinese. In the face of death. They sing.'

Needless to say, that doesn't silence them. Seems nothing will. Israel is speaking now, reminding him, in his Polish-accented English, that he's headed for Hong Kong to work with Chingling and her Defence League. Rewi might have known someone would bring Chingling into it. Everyone knows how he feels about her.

'The Burma Road,' Israel is saying. 'They're saying the British will close it to stop the Japs getting any further south. If that happens ...'

All right, all right, Rewi says to himself. I get the message. The Burma Road is the only reliable route to the Red Army. The Defence League relies on it. What will happen if it's closed doesn't bear thinking about. China will be forced to rely on what's left of its industrial base – which, as everyone knows, is bugger all! So of course it makes sense to move as much industry as possible into unoccupied China. What doesn't make sense is thinking I'm the man to make it happen.

'Factories run as co-operatives ...' Peg says, echoing Israel. 'Can't you see it, Rewi? There'd be no shortage of workers. Refugees will jump at the chance of a job.'

Come on, Rewi ... It's Old Man Bailie he's hearing now, not his co-conspirators. The one man he can never say no to ... We've talked about this. Co-operation is the key. And schools. To train workers. It's what China's been waiting for. The quiet revolution ...

'So you'll do it?' Ed says, leaning across the table.

Rewi stares at the ceiling. Not that it helps. When did he agree to this? Has he agreed to it?

'You've left me no choice,' he answers.

*

Rewi doesn't believe in Fate but he'll look back on that evening as the moment when everything in his life changed.

Thanks to the bottle of bourbon Ed produced, the rest of the night passed in a warm haze of talk and excitement. But he was clear as to what his first step was to be. A quick re-write of his Wuhan report, demonstrating the ability of the Chinese to work co-operatively, to be ready for publication in the next *Weekly Review*. Ed was convinced there was a lot of potential support out there, nationally and internationally, for the idea of reorganising China's industry – or what could be salvaged of it – along co-operative lines. 'The Japanese may see China as a vassal state but they can never police the whole of the interior,' he'd reminded the group, words Rewi would recall in the years ahead when bombs rained down on his co-operatives.

Only when Ed started listing the things the army needed – everything from trucks and tractors to soap and candles – did the scale of what Rewi had signed up to start to dawn on him. Bullets, uniforms, blankets, boots … The list was as long as his arm.

'It's a barefoot army in all but name,' Ed had explained. 'Not even Mao has boots. Wears straw sandals like everyone else.'

'No good at thinking on my feet,' Rewi grumbled when pushed for a response to yet another suggestion as to how to turn this crazy notion into a reality. He needed to get to his typewriter. Whoever said you only discover what you think when you see what you write spoke the truth. 'Give me a piece of wire and a bust machine and I'll come up with answers' – they'd all heard him say it – 'just don't expect me to answer hypothetical questions …'

It was close to midnight when Agnes asked him if he knew Kathleen Hall. Well, he knew who she was, of course. She's his countrywoman, so it can only be a matter of time before they run into each other. Wonderful woman by all accounts. Runs a mission hospital in Songjiazhuang on the outskirts of Peking. Lately she's taken to ferrying medical supplies through Japanese lines to the Red Army. That a Christian nurse should take such risks on behalf of the communists has led to all sorts of speculation. The explanation most people (including Agnes and Peg) favour is that she's fallen in love with the boozy, brilliant Canadian doctor, Norman Bethune, who's been travelling with the Reds since he arrived in China from the war in Spain. Rewi is sceptical. A missionary nurse falling for a drunken doctor with a reputation as a womaniser? Unlikely. Bethune (or Bai Qiu En, the Light who Pursues Kindness, as the Chinese call him) is fast becoming a legend in China, riding on his white horse, a gift from a grateful general, tending the wounded. 'I have met an angel,' he's reported to have said after meeting Nurse Hall. 'If she isn't an angel what on earth does that word mean?'[2]

(Years later – by which time the two New Zealanders have been friends for decades – Rewi, on a visit home, will ask Kath, who's been living in New Zealand since 1941, why she ever agreed to ferry medical supplies to Bethune. It was practically a suicide mission. Her answer is simple: 'God loves communists too'. Presumably Rewi didn't ask if any other kind of love was involved. He Mingqing, as the Chinese called her, was entitled to her privacy. But he must have wondered. In her book on Bethune, Adrienne

Clarkson claims that women fell in love with the charismatic doctor all the time. One of 'the most aggressively male creatures I had ever encountered' is how one woman who succumbed to his charms described him.[3])

'What is it with you New Zealanders?' Agnes had teased him. 'Cats with nine lives the lot of you.'

Agnes's explanation for Nurse Hall's derring-do had annoyed Rewi. 'I think my countrywoman would give God the credit,' he'd snapped, stifling a yawn. He wished they'd all go home. He needed to think. He needed to sleep. Agnes's description of Nurse Hall hitching rides on mule carts, yellow-fishing on trucks, striding across the North China Plain with her big yellow dog – a present, like Bethune's horse, from a grateful general – had worked on him like a drug. If a lone woman could walk across half of China in the service of its revolution then he could do what was being asked of him. The thought of her making her way through that desolate, bandit-and-wild-animal-infested wilderness, pursued in all probability by Japanese spies, the precious medicines marked 'International Peace Hospital' sewn into her padded clothes, had stiffened Rewi's resolve. Cats with nine lives had nothing to do with it.

*

By the next afternoon Rewi has the Wuhan material ready to give to Ed Snow. One step ahead of him, Ed has already dug out photos of the destruction in Shanghai to accompany the article. 'Powell will publish,' he assures Rewi. 'It'll be in the next edition of the *Weekly Review*.'

The reaction, when the article appears, is even better than the group had anticipated. Within days, news of the infant movement has spread from Shanghai to Hong Kong, Beijing and beyond. Chingling writes enthusiastically from her Defence League headquarters. Ida Pruitt, employed by the Department of Social Services at the Peking Union Medical College, offers to help with raising funds. Donations are pledged, from America, Britain, Australia, New Zealand, Canada, the Philippines … INDUSCO, charged with promoting the co-operative idea internationally and raising funds, comes into being. The British ambassador, Sir Archibald Clark-Kerr – 'a good Scotchman fallen among diplomats', Agnes Smedley would tell anyone who asked[4] – invites the movement's two spokesmen, Edgar Snow and Rewi Alley, to a meeting. Over tea served by the ambassador's Chilean wife Tita, Rewi, whose dander is up now talk has been replaced by action, explains that the idea is to build hundreds – eventually thousands – of small co-operatives in the unoccupied areas of China. Flashing the list of the essentials needed for the survival of the Eighth Route Army, he assures his hosts this is not a business they're setting up, it's a system of production to help win the war and bring new life to rural China.

The ambassador is impressed. He runs through the list of regulations Rewi has drawn up: a minimum of seven co-operative members; every member to own at least one share; members to determine their hours and rates of pay; a chairman to be elected from among the members; regular meetings to discuss problems; misconduct to be dealt with by all members; financial decisions – the repaying of loans, distribution of profits, re-investment – to be made democratically … 'Well, gentlemen,' he says. 'You seem to have thought of everything.'

From that day on till his recall in 1942 Ambassador Clark-Kerr – who will describe Rewi as 'a perpetual motion machine', while Rewi, reverting to Kiwi vernacular, describes him as a 'decent old bird' – will be one of Gung Ho's most influential supporters.[5] Warned by one of his staff that Rewi Alley is no better than 'a will-o-the wisp', his testy response is, 'Might not be a bad idea if more people pursued that will-o-the-wisp.'[6]

*

Now that the ball is rolling, 'study group' meetings take place on an almost daily basis. Rewi has come up with a motto – 'One for all and all for one' – lifted from *The Three Musketeers*. But so far he hasn't been able to think of an emblem, something that will get the message across without words. The answer comes to him as he's walking home from a meeting with Bill Powell. The Chinese character for Gung Ho (Gong He) 工合 means 'work together'. By the end of the month enamel badges bearing the emblem have been circulated to hundreds of friends and supporters. Thousands more will follow.

It nearly didn't happen. The impetus behind the movement was to supply the troops fighting the Japanese, but the KMT, still hankering after appeasement, disagreed that there was a need to move Chinese industry away from the eastern seaboard. Wouldn't it be better to negotiate with the Japanese? Find a way to keep essential businesses running in their existing locations? Rewi barely managed to keep his temper. Without KMT support he'd never get Gung Ho off the ground. Wheedling his way into Chiang's good books – Rewi was not the only one who called him *Chiang Fei*, Chiang the Bandit – went against the grain, but for now there was no alternative. The KMT were the government. Nothing could happen without their say-so.

In the event he got more than he hoped for, at least for a while. Having consulted Zhou Enlai, Rewi proceeded to request a meeting with Chiang's Australian adviser W.H. Donald, his finance minister H.H. Kung (married to Ailing, Chingling's sister) and Soong Meiling, Chiang's wife (Chingling's other sister).

The meeting takes place in the boardroom of the Yokohama Specie Bank in Wuhan. Rewi, who of course knows Wuhan well, wonders if he's the only one seeing the irony in the bank's name. He has just finished outlining the plans for Gung Ho. A silence has fallen. Suddenly Dr Kung bangs his fist on the table. 'You know what this hare-brained scheme of yours would do, Alley, don't you? Put economic power in the hands of the peasants. That what you want?'

'That's exactly what I want,' Rewi answers calmly.

'Chinese peasants are pro-communist. You thought of that?'

'Chinese peasants are pro-China,' Rewi responds. 'They believe in the United Front.' He looks around the table, gauging the measure of support. Kung is against, obviously, and there's no point appealing to Donald. A compromised Australian if ever there was one. Perhaps Meiling …

Meiling catches his eye. She claps her hands for tea to be served. She is the First Lady of China. She knows how to behave …

'I'm sorry Hsiang-hsi,' she says to her brother-in-law when tea has been poured, 'but I'm going to insist. You're always vetoing my projects. Well, you're not going to veto this one. I'm sure my husband will agree with me. Establishing co-operatives to help with the defence of our country is a splendid idea. Rewi, you have my full authorisation to proceed with Gung Ho.'

A stunned Rewi starts to thank her, but she waves his words away. 'Off you go,' she says to the other two men in the room. 'I want to talk to Rewi.'

'Darling Rewi' … Is this where that rumour started? My mother was convinced Rewi and Madame Chiang were great friends. And so they were, for a while. Rewi didn't just need Madame Chiang's blessing for Gung Ho, he needed financial support. The meeting in Wuhan secured that – but, like the friendship, only for a while.

*

So Gung Ho begins its life in Wuhan – the name given to the triple cities of Wuchang, Hankou and Hanyang – a place that is already part of Rewi's story. Thanks to Meiling, Rewi is able to establish temporary headquarters on the top floor of the same bank where that first crucial meeting took place. Deng Yingchao, Zhou Enlai's wife, employed by an organisation committed to helping the working women of Wuhan, works on the ground floor. Rewi is delighted. What could be better? Gung Ho is not politically aligned but it has the blessing of his friend Enlai. Rewi, whose official title is Technical Advisor to the Executive Yuan, can't wait to get started.

His first job is to supervise the removal of Wuhan's essential industries to Baoji in the northwest. Since the fall of the wartime capital Nanjing, and the blockading of the new capital Luoyang, the government has been conducting its business from Wuhan, making it a target for Japanese bombs. But the northwest – thanks to the battle of Pingxingguan in September 1937, the first Chinese victory against the Japanese – is, at least for the time being, safe. With no time to lose Rewi organises transport to carry thousands of cases containing tools, machinery, boilers and generators from Wuhan to Baoji. Later he will return to supervise the dismantling of Wuhan's cotton mills. Shanghai's industry, what can be recovered of it, will eventually be moved as well, but it's going to take time and stealth to get the materials out from under the noses of the Japanese.

As soon as the ancient Soviet trucks, laden with equipment, have set off on their long journey westward, Rewi takes the train to Baoji to begin the process of setting up Gung Ho's regional headquarters. Once that's up and running he can start arranging loans for the first co-operatives. Within a few weeks, more than a dozen have sprung into life, producing blankets, towels, surgical cotton, gauze, shoes and foodstuffs.

'We're onto something,' Rewi confides excitedly to Yingchao. 'This thing could spread across the whole of China.'

CHAPTER THIRTY-TWO
10 July 2017

SINCE starting this book I have become like a squirrel hoarding nuts – any and every piece of information I can find about China gets copied into my bulging files. Trouble is, so much of this information is contradictory. 'Alternative facts' abound. Today I have been reading about the poet and Nobel Laureate Liu Xiaobo. Jailed in 2009 for allegedly trying to topple China's one-party state, he is now in the final stages of terminal liver cancer. Not an alternative fact, a true one, verified by photos of the emaciated poet with his wife. Rumours of the persecution Liu and his family have suffered at the hands of the state – doubt has been cast on the effectiveness of the medical treatment he received in prison – are contradicted by a 7 July report in the state-run tabloid, the *Global Times*. Describing Liu not as a 'political prisoner' but as a 'convicted criminal', the paper insists that 'a team of medical experts from all over China, headed by a renowned surgeon from Beijing', has been sent to Shenyang, where Liu is in hospital, to try to save his life.

I dig deeper. Discover that China claims to have no political prisoners, only criminal ones. But in what way is Liu Xiaobo a criminal? A writer, critic and human rights campaigner, his 'crime' is his support for democracy and opposition to one-party rule. If China has no political prisoners it's because dissidents are invariably charged with 'crimes' other than dissent. When Liu Xiaobo was arrested he was charged not with dissidence but with 'inciting subversion of state power'.

This raises another question. President Xi has declared it his mission to rid China of corruption. But is that really what he's doing, or is he using his anti-corruption crusade to weed out 'enemies' like Liu Xiaobo (and the Falun Gong)?

Five weeks after reading that report on China's Nobel Laureate I hear on the radio that he has died. He was 61.

*

Over the next few months I gather a lot of nuts, but it's not until November that I stumble on one that addresses directly the question I've been asking myself about President Xi's anti-corruption campaign. In the 9 November edition of *Time* magazine, journalist Ian Bremmer describes Xi's fight against corruption as 'Swamp Draining with Chinese Characteristics', a reference both to President Trump's promise to 'drain the swamp' of Washington and Premier Deng Xiaoping's transformational 'Socialism with Chinese Characteristics' introduced in the 1980s.[1] Xi's promise to 'catch both the tigers and the flies', the top officials and the underlings, was made two months before he came to power.[2] Over 400,000 officials have been censured since that promise was made. The former head of public security, Zhou Yongkang, was sentenced to life imprisonment in 2014. His crimes ranged from abuse of power to bribery and corruption. Other leaders in the military have been targeted as part of Xi's drive to ensure that control of China's armed forces remains in the hands of the state. Yet it is under Xi's leadership that the rich have become spectacularly richer. The combined wealth of the 200 wealthiest Chinese citizens – all of them Communist Party members, most of them parliamentary delegates – almost equals the total GDP of Belgium. That's $NZ720 billion in hard cash.

There can be little doubt that Xi's concern to root out corruption is genuine, but he is also concerned to root out opposition. His methods are not the obvious ones of a man seeking absolute power. He prefers Mao's policy of steady infiltration – 'mixing the sand into the hardened soil'[3] – to guns and prison sentences. But that is little comfort to the human rights activists, the lawyers, artists, academics and booksellers, the Uighur protestors and Falun Gong practitioners who have been arrested from Hong Kong in the south to Urumqi in the north.

Inevitably Xi's anti-corruption campaign has been compared to Mao's now infamous Hundred Flowers Movement. 'The policy of letting a hundred flowers bloom and a hundred schools of thought contend is designed to promote the flourishing of the arts and the progress of science', Mao announced at the launch of the movement in the summer of 1956.[4] Within months almost all the individuals – artists and intellectuals for the main part – who had come forward with ideas and criticisms were either in prison or dead.

On a recent visit to Hong Kong, President Xi made clear his determination to treat the former British colony no differently from the rest of China. The 'one country two systems' agreement with the British, made when Hong Kong was handed back to China in 1997, has been torn up with not a word of protest from the UK. Britain's economic dependence on China, like our own here in New Zealand, stifles protest at the highest levels. Those brave democracy advocates in Hong Kong, members of the Umbrella Movement founded in 2014, some of whom have already seen the inside of a prison, are now effectively on their own. The West appears to be united in its desire not to offend China.

'I believe the greatest dream of the Chinese people in modern history is the great renewal of the Chinese nation,' President Xi declared in a speech in 2012.[5] Under his leadership the country we call China but which the Chinese know as *Zhong Guo*, Central Kingdom, has grown to become the second largest economy in the world. 'From time immemorial the Chinese people have viewed China as the centre of the world,' acclaimed novelist Yan Lianke has his 14-year-old protagonist declare in *The Day the Sun Died*. What Lianke goes on to say constitutes a coded warning both to his own people and to the world. The message buried in his mesmerising novel is that Xi's much vaunted Chinese dream *(Zhong Guo Meng)* is not all sweetness and light. The system of government over which Xi presides – described by Eric X Li in his 2013 TED Talk, 'A Tale of Two Political Systems', as 'responsive authoritarianism' – has a dark side.[6] By revealing that darkness, Yan Lianke hopes to awaken readers from what his translator, echoing James Joyce, calls 'the nightmare of history'.

Exiled Chinese novelist Ma Jian goes further. His 2018 novel, ironically titled *China Dream*, has been described as a 'fearless epic of history and memory'. In 'scene after scene of black satire, lyric tenderness and desolating tragedy … [*China Dream*] establishes Ma Jian as the Solzhenitsyn of China's forgetful drive towards world domination.'[7]

CHAPTER THIRTY-THREE

WUHAN, China's capital in 1938, is a city seething with rumour and intrigue. Journalists from all over the world rub shoulders with writers and adventurers. W.H. Auden is here, writing his peerless poetry, accompanied by his friend Christopher Isherwood. The Jesuit priest and paleontologist, Pierre Teilhard de Chardin, has been and gone. As has Peter Fleming, brother of the more famous Ian, and his actress wife Celia Johnson. A young Robert Capa, fresh from the war in Spain, turns up clutching a roll of film taken on his travels with the Red Army. Ernest Hemingway has been creating a stir, performing sword and dagger tricks for the amusement of the locals ...

In inns and hotels, tea houses and boardrooms, people plot everything from the overthrow of the government to the destruction of the red bandits. Some plot to do a deal with Japan. They agree with Chiang's assessment that while Japanese are 'a disease of the skin', communists are a 'disease of the heart'.[1] Others are committed to driving Japan out of China. A few diehards, nostalgic for the way things used to be, dream of a China partitioned among the Western powers. And here, in the business areas of Wuhan, are Rewi's 'big greedy people', frightened out of Shanghai by the Japanese, holding banquets and making deals, seizing the opportunity war has provided to increase their fortunes.

The streets are packed with refugees. As in Shanghai, a 'Himalaya of suffering' exists alongside comfort and privilege.[2] The summer of 1938 is exceptionally hot. People die in the streets, their bodies left to decompose till the government orders a clean-up and the corpses are tossed into the river. The KMT, not satisfied with mass shootings and decapitations, devises new ways to punish its enemies. Officially nationalists and communists are part of the same army now but that doesn't stop the arrests on false charges of treason, nor the ghastly punishments meant as a warning to others. Men condemned to be shot are castrated and their genitals stuffed in their mouths. Their mutilated bodies are left hanging for all to see. And all the while, government officials, bankers and diplomats, missionaries and military advisers visit each other's houses, take tea and discuss the politics of the day.

But in the evening the oppression lifted;
Tall peaks came into focus; it had rained:

Across wide lawns and cultured flowers drifted
The conversation of the highly trained.

Thin gardeners watched them pass and priced their shoes;
A chauffeur waited, reading in the drive,
For them to finish their exchange of views:
It seemed a picture of the way to live.

Far off, no matter what good they intended,
Two armies waited for a verbal error
With well-made implements for causing pain,

And on the issue of their charm depended
A land laid waste with all its young men slain,
Its women weeping, and its towns in terror.[3]

*

'Rewi!' The name slices through the fetid afternoon air. No doubt whose voice it is. Agnes Smedley. Here to record the mayhem in China's temporary capital. And catch him at work dismantling Wuhan's industries.

She's wearing a crumpled shirt with a red star embroidered on the pocket. A dark hank of hair droops over her forehead. The rest is concealed under her cap, emblazoned with another red star. Rewi smiles. Wouldn't surprise him if she'd followed the example of her hero, General Zhu De (like Rewi, Agnes would have used the old spelling Chu Teh), who had the Chinese characters 八一 Ba-yi (1 August) – the date of the 1927 Nanjing uprising against the KMT, sewn into the lining of his cap.

Rewi is as anxious for news as Agnes, but with the day still young this is not the time for talk. So they arrange to meet that evening in the Marco Polo Hotel where, Agnes tells him, James Bertram, fresh from his sortie into Burma on behalf of Chingling's Defence League, is staying. 'You don't still think he's a spy do you?' Rewi teases, disguising his delight at the thought of reuniting with his old friend. 'Thought *you* were one for a while,' Agnes shoots back.

Jim Bertram isn't the only member of the Shanghai study group staying at the Marco Polo. Ed and Peg Snow are there as well. Agnes, immune to Peg's charms, has taken to calling her 'the revolutionary butterfly'. Be quite a get-together, Rewi tells himself as he heads back to work.

Not one to ask others to do what he isn't prepared to do himself, he hoists a section of the dismantled Ghosh cotton mill onto his already aching shoulder and heaves it aboard the waiting truck. Japanese bombs could start falling on Wuhan any day, so the sooner the job is done the better. Rumour has it that Chiang, aware of the rich pickings this triple city provides, is planning to move the capital to Chongqing. No doubt the rumour will be picked over tonight at the Marco Polo. Agnes has warned him to expect questions about his 'tiffin with the Dragon Queen' – her cheeky description of his meeting with Madame Chiang. 'You're the talk of the town, Rewi,' she informed him, ominously. 'You should hear what people are saying.'

*

They meet in the bar as the sun's going down. Agnes, still wearing the same attention-getting shirt, greets Rewi with a shout. Jim Bertram shakes his hand warmly. Rewi can see the exhaustion in his friend's eyes, but with his carefully combed hair and trim moustache he still manages to look as if he's strolled in from the office. 'You just caught me,' he murmurs. 'I'm back to HK tomorrow, then on to London.'

'How's Chingling?'

'Worn out. Defence League takes up all her time. But she's a hundred per cent behind Gung Ho. Well, I assume you know that.'

Rewi has been asking himself if the reason his meeting with Madame Chiang went off so well had something to do with Chingling, but he knows better than to give voice to the question. The less he says about that particular encounter the better.

He's about to ask Jim for news of his Burma adventure when a shout from Agnes pulls Jim away. Smiling to himself – no one says no to Agnes! – Rewi heads for the bar. Perhaps I'll spot those poets she mentioned, he thinks. Not that she told him much. Friends of hers, young, English – that's all he knows. Most of the bar patrons are foreign but there are clusters of wealthy Chinese, as well as the now ubiquitous Japanese officers in their high black boots and white gloves. These places give me the pip, Rewi mutters. Aimed at Westerners, they manage to produce the worst of both cultures. Too much glitter. Too many chandeliers. Too many dragons.

'Rewi!' Another voice he'd know anywhere. No need to look around. The arms circling him from behind smell of jasmine.

'Evening, Spark-plug,' he says. Peg moves to sit beside him. She's wearing a blue cheongsam and a thing on her head he supposes is called a hat but looks more like a mini swan's wing come to rest. He glances down at his grubby shorts and scuffed sandals.

'You haven't changed,' Peg laughs.

'Where's your dog?'

Peg tips her head to one side. She knows what's coming – a lecture about riding her bike around Peking with her big white greyhound in tow. Drawing attention to herself. That's what Rewi will say. Spoilsport! If you can't have a bit of fun because there's a revolution going on, what's the point of the revolution?

'No you don't,' Peg says, when Rewi mentions the dog again. 'We've more important things to talk about. Tea with the First Lady of China. Come on, Rewi. Spill the beans.'

Rewi lifts a finger to his lips. 'Later,' he says. 'After we've met these poets of Agnes's. Any idea who they are? Way she's carrying on you'd think she had Yeats hiding in her bedroom.'

When Rewi hears the names – Christopher Isherwood and Wystan Auden – he lets out a delighted whistle. He doesn't know Isherwood's work but he's read Auden's debut collection and been impressed. '"Look, stranger, on this island now ..."' he quotes, but goes no further. Poetry isn't Peg's thing.

Learning that the two poets are stringers for an English newspaper – Peg isn't sure whether it's *The Times* or the *Telegraph* – Rewi feels a rush of gratitude to Agnes. It was she who introduced him to Lu Xun. Now, thanks to her, he's going to meet two of England's brightest young wordsmiths.

Moments later, by which time Jim and Agnes have joined them, the two young poets walk, or rather bound, into the bar. Isherwood, Rewi decides, is like a frisky puppy; Auden, the taller of the two, like a young giraffe. It doesn't take long for the talk to turn to war. Both men seem genuine in their desire to learn. Is it really true the Chinese had nothing to fight with at the Battle of Pingxingguan but a few grenades and some clapped-out rifles?

'Ask Agnes,' Rewi answers. 'She was there.'

Words fly about like startled birds. Rewi is loving every minute of it. Eventually they start talking about Gung Ho, which the two Englishmen, to Rewi's surprise, seem to know quite a lot about. Peg wants to label it a 'middle way', a bridge linking communism and Western-style democracy, but Agnes isn't having a bar of it. 'Mix flour and water and what do you get?' she bellows. 'Paste? Chinese can't live on paste!'

When Auden asks Peg if advocating a 'middle way' means she doesn't trust the communists, she becomes almost as incensed as Agnes. 'The CCP is doing more than anyone in China to get the country out of the mess it's in,' she answers hotly. 'It's creating a new way of thinking, a new people. And it's happening here, now, in the very heart of the most changeless civilisation on earth …'⁴ She waves her elegant hands.

Auden stretches out an arm as if to pull her into a dance, but – wisely, in Rewi's opinion – does nothing. Peg likes to lecture. And she doesn't like to be interrupted.

When the homily is over it's Agnes's turn to take the floor. 'Peg's right,' she declares. 'People study the history of Europe until they're blue in the face when they should be paying attention to the history of Asia. It's more than half the bloody world, for God's sake! How much do you think Roosevelt knows about China before the Nanking Treaty? Or Chamberlain? Or anyone else in government, come to that?'

As their talk becomes more animated, attracting the attention of people at the bar, they're joined by a man called Carlos whom Agnes describes as a pal of Teilhard de Chardin.

'Is there anyone you don't know?' Rewi asks, when Agnes has dealt with the introductions.

'Teilhard de Chardin,' Isherwood says, slurring the words. He's not the only one who's more than a little drunk by now. 'Isn't he the Peking Man chappie?'

'And who are you a stringer for?' Peg asks Carlos. It's that stage of the evening when questions are asked but seldom answered.

'Pope Pius,' the young man answers, grinning.

The arrival of Carlos has sent the conversation off in a new direction. Paleontology, evolution, China's ancient history, the Catholic Church … but with so many opinions vying for ascendancy it's hard to keep track of the arguments. '"Humanity is still in its infancy,"' Agnes shouts. 'Who said that. Was it Freud?'

Jim shakes his head. 'Freud is convinced humanity has come of age,' he corrects.

'Not any more surely,' Auden comments gloomily. 'He's a Jew.'

Jim is the first to leave. Rewi, watching him march out of the room, gets to his feet, determined to call it a day. Conversation is all very well, but it won't stop the sun rising and it won't get tomorrow's work done. He's given Auden his Shanghai address. If he and his friend make it to the city and he's at home, neither of which are at all certain, he'll show them around. (As it happens they do meet. Years later Rewi will recall his time with the two poets: 'Nice couple o' fellas ... Things were pretty unstable but they bore up well. I showed them some rough places. At times we were in real danger ...'[5])

Rewi is already out the door when Agnes's voice stops him for the second time that day. Unbelievably, she wants him to come back, meet another of her friends, some fellow who's just turned up. 'Name?' Rewi grunts. It's almost midnight, he has a gruelling day ahead of him, and his shoulder is aching.

'George Hogg. English. Something about him. Been travelling with the Red Army as a stringer for United Press. Met all the bigwigs. Mao. Zhou. Chu Teh. Keen to do more. Bit like you, Rewi. Writing articles not enough.'

Rewi peers at his friend. What the expression on her face is telling him is that she's fallen for this Englishman. Wouldn't be the first time.

'That's him. Leaning against the bar. Gorgeous, isn't he?'

*

An hour later Rewi makes his way back to the inn where he's been staying. He doesn't know it yet, but he's just met the man who will help make his vision of a school to train workers for the Gung Ho co-operatives a reality. He has also just met the man whom he will grow to love as a son (George is 23, Rewi is 41). Agnes was right, he thinks, as he picks his way over sleeping – or dead – bodies, accompanied by the usual pack of stray dogs and noxious odours, there is something about him. He'd call it innocence if that didn't sound patronising. Goodness, maybe. The same kind of goodness he has ascribed to Kathleen Hall.

CHAPTER THIRTY-FOUR

FEBRUARY 1939. George Hogg is on his way to Baoji. 'If you're looking for a job that will help China then you should make your way to Gung Ho headquarters,' Rewi Alley had said to him that night in the bar of the Marco Polo Hotel. George hadn't known quite what to make of the stocky New Zealander but he'd been impressed by his directness. 'There'll be no salary and you'll have to work your backside off, but you'll be making a difference. If that's what you want.'

Over the next few months, travelling around China gathering stories for United Press, meeting Red Army leaders, parleying with KMT officials, George couldn't get Rewi's words out of his head. He'd come to China by accident, dropping off from a world tour with his Christian pacifist aunt. He'd only intended to stay a few weeks. Now here he is, a year later, on his way to Baoji to look for a job that will probably keep him here indefinitely. He knows what the Chinese call him – *yang guizi*, foreign devil – but after his marathon journey across unoccupied China he's beginning to feel more Chinese than English. He meant it when he told Rewi he wanted to do something practical to help. Where else in the world would you find such cheerfulness in the face of almost universal injustice and deprivation? Telling China's story to the world had seemed like a good thing to be doing, now it mostly seems pointless. No one's listening.

George doesn't know where Rewi is – all he's been able to find out is that he's constantly on the move – but he knows where Gung Ho's HQ is: a good thousand kilometres away, some of it over mountains twice as steep as the highest peak in England. He doesn't own a bicycle, so it will be either shanks's pony or, if he's lucky, yellow-fishing on a truck. But he's made his decision. For better or worse he's going to throw in his lot with the man whom Agnes seems to regard as some kind of secular saint. George is a Quaker, so he doesn't have much time for saints, but he knows a good man when he sees one. If you *are* a saint, Rewi, he says to himself as he kicks the dust from his sandals, then you're a mighty irritable one. Wouldn't want to get on the wrong side of you!

George knows what's ahead of him. As a roving reporter he's spent dozens of nights in flea-infested inns, or sleeping wrapped in his embroidered blue bedroll in caves or under trees. He's already had a bad bout of typhus, contracted when he was in Yan'an with the Red Army, but he's fit now and he can get by in the language. So long as he doesn't run into bandits – the real ones, not Chiang's Blue Shirts who so far, thank God, have shown no interest in him – he's confident he'll reach Baoji unscathed.

Ten days into his journey he falls ill. He knows at once what it is. Typhus back again. He'd been feeling feverish for several days but had chosen to ignore it. So long as there was no rash, he could tell himself he was simply suffering the effects of hiking over rough roads and of a far from adequate diet. But there, spreading across his chest, is the telltale rash.

He turns back, knowing his only hope is to get back to the inn where he spent the previous night. With luck he'll sweat the illness out. Later he will remember almost nothing of this retracing of footsteps, staggering along the road, mouth full of dust, eyes deceiving him as the distant mountains mist over and become menacing – an army of soldiers with spiked hats; tigers baring their teeth; sabres drawn above his head …

'Hullo. Can you hear me? Hullo.'

George hears the voice but is unable to respond. Is he in heaven? How wonderful. The angels speak English!

'My name is Kathleen Hall. I'm a nurse. I'm going to help you.'

The next thing George remembers is the sound of a donkey braying. He's not at the inn any more, lying on his straw mat drenched in sweat. He's in a donkey cart. An angel is walking beside him. She gives him water; tells him she's taking him to her hospital.

When he wakes, finally, he's in a bed with sheets, surrounded by hospital smells and the murmuring of nurses – or are they angels too? He tries to open his eyes but they're glued shut.

Someone takes his hand. 'Thank God,' a soft voice says.

'My eyes …'

'Here …' A cool flannel settles on his forehead. 'I'm afraid you'll have red eyes for a while, but you're not blind.'

'Where am I?'

'Mission hospital. You've had typhus.'

'You saved me …'

'God saved you, George. I was just His instrument.'

'You know my name.'

'The letter to your parents. It was in your jacket pocket.'

'Thank you.'

'What for?'

'Saving my life.'

Two months later an impatient George – his recovery has been punctuated by Nurse He's repeated threats to tie him to the bed – is back on the road to Baoji. But it will be another eight months before he catches up with Rewi. The information he'd been given before setting out on his journey was accurate. Rewi no longer has a fixed address. Darting from one place to another on his rusty bike, he's as hard to pin down as a balloon broken free of its string. His official title – Technical Advisor to the Executive Yuan – is misleading. It makes it sound as if he's sitting at a desk dishing out good advice. In reality, he's covering vast areas of China, setting up co-operatives, negotiating with obstructionist KMT officials, writing letters to anyone who might help Gung Ho's cause. Within the space of a year he's become a legend: a man with a price on his head, managing on a daily basis to escape bandits, Japanese spies, KMT thugs, and the ever-present threat from wolves, jackals, tigers and wild dogs.

*

What George Hogg doesn't know as he navigates his way to Baoji is that the man responsible for his making the journey has also fallen ill. May 1939. Rewi, like George, was struck down while still on the road. Diagnosed with a combination of typhoid and malaria he has, thanks to the good offices of his friend Bishop Hall, been transported to the mission hospital in Ganzhou. Informed by his doctor – who will go on to describe him as a 'saint'[1] – that he is unlikely to recover, Rewi falls back on his mantra. 'Well that's it, I don't care.'

> Then came a hospital bed, surrounded
> by kindliness, but bringing realization
> that somehow one had not learnt how
> to live; a feeling anyway that only
> a start had been made at learning
> of any kind; for only now did the veil
> of incrusted tabu begin to lift
> and around one reality stands in all
> its youthfulness ...
> and I wondered why when young I felt old,

yet now felt young and adventurous
again, though with so brief a time
in front of me ... [2]

Rewi has been writing poems for some time now. Lying on the hard earth, huddled in a makeshift shelter, waiting on a roadside for a passing truck to pick him up, sharing a *kang* with a peasant family, the lines have been coming, sometimes as letters home, sometimes as a relief for pent-up emotions, sometimes as a way of slowing time, a breather between one rough, erratic day and the next. As often as not these random lines are forgotten, but some have found their way onto paper or ragged strips of material. Some have even managed to stick, waiting for their moment when life is quieter – as now, in hospital – to be shaped into poems that will last.

'There's a tree by my window that's full of birds,' he writes from hospital, in a letter designed to reassure his family. 'They cheer me immensely.'[3] He's been encouraged by a visit from his friend the bishop, who brought with him a letter from Mao Tse-tung praising the work of Gung Ho. Singling out the industrial co-operatives in the guerrilla northwest for special mention, Mao wrote, 'Their help is greatly appreciated and warmly welcomed by the Eighth Route Army. Gung Ho's contribution to our struggle is incalculably great.'[4]

On the insistence of the American nuns nursing him, Rewi is fed on a diet of *mitang* – rice gruel soup – and nothing else. It works. He starts to recover, surviving not just the double whammy of typhoid and malaria but also the Japanese bomb that nearly destroys the hospital. He doesn't wait to be discharged. As soon as he can walk again he's back on the road, 'midwifing' the co-operatives proliferating all over China.[5] He can't bear to think of Alan and Mike. For all he knows they could both be dead. So he thinks of his friends, and how much he misses them. He misses both the scintillating company of the Snows and the calm wise presence of Ma Haide. And he misses Agnes, his old sparring partner. He even misses her rages. Most of all he misses Chingling. He's always felt complete in her presence. If he could see her, just for an hour, his loneliness would evaporate like steam from a kettle.

CHAPTER THIRTY-FIVE

IN September 1939 Britain declares war on Germany. The news doesn't reach Rewi till the end of October. By then, having zigzagged his way across China, he will have notched up more than 17,000 kilometres. Yellow-fishing, walking, cycling, riding hard class on the railways, stowing away on ferries, piling onto buses powered by charcoal, by Chinese New Year that figure will be closer to 20,000.

As the news – conveyed to him by a group of soldiers on their way to Yan'an – sinks in, Rewi feels as if his lungs have collapsed. Scenes of the slaughter on the Somme have risen like ghosts, reminding him, not that he needed any reminder, of what war does. He hadn't realised how much comfort he'd got from the thought that not every country was suffering as China suffered. He had only to conjure up the scented garden at the convalescent hospital in Wiltshire, the elms, oaks and plane trees that are the lungs of London, the Thames that bears witness to the history of England as the Yangtse does in China, to have his hope in the future restored. Now the madness is starting again in Europe, and New Zealand will be caught up in it, as it was before, as *he* was.

The world will forget China now, he says to himself bitterly. 'It's so hard to make the West take the East even a little seriously.'[1] Not his words – Iris Wilkinson's, a New Zealand journalist, better known as Robin Hyde, whom he encountered in Beijing before setting out on his latest marathon. Funny he should think of her now. He hopes she's somewhere safe. Having ignored his advice to go south, away from the advancing Japanese, the wretched woman got herself captured and was raped.[2] Ghastly business, but she should have listened to the people on the ground. Not gone off on her own like that.

Rewi has grown used to the sound of sirens – *jinbao* – or bells, or both, announcing another air raid. Europe is only just waking up to the reality of war, but China has been living with it for the whole of the century. Ever since the bombing of Shanghai in 1932 the country has been used as a laboratory for what's being described as the future of military conflict – war from the air. How else to describe the insane bombing of paddy fields and clusters of mud huts with no military significance whatsoever? In towns and cities, where dugouts have been excavated, it's possible to avoid the full force of the raids, but no such amenities exist in the villages where Rewi spends most of his time these days. So he does what everyone else does, and runs to the nearest ditch. He seldom feels fear. It's as if the stoicism of the people around him has entered his blood stream. (One story has him caught in a bombing raid in Chongqing, calmly finishing his meal while everyone else runs to the shelter.[3])

Will things get worse now that Europe is at war? No doubt America will go on supplying the Japanese with iron ore, ignoring the inherent contradiction in that policy. But Britain will have little time for Chinese affairs. Which will probably mean the recall of Ambassador Clark-Kerr, whose support for Gung Ho has been crucial to its success. All in all a bad day, he thinks, as he flags down a passing truck and starts the tedious business of negotiating to yellow-fish. He needs to get back to Baoji. Reassure the people at HQ that the war in Europe will not affect the running of Gung Ho.

*

'I only came to China to have a look,' George Hogg says, snorting with laughter. 'Now look at me. A full-time, unpaid employee of Gung Ho.'

Rewi grins. He remembers that laugh from the meeting in Wuhan. According to Agnes – whose designs on Gung Ho's newest recruit seem to have come to nothing – George was called Pig at school not because of his surname but because of that snort of his. 'My parents expect me back,' George goes on. 'They think I'm just doing what lots of young men do, post-Oxford. Amusing myself with a bit of travel until Real Life takes over.'

They're talking in the room Rewi stays in when he's in Baoji – the nearest thing he has to a home. A bed, a table and chair, a washstand, a fire burning in the grate – luxuries compared to what most people in China have. A small bronze Buddha stands on the table next to Rewi's battered Remington typewriter, along with a pile of dog-eared books, pen and ink, and a few sheets of scribbled-over paper.

Inevitably war is their main subject: the Japanese advance; the stalled war in Europe; the difficulties besetting the United Front. But Gung Ho is never far from their minds. With the creation of INDUSCO and the success of Ida Pruitt's drive to get branches established around the world, there is reason for optimism. Not that George is ever anything but optimistic. When Rewi announces that Ida has succeeded in getting the American president's wife onto the board of INDUSCO, George lets out another of his delighted snorts. 'She's even press-ganged the owner of *Time* and *Life*,' Rewi goes on. 'Not that

I think much of Henry Luce and his millions. Altogether too keen on putting Chiang on the cover of his magazines.' (He appeared 10 times.) 'I'll take his money though. No scruples on that account.'

They do the numbers, calculating that the 3000 co-operatives already up and running will have grown to a 100,000 by the end of next year. Especially if Ida succeeds in signing up more of Hollywood's Big Names as donors. She's already nailed Sam Goldwyn and David Selznick. Now she's got Louis B. Mayer in her sights.

'Can I ask a question?' George says as Rewi gets up to make tea. 'Are you being paid?'

Rewi gestures round the room. 'Does it look as if I am? The KMT only let me use this because they like to keep an eye on me. Every time I come back I expect to find my typewriter gone and someone else shacked up here.'

George nods. He knows how Rewi lives. It's how he lives himself when HQ send him out on inspection tours. Without the generosity of the peasants he would die of starvation.

'Funny what you can get used to,' Rewi muses. He's thinking of his comfortable Shanghai life and how the thought of living like the Chinese used to scare the bejesus out of him. Now all the things that used to spook him – bed bugs, cockroaches, mosquitoes, rats, lice – are just part of daily life. It's because of the lice that he now shaves his hair.

For a few moments, while their tea infuses, they talk about the best ways to counter the ever-present threat of malaria. Rewi, whose supply of Keatings Insect Powder has long since run out, swears by the old method of tying a piece of cloth dipped in insect repellant to the bedpost. George reckons burning paraffin is more effective. They don't say anything about typhus. They both know there's no way they can protect themselves against that pernicious predator.

When they finally part for the night Rewi, listening to George's retreating footsteps, feels a pang of sympathy for Agnes. Easy to see why she fell for him. Six feet tall, a mop of fair curly hair, penetrating blue eyes ... 'Those whom the gods love ...'

CHAPTER THIRTY-SIX

IN the months following his meeting with George Hogg, Rewi will continue his travels across China, pushing himself to the limit of exhaustion, sustained by the kindness of the people he meets, the beauty of the mountains, the seasonal costume changes of the trees and, come summer, the delight of jumping into a lake or river when heat overcomes him. Sometimes it's not just heat that overcomes him: it's homesickness, not for New Zealand – his home is China now – but for his boys. He'd felt sick when they left. Alan was the first to go. Then, following in Elder Brother's footsteps – just as Rewi had done 20 years earlier in New Zealand – Mike walked out the door. Now, when he thinks of his sons, the nausea returns. There's been no communication for over a year. If he knew where the Eighth Route Army was he might be able to find them, but no one knows where it is from one day to the next. So he keeps moving. With thousands of co-operatives to visit, meetings to attend, loans to arrange, training schools to establish, self-serving officials to pacify or fob off, he has no choice. Will he ever be part of a family again?

*

By the middle of 1940 Rewi has become a cog in a wheel, admittedly an important cog but no longer the prime mover and shaker. His biggest problem is making sure the money raised by INDUSCO gets to the right places. The Alley temper is never far away when he thinks how much has been squeezed from the latest worldwide 'Bowl of Rice' campaign organised by Ida. Ten thousand US dollars – much of it funnelled through Dr Kung's bank – reduced to half by the greed of KMT officials. He can't complain, not officially. He knows how business is done in China. It all comes down to personal relations. 'If you are on good terms everything is made convenient, if not you can never get anything done at all.'[1]

But Gung Ho is a success. Co-operatives close to the Red Army base in Yan'an are keeping up the supply of blankets, clothing, medical supplies, candles, paraffin, oil, canvas, mosquito nets, boots, bullets (the soldiers call them 'black dates'), casings for grenades … Others, spread across the country, are producing coal, steel, pottery, tools, textiles, sugar, ink, agricultural equipment, fertiliser, glassware, paper, leather goods, rice flour … 'Amazing what the possession of a couple of old lathes, a hand drill press and a few bench tools can do for a whole bunch of refugees,' Rewi writes in a letter home.[2] 'Co-operative days, co-operative nights / Co-operative lice, co-operative fights ...'[3] The lines come unbidden, stored in his memory till he can find a moment, and a scrap of paper, to record them.

Writing reports on the progress of Gung Ho, Rewi is careful to emphasise the positive. Too many people in the KMT want him to fail. When a co-operative collapses, either through bad leadership or because a landlord, seeing a chance to make a profit, has wangled his way in and taken over, Rewi dismisses it as an aberration. But in the wee small hours of too many sleepless nights, he's not so sanguine. Typhus, malaria, cholera, liver-fluke, beri beri, blackwater fever, scabies – how can Gung Ho hope to survive when even nature is so keen on killing?

'Second night on this boat I suddenly feel very much alone,' he writes in his memoir, quoting from his diary of the time. 'A feeling I dread rather and try to avoid by being busy – usually very unsuccessfully. But a day – a cold day of inaction – does not improve things and I am left wondering what sort of a Don Quixote I am tilting at windmills all over the place ... I am concerned as ever of the immense importance of our job under any circumstances – war or peace. It holds the seeds of a real future. But I wish I did not feel so futile in the face of it all.'

The one thing he never feels is self-pity. He only has to think of the children he encounters every day to put that bogey to rest: babies dying of starvation; girls sold into brothels or as sex slaves to landlords; buffalo boys whipped for the loss of an animal in a flood; black-faced 'ants' emerging from coal, copper and tin mines; the factory children he saw in Shanghai ... One boy in particular haunts him – a lad who looked about six but was probably much older, his body covered in scabies, his legs swollen from the beri beri that was surely going to end his life within months. Rewi, in his role as factory inspector, had managed to get him and one other little boy into hospital. With nothing to call his own but three tiny torch bulbs, the boy insisted Rewi take them as thanks. 'Please ... they are good fun to play with.'[4]

Rewi kept the bulbs – two red, one green. They were his corrective; the lasso that captured and killed the demon doubt.

CHAPTER THIRTY-SEVEN

'REWI!' George, jumping up from his desk at Gung Ho headquarters, opens his arms as if about to hug him. But he's English, so he doesn't. 'Where've you been hiding?' he asks. 'Last I heard you were up near Yan'an.'

'You look well.'

'More than I can say for you.'

It takes less than a minute for Rewi to agree to spend the night at George's lodgings. His own, as he'd predicted, have been commandeered. 'I don't have a proper bath but there's a tub of sorts,' George says. 'And I make a mean pancake.'

'You telling me I need a wash?'

'How long is it since you had a shave?'

'Lost my razor,' Rewi answers.

Walking back through the rough streets of Baoji, huddled in their padded jackets – autumn has arrived early this year – George talks excitedly about his work for Gung Ho and the articles he's been sending back to England for publication. They seem to have agreed not to talk about the war in Europe. With news so hard to come by, all they'd be doing is speculating.

As they approach the railway line with its sorry crowd of refugees, George starts muttering, more to himself than to Rewi. 'The world has to know what's happening here,' he says. 'We can't fix this on our own.'

'I'm afraid the world has other things on its mind,' Rewi answers glumly.

For a while after that they're silent, but then Rewi, in an attempt at distraction, asks George how much he knows about the history of Baoji, one of the oldest cities in China. The stratagem works. Conjuring up the Baoji of the Zhou dynasty, when it stood at the centre of the trade network along the Old Silk Road, they manage, for a few precious minutes, to forget the misery that surrounds them.

'"Sweet to ride forth at evening from the wells …"' George quotes.

Rewi looks at him in surprise. '"When shadows pass gigantic on the sand …"'

'You know it?'

'Learned it as a boy.'

George reaches into his pocket and takes out a copy of *Palgrave's Golden Treasury*. 'My bible,' he says. He opens it at a dog-eared page. Rewi recognises the poem they've just been quoting – James Elroy Flecker's 'The Golden Journey to Samarkand'. Only the best-known verses are printed in the book, but that doesn't stop them stumbling through the rest, making up what they can't remember.

George's lodgings consist of two sparsely furnished rooms in a boarding house in the Chinese part of town. But, as promised, there's a tub for Rewi to wash in, and a primitive stove on which George sets about making willow-flower tea. Rewi's guessing he must have smelt pretty bad because George is still going on about it, shouting from the other room, telling him what he already knows – that the Chinese think Westerners, even the clean ones, smell bad. 'You know what they call us don't you?' George says.

'*Yang guizi*?' Rewi guesses.

'Pale-skinned nomads.'

'Well, I'm a nomad all right but hardly pale any more. More like a redskin.'

Rewi had forgotten how easy it was to be with George. Not usually one to hold the floor, he finds himself, over a meal of pancakes and Chinese cabbage, telling him about the cave house, the *yaodong*, he's built in Shuangshipu, a village 80 kilometres or so south of Baoji. It's part of the training school he's established there. Trouble is, the school is failing. A succession of disastrous headmasters, coupled with the refugee crisis in the village, has brought it to the brink of closure.

As he talks a plan starts to form in his mind. It's not the location of the school that's the problem – the Japanese have shown no interest in bombing Shuangshipu – it's the leadership. What if George were to become headmaster? Other schools – in Baoji, Luoyang, Lanzhou, Chengdu and Chongqing – are also struggling, but if the school at Shuangshipu were to be run efficiently, it could become the benchmark for all the others.

Like Rewi, when ambushed by other people's plans for him, George resists at first. He doesn't see himself as headmaster material. He's not even a trained teacher. Besides, he already has a job, an argument Rewi once made himself but now brushes aside. 'You'll achieve far more as a headmaster than mucking about here,' he insists. ('When Alleys want you to do something …')

That night Rewi sleeps on George's mattress while George wraps himself up in his bed roll on the floor. In the morning, over a bowl of congee, Rewi, afraid that George might have had second thoughts, launches into a description of Shuangshipu's hauntingly beautiful mountains, shaped and moulded from the thick dust blown south by Gobi desert winds. The caves hollowed out of the loess hills will be familiar to George. Baoji's hills are full of them. What might not be so familiar is the history of those caves, providing shelter – cool in summer, warm in winter – and protection from rapacious landlords and murdering bandits for more than 4000 years. Right back to the Shang dynasty.

'I take it you're thinking Baoji will fall to the Japanese,' George says, when Rewi finally runs out of steam.

Is that what clinches it? Rewi will never know. But moments later he is shaking hands with the new headmaster of the Shuangshipu Bailie School.

CHAPTER THIRTY-EIGHT

'HO-KE, Ho-Ke!' The boys of the Shuangshipu school choir swarm around George, pulling him up on to the stage, urging him to sing one of his own songs. George, their chorus master, snorts with laughter. They have just sung, for the benefit of visiting officials, a medley of songs ranging from 'Old McDonald had a Farm' to songs from the Taiping rebellion and the current war of resistance.

It's August 1943. George has been headmaster of the school for nine months. The difference in the way things were before his arrival and now can be measured in the smiles of the boys, and the daily buzz from the power plant, the cotton-spinning plant, the engineering factory, the machine shop, the brick-making factory, the kiln, the tannery, the leather shop, the flour mill and the printing press. Production is up by 500 per cent. What was a barely functioning training school is now an essential cog in the war machine. There are new dormitories, a brand-new clinic stocked with plentiful supplies of sulphur ointment (principal weapon in George's war on scabies), a revamped bathhouse, several new classrooms, a baseball court and a kitchen garden. The sign displayed in the classrooms can be seen in all the schools Rewi has established: 'Create and Analyse. Hands and Minds' – a quote from Joseph Bailie.

Rewi, sitting among the 60-plus pupils, knows he's in for a treat: George is a fine baritone. He watches as George gently persuades the accompanist, who is keen to join in on the school's only musical instrument, the two-stringed *erhu*, that he's better off singing alone. Then, adopting a mock-heroic pose, he starts to sing:

A life on the ocean wave, a home on the rolling deep,
Where the scattered waters rave, and the winds their revels keep …

The applause that follows this song of a sea none of the boys has ever seen brings tears to Rewi's eyes. This is happiness, he thinks. This is the elixir that silly old Emperor Qin spent his life searching for. Youth. Hope. The future. Best thing I ever did, pushing George into taking over the school. If I could I'd spend all my time here. Not be dashing from one struggling co-op to another.

The war is getting closer. Every day more refugees pour into Shuangshipu. People are living on what they can scavenge – herbs, weeds, insects, tree-bark, straw. Tales of Japanese brutality circulate like dust – prisoners bayonetted, women raped, whole cities burned to the ground. 'The most terrible thing,' Rewi writes in his diary, 'is how the Japanese seem to enjoy the whole torture business. Squeezing blocks of wood between prisoner's fingers; feeding gasoline and pepper up their noses …'[1] So acute is the food shortage George has several times had to bike over the bandit-infested Qingling mountain pass to Baoji to plead for cash to feed the students. One small kitchen garden is hardly adequate to feed 60 growing boys. Rewi knows the risks George takes – he faces the same threat as he travels around the co-operatives. Luckily, the one time George was ambushed he managed to fight off his attackers, leaving the cash, sewn into the lining of his trousers, untouched.

But there are no bombs. No flags flying on the mountains to warn of the approach of war planes. No enemy soldiers marching up the Jialing Valley. At night the setting sun turns the tawny hills red, spreading beauty over the workaday world. There's no end to the pitiful flow of refugees, but there's usually a child or two flying a kite, waving it at the sun as it disappears over the peaks. And on warm evenings men squat on the pavements, playing chequers, while others bring out their caged song-birds, filling the air with a chirruping chorus not unlike the singing in a Chinese opera, an art form Rewi has grown to love. On the steps of the old Buddhist temple the better-off refugees have set up stalls selling cigarettes and cheap cloth. They call out to Rewi, a familiar sight on his bicycle, ribbing him about his big nose, demanding to know how he manages to eat rice with such an obstruction in the way.

Not for the first time Rewi marvels at the Chinese ability to laugh in the face of daily misery. Last Chinese New Year when a puppet show came to the village the atmosphere was positively festive. A large crowd of locals and refugees, with Rewi, George and the boys from the school in excited attendance, gathered in the market square to watch the unfolding of the story of the cheeky, wand-waving Monkey King. Death, constant companion of the refugee, took a back seat that day.

Nothing can be done, of course, about the fleas and sandflies that keep up their relentless biting, but the boys, thanks to George's insistence on hygiene, are free of lice. Free of evil spirits too, if the women waving their willow branches outside the school gates are to be believed. Whenever they see Rewi, they grin and wag their fingers at him. They like the high nosed foreigner even if he doesn't believe in their spirits. Rewi wishes they'd wave their willow branches at the KMT officials who keep turning up unannounced on their doorstep, bent on conscripting the older boys into their rotten army. George has devised a signal to warn the boys when the KMT come sniffing around. Two short blows on the whistle and the older boys quietly leave their machines and melt into the hills. Rewi's approach is not so subtle. He assumes the white-man arrogance he so conspicuously lacks and orders them off the premises. 'This is a KMT-funded school,' he shouts. 'Madame Sun Yatsen is our patron!'

So far they haven't lost a single boy, but Rewi is under no illusion. His claim that the school is KMT funded fools no one. These days it's not just Rewi whom Chiang suspects of being a communist, it's also the young English headmaster, George Hogg.

'They're not getting their grubby hands on a single one of our lads,' Rewi mutters, joining George in the cave house at the end of the concert. 'They'll have to kill me first.'

George stoops to light the fire under the *kang*. It's been a long day. The arrival of the officials from HQ was preceded by a far less welcome visit – from the KMT's 'running dogs', as Rewi calls them. Such visits are becoming an almost weekly event, forcing both men to face the likelihood that they will have to move the school even further into the interior. The boys know the score. The communists – whom many of them will join when their training is finished – have no need to conscript. They don't leave their sick and wounded to die, or abandon them when the food runs out. George, whose Quaker beliefs are central to his character, is uneasy about the communist insistence on dialectical materialism as both explanation and remedy for the suffering in the world, but he can't deny the evidence of his eyes.

'Did you listen to the shortwave today?' he asks as the heady smell of burning dung fills the room. 'You were right. Japs are practically on our doorstep.'

'Then we're between the devil and the deep blue sea,' Rewi comments gloomily. 'Either the KMT come and take our boys away, or the Nips come and it's "Goodnight Irene".'

*

The Alley temper, occasionally on show when a boy ignores instructions, is never far away when the subject of KMT conscription comes up. Rewi has seen too much of it. He knows their methods and he knows what awaits the unfortunate lad hauled away from the fields on the order of the local warlord or conscripting officer. He saw it when he lived in Shanghai. Now he's seeing it again in this remote corner of China. What sickens him is the knowledge that forced conscription has been going on for centuries. It's there in the songs and the poetry. If for no other reason than to bring such practices to an end, a revolution is looking more and more like a good thing.

'If Rewi Alley didn't come back with a new conscript story himself, the people who had been out with him were sure to have one: the young boy shivering with malaria and covered with scabies whom Rewi hauled up onto the truck, despite the outraged admonishments of the local press gang; the officer be-labouring a sick conscript with a pole whom Rewi laid flat in the dust ...'[2]

Years later Rewi will translate a poem written by the thirteenth-century poet Song Chiu-Chia, and invest it with some of his own fury on the subject of forced conscription:

Lazing away the day
under the shade of a willow tree,
wearing neither cap nor socks;
drinking wine in the morning
in one village, then again in the evening
in another; suddenly being seized
escorted to an office,
shoved onto a blind horse
promptly marched off to the very centre
of the battlefield ...[3]

*

Through the winter of 1942–43 life at the school in Shuangshipu goes on smoothly enough. But by the time summer comes it's obvious to Rewi and George they've reached the point of no return. Rewi's dismissal in September 1942 from the post of Gung Ho's Technical Advisor to the Executive Yuan, a move engineered by the KMT, was the clearest signal yet that the government was gunning for him and his school. He still has to report to INDUSCO on the progress of the co-ops, but in government circles his voice is no longer heeded.

When Rewi suggests that the school be moved further west, into Mongolia if need be, George agrees, though he considers Gansu province on the Mongolian border far enough. Rewi doesn't argue. Gansu is rich in minerals. It has coal and copper and oil. And the Japanese are unlikely to drop bombs so far from their bases.

Trouble is, Rewi thinks, as he lies awake on the *kang*, moving the school, lock stock and barrel, is a transport nightmare. Even if we had a place to go to. And given how things stand with the KMT, our chances of getting funding are less than nil … A miracle, that's what's needed, he concludes, as sleep starts to claim him. The kind Nurse He believes in.

CHAPTER THIRTY-NINE
15 April 2017

ONCE again we are visiting places in geographical but not chronological order: Beijing before Shanghai, now Shuangshipu before Baoji. Rewi had been coming and going in Shuangshipu as early as 1938, but it was not until 1941 that he really started to think of his cave house there as home.

We have been staying in the Shangri-la Hotel. Because of yesterday's delay we are being taken on a lightning visit to the house Rewi shared with George Hogg – we should have seen it yesterday afternoon. After this we will be driven to Baoji, where we are to board the overnight train to Shandan.

There's a certain amount of tension about. Some of us can't get a clear answer as to exactly where we are. Is this Shuangshipu or Fengxian? One appears to be the name of the village, the other the name of the county, but then we're told the village and the county share the same name, so we're no wiser. This will happen again as we move closer to the border with Mongolia. Village names become interchangeable with newly created county names. To add to the confusion, names from the past exist alongside their present-day replacements, common practice having proved stronger than government decrees. As for spelling, that too is all over the place. We're headed for the place most closely associated with Rewi, where he established his most famous school. But is it San Dan, or Sandan, or Shandan or Shan Dan? Most likely it's all four. In this remote corner of China names are as fluid as history itself.

On the way to Rewi's cave house Dave tells us about the work the NZCFS is doing in this area: supporting the newly revived co-operative movement; helping with disaster relief after earthquakes – a regular occurrence in this part of China. Rewi, the inspiration behind the various China Friendship Societies all over the world, would be quietly gratified. When, post-Liberation, his Shandan Bailie School was taken over by the Oil Ministry, leaving him effectively without a job, his heart was broken. 'One does die quite a number of times before the actual demise,' he wrote in a letter home. 'We go in stages I guess.'[1]

(Thirty years later the co-operative movement, kick-started by the then 85-year-old Rewi, was revived. Rewi had waited a long time for Gung Ho's phoenix to rise from the ashes. Finally, at the end of his life, it happened. Three things contributed to this miraculous re-birth. The first was Rewi's growing fame, fuelled by his friendship with Premier Deng Xiaoping. The second, a consequence of that friendship, was that he'd recently been made the first ever honorary citizen of Beijing. The third was the involvement of China Friendship Societies around the world, all of them eager to see Gung Ho up and running again. Within just a few years the school at Shandan was re-built, George Hogg's grave, defiled during the Cultural Revolution, was restored, and Rewi was once again the titular head of Gung Ho – 'Honorary Advisor to the Association of Chinese Industrial Co-operatives', to give him his full title.)

It will be many weeks before I manage to stitch together the pieces of the Gung Ho story, its rise and fall and rise again, mirroring that of its famous 'midwife'. Snippets, dropped like coded messages into the conversations I have at Rewi's cave home, make sense only when the various threads come together.

As we walk up the hill to the house Rewi shared with George Hogg, we are accompanied not just by officials but by local people anxious to shake our hands and tell us, in fractured English, or with the help of a translator, about their memories of Rewi. 'Without Rewi I would not be here,' one woman tells me. Her father was one of the many boys Rewi and George rescued from abandoned orphanages, coal mines and factories where few survived beyond their teens. 'Without the Communist Party there would not be a new China,' a man walking beside me asserts. Near the top of the hill a group of women are busy stripping the flowers from willow branches. 'For tea,' they inform us in Mandarin. 'Delicious.'

*

Shuangshipu today is a thriving market town, but when Rewi and George lived here it was an insignificant farming village with a population, before the influx of refugees, of less than a thousand. It was not, however, insignificant to the communists. In 1932 it was the scene of a successful uprising against the KMT. Two years later it became a place of refuge for Mao and his troops on the Long March. Even if nothing else had happened, Shuangshipu's place in China's revolutionary story would have been assured.

But more did happen. After he persuaded George to take over the running of the school, Rewi was faced with the task of moving as many of Baoji's co-operative factories as possible to the comparative safety of Shuangshipu. Having already moved everything from Wuhan to Baoji, he knew what to do.

And this time, having made many journeys between Baoji and Shuangshipu in the course of his Gung Ho work, the route was as familiar to him as the back of his hand. Driving a truck over the bandit-infested mountains would be a breeze compared to riding a bicycle, his usual form of transport. (I picture Rewi, pushing his bike up the very hill we walked on, sweat pouring down his back, relief that he has arrived unscathed washing over him as he pushes open the cave-house door. And I picture him jumping down from the cab of the old Soviet truck he has managed to purloin, similarly relieved that the precious convoy of donkey carts piled high with factory equipment has survived bandits and wild animals to reach its new home in Shuangshipu.)

By the end of 1942 Shuangshipu's caves are echoing not just with the voices of students eager to learn but to the clatter and thump of machinery. On cave walls the words 'Create and Analyse. Hands and Minds' have appeared alongside slogans left behind by Red Army troops: 'Resist the Enemy'; 'Down with Landlords'; 'Divide the Land'. Sometimes, beneath the slogans, older markings have revealed themselves – frescoes painted by refugees from earlier wars and famines, a palimpsest of Chinese history spanning 4000 years. In one particularly striking illustration, Rewi has identified what looks like a black cloud moving in flying formation above a field of wheat as a swarm of locusts poised to strip the fields of every last bit of nourishment.

In the course of his work at Shuangshipu, Rewi will befriend a Red Army officer named Xi Zhongxun. He will not live long enough to see his friend's son – Xi Jinping – become 'President of China' (one of 12 official titles bestowed on him), but he will see Xi Zhongxun, a founder member of the Communist Party, declared an 'immortal'. When, in 1947, at the height of the civil war, Xi Senior agrees to become an honorary principal of the school at Shandan, Rewi feels – wrongly – that his Gung Ho training programme is now safe. The KMT will go on trying to take it over or shut it down, but Rewi has no doubt who is going to come out on top in the current struggle. With the KMT defeated the school, surely, will live forever.

*

And now here we are, standing outside Rewi's house. I try to feel his presence but there is too big a crowd and too much information, written and spoken, to feel anything more than slight irritation. The place has become a shrine. The house, built out from the cave entrance, is neatly bricked and cleaner than it would have been when Rewi and George occupied it. There were no bricks then, just wattle and daub. With its freshly swept courtyard and herb garden this could be any well-kept local cave house. Its one distinguishing feature is the yellow Gung Ho symbol hanging over the front window.

When Rewi lived here he would sometimes wake to find his profile, or George's, complete with large, hooked nose, painted on the outside wall. At other times well-wishers would paint white circles on the door to scare away wolves, or *yinyang* signs to encourage prosperity. Rewi always left this well-intentioned graffiti untouched. He was not superstitious, but he respected the old ways. Everywhere he went in rural China he encountered *Tai Shan* stones placed at the entrance to villages to ward off evil spirits. 'Don't Dare' were the words carved into them. Living under the yolk of feudalism, with flood and famine ever-present threats, country folk needed all the help they could get.

Stepping inside I shrug off my irritability and set about trying to imagine Rewi's life here. A simple table and chairs, a paraffin lamp, a desk with an old typewriter sitting on it, a bedroom with a heated *kang*, an outhouse … But it's too clean, too tidy. The windows should be made of paper, not glass. Where are the photos of Peg Snow and Ida Pruitt, of Henry Luce and his wife, snapped outside a towel-making co-op in Baoji? What we're seeing on the walls today are placards, maps and photos, displayed for the benefit of tourists. There are no fleas, no rats (so many, Rewi complained, they were like household pets), no lime spread on the floor as disinfectant. Wall niches hold artfully placed lamps, not the ancient figurines and tiny Buddhas, unearthed during the building of the house, that Rewi liked to have around him … Photos of Rewi and George Hogg, displayed like icons, confirm that the home they shared has become a sacred space, the last thing either of them would have wanted.

'This way please, Alley whānau, this way.'

We are on a tight schedule. I sense that someone might be blamed if we don't make up the time lost because of yesterday's delays. Perhaps that's why I can't dream my way back into the past …

Deep purple hills, clear-cut ridges
against a moonlit sky, from out
of the valley centre, the little hill
rising like some ancient grave-mound;
and a thousand memories strong, moving,

return in force to me;
coming through the tall corn
after a singsong in the school
on a summer's Saturday evening,
and Chang Yu-lin jumping down from
the terrace above, square on my back,
full of the joy of being fourteen ...[2]

*

Statistics. Handed out to us like sweets. We are on our way to see the factories Rewi built in the early days of Gung Ho, deep inside Baoji's network of caves. In all, 26 caves, each measuring around 100 metres deep and five metres wide, were commandeered to house machinery. Connected by tunnels, they became hubs of industry, with over 10,000 workers employed making munitions, blankets, textiles, supplying the Red Army with the means to survive. Baoji, as Rewi had predicted, was bombed, but not one bomb fell on the factories hidden in the caves.

We are surrounded by officials. Speeches are made inside the caves, swept clean (we suspect) for our arrival. The echo created by the tunnels stretching behind us adds to my feeling of claustrophobia (vertigo's twin). There are lights, and remnants of the machines that would have made the mountains hum, but this place too has become a shrine. I try to fill it with real people doing real work, but imagination fails me.

Emerging into the clear mountain air, we are surrounded by even more people. Locals, curious to see what's going on, have joined the army of officials. At one point Irene comes up and whispers in my ear. 'I have a story for you.' We agree to sit together on our next long bus ride.

'The caves were abandoned after the war,' a man with good English informs me. 'Forgotten about. It's only recently they've been opened up again.'

Not for the first time I wonder about the way history is used not just by the Chinese government, but by all governments, as a tool to promote their policies and cement their hold on power. That Rewi has been a convenient propaganda tool for governments after the Cultural Revolution is obvious. What we have seen so far – the elevation of this Foreign Friend of China to almost divine status – has left us in no doubt. Rewi the Internationalist has become part and parcel of China's drive to establish itself as the dominant trading power in the world.

It's hard to imagine what Rewi's role would have been had he lived into the twenty-first century. It is not just the word *tongzhi* (comrade) that isn't heard any more, it's the ideas associated with that word. Rewi fought hard for the co-ops to be non-profit making. He could see no justification for a profit incentive unless the intention was to plough money straight back into the venture itself. When the co-operative movement was revived in the mid-1980s he described it, with some of his old fervour, as an alternative to the 'turbo capitalism' taking hold in China as a consequence of Deng's reforms. 'At present, internationally, an evil wind is blowing which says that China is rapidly becoming a capitalist economy,' he wrote in *Rewi Alley on Gung Ho*. 'Gung Ho revival will counter this. We either have Gung Ho co-operatives or purely capitalist companies – we cannot have both.'

Perhaps Rewi didn't understand the Chinese as well as he thought he did. Money, in twenty-first-century China, is central. Greed hasn't disappeared, it's widened its scope. Not everyone is greedy. But the struggle to survive is still too recent for anything, even food on the table, to be taken for granted.

The poster that followed us around China.
Photo by Zeke Alley

In Tiananmen Square on our first day in China.
Photo by Ken Watkin

Whanau at the Beijing home of Madame Sun Yatsen (Soong Chingling). Michael Crook at left with red cap, Dave Bromwich on far right. Jocelyn is sitting on the swing at right, and I'm on the other swing. Photo by Zeke Alley

Zeke in Rewi's chair in his Beijing apartment. Photo by Zeke Alley

Dave Bromwich talking to the whanau on the tour bus.
Photo by Zeke Alley

With Rewi's foster son, Lao San.
Photo by Ken Watkin

The whanau enjoying a riverside lunch, en route to Shuangshipu.
Photo by Ken Watkin

Ross and Judy
(brother- and sister-
in-law) on the train
to Shandan.
Photo by Zeke Alley

Photo by Ken Watkin

Cousins Sarah and
Rachel riding camels
in Gansu Province.

Photo by Maurice Alley

ABOVE: Statue in Shandan celebrating the revolutionary struggle. Rewi in at front left, next to Xi Zhongxun, father of China's current leader, Xi Jinping.

Photo by Zeke Alley

With my three first cousins in Shandan: from left Jocelyn, Ross, myself, Zeke. Behind us is a statue of Rewi and George Hogg.

Photo by Ken Watkin

With Rewi's grandchildren, Hailong (Mike) and Haiying.

Photo by Ken Watkin

With Michael Crook in Lanzhou.

Photo by Ken Watkin

BELOW: Ross and Jocelyn (brother and sister) reading one of Rewi's poems live on national television.

Photo by Ken Watkin

Waiting for our train at Beijing Railway Station.

Photo by Ken Watkin

Ross on the piano at our Shanghai hotel.

Photo by Zeke Alley

CHAPTER FORTY

WHEN Rewi, in September 1942, was sacked from his executive position in Gung Ho, his former champion, Madame Chiang, did not come to his rescue. With the number of co-operatives countrywide reckoned to be over 100,000, Gung Ho had become too successful. Learning that the Number One Red Bandit, Mao Zedong, had declared the movement 'a revolution in productivity development' must have sent Chiang into a tail spin. 'It is worthwhile for us to consider whether this co-operative method can be widely applied in our factories and farms,' Mao wrote.[1] To Chiang those words were treason. Gung Ho wasn't just a communist cell, it was a government in waiting!

Perhaps Madame Chiang did attempt to defend Rewi. We will never know. What we do know is that Rewi, shadowed by Chiang's spies, travelled to Yan'an in January 1942 to meet with Mao. They talked through the night about the war of resistance, Gung Ho's contribution and the future of China. 'Why would he go to Yan'an if he weren't in league with the communists?' I can hear Chiang shouting at his wife. Would she have reminded him that the KMT were in league with the communists too? That there was a United Front? I would like to think she might have tried.

But Chiang, for all his power, can't get rid of Rewi. He still has his position as secretary of INDUSCO's international committee. Not even the Generalissimo can sack him from that. Too many powerful Americans involved, people who think Rewi is God's gift. Chiang is no fool. His government is dependent on American aid and American arms. All he can do is paint Rewi as a communist – the 'enemy within' – and wait for the Americans to come to their senses.

'The number of people who want to knife me and everyone who works in our show seems to be increasing,' Rewi writes in a letter home. 'Jap planes are the smallest of our annoyances – politics the worst by a long shot.'[2] From this time on, as China drifts in and out of civil war, he is a man with a price on his head. In a script written by Chiang's propaganda machine, the one-time friend of Madame Chiang and partner, at least in theory, of the KMT, has become 'a British agent trying to get hold of Chinese industry, a diabolically clever engineer, a sentimental religious adventurer out to make a name for himself at the expense of the Chinese people, a sex maniac with a wife in every city, a Japanese agent, a communist sympathiser, and a gangster who was piling up a fortune in banks in India …'[3]

The truth of these accusations didn't matter; it was the spreading of 'alternative facts' that counted. During one of Rewi's many inspection tours of the co-ops, he was stripped, beaten and left on the roadside to die. During another he was taken prisoner, with what could have been fatal consequences had he not managed to escape by disguising himself as a Buddhist monk. No wonder he wrote home advising his family not to believe all the negative publicity about him. What he didn't reveal was that the KMT, having failed in its attempts to intimidate him, had offered him a large sum of money and a first-class fare back to New Zealand. 'Don't care what it costs,' I imagine Chiang shouting. 'Just get that red-haired bandit out of the country!'

That Rewi, following his sacking from Gung Ho, simply carried on his work for INDUSCO must have sent Chiang into a tailspin. With his nemesis no longer in a position to harass officials handling Gung Ho's overseas funds, he'd hoped the organisation would simply starve to death. Again he was wrong. Gung Ho, now indelibly tarred with the communist brush, may have lost credibility as a 'middle way', but that didn't seem to bother its mostly American donors. The syphoning off continued, but enough got through to keep Gung Ho going for another decade. As for Rewi, being labelled a communist didn't bother him in the least. 'I never had time to play politics,' he writes in his memoir, 'being quite ruthless in pursuit of a goal.'

After the initial encounter in Yan'an, Rewi would meet Mao again several times. There's a photo of him and Edgar Snow sharing a birthday meal with Mao; another of the two men shaking hands. But Rewi has nothing to say about these meetings. 'I'm not like a journalist meeting the great, hanging on his lips,' he will say to Geoff Chapple when pressed for details. Perhaps, after his firing by the KMT, he got a chance to tell Mao not just about Chiang's bribe but also about the invitation he'd received from the New Zealand Labour Party, which he suspected Chiang might have engineered. 'What invitation was that?' Mao asks.

'One that frightened me to death,' Rewi answers. 'To stand for parliament.'[4] I like to think it would have raised a laugh.

*

Politics is not Rewi's only headache in 1942–43. More immediately urgent is the problem of moving the Shuangshipu school to a place of safety.

Unsurprisingly, given his recent demotion, Rewi gets the brush-off from Gung Ho officials in Baoji. He's made enemies, notably Peter Townsend, INDUSCO's publicity secretary, who objected to his insistence that funds go to the schools in preference to the cooperatives. Many in the organisation agree with him. The international donors, on whom Gung Ho now depends, gave money in the belief that it was going to co-ops. But Rewi is adamant. If the schools fail the whole movement will fail also. He knows what people are saying about him – that he's become a fanatic – but he doesn't care.

Then one day, late in the summer of 1943, an Englishman turns up on the doorstep of the cave house at Shuangshipu and a way ahead is found. *Yo Banfa!* – there is a way!

It will become the title of Rewi's first published book.

*

'You have a story to tell me,' I remind Irene when, the day after our visits to Shuangshipu and Baoji, I manage to sit next to her on the bus. 'Something that happened at the cave factories?'

Irene smiles. She's one of those people who, like Jim Bertram, manages to look elegant no matter how hot and dusty the day. The story she has to tell will unsettle me. Like so many of the things I hear in China it doesn't fit with other things I've been told. We have come to the land of paradox, I decide. Things aren't supposed to 'fit'.

Her story centres around a young Chinese man she got talking to during our tour of the Baoji cave factories. She'd noticed him when we first arrived, standing with a woman she'd assumed to be his mother. But when, at the end of the tour, she went over to him and said, 'Ni Hao', he answered in Australian-accented English. 'He seemed nervous,' she tells me, in her own charmingly accented Danish-English. 'Kept looking over his shoulder.'

His name is David. Brought up in Australia, he's come back to China to claim his land – the land we are all standing on. The factories have been scheduled by the county for demolition, that's why he's come. He opposes the decision. He wants the factories to be preserved …

I interrupt Irene. What she's just said doesn't make sense. Surely the officials who showed us around the cave factories would have told us if that was what the county was planning? Or is this another piece of the past destined to be quietly erased, like the Tiananmen Square massacre? Perhaps the fact that the factories were the brainchild of a foreigner, however revered, explains the county's decision. But that presupposes that David's story is true, and I'm not sure I think it is.

Irene, of course, is as unable as I am to answer these questions.

She goes on, telling me that the conversation she was having with David was interrupted by the sudden re-appearance of the woman she'd seen with him earlier. 'Your mother?' she enquired, indicating the woman hurrying towards them. 'My minder,' he murmured. 'Better make yourself scarce.'

Irene looks at me, gauging my reaction. I shrug. *Minder.* Ominous word. But I'm still confused. There's no private ownership of land in China, so how can David claim the land is his?

Things will become a little clearer after another bus conversation during which Dave gives us a snapshot of how property law works in China (though, like so much else in this challenging country, the law isn't a fixed thing, it's 'evolving'). As to the question of why David, returning to his native land, had to have a minder, there's no answer to that.

'It's important to be comfortable with uncertainty,' the contemporary Chinese-British novelist Xiaolu Guo has declared.[5]

I'm beginning to see what she means.

CHAPTER FORTY-ONE
15–16 April 2017

OVER the next 24 hours I manage to talk with both Sarah and Rachel. We share the usual travellers' complaints: delays; swipe cards locked in rooms; mislaid tickets; lost sunglasses; the lack of internet access; the lack of world news, of news from home, of antibiotics, of decent coffee; the relentless adherence to a timetable we had no part in devising ('Hurry now please, Alley whānau. This way …'). Everywhere we go we are given presents, usually books about Rewi, but sometimes objects so bulky we have no choice but to leave them behind. In Shandan we are presented with red felt horses – the horse is Shandan's symbol – the size of small dogs. Burdened as we already are with luggage, most of us opt to leave them in our hotel rooms. We are hardly out the door when hotel staff, clutching the abandoned gifts, come running after us. 'Please Lady, Gentleman, wait, please. You leave behind …'

There are times when mild hysteria threatens. We've all got colds. We are all sleep-deprived. Even Ross, the party animal, has declared a truce on evening carousing. He's going to miss dinner and sleep for 12 hours. Spoonerisms abound. Maurice and Dorothy have become Doris and Morothy. Our mangling of Chinese names has progressed from embarrassing – which is the surname, the first word or the second? – to catastrophic. I call Carol Christine and vice versa. Our poor guide is asked the same question half a dozen times. Information is received, and within five minutes forgotten. I get a headache trying to hold the Alley family tree in my head.

Rachel talks to me about her grandfather, John, my mother's younger brother. John was never talked about much in my household so I'd assumed he was something of a black sheep. But I was wrong. My mother, I will learn, nursed him back to health when he had Tb. More than that, she encouraged him to get an education. 'Look at it this way,' Rachel says. 'I'm a librarian. Maybe I wouldn't be if it hadn't been for your mother.' Not for the first time I see my mother in a new light and wish I'd known her at a different time in her life, in a different place.

Rachel's husband Stewart works for the New Zealand dairy company, Fonterra. He tells me about the company's dominant position in China. At one point we pass a Fonterra milk treatment factory. 'People think the

Chinese are coming into New Zealand and buying it up,' he says. 'But it's not all one way. We have a pretty big presence here as well.'

'But we can't buy land, can we?' I say.

At which point Dave enters the argument. No one can buy land, he reminds us. Not even the Chinese. Land belongs to the State.

More voices are raised. We all saw the millionaire mansions in Beijing. So does the State own them too?

Dave laughs. Explains that the millionaires – billionaires! – pay rent to the State. They own the buildings but not the land. 'Think of it as rates,' he says. 'We all pay those.'

Now several people are speaking at once. They all seem to have the same question. So could the State, in theory, take possession of the buildings, since they own the land?

Dave agrees this could happen, though he considers the prospect remote. At present leases can last for up to 70 years. What will happen when they expire has still to be worked out. 'All this is pretty new for China,' he explains. 'That's what you have to understand.' There's silence for a few moments, then Dave introduces another topic – the *hukou* system, the Chinese form of household registration, by means of which a citizen has access to education, health care and permission to marry. Based as it is on ancestral land rights, all sorts of problems occur when an individual moves from the country to the city. Given that millions have done just that in recent decades it's hardly surprising there have been hiccups.

My mind starts to wander. How can a system that came into existence when the first communes were set up be expected to work in a quasi-capitalist, entrepreneurial society? The answer is it can't. Those millions who left their villages to seek their fortunes in the city left behind more than just an ancient rural way of life – they left their *hukou* rights. Our Beijing guide would tell me the situation is evolving. Things will get better! But it's hard to see how a system designed when China was 80 per cent rural can 'evolve' to answer the needs of an exploding urban population.

I get my chance to talk to Sarah when we're sitting in spring sunshine outside a Buddhist temple in Shandan. Sarah is suffering from a cold but is not going to let it deter her from seeing and doing everything on offer (including joining her cousin Rachel on an uncomfortable and highly pungent camel ride). Having already exchanged stories about our childhood, and found similarities, Sarah and I have established a rapport. Other things we have in common will surface as the journey progresses. Sarah, who works for the Christchurch City Council, shares the Alley passion for education. She has come through the earthquakes that devastated her city determined to spend the rest of her life as a learner, just like Rewi.

'What did Rewi mean to you growing up?' I ask her. 'You met him, didn't you?'

'I did but I don't remember. I was too young. What I do remember is the giant panda bear he gave me. It was bigger than I was.'

Everyone Rewi visited on that 1971 New Zealand visit received presents. How did he keep abreast of us all?

Sarah's father Buck, and Digger – father of Zeke, Jocelyn and Ross – travelled to China in 1988 to witness the scattering of Rewi's ashes from a helicopter flying over Shandan.

Even if we wanted to, we can't, as a family, get away from this man.

CHAPTER FORTY-TWO

THERE was 'no limit to Rewi's love for his friends and family,' Ma Haide wrote in the wake of Rewi's death in 1987. He was a 'deeply emotional person … a very dear comrade, friend and mentor … a man who reached for the stars'.[1] Throughout the tumultuous years of the wars of resistance and liberation Rewi never forgot his family and he never forgot his friends. Tramping over all the roads of China in the service of Gung Ho, he would post letters to Alan and Mike, to Lao San and his brothers, to Chingling, to the Snows, to his family in New Zealand, to Agnes Smedley, to Han Suyin … He had no real hope that these letters would reach their destination, but he mailed them anyway. Very few reached him in return. (I had similar doubts when, some 30 years after the demise of Gung Ho, I posted a letter to Rewi in a tiny Victorian-era post box built into the wall of a Devonshire stately home. Part of me thought it would never leave the box, one of only a handful left in Britain with VR inscribed on it. It reached Rewi in Beijing three days later.)

As for his enemies – of whom there were plenty – he had a lively vocabulary of New Zealand vernacular to help him deal with villains both past and present. They were 'scamps', 'scalawags', 'loafers', 'rat-bags', 'fat bastards', 'running dogs'. Imperial sovereignty was a 'rule of rascals'. His stubbornness exasperated people. His prickliness got up their noses. His impatience saw him described as a 'brow-beater'. Nor was criticism of him confined to his enemies. When Jim Bertram was asked for his views on Rewi's books, he dismissed them as 'violent and simplistic'. Reviewing Rewi's *Man Against the Floods* he wrote, 'The tone of this account is partisan … too unremittingly heroic for those unwilling to accept the emphasis here given to the dynamic of the Communist Party leadership'.[2] Rewi's riposte was cutting: 'I don't write for New Zealanders, I write for Asians. Whoever's century this one is, the next one will be Asia's'.[3] His judgement of Bertram's literary oeuvre was equally undermining. In his opinion Jim had written only two good books. Given that Bertram had written eight, in addition to his many academic publications, this was less than generous.

But literary rivalry, if that's what it was, was never going to separate the two friends. Rewi the country bumpkin, and Jim, the Shakespeare-quoting gentleman, with his matching cravats and handkerchiefs, would stay in touch throughout their lives. When Rewi failed to return to New Zealand after the civil war, Bertram's disappointment went deep. Who else could he talk with about the China they had both experienced, or about Chingling, whom they both loved?

Two years after the meeting at the Marco Polo in Wuhan, Jim, charged with bringing China Defence League supplies into the north via the Burma Road, completed his task and returned to Hong Kong. The European war was heating up. His loyalty now was to New Zealand. Arriving back home he immediately presented himself to the army. The army rejected him. Further rejection followed when he tried to get a job as a war correspondent. No one, it seemed, wanted him, and no one wanted to hear what he had to say about the Japanese threat and the resistance of the Eighth Route Army. So he returned to China to work again for Madame Sun. Caught in Hong Kong – the first British territory to surrender to the Japanese – when Pearl Harbour was bombed, he would spend the rest of the war in a prisoner-of-war camp. Chingling, whose Defence League was based in Hong Kong, only just managed to avoid capture.

There's no way of knowing when news of the fate that had befallen his friends reached Rewi. Given his peripatetic life at the time it's a wonder news of any kind got through to him. His anxiety on Chingling's behalf he would endure in silence. ('I don't talk about Madame Sun because she doesn't like being talked or written about,' Rewi told Geoff Chapple.) His fears for Jim, suffering, as all Japanese POWs did, from ill-treatment and malnutrition, probably had to be kept to himself too. Living so far from his former companions, who would he have confided in?

Returning to New Zealand in 1945, instead of being welcomed as a survivor of the waking nightmare of Japanese imprisonment, Jim was once again greeted with suspicion. Grateful for America's defence of the Pacific, New Zealand was anxious to please its powerful ally. That meant looking at men like James Bertram (and Rewi) through American Cold War eyes. China, according to the *New Zealand Herald* of the day, was 'an aggressive giant … seeking to foment strife and turmoil on the way to world conquest'. Anyone associated with that 'aggressive giant' automatically came under suspicion. So, like his old friend from his China days, Jim would be shadowed by the SIS. And he would be asked, when he applied for positions at both Christchurch and Otago universities, if he was a communist. His answer was no, but the posts went to less-qualified applicants.

Eventually, in 1947, Bertram was taken on as a lecturer in English by Victoria University in Wellington, a position he would hold until 1971, when he was appointed professor.

For old China hands returning to the US, things were a great deal worse. 'We are paying the price for China now,' Peg Snow wrote to Jim Bertram. 'We have been barely able to survive here these past few years.' 'We have been smeared and blacklisted,' her by-then estranged husband confirmed in a later letter.[4] Penniless and jobless, Edgar Snow would flee the United States in 1959 accompanied by his second wife Lois Wheeler. He would never return.

An even sadder fate awaited Agnes Smedley. Forced after Pearl Harbour to leave the country she loved, she took comfort from the fact that she had a new mission, one entrusted to her by her friend General Chu Teh. 'Tell your countrymen about China, Agnes,' he urged. 'Tell them what's happening here.'[5] But Agnes's compatriots, caught up in a war they'd hoped to be able to ignore, didn't want to know. The only people interested in what she had to say were the FBI. Two years before the communist victory changed United States policy forever, Agnes was accused of espionage. The charges were never proven but the stigma remained. Like Edgar Snow she could no longer find work in her home country. In 1949 she fled to Britain. A year later, following a failed operation, she was dead.

Rewi would attend the memorial service for Agnes in Beijing in May 1951. He would bow three times as her ashes were laid to rest on the Hill of Eight Values in the Babaoshan Revolutionary Cemetery. Inscribed above her name was the red star she sometimes had to hide from view but, post-Liberation, wore so proudly on her cap. Buried next to her was a young communist executed by the KMT. Rewi found it oddly comforting. What better companion could there be for his wild, free-spirited friend than a hopeful young revolutionary, happy to lay down his life for his country?

'Some people leave home in order to find it,' James Bertram wrote in 1956 to his school friend Ian Milner, another radical who left New Zealand before the war and, like Rewi, opted not to return. 'I think Rewi is one of those.'[6] Like so many of his generation Milner followed the socialist dream, believing it to be the only way to defeat fascism. A generation defined by the Spanish Civil War – a war which W.H. Auden believed had 'x-rayed the lies upon which our civilization is built'[7]– found itself cast in a very different light by the politics of the Cold War after 1945. Rewi, who lacked the political motivation of Bertram and Milner when he set out from New Zealand, would nevertheless be viewed through the same anti-communist lens as they were. Communism had become the new bogey-man. In the fight to rid the world of this scourge, millions would die in a series of wars that show no sign of ending.

'The reason so few of us returned to New Zealand in the thirties,' Bertram maintained in a letter to Milner, 'is that there was nothing to return to.'[8] Tempting though it is to see Rewi as part of this pattern – radicals leaving the country described by Rudyard Kipling as 'last, loneliest, loveliest, exquisite, apart' to find meaning and purpose elsewhere[9] – I don't see him fitting the same mould as the four Rhodes scholars – Milner, Bertram, Davin, and diplomat and linguist Paddy Costello – all of whom were prompted to flee their native land by their strong left-wing views. For Rewi, radical motivation came after his departure from New Zealand. His trigger was the failure of his farm and the lack of opportunity in his homeland. He left New Zealand to find adventure and a job, not to save the world. When asked near the end of his life why he left, he answered, 'The price of wool!'[10] ('I came on to China because of a wool slump and the returned soldiers' land policy,' he explained in a June 1952 letter to the *Dominion Post*.)[11]

Bertram's decision to return to New Zealand didn't mean he'd given up on China. On the contrary, he leapt at any chance to visit, keeping up a regular correspondence with Rewi as well as with others met during his adventurous years as a journalist-at-large. 'Think of those supermen like Rewi and his friend Ma,' he wrote to Milner in his exile in Prague. 'They discharge themselves after major ops and are next heard of climbing Coal Hill [an artificial mound built during the Ming dynasty from mud excavated to make the Imperial Palace moat], walking around the palace walls and generally disporting themselves like eagles on the updraft.'[12] After that first postwar visit in 1956, Jim had to wait 30 years for a second invitation – this time to attend the celebrations marking the fiftieth anniversary of the Xi'an Incident. His role in bringing that extraordinary story to the attention of the world had not been forgotten. Nor had the story itself. Had Chiang not been captured, had the United Front not been cobbled together as part of a deal to secure his release, the map of the world might well look very different.

*

When visiting China in 1986 James Bertram is given VIP treatment. He is reunited with Rewi. The two old friends, meeting in Rewi's Beijing apartment, talk far into the night. China may have changed in the 30 years since I was last here, Jim thinks, looking around at Rewi's crowded bookcases, the scrolls and drawings covering the walls, the shelves where vases and figurines and moon-faced Buddhas sit in jumbled splendour, but this room hasn't. The fact that it's on the ground floor and not the first, where Rewi used to live, is irrelevant.

Over tea and biscuits brought from New Zealand, Jim tells Rewi he's not happy with what he's seen so far of Deng Xiaoping's China. The newly enriched fat cats cruising the streets of Beijing in their foreign cars remind him of the bad old days in Shanghai.

Rewi disagrees. Deng is his friend. Creating a few fat cats is the price that has had to be paid to raise the people out of poverty. 'People who come to China are far too quick to judge. Even you,' he scolds. 'You only have to think about what went before to see how far China has come.'

Jim starts to protest, then changes his mind. Rewi's unease is as tangible as that of the lovelorn young man man featured in the scroll painting on the wall opposite. He suspects his friend is as worried as he is about these reforms (he is: 'we either have Gung Ho co-operatives or purely capitalist companies – we cannot have both'), but it's clearly not something he wants to discuss. So Jim changes the subject. In all the years he's known Rewi the one thing guaranteed to fire him up, apart from Gung Ho, is the art of China's past. Just so long as I'm not asked to take anything back home with me, he thinks, as he questions Rewi about his latest acquisitions. Some of the things in this room look priceless – that jade pendant, for instance, and that bronze Ming dynasty bodhisattva which, sure enough, Rewi turns to next, pointing out the detail on the lotus flower on which the bodhisattva is sitting.

As the evening wears on Jim's mood shifts from the euphoria of reunion to a creeping sense of melancholy. It's not the fact that Rewi's aged since their last meeting in New Zealand – he'd come prepared for that, he's over 80 after all – it's the look in Rewi's eyes that's disturbing him. Since when was the man Edgar Snow compared to Lawrence of Arabia – 'where Lawrence brought to Arabia the destructive technique of guerrilla warfare, Alley is teaching China the constructive organization of guerrilla industry'[13] – given to resignation? What happened to you in the Cultural Revolution? Jim wants to ask. Can we talk about that? You've called it a 'bitter interlude to learn from', claiming that everybody underwent what you described, with breathtaking understatement, as 'a good deal of unpleasantness'.[14] But you've steered clear of the details and that, as we both know, is where the truth lies. I know you blame the Gang of Four. Everyone does now. But they were only the last act in a show that had been playing for nearly a decade.

'Nothing in China is what it seems to be on the surface.' The old Rewi would have agreed. But the man sitting opposite him seems to have chosen to look away.

'So you think Deng will stay honest, do you?' Jim challenges some time later, steering the conversation back to where they started. 'Not succumb to the temptation to enrich himself?'

'Speculation,' Rewi scoffs. 'Waste of time. I leave that sort of thing to the China watchers in Hong Kong. Much safer for them on the periphery than for me here.'[15]

The desolation behind those words hits Jim like a punch in the gut. It's not just Rewi who's lost his way, he thinks, it's China. When he met Mao Tse-tung in Yan'an in 1937 he was convinced he'd met the man who would lead China to greatness. 'No one … has ever given me such a strong impression of intellectual energy, concentrated will power, and easy mastery of the whole range of Far Eastern Politics,' he wrote in *Capes of China Slide Away*. When did Mao, so admired and loved, become the monster who unleashed the Cultural Revolution?

Neither man wants the evening to end, but inevitably it does. Throwing off his years, Rewi insists on accompanying Jim back to his hotel. As they walk through the murmuring darkness, Jim keeps asking himself the same question: how much of the China I believed in remains? The more he tries to answer it the darker his mood becomes. Only you, Rewi, he decides. And Chingling, of course, the beautiful heart of the revolution. You two sitting together in a small room, that's all that's left.[16]

Back at his hotel Jim takes out the poem Rewi had slipped into his pocket as they were leaving – one of his better ones, as it turns out – and reads it aloud. It's called 'Home':

I look at the old Ishing teapot,
the blue cup and saucer, the
plates from Chingtehchen, each
morning and smile; home is a place

where bits and pieces one has loved,
collect; where friends and family
come around, making walls echo
with sounds of laughter ...[17]

A reminder, not that he needs one, that his old friend is in China to stay.

CHAPTER FORTY-THREE

WE are learning about train travel. Trains stop for a pre-set number of minutes then depart whether the passengers are on board or not. So when we board the overnight train that will take us to Shandan, Dave has us marshalled into ranks, heavy luggage lined up with the men, women clutching as much hand-luggage as they can carry. We tease Christine, who seems to have more bags than any of us (she's a keen shopper), but really we're just trying to look nonchalant, faced with the prospect of being left behind on the platform.

In the end all is well. Not even a carry-bag is left behind. We stagger down the narrow passageway to our designated carriages: six to a carriage; three bunks, one on top of the other with a narrow space between; a thin mattress to sleep on; a 14-hour journey ahead of us. Not many of us will sleep more than fitfully, but such is our camaraderie by now that no one complains. 'Don't drink too much,' a voice from the next carriage warns. 'Toilets best avoided.'

We smile at our fellow passengers, many of them Tibetan, identifiable by their red cheeks and friendly smiles. We're trying to look as relaxed as they are, not what we know ourselves to be – a bunch of pampered Pākehā forced to travel hard class.

Waking to see through our window what Rewi saw when he first came here in 1943 – a scene that resembles a snow-covered Canterbury Plains with the Southern Alps in the distance – our stiff muscles and aching joints are forgotten.

> Do you have mountains like these?
> Farmers as ours? I look across at the
> Towering peaks of Chi Lien Shan
> Over wavering tussock, bits of marsh to their snows …
> As Castle Rock over to Five Rivers, The Dome
> And windy Waimea Plains …
> In Southland there would be wire netting
> To keep out rabbits. Here stones lie ready on tower
> Tops, to drop on intruders; the human struggle is
> More at hand …[1]

*

August 1943. The man standing at the door of the Shuangshipu cave house introduces himself as Joseph Needham.

'Frightfully sorry to bother you,' he says to Rewi. 'I was told there was an Englishman living here …'

'That's George. I'm a New Zealander. Rewi Alley.'

'Oh, I know who you are.'

'Sounds ominous. You're not a spy, are you?'

'Nothing so exciting. I'm a scientist. With a particular interest in …'

'You'd better come in.'

Rewi leads his unexpected guest into a room where half a dozen boys lie spread-eagled on the floor, engaged in a game involving small pieces of bone. 'Knucklebones,' Rewi explains. 'Used to play it as a kid … Vamoose!' he says, in English, waving an imperious hand at the boys. Then he says what Needham imagines is the same word, in Chinese. The boys get up reluctantly, gather up the cat that has been sprawled on the floor with them, and head out the door.

'So what's the problem?' Rewi asks as he sets about making tea. He can guess the answer. Whatever vehicle Needham is travelling in will have broken down. Happens all the time. China's roads in this part of the country are not really roads, they're donkey tracks.

Needham confirms that indeed his truck has broken down, but then goes on to explain what he's doing in Shuangshipu. He's en route to the Yumen Oilfields on an assignment for his employers, the Sino-British Science Co-operation Office. 'Been with them six months,' he tells Rewi.

'Where are you based?'

'Chungking.'

'That cesspool.'

'I try to ignore the politics.'

'So do we. Trouble is, it refuses to ignore us.' Rewi grins and blows the steam from his tea. It's been a while since he's welcomed a visitor to the cave house. Most of the people who come knocking are KMT scoundrels intent on capturing recruits for their army. Needham, whose truck has a broken spring – something the boys from the workshop will have fixed in a jiffy in the morning – will have to stay the night. That means conversation, a rare treat. He's just sorry George will miss out. He's in Baoji, begging for funds.

Needham doesn't disappoint. Over a meal of corn-on-the-cob, bread and honey, he confesses that what really brought him to China – the job was just an excuse – was his fascination with the country's long history of scientific and technological achievement. Man after my own heart, Rewi thinks, as his guest expands on his interests: pottery, movable type, the magnetic compass, clocks, all of them invented in China while Europe was languishing in the Dark Ages. 'You know the Russians called China Serica, the Land of Silk?' he says.

'And we called it China, the Land of Porcelain,' Rewi counters.

'Proves my point about China's reach,' Needham says, grinning.

Rewi laughs. 'My students would tell you you're wasting your time,' he says. '"Junk of the ages". That's what they call the stuff I dig up.'

Their talk goes on past midnight. Over several mugs of green tea they speculate, none too happily, about the progress of the war in China (the ambushing of the New Fourth Army by KMT troops in January 1941 has once again placed the United Front in jeopardy). As for what's going on elsewhere in the world, they give up trying to second guess where it's all headed, and return to their original subject.

'Incredible when you think about it,' Needham muses. 'The Chinese had it all back then. Light-years ahead of the West in just about everything you can think of – astronomy, mathematics, architecture, science, technology, gunpowder ...'

Rewi waves a hand. 'Word of advice,' he says. 'Don't congratulate them on the invention of gunpowder. They'll take offence. They say *we* invented that. What they invented was fireworks. It's one of their many jokes at our expense.'

Curious to know how Needham knew who he was when he opened the door, Rewi is dealt a not altogether pleasant surprise when he learns it's not just Gung Ho that's become world-famous, it's Rewi Alley. Edgar Snow's enthusiastic publications have ensured that his face has been featured in newspapers in almost every Western country. 'Red hair streaked with grey, sharp Roman nose, vivid blue eyes, I'd have known you anywhere,' Needham says. 'Though I was expecting you to be taller.' (Rewi's SIS file gives his exact height – five foot six and three-quarter inches.[2])

'You know, you can try all you like to avoid politics,' Rewi says, through a yawn. 'But this is China. Sooner or later you have to choose which side you're on.'

Next morning Rewi wakes with a plan in his head. George is due back today. If he agrees, Rewi will hitch a lift with Needham to Gansu province. Somewhere in that vast empty wilderness there has to be a safe place for the school.

CHAPTER FORTY-FOUR

THE journey from Shaanxi province to Gansu should have taken less than a week but Needham's truck kept breaking down, obliging Rewi, the 'god of running repairs' to improvise with whatever materials he could find in his kit bag, or lying on the roadside, to keep them moving.[1] At various times, a piece of cotton torn from a shirt is used to fix a broken fan belt, cellulose and glue are employed to mend a cracked piston, and a tyre scavenged from a wrecked Soviet truck solves the problem of a puncture. They've been driving for three weeks, following the line – what remains of it – of the Great Wall. Rewi's skin is itchy from the bed bugs that have plagued them in every inn, insect repellant proving useless in Gansu's ancient hostelries. Clay floors, holes in the roof to let out the smoke, cockroaches lazing their way across the floors, rats stealing their soap, eating their shoes and papers, scuttling across them as they slept … 'Like something out of the Middle Ages,' Needham had complained on the first night. Three weeks later, jammed into the cab of the truck, windows closed to keep out the dust, he's stopped complaining. He knows he must stink as badly as Rewi, so what's the point of drawing attention to it.

As they head down the dusty Gansu corridor, Rewi, whose turn it is to drive, asks Needham if he's heard of Ma Bufang, the local Moslem strongman. 'Nasty bugger,' he says. 'Does the KMT's dirty work for them.'

Needham wants to know more. So Rewi launches into the story – an all too familiar one – of peasants forced by warlords, in this case Ma and his thugs, to dig up crops and plant poppies instead. It's been going on for a century and more. Ever since British merchants forced the Chinese to buy opium from their vassal state, India, then whacked on huge tariffs when addiction upped demand.

'You telling me it's the peasants who get addicted?' Needham asks.

'Of course. With part of their wages paid in kind it's inevitable.'

Needham shakes his head. 'We British have a lot to answer for,' he says.

Rewi doesn't argue. 'Well, now the Japanese are up to the same tricks,' he mutters. 'Dishing out opium like it's a lolly scramble.'

They drive on through the grey landscape, saying nothing as fields of poppies, ready to harvest, come into view. Peering through the dirt-encrusted windscreen, Rewi isn't sure whether what he's seeing – camels laden with tea,

spices, silks, jade, porcelain – is a mirage, or a figment of his imagination
… Chinoiserie. All the rage in nineteenth-century England and France. The
'lure of the Orient'. Whoever came up with that sales pitch should be dumped
in the middle of this wilderness and left to fend for himself.

Now, on either side of them, ancient Han towers have appeared, stretching
across the steppes like crumbling telegraph poles, evidence that there have
been cities here for thousands of years.

Shandan, Needham announces, consulting the map. Rewi's heard of it.
A bustling metropolis 2000 years ago, famous for its veggie gardens. The
characters for Shandan mean Golden Mountain. Probably something to
do with the sunset. Could this be the site of the new school? It has all the
necessary ingredients – water, coal, iron, copper, oil. Not to mention the fact
that there are bound to be other cities even more ancient than this one under
these shifting sands … As the walls of the town emerge through the haze, his
heart starts to race. The place is a ruin. He can tell that even from a distance.
That means it will be littered with building materials.

They approach cautiously. Shandan may be a ruin but there will be people
eking out an existence within its walls. Rewi identifies a large beehive-shaped
structure on the skyline as a *dagoba*, a building for storing Buddhist relics.
Something tugs at his memory. Then it comes to him. *Fatasi*, Temple of the
Hair. Built to house hair taken from the head of an Indian king, ruler of this
part of China in the Ming period. As they pass through the ruined gateway,
Rewi spots a second almost-intact structure – the more familiar pagoda, no
longer in use judging by the state of its walls.

'No sign of your warlord and his merry bunch,' Needham says. The
people staring at them from the roadside – dirt-poor peasants, many pushing
wheelbarrows containing small heaps of dried fruit and wheat cakes – have
the worn-down look Rewi has seen on faces all over China.

'They'll be lurking somewhere,' Rewi cautions.

They pass a line of trees which Rewi identifies as persimmons. Another
cluster, leaves already turning, have been stripped of their fruit. 'Walnuts!' he
says out loud. Snow-capped mountains, walnut trees – no wonder he feels as
if he's arrived in a familiar place. Above their heads an eagle circles.

Rewi winds down the window. Not a good idea, given that dust will get
sucked in the way a swimmer sucks in air, but he can hear singing. A strolling
minstrel perhaps? In this hushed, forgotten place he could almost believe it
was an angel singing.

'All the world is full of poor but none so poor as I ...'

Rewi smiles. 'The Song of the Little Cowherd'. Heard all over China. A love song. Thousands of years old. If his throat weren't so dry, he'd join in.

He stops the truck in the shade of a gnarled jujube (date) tree, which he eyes approvingly. A good food source, even if it has seen better days.

Jumping down from the cab, it's not singing he hears but shouting and the braying of animals. He frowns at Needham. Ma Bufang? If it is, they better get ready to do some fast talking. When he sees a group of Mongol shepherds approaching from the north gate riding camels, his relief triggers a splutter of laughter. It's a grand sight. The colourful rugs draped across the camels' backs remind him of the banks of azaleas he used to take the boys to see outside Shanghai. This is what China does. Just as you're beginning to think you'll never see colour again, a hillside blanketed with pink and white blossom bursts into view; a rug displaying the colours of the rainbow trots right past you ...

Rewi reaches back into the cab for his trusty Box Brownie camera. This has to be recorded: the gaily dressed Mongols; the ungainly camels with their look of tortured dignity; the wild dogs snapping at the camels' heels; the crows and pigeons circling the air above them. He looks around for the eagle but it's disappeared.

'Smelly buggers,' he says, as the stately caravan sways past them.

'Where do you think they're headed?'

'Marketplace?'

Needham shakes his head. The people they've seen so far look as if they can't afford food, let alone a hand-woven rug of many colours.

Over lunch – steamed bread and apples – eaten on the banks of the first river they've seen in days, Rewi announces he's going to stay on in Shandan. Needham doesn't have to ask why. They've only been here a few hours but Rewi, who lost no time throwing himself into the water, has already got it marked as the site for his school. Is it madness or genius, Needham wonders, to imagine you can build a school in a ruined town on the edge of the Gobi desert, where half the population is addicted to opium and the other half is in the pay of warlords?

Ten days later, having finished his work on the oilfields, Needham reappears in Shandan and gathers up an excited Rewi. His conversations with the locals have gone well. Opposition to the school might come from Ma Bufang, but it won't come from the people of the town. Shandan, Rewi declares, is exactly what he's been looking for.

This time the long drive back to Shuangshipu passes without incident. They only have to make six overnight stops. Staying for the second time at the Inn of Eternal Prosperity, Rewi explains that the names given to these flea-ridden wayside hostelries are not meant to be ironic. They reflect the deep-seated Chinese belief that things will get better, if not in their lifetimes then in the lifetimes of their children.

'Amen to that,' says Needham.

*

Needham will stay in China until 1946. No compulsory exile for him. During that time he will make numerous trips to the northwest, gathering artefacts and information, recording the evidence of China's ancient, world-changing inventions. On one trip, during which he would almost certainly have visited Rewi, he discovers a copy of the Diamond Sutra, the earliest-dated printed book, in one of the caves at the Dunhuang Grottoes (a favorite haunt of Rewi's).

Returning to England in 1946, Needham is made head of the National Science section of UNESCO. From that time on, both as a UN official and, later, as a Fellow of Gonville and Caius College in Cambridge, he will devote his energy to the history of Chinese science. As well as writing about the big things China invented – printing machines, clocks, telescopes, compasses – he itemises the small domestic and agricultural items that did so much to change the way people lived and worked – the wheelbarrow, the loom, the kite, harness for horses.

At the end of the Korean War Needham will be recruited by Zhou Enlai to test the allegation that the US had used biological weapons in the Korean War. His report will confirm the presence of anthrax in North Korea. As a consequence he will be blacklisted by the US government, a restriction that will last until the mid-1970s.

When Rewi publishes his first book Yo Banfa! in 1952 he asks Needham to write the preface. 'I never tired of listening [to Rewi],' Needham will write, describing their long journey into China's northwest. 'Over a roadside breakfast off the truck bonnet he descanted on the strategy of the Three Kingdoms; in ancient inns he recounted his experiences among the dark Satanic mills of Shanghai, and explained the system of gangsters and secret societies; during breakdowns on desert tracks he spoke of the profound humanity of the Chinese folk, and the revolutionary activities of those who were determined [China] should blossom forth in fullness and freedom from age-old oppression … Now for the first time whoever reads this epic book will be able to accompany Rewi on such a journey as I did and hear him expounding in seemingly casual commentary the background of what future historians will surely regard as the greatest movement of this age.'

Rewi and Needham will remain friends throughout their long lives: Needham, too, lived to age 90. An Anglo-Catholic with strong communist sympathies, he also saw himself as an 'Honorary Taoist'.[2] It's a claim Rewi, a communist who respected Christians who put their faith into practice, could have made about himself.

CHAPTER FORTY-FIVE

Queer to come to a place
so well known, finding sameness
Yet so many differences ...[1]

'IT was like coming home,' Rewi rhapsodises. 'Did I mention there are walnut trees?'

George grins. Rewi in the grip of an idea is unstoppable. They've talked of nothing but Shandan since he walked through the door three hours ago.

'And you know the best part? No Jap planes. I doubt they even know of Shandan's existence.'

In Rewi's mind they are already there, the 60-plus boys, the machinery, the books and tools, desks and bunks, pots and pans – even the apple tree he planted five years ago and has no intention of leaving behind now it's starting to bear fruit. But George is worried about earthquakes – a common occurrence in northwest China. He's even more worried about money. Unless Gung Ho comes to the party they won't be going anywhere, and the signs from that direction are not good. Rewi has talked eloquently about Shandan's part in the Long March, giving shelter to soldiers of the Fourth, Fifth and Sixth Armies on their way to Yan'an. Joining in the fight. 'Lots of kids died,' he's pointed out. 'Establish a school there and they won't have died in vain.'

George has no wish to rain on Rewi's parade, but he needs him to at least think about the earthquake risk. And to start working out how they're going to pay for the move if Gung Ho shuts the door.

*

Three months pass before anything happens. Rewi's next attempt to persuade Gung Ho officials that moving the school and its associated factories is essential produces the same result as before. Not even the news that a site has been found and the support of the local community secured swings things his way. Inflation is running at record levels. The simplest purchase costs thousands of yuan. Maintaining existing co-ops is difficult enough; how on earth can they be expected to find money for an undertaking of this size?

So Rewi changes tack, writing letters to anyone and everyone who might support his cause, meanwhile impressing on George and the boys that they are not to talk about their plans to anyone. If questioned, they are to say that the school is running along normally. He may not think he's playing politics but he is. It's bad enough haggling with Gung Ho without having the KMT in on the case. Fear that word of the proposed move will get out and KMT conscription officers will descend 'like the wolf on the fold' dominates his thinking.[2]

In the end he gets enough of what he needs to make the move possible. It's not a great deal – one truck instead of three; half the money he wanted, raised not by Gung Ho but by New Zealand Corso – but it will have to do.

Early in November 1943, leaving George to pack up in Shuangshipu, Rewi travels to Shandan to begin work on the basics – food and shelter. George is determined to bring everything – the Ghosh cotton mill, the milling and planing machines, the school lathe, the diesel engine, the shaftings and pulleys, the sewing machine … They couldn't be travelling at a worse time. Winter is beginning. Temperatures can be expected to plummet to minus 30. George and the boys will be travelling in an old Soviet truck and on mule carts. Their route will take them over mountain passes thick with snow and ice. What will happen if the truck breaks down? (It does.) What if they get attacked by bandits? (They don't.) What will happen if the boys get sick? (Some do.) Typhus germs thrive in the mud floors of peasant huts. If they need to throw themselves on the hospitality of villagers, all their hard work at Shuangshipu, instilling principles of hygiene into the boys, will go for nothing. The only thing George doesn't have to worry about is Japanese bombs. Why would anyone want to bomb such a makeshift cavalcade?

In the event, most of what Rewi had imagined could go wrong doesn't happen. They do lose one boy, but not through infection: he has a heart attack. The day the truck, piled high with machinery, rumbles into Shandan, the boys perched on the roof shout, '*Daoliao!*' 'We've arrived!'

*

In 2009 a film titled *The Children of Huang Shi* (also known as *The Children of the Silk Road*) was released in Australia. It purports to tell the story of George's 'little long march' over the Huajialing mountains, taking the boys from an 'orphanage' in Shuangshipu to Shandan. It's so wildly inaccurate as to be almost laughable – there's no Rewi in the story, and Kathleen Hall, who wasn't there, has been reinvented as a pretty young American nurse called Lee. George, naturally, falls in love with her. Death-defying adventures take place – not in themselves remarkable since northwest China in 1943 was home to tigers, jackals, wolves, bandits, snakes and extreme weather – but the events depicted in the film bear little or no relation to the truth.

'We were all very tired and disappointed,' George's youngest son, Nieh Guangpei (Lao Si), will tell people years later, describing the day of their arrival when he was just six years old. 'There was nothing in the temple [the semi-ruined pagoda Rewi had adapted as a temporary dormitory], hardly even a roof. It was filthy and cold ...'[3]

But Rewi is not disheartened. He knows the size of the task ahead of him but he's ready for it. Here in Shandan there is beauty and there is suffering, but there is also hope. The school they left behind in Shuangshipu, built into caves that protected them from the elements, might have seemed like paradise lost to Lao Si, but to Rewi, looking out at the chocolate-coloured hills, watching a file of peasants moving swiftly and silently back to their village, Shandan is paradise regained.

CHAPTER FORTY-SIX
16–17 April 2017

WE are staying at Shandan's Alley International Hotel. After our overnight ordeal on the train we're looking forward to a shower and a rest before lunch and our scheduled visit to the Shandan Bailie School for yet another commemorative function. But the programme has been changed. A lunchtime banquet has been arranged in our honour. We are to be ready, dressed in best bib and tucker, in 10 minutes.

Rebellion breaks out. Ross refuses to adhere to the timetable. I twice send the young man who knocks on my door – 'Hurry please, Lady. No time' – packing. I'm close to tears. I'm dirty, sleep deprived, and have almost lost my voice. I'm tired of being told to hurry, to move along, to go here but not there, to present a written copy of the speech I'm scheduled to give this afternoon. How can I write a speech when I have no computer and there's been no time to think about what I'm going to say? The day inches towards disaster …

'We seem to be at war with North Korea,' an eerily calm voice announces. (I remember the words but not who said them. Most of us have given up trying to get internet access.) We're gathered – those of us who've heeded the call – in the hotel foyer 15 minutes behind schedule. Our minders – one assigned to each person – are visibly unhappy. I assume their agitated chatter is not about North Korea but about whether to shepherd us into the banquet or wait for the stragglers.

A collective gasp/nervous giggle issues from the whānau. We're on the border of Mongolia. Does that mean we're in the line of fire? Questions fly about like released cage birds. 'Who started it? Was it Trump? What if it goes nuclear? Are we going to have to fly home?'

I don't remember much about the banquet, just that by the end, when the toasting and the speeches were done, we knew we were not at war. Sharp words have been exchanged between Presidents Trump and Kim Jong-un, threats have been made, but so far no bombs have been dropped.

We travel with an official escort, celebrity-style, to the school. Banners in the streets proclaim Rewi's triple anniversary – 120 years since his birth, 90 since he arrived in China, 30 since his death. I am worryingly nervous. I dislike making or listening to speeches that are read out, but I realise, too late, that the reason I was asked for a written copy of my speech was to facilitate translation. What follows is a low point for me and I suspect for some of the others as, amidst great formality, seated in a packed auditorium of students, teachers and officials (over 500, we're told), we're obliged to listen to speech after speech saying more or less the same thing. There is even a message from President Xi, hailing Rewi as China's 'old friend', 'good friend'. By the time it's my turn to take the stand I'm drunk with boredom and exhaustion and the realisation that I've screwed up. Speaking extempore is not done in China. I stumble through, drawing on my childhood memories of Rewi, but with very little awareness of what I'm saying. I apologise to the translator and stagger back to my seat.

The rest of the day should have been a highlight. This is where Rewi spent the happiest years of his life. We are taken to see a huge statue of him and George. Then it's on to the *lei tai* – an elevated platform, site of an ancient wrestling ground – where Rewi's cottage, now a museum, is situated. I look at the modern, airport-style gangway leading to the brightly painted museum, red with gold facings, and can see no resemblance to the photos I saw as a child. Where are the mud walls, and the courtyard that separated Rewi's living quarters from those of the children too young to sleep in the school dormitories? Where is the stone bench where Rewi liked to sit in the evenings? Where is Skimpy the dog and Muggins the cat? And why is there a young Chinese woman dressed in spotless black and white, standing, hands clasped like a singer about to give voice, at the side of the platform? I smile at her but there is no response. Her eyes are focused elsewhere, while mine are focused on Rewi, wearing a fur cap and sheepskin coat, a couple of small boys perched on his knees – an image familiar to most of the family – and sitting on a very different *lei tai* from the one in front of me.

Houses that have become museums, statues that sanitise the blood, sweat and tears of real life – is this why I remain unmoved, or is it just travel-weariness? Judging by the number of photos being taken, others are finding this experience more rewarding than I am. Later we will be taken to the site of the new museum being built to house Rewi's art collection. Confronted by yet another enormous statue – this time of Rewi and a group of children with, among other dignitaries, Xi Zhongxun, the president's father, in his role as honorary principal of the Shandan Bailie School – the cameras come out again in force. 'In their well-worn serenity, statues have the appearance of denying controversy, placidly asserting their innocence,' Tom Crewe wrote in the September 2017 issue of the *London Review of Books*. Perhaps that's why

I'm unmoved. There is no hint of the dark periods in China's recent history in these heroic figures. Nor can I place Rewi, the man Geoff Chapple described as 'the god of digging the long drop where it could not contaminate the well water', in this polished, theatrical setting.

*

The next day is better, though I am still bothered by this sanitised version of Rewi's life. We are taken to the mausoleum (even the word feels wrong) built to commemorate the life and work of George Hogg and Rewi Alley. As the wreath-laying ceremony and accompanying speeches get under way, I close my eyes so I can picture Rewi's last will and testament. 'No fuss', he insisted. 'It is just one more soldier marching on.'[1] What would he have made of these solemn speeches and this carefully staged pageantry?

I try to summon the appropriate emotions but I can't get that scrap of paper, witnessed by his friend Sid Shapiro, out of my head. It's only when we're each given a yellow chrysanthemum to lay on the mausoleum that a lump forms in my throat. 'Sorry', I whisper as I lay my flower beside the others. 'I've come too late …'

Herded back onto our bus after the obligatory group photo, we're whisked away to a farming co-operative to see the descendants of 25 Corriedale sheep sent to Rewi from New Zealand in 1947. There are thousands of them now, feeding on the grasses of Gansu province. Watching them being shorn in readiness for summer gives me a queer feeling of déjà vu. Where am I exactly? Dave has been telling us about the work the NZCFS is doing in this area: supporting the newly revived co-operative movement; helping with disaster relief after the all too common earthquakes. Is this why I feel I've been here before? I live in a city and a country as prone to earthquakes as the land we are passing through. WELCOME HOME TO CHINA, the placards at the Bailie school in Beijing proclaimed. So am I at home now?

But I know where I am with the next place we visit – a temple housing the largest Buddha in the world. We are encouraged to walk (actually we have to crawl) through the narrow passageway underneath the Buddha's backside. I take a deep breath, tell myself, 'I don't care', and slither as quickly as I can from one side of the gigantic statue to the other. I'm hoping my temporary overcoming of claustrophobia will bring me good luck.

Then it's on to the Exhibition Hall of Cultural Relics, where Rewi's collection of artefacts, left to Shandan in his will, is housed. Four thousand of them, we're told. But there are many more packed away, awaiting the completion of the new museum.

It's hard in this building – which could be a museum anywhere in the world – to picture Rewi wearing either his shorts or winter's padded clothes, setting out from Shandan on one of his regular treasure hunts. With so much 'junk of the ages' lying around, he almost never came back empty handed. One of his favourite places to explore was the famous Grotto Temple in nearby Yulin, where the chances of stumbling on a figurine dating back to the Tang or earlier lurked beneath every stone. A similar prospect awaited him at the Dunhuang Grottoes. 'Laugh all you like,' he'd say to the lads who teased him. 'The day will come when you'll be proud of your ancestral junk.'

I refuse to be hurried. Something is emerging here that needs time to show itself. In his essay on Anna Louise Strong, Rewi once said that the history of China was like a 'great long Chinese scroll, its beginnings known but its full length as yet unfurled.'[2] As my eye travels around each room with its glassed-in displays, I feel I'm watching the scroll of Rewi's inner life unfurl. This was the man who served the New China while quietly, and at times secretly (as during the Cultural Revolution), celebrating the old. It wasn't just the old poets he admired, it was the pottery (ceramics in particular) and painting; the tales of gods and emperors, warlords and rebellions, love and duty; the jewellery and deftly fashioned tools rescued from the ruins of palaces and temples all over China.

> … yet the mountains seem to approach,
> Bits of pottery, tripod legs, bits of funerary urns,
> Relics of ancient furnaces of prehistoric men show up to shout
> Of the creative art of ages past …[3]

*

'Please will you give me some space?' I've lingered behind in the Hall of Cultural Relics. An official has been following me, urging me to join the others. Now he is so close I can smell his breath. 'I'm a writer,' I explain, uselessly. 'I'm taking notes.'

The official smiles and stays exactly where he is.

I move to the next glass case. He moves too. I'm trying not to feel spooked. What I want to do is record an object from every dynasty. I want to prove that Rewi's love of the past, his appreciation of beauty, his sensitivity to what art tells us about past civilisations and about ourselves, came from the deepest part of him. I would rather spend time here than almost anywhere else we have been. But I'm not going to be allowed to do that. The hand on my arm is firm …

I head for the door.

Most of the whānau are outside by now, enjoying the spring sunshine – winter's breath still hovers over Shandan, so the warmth is welcome – but a couple are loitering in the final gallery, looking at Rewi's more mundane possessions: his bicycle, his typewriter. The bicycle, unsurprisingly, is about as basic as a bicycle can be. I picture it laden with necessities, Rewi pushing it up an unforgiving mountain pass; or, when luck is with him, hitching a ride by clinging to the back of an unsuspecting truck, letting go when he reaches the summit and free-wheeling down the other side … The typewriter – which he claimed, in a 1970 letter to Pip, 'never learned to spell properly' – makes me smile.[4] It's like pieces of the True Cross. It keeps popping up in unexpected places. We've seen three so far: one in Rewi's Beijing apartment, one in the cave house, and now this one. All three are, of course, the 'real' one. (I wish I'd thought to check if they were all Remingtons. After Liberation, a typewriter known as the People's Welfare Typewriter was manufactured in Shanghai. Designed to print Chinese characters it could only be used by people trained to operate it. Rewi makes no mention of such training. Perhaps he didn't need it. For the last two decades of his life he had the help of a Chinese secretary who would, presumably, have had no problems using the People's Typewriter.)

I opt out of the evening entertainment. I need to try to make sense of the day's revelations. Is it fanciful to see Rewi's love of art as the ground of his being? In several of his books there are sketches that I'd initially assumed he had done himself. Not so. Like me, he apparently couldn't draw to save himself. Again like me, he failed art at school. But he knew the real thing when he saw it. He could tell the sheep from the goats.

According to Deng Bangzhen, one of Rewi's five foster children, now a well-known artist in China and New Zealand, Rewi was not satisfied with the quality of the drawings in his books, so he asked his foster son to re-do them. The sketches we have now are vivid, humorous, poignant. The drawings in *Fruition*, the book Rewi wrote in memory of George Hogg, give tangible expression to the love and admiration Rewi felt for the charismatic young Englishman. The same is true of the drawings of children. Their delight in the natural world – especially when it involved swimming – reflects Rewi's abiding love for, and belief in, the young. 'Children more than doves rank as the symbol of peace ...'

'You cannot divorce architecture from medicine or medicine from politics and art,' the old Chinese doctor that Rewi travelled with during the war said to him. 'The earth has a pulse, everything is vibrating, everything with its own combination of yin and yang ... they are not two as some suppose, they are one. The yin is the cause of the yang and the yang is the cause of the yin.'[5] As with so many things, holistic medicine was being practised in China long before it took hold in the West. Nor were herbs and acupuncture the only addition to the medical pharmacopeia. As the old Chinese doctor explained to Rewi, he and his fellow practitioners also healed with art.

What Rewi found in the art of China was the essential harmony of body and spirit; of yin and yang, beginnings and endings, life and death. Confucianism, Taoism, communism, Buddhism, Christianity – none of these, on its own, yielded up the kind of treasure he unearthed in the work of China's artists stretching back 4000 years. The boy who spent hours poring over exhibits in the Canterbury Museum, the man who claimed never to have grown up, the 'slow learner' grappling with new ideas embraced communism not as a cast-iron belief system, but as a way to solve practical problems. (To set the record straight: Rewi never joined the Chinese Communist Party, though he did apply, twice. Perhaps he should have tried harder. Xi Jinping applied 10 times before he was accepted!)

Rewi read and was influenced by the works of Marx and Lenin, but it was what he saw around him in China that changed him from a soldier in the service of empire to a humanitarian in the service of others. Like the country our Beijing guide described, Rewi's views were constantly evolving. Throwaway remarks made in conversation with family members and others bear this out. As do his later recollections in his memoir. His role as an apologist for the government during the Cultural Revolution was almost certainly not one he chose, though his attacks on the West for the wars in Korea, Vietnam and Malaya were clearly genuine. What has to be remembered is that the Rewi Alley of 1966–76, the decade of the Cultural Revolution, had seen and done things that would have been unimaginable to the Rewi of 1927. If he is to be judged, it must be in the context of those experiences.

*

271

If Rewi's love of art was seeded in his childhood, it was in China that those seeds bore fruit. One of his books, *Peking Opera*, was for many years regarded as the standard work on the subject.[6] Unlike Western opera, the Chinese version is not an elite form but one that reaches across social divides. Mao's insistence that opera and drama be part of the daily life of his soldiers, even when there was almost nothing to eat, was not a quirk of his personality but a reflection of the way the Chinese peasantry lived. An opera performed during a village festival would not have the magnificent masks and costumes of the famous Peking Opera but it would tell the same stories. When, in the days immediately after Liberation, students from Rewi's Shandan school were helping to transport the People's Liberation Army to the Yumen oilfield, they were treated to two operatic performances by the army's dramatic group. Verbatim reports testify to the effect these performances had on the newly liberated students. What had been understood in the head was now understood in the heart. Peasant poverty and landlord wealth were not inevitable, they were the consequences of a corrupt system going back centuries. As the opera reached its victorious conclusion, the prolonged, emotionally charged applause was not just for the actors, it was for the new China the students saw coming.

Rewi's description of Chinese opera as 'the most perfect thing of its kind existing in our world today' is testament to his abiding love for this uniquely Chinese art form. In the preface to the 1981 edition of *Peking Opera*, he described how traditional opera was almost destroyed during the Cultural Revolution when the classics, like so much else, were forbidden, and only new culturally approved works could be performed: 'actors, actresses, costume and wardrobe people, stage crews, directors … were severely criticised, made to do manual work in the rural areas of China and even imprisoned.'[7]

Yet only a few years earlier, with the Cultural Revolution in full swing, Rewi was claiming, in a letter to Pip, that there was an extra dimension to the enjoyment of opera because 'corruption has gone for good and the country is united' – a statement completely at odds with his expression of dismay at the punishments meted out to artists.[8] After the overthrow of the Gang of Four, when traditional opera was revived, Rewi made no secret of his delight. Now this 'perfect thing' combining music, drama, ballet, mime and acrobatics could be enjoyed again, and the old stories of corrupt officials and greedy landlords, of gods, lovers, enchanted snakes, deathless spirits, emperors, generals, and animals with magical properties, told all over China.

So was Rewi simply being 'flexible' in his public statements, or was his support for Mao's policy genuine, at least at first? Probably both are true, since it's clear from his written words that he was initially in favour of the revolution. ('In China a great spring cleaning has been put into effect throughout the past two years of the Cultural Revolution,' he wrote in the preface to *Poems of Protest*.) Breaking up power factions, keeping officials grounded: how could he not approve of these things? It was only when his friends started disappearing, and his own life came under threat, that he began to see things differently. But by then he was trapped in the role of mouthpiece.

*

Next morning we check out of our Shandan hotel. I feel like a child who has been served ice cream only to have the bowl snatched away. Rewi is so close here. Now, with a day given over to more visits to co-operatives, plus a tour of a geological park, my cousin will become a ghost again.

Ironically, for the first time we will be travelling in the same direction as Rewi. In 1952, under orders from the government, the Bailie School was moved from Shandan to Lanzhou, capital of Gansu province. It would no longer be a school teaching a variety of trades based on the principle 'Create and Analyse'; it would exist solely to train workers for the oil industry. Even the name would change, the Bailie School becoming the Petroleum School. For Rewi it was a kind of death. 'It may be that just as I have seen the last of Shandan I may see the last of China,' he wrote in his diary. 'It has all been so much a part of me that one does not have much of an appetite for anything else.'[9] They are the words of a man whose heart is breaking. Because it isn't just the school he's lost. It's his family. Alan and Mike, married with families of their own, are leading independent lives. Lao San and his brothers have been reunited with their father.

The final blow comes in 1954 when Rewi learns that Shandan has been virtually destroyed in an earthquake. 'A piece of one's life and experience blown over the desert,' he laments in his diary. From that time on, until the revival of the co-operative movement in 1983, the school where he spent the happiest years of his life is nothing more than a heap of rubble.

CHAPTER FORTY-SEVEN

TODAY, 18 October 2017, I read the following in the *Guardian*:

Xi Jinping has heralded the dawn of a 'new era' of Chinese politics and power at the start of an historic Communist party congress celebrating the end of his first term in office. Speaking in the Great Hall of the People in Beijing, at the start of the week-long 19th Party Congress, Xi told delegates that thanks to decades of 'tireless struggle' China stood 'tall and firm in the east'. Now, Xi said, it was time for his nation to transform itself into 'a mighty force' that could lead the world on political, economic, military and environmental issues.

The report went on to say that Chinese state media had announced the decision to grant Xi his own eponymous school of thought – the Xi Jinping Thought on Socialism with Chinese Characteristics for a New Era. 'This represents a momentous occasion in Chinese politics and history,' the report concluded. 'This new body of political theory bearing Xi's name will be written into the party's constitution.'

This is no mere legality. To the Chinese, the Thoughts of their paramount leader are a template instructing them in how to regard the past and what to expect in the future. Thoughts, even those of lesser mortals, travel, so the Chinese believe, down the road that writing makes. So from now on Xi's Thoughts, published and disseminated throughout the land, will travel from his mind straight into the minds of China's millions.

After the Cultural Revolution steps were taken to make sure the abuses of power that destroyed so many lives during that dark decade could never happen again. Deng Xiaoping was allowed his Theory – 'Socialism with Chinese Characteristics' – but it was understood that no one would again aspire to the height of Thoughts. Now it looks as if Xi, the 'Headline Prince', is heading in the same direction as Mao, whose Thoughts were required study for all Chinese. No one laughed at Mao and no one now laughs at Xi. The man who was for a time gently mocked for his likeness to Winnie the Pooh has ordered the recently released film *Christopher Robin* to be banned in China.

'The five most important people in China today,' those brave enough to voice their discontent joke, 'are Xi, Xi, Xi, Xi and Xi!'

*

How to write about happiness? A problem writers have faced since story-telling began. Rewi, wisely, didn't even try. But it's clear from what he did write about his years in Shandan that he looked back on that time as the happiest period of his life. Which isn't to say it was trouble-free. Even so far from Shuangshipu, the KMT continued to threaten. With so many nationalist soldiers dying from untreated wounds and malnutrition, the need for conscripts was more urgent than ever. But the real threat came from Shandan's proximity to the valuable Yumen oilfields. Chiang knew as well as anyone that what was coming, once the Japanese had been driven out, was civil war. Tightening his grip on the oil supply was essential if that battle was to be won.

For a time, though, with the Japanese well in the rear, and the nationalist army otherwise occupied, there's a semblance of peace. George, at the end of his epic trek over the mountains, can congratulate himself on delivering both boys and equipment safely to the site of the new school, and Lao Si, thanks to the padded clothing Rewi has purchased, has stopped shivering. Most importantly, there's enough to eat, chiefly steamed bread, potatoes and millet soup, but Rewi has promised there'll be meat soon. He's a hunter after all. He can point his gun at a yak just as easily as he once pointed it at rabbits and wild pigs.

After a few uncomfortable nights sleeping together in the ruined temple, Rewi manages to hire houses for the boys to sleep in. Now the temple, the only large building with a roof, can be used to house machinery. 'Out come the Buddhas. In comes the boiler', he boasts in 'Boiler in Sandan' – the poem my mother read out to me. The locals look on with amazement and disapproval. Their temple may be ruined but they are still Buddhists. Rewi has to promise to leave the largest Buddha – six metres high – untouched, to prevent a riot breaking out.

By the summer of 1944 the school is almost back to where it was when they left Shuangshipu. The Ghosh cotton-milling plant has been installed in pride of place at the Buddha's feet. Now, instead of chants and the ringing of bells, the old temple echoes with the clatter of machinery and the chatter of the boys in charge of this, the school's most precious possession. Other hastily restored buildings house the pottery, tannery, machine shop, printing press (the local chi chi grass is proving excellent for making paper), leather shop, brick-making section, engineering division, glass-blowing factory, bathhouse, and a growing number of classrooms. More pupils, including girls – 40 of them, brought from an orphanage closed down by the KMT in Baoji – have been taken in. From 60 the numbers soon swell to 600. George, writing home to his family, declares proudly that at Shandan they take in the 'poorest of the poor ... If the children were sub-consciously searching for their parents, we were sub-consciously searching for children ...' 'Thank God we are dirty,' he writes in another letter, meaning thank God we no longer look like *yang guizi*, foreign devils. 'It's a comforting thought.'[1]

Power is generated by a restored water wheel. Coal is mined from a shaft in the loess hills. A vegetable garden has been planted; a clinic established; a plant built to turn their first crop of beets into sugar. Best of all, in the opinion of the students, George has created a basketball court outside the south gate.

As at Shuangshipu, the working day is divided between practical work and theory. The day begins with the striking of a gong – a suspended truck wheel beaten with an iron bar – at 6am. Then, after the raising of the Gung Ho flag over the *lei tai*, George leads the students, dressed in white shirts and blue shorts, in exercises. Afterwards they all share the same breakfast – congee and steamed bread. For lunch they will eat rice and vegetables, with bean curd and onions – or rice gruel when times are hard – for supper. Sometimes, if Rewi has been out with his gun, there is yak or goat meat. Occasionally, after the New Zealand sheep arrive, there is mutton. But mostly the diet is simple, even sparse. In summer melons, persimmons, pears and wild strawberries are plentiful, but in winter they have to make do with dates and walnuts harvested in the autumn, and Rewi's famous plum puddings made from persimmons (an improvisation from his mother's recipe).

When the students complain of being hungry Rewi reminds them that the teachers are hungry too. 'No difference between our diet and yours,' he points out sternly. 'And I've told you the best way to overcome hunger. Singing!'

> In the dense forests,
> Our comrades set their camps.
> On the tall mountains,
> Our countless brothers are there.
> Nothing to eat, nothing to wear?
> The enemy will supply us.
> No guns, no cannons?
> The enemy will forge them for us ...[2]

These Red Army guerrilla songs are the boys' favourites. But there are girls in the school now. So George is extending the repertoire to include the old folk songs – the ballad of Meng Jiang, the faithful wife, weeping for her dead husband at the Great Wall; the song sung by the peasants of Sichuan: 'Old men of the mountains/ Living by cutting fuel/ Nothing to eat except what comes/ From the sale of firewood ...'[3]

Watching George as he moves around the school, conducting the choir, joining in games of volleyball and basketball, cradling the head of a boy learning to swim, supervising candlelit study in the long winter evenings, Rewi acknowledges his dependence on the young Englishman who is now his closest colleague and companion. When he hears a rumour – fuelled by KMT officials determined to discredit the school – that he and George are lovers, he bursts out laughing. George is in love all right, but not with him. The object of his affection is Xiao Ren, a young woman soldier in the Red Army. On the days when a letter arrives from Ren, George's face 'lights up, and he laughs all day, pulling the letter out a hundred times until it falls to pieces'.[4]

*

The 'accusation' of homosexuality – it didn't stop being a crime in New Zealand until 1986; in China it took a decade longer – will rear up again after Rewi leaves Shandan. This time it comes from New Zealand. It's the early 1980s. George is dead, so the finger-pointing is reserved for Rewi alone. 'So [I'm] an old queer eh?' is Rewi's response when the rumours are conveyed to him by David Mahon. 'Well I'll tell you what, I couldn't be any use to a woman or a bloke if I tried. I was shot through the arse in the First World War and it did a bit of other damage.'[5]

By this time the two New Zealanders, Rewi in his eighties, Mahon half his age, are comfortable enough with one another to talk easily. ('I like the fact that you are one of my few visitors who never ask me for anything,' Rewi has said. 'So many come on their official visits and they want the Chinese to give them something so they wheel me out.')

'Did you know they once tried to paint you as a pederast?' Mahon asks.

'Well I call that a low move,' Rewi responds quietly. 'I've been a family man through adoption. I have sons and I am a father. Can you think what a country like this would have done to me if I'd been interfering with little kids?'

'It matters to me if people around me get hurt,' he says later in that conversation. He makes no mention of how hurt he himself must have been by these accusations.

'Rewi was a very, very virtuous man,' Ma Haide's wife Su Fei (Sophie) stated when interviewed for the Chinese documentary *Rewi Alley*.[6] As the wife of Rewi's oldest friend in China and a frequent visitor to his home, as he was to hers, she was speaking as someone who knew him intimately. The story she tells confirms David Mahon's report. Rewi never married because his injury meant he couldn't be a husband in the full sense of the word.

CHAPTER FORTY-EIGHT

'YOU know, Rewi,' George says to him one night after the boys have gone to bed. 'All this' – he sketches a circle with his arms – 'Sandan, it's the best of all the worlds I've lived in so far. Knocks Oxford into a cocked hat.'

Rewi smiles. He's been trying to type up his weekly report but his cat Muggins keeps climbing onto the typewriter. George has called him a softie where animals are concerned, but it's only Muggins and Skimpy, the skin-and-bone Alsatian Rewi found wandering through the ruins of an old Taoist temple, that he treats as pets. Lions, tigers, camels, buffaloes, the wolves, jackals and wild dogs whose howling keeps them awake nights, the eagles that circle menacingly overhead – no one in their right mind would be a softie around them.

'Wait till you've gone through another winter,' he answers. 'Might change your tune then.'

George, perennially upbeat, waves the objection aside. 'O wind, if Winter comes, can Spring be far behind?' he quotes.[1]

It's Rewi's favourite time of day, the hour before sleep when there's time to write. If he's up to date with his reports he'll write letters or dabble in a bit of poetry. What George scribbles in the red notebook he carries with him everywhere, and is busily writing in now, is a mystery. Would he have recorded his reaction on hearing that he, like Rewi, has a price on his head? The news reached them at the beginning of the week. Ma Bufang was behind it of course, no doubt obeying orders from the KMT who'd love nothing more than to see the school closed down and its teachers dead and buried. Nothing he and George can do about it, apart from crossing their fingers and encouraging the rumours, started by the villagers – who've become their most ardent supporters – that the school is heavily armed. Five old rifles and a pack of kids who'd rather die than let Ma and his henchmen through the gates – some defence!

Neither man needs to be reminded of what the KMT's bully boys do to people they don't like. They've both had first-hand experience. George's close encounter happened just before the school shipped out from Shuangshipu. A KMT officer, who must have got wind of the move, tried to pressgang some of the older boys into the army. George, apparently, flew into a rage. Upshot was, George was hauled off to Baoji, where guards tried to beat him into submission. Miraculously, they let him go. Even more miraculously, the KMT 'scamps' melted away without having acquired a single soldier for their rotten army.

Looking at George now, Rewi mutters a silent prayer to the God he doesn't believe in for putting this man in his path. With four boys dependent on him, George's commitment to China would seem to be on a par with his own. Watching him horsing around with his two youngest at bath-time, threatening them with dire punishments if they don't wash behind their ears, his familiar snorting laugh triggering a frenzy of ear-twitching from Skimpy, Rewi has several times had it on the tip of his tongue to ask about his long-term plans. But something has always stopped him.

'I've made a decision,' George says suddenly, when Rewi gets up to make tea.

Rewi swivels around in astonishment. If this is what he thinks it is, then the man is a mind-reader.

'Actually I made it months ago,' George says, 'but I've been waiting for the right moment. I'm not going back. My parents expect me to return when the war's over but I'm not going to do that. I'll visit. I owe them that. But Shandan is my home now. The place where I will live and die. For better or worse, I'm raising my sons here.'

*

Rewi watches George as he conducts the choir singing an old Sichuan folk song that's been around since the beginning of time. It's their second spring in Shandan. The school is running well, thanks to George's skill as headmaster, and the support of ICCIC and NZ Corso (spurred on by my mother). The teaching staff has grown along with the school roll. Teachers from England, New Zealand, Australia, the US and Canada work alongside Chinese teachers, turning out young men and women ready to work and train others in the ever-growing number of co-operatives established throughout unoccupied China. *Peili*, the Romanised form of Bailie, which Rewi translates as 'dawn of training', is the message they take with them.

The biggest problem facing the school, apart from ongoing KMT and warlord harassment, is getting materials through Japanese lines. Rewi's aim is to make the school self-sufficient, but in the meantime he and George have to rely on funds and essential supplies smuggled in from overseas. A great deal of it never reaches them. The first flock of sheep sent from New Zealand ended up in India! With Hong Kong in enemy hands and the Burma Road closed, goods have to be carried clandestinely, at great risk to the carrier. Inflation is through the roof – a single packet of nails costs thousands of yuan – so money that used to come in the form of cash now comes as gold bars. Were it to be sent as cash it would require a whole caravan of donkey carts to transport it.

But there's no shortage of hope, or of laughter. Concerts, like the one George is rehearsing for now, are a regular feature. As are dramas, acrobatic performances and Yoko dancing. Recently, under George's direction, the students put on a play about an opium smoker and his family. It went down a treat. Opium is the staple crop of Gansu province and will remain so while the warlords are in control, so many of the boys have had first-hand experience of the drug's devastating effect on family life. When the opium-smoking father in the play finally sees the error of his ways and throws his pipe away, a loud cheer rose from the audience.

George has decided the next item on the agenda should be an opera. The boys want a story with lots of fighting so they can practise their martial arts. So do the girls! But George has other ideas. He wants them to think about something other than war. So he's chosen 'The White Snake', a story of magical transformation and thwarted love. Rewi stayed schtum when the announcement was made. He knew what lay behind it. More than six months have passed since George last heard from Xiao Ren. Staging 'The White Snake' is his way of coping with his fears for her. Personally Rewi thinks the kids are right and they should put on a story in which peasants fight for justice against a cruel emperor or warlord. At least those stories usually have a happy ending.

Lift your veil
So that I may see your eyebrows
Long and narrow like a half moon …

It's Rewi's favourite song, an ancient Uyghur melody from Xinjiang province. He'd asked for it to be sung at the end of the concert.

Lift your veil
So that I may see your eyes
That shine bright and move my heart ….

He thinks of his mother, so far away yet so near in her letters and her support. ('Sorry my letters are torn,' he writes. 'Perhaps not surprising. So many people seem interested don't they?'[2]) He thinks of Chingling, who's moved from Shanghai and is now living in Chongqing, the wartime capital. Her letters to him, those that reach him, are, like his letters home, censored. But he carries them, with the poems of Lu Xun, next to his heart.

Lift your veil
So that I may see your face
Red and round
That resembles an apple in autumn ...[3]

I will hear this sung by Rewi's grandchildren and great-grandchildren at the family reunion held at Wharenui School – where Rewi was a pupil and his father headmaster – in December 2017. It is 46 years almost to the day after Rewi, on a return visit in 1971, opened the library named in his honour. My eyes will fill with tears. Sitting around the table with my Chinese cousins, the person I see as the veil is lifted is Rewi.

CHAPTER FORTY-NINE

'SHANDAN in summer is one of the most beautiful places in China,' Rewi writes in *Yo Banfa!*. Never was that more true than in the summer of 1944, when the larks seemed to sing more sweetly than ever, and the crane – symbol of longevity and peace – standing guard over the swimming hole became, in Rewi's mind, one with the birds captured on parchment by artists over the centuries. The war with Japan was coming to an end. Despite their distance from the conflict, George and Rewi, ears glued to the short-wave wireless, can read the signs. But that doesn't mean they can let up on their production of goods for the Red Army. Another war waits in the wings, the outcome of which will determine both their personal futures and the future of their adopted home.

News of the German surrender reaches Shandan at the beginning of their second summer. May 1945. Rewi orders the school gong to be sounded for an immediate stop-work. An impromptu celebration follows. Hastily created banners are erected on the *lei tai*, where the Gung Ho flag flutters in the spring breeze; drums and cymbals are hauled out onto the square; an impromptu dance is performed. Even the animals join in: camels braying, perhaps in protest at the clamour; buffaloes grunting and snorting; Skimpy dashing around, barking furiously, as if stung by nettles. Finally George gathers up his choir and leads the school in the singing of the new Chinese anthem, 'The East is Red', adapted from an old Shaanxi folk song. Rewi mutters a quiet thank you to the gods that the suffering in Europe is over. Though of course he knows it isn't. Look what happened after the last war – the flu epidemic, the financial collapse, the millions thrown out of work …

The anthem comes to an end. The assembly starts to break up. Everyone is smiling. The students know what this day means. They've heard Rewi say often enough that 'the purpose of co-operation is to build the kind of human structure that will outlast the "follow the leader" psychology of fascism'.[1] So they have every reason to be happy. Trouble is, Rewi can't forget what he knows – that the nationalist army, one eye on the oilfields, the other on the southward surge of the victorious Russians, is hovering.

We're kittens in the path of a tiger, he thinks, as he follows the students inside.

*

By July, with Japan still in the war and the nationalist army closing in on the oilfields, Rewi has no choice but to alert staff and pupils to the danger facing the school. Teachers from overseas are offered the chance to leave. No one takes it up. The key word now is vigilance. They may not have much in the way of weapons, but they are well supplied with cunning. Forewarned is forearmed.

Obliged to keep up the pretence of good relations, Rewi and George attend a banquet hosted by KMT officials visiting Shandan. 'A chance to discuss the school's progress' is the reason given for the invitation. 'Bunkum!' Rewi snapped when he read that. 'It's just an excuse for those loafers to throw a party.'

'Or spy on us,' George muttered.

The banquet goes on for hours. Walking home through the cicada-humming darkness, Rewi takes out his frustration by kicking stones, till George asks him to stop because the dust is making him cough. 'Do they really think we don't know what they're up to?' Rewi grumbles. 'All that tucker was paid for by Gung Ho funds.'

'Well, whoever paid for it it's left me feeling rotten.'

'It's eating too much. After what we're used to. You'll be fine by morning.'

But he's not. He feels worse. Food poisoning? Rewi wonders. George doubts it. It's his toe that's sore, not his stomach. He stubbed it playing basketball.

Rewi tells him to get it seen to, and hurries off to work.

As he goes about the day's business, cycling from one part of the school to another, Rewi forgets about George. He's tough, he'll throw this thing off. Looking green around the gills is to be expected from time to time …

It's his friend Evans Carlson, a former US marine intelligence officer (later a brigadier-general) whom he'd met back in 1938 in Wuhan, who's on his mind this morning. It's an unlikely friendship, but then Carlson was never your typical Yankee officer. 'I am an American soldier working in army intelligence,' he told his Chinese hosts when he visited the Red Army in Yan'an. 'I do not want to pry. Anything you want me to see please show me and I will be content.'[2] No wonder Rewi liked him. Now the man whose support for Gung Ho was reflected in his decision to call the soldiers he led in the Battle of Guadalcanal the Gung Ho Raiders is not answering his letters. Nor is his former boss in China, General Joe Stilwell, the soldier who persuaded President Roosevelt that the war in China was pivotal to the success of the war in the Pacific.

So what's going on? Have the hero of the first major Allied victory in the Pacific, and the general who led his troops out of Burma when it fell to the Japanese, been silenced? It would never have happened under Roosevelt, whose death four months ago sent the Chinese–American relationship into a tailspin. God knows what's going on in President's Truman's White House. Or what poison's being poured into the ear of the new commander in chief. Plenty, if the amount of military hardware being sent directly to the KMT is anything to go by.[3]

I need a dose of George's optimism, Rewi thinks as the day draws to a close. George blames the lack of communication from Carlson and Stilwell on wartime censorship. He's also convinced that's the reason he hasn't heard from Ren. Rewi doesn't have the heart to disabuse him. What possible interest could George's romance be to the censors? Though he'll never say it, the most likely explanation for her silence is the one George cannot bear to hear – she's dead. As for the silence of his American friends, if his hunch is right then it means President Truman has abandoned the 'two governments' policy, Roosevelt's name for the knife-edge diplomacy required to hold the United Front together. Which also means whoever is advising him is lying. Why else would the leader of the most powerful nation in the world side with a government that's about as popular in China as the plague? Does Truman even know how many provinces are now defiantly communist? The KMT may have the weapons, but the communists have the numbers. The president should read his history. Napoleon had the weapons too, but the Russians had the numbers. More than that, they had right on their side. Which is precisely what the Chinese people have.

He'll feel better after he's talked with George. His optimism may be misplaced, but that doesn't stop it acting like a tonic.

But George, when evening comes, is not up to serious discussion. Saying he feels 'fluey', he takes himself off to bed, insisting he'll be fine after a good night's sleep. He isn't. Rewi, more concerned than he cares to admit, wonders if George might have contracted dengue fever. He's just recovered from a bout of it himself, picked up when he stayed at a particularly unsavoury inn on the way back from Lanzhou. Whoever called it the Inn of National Construction was even more of an optimist than George! The place was barely standing. But George doesn't think its dengue fever, and he's certain it's not malaria. 'Had that, and this ain't it,' he says, pushing away the bowl of congee Rewi has just dished up for him.

Rewi had been planning to bring up the subject of Lao San, George's Number Three son, over breakfast, but with George looking so ill he thinks better of it.

Lao San is old enough now to move into the dormitories. George isn't going to like it. He'll argue that the brothers shouldn't be separated. Whereas the truth is, it's George who can't bear to be separated from his boys. Lao Da and Lao Er, Number One and Two sons, are almost fully grown. Lao Da has announced his intention to join the Red Army. Lao Er is bound to follow suit. God knows how George will cope with their absence and the almost certain silence that will follow. There's been no news of Alan or Mike for over two years now. 'My poor heart,' George wailed the other night, thumping his chest in mock despair. 'It's not used to all this loving.'[4]

By the end of the day George is worse. His jaw is hurting. He has difficulty swallowing. Damn and blast, Rewi says to himself. Tetanus. Should have spotted it earlier. The school clinic doesn't have any serum, but there should be some at the clinic in Shandan. A boy is dispatched immediately. But the town clinic has run out. So Rewi sends telegrams to all the clinics and hospitals in the Gansu Corridor, stressing that the need is urgent.

Next morning, having had no reply to his telegrams, he sends out trucks. 'Drive like the wind,' he tells the transport boys, ordering them to go as far as Lanzhou if necessary. The irony in urging the boys to throw caution out the window when he has always emphasised the need for vigilance in driving over Gansu's dirt roads is not lost on him. But the boys know the score. If the serum isn't found, their beloved teacher will die.

Rewi stays by George's side all night, wishing there was someone to pray to, but praying anyway because there's nothing else he can do. George has asked him to read aloud from Ed Snow's *Red Star Over China*. Every so often he whispers 'yes' in agreement. 'I see it all now,' he murmurs at one point.

Eventually the life-saving serum is located. 'Not long now,' Rewi says, bending close so that George can hear him. When no reply comes, he lowers his head to George's chest. His breathing is ragged. There are long gaps when he doesn't breathe at all. Rewi looks at his watch. Calculates the time it will take to drive from Lanzhou.

'Please,' he says out loud. 'Please please …'

Half an hour later, George is dead. Rewi, having failed to resuscitate him, sinks back into his chair, too stunned to do more than gasp for breath. George is 30 years old. He has four adopted sons. He's in love with a beautiful Chinese girl. How can he be gone?

He stays by George's side till dawn. Then, with the striking of the gong, he makes his way to the room where Lao San and Lao Si sleep. He tries to find the right words but there are none, so he holds them tight, pressing their small heads into his chest. 'You're my sons now,' he tells them. But they can't hear him. Their hearts, like his, are breaking.

The only work that is done in the school that day is the digging of a grave outside the South Gate. 'My all to the Bailie School,' George, unable to talk, had scribbled across the cover of Ed's book.[5] What that meant in material terms was a typewriter, his precious red notebook, a camera, his patched blue bedroll and his shortwave wireless. What it meant in spiritual terms was a legacy that would play out down the years, fading through the decade of the Cultural Revolution, only to revive again in the re-birth of Gung Ho in the 1980s. George Hogg, like Rewi Alley, would live on as a 'Great Fighter, Old Comrade and Loyal Friend of China'.

*

The following day the whole school gathers at the graveside to farewell their teacher, friend and father. They lay the Gung Ho flag on the coffin. They sing the school song. Then they bow three times. Forty years on Rewi will describe the scene, still as vivid to him as it was on that bright summer day so long ago, in his memoir: 'The boys in their white vests and blue shorts stood silently around. The Nanshan mountains gleamed white through the green of the trees. I could not say a damned thing.'

Next morning Lao San and Lao Si get up before the gong sounds and carry fresh coffee and steamed bread to the graveside. ('We had never met anyone like him,' Lao San will say to me about his father. 'We never will.') They are still sitting there when Rewi comes to call them to breakfast. He lifts them to their feet, takes a hand in each of his, and leads them up the hill to the school. Don't worry, George, he says, addressing an absence he cannot comprehend, I'll take good care of them for you.

> ... Sunset, and from behind the peaks
> red rays spread over the Old Silk
> Road below, stealing around a grave
> by a stream; an evening wind rises;
> in it still the sound of the singing lads
> he loved and worked with, comforting him ...'[6]

Rewi not only kept his promise to George, he wrote regularly to George's mother in England to update her on the progress of her grandsons. 'Lao 4 was here for a month's holiday,' he tells her in a July 1966 letter, 'George would have been proud of him.'[7]

CHAPTER FIFTY

'**IN** Shandan after the passing of George Hogg I felt a kind of loneliness,' Rewi writes in his memoir. Admitting that he had never met anyone 'who could enter others' lives as George could', he would talk of him for the rest of his life. From this time on the word 'lonely' keeps cropping up in Rewi's writing, not as a bleat of self-pity but as an acknowledgement of what is missing. Fortunately he is too busy to spend much time dwelling on his emotions. He carries on as he's always carried on, throwing himself into the demands of each day, ignoring the pleadings of his heart.

In addition to the day-to-day running of the school, a job George made look easy but that Rewi will soon learn is anything but, he is now responsible for George's four grieving sons. He can't stop Lao Da – nor Lao Er when his turn comes – heading off to Yan'an, any more than he could stop his own sons. But he worries about the two younger boys. They've lost their father; now they're having to cope with losing their older brothers.

'These children did more for me than than I could do for them because they [moved] me from loneliness,' he writes in his memoir. It's not just the Nie boys he's thinking of, it's all the students. He never tires of watching them learn, marking the transformation of each boy and girl from illiterate, half-starved child to eager-to-learn, healthy young adult. Sometimes, when teachers leave and replacements can't be found, he has to fill the gaps himself, teaching everything from animal husbandry to truck maintenance. But he doesn't mind. Like his father he is a natural teacher.

As July merges into August, Rewi finds comfort where he can: sharing a compote of frozen pears, dried apricots and ginger around the iron stove in the bathhouse; joining the kids in games of basketball and volleyball, surprised to find that the competitive streak instilled by his father is still alive and kicking; reading letters from his mother, from Pip, from Chingling; retreating to his cottage on the *lei tai* at the end of the day to be welcomed by an excitable Skimpy, while Muggins, more interested in food, purrs around his ankles.

Midnight – Muggins the cat puts out a paw, taps my face;
I turn and find Skimpy the Alsatian licking my hand,
And whining a little; so get up and open the door,

> And with these oddly assorted two climb the Lei Tai
> Into the Central Asian moonlight ...[1]

*

On 6 August 1945, at 8.15am, a nuclear bomb code-named 'Little Boy' is dropped on the Japanese city of Hiroshima from an American B29 bomber. An estimated 70,000 people, including 20,000 Japanese combatants and 2000 Korean slave labourers, are killed. By the end of the year that number will have grown to over 150,000.

'The force from which the sun draws its power has been loosed,' President Truman announces from the White House. 'The basic power of the universe' has been harnessed. Should Japan not agree to surrender, this 'new and revolutionary increase in destruction' will be used again.[2]

Three days later a second nuclear bomb is dropped, on Nagasaki. The Japanese surrender follows on 15 August. General MacArthur, the American Supreme Commander in the Pacific, orders the Japanese forces in China to surrender to the Kuomintang, the government led by Generalissimo Chiang Kaishek.

Rewi, struggling with a toxic mix of shock, horror, outrage and sheer incredulity, loses his battle to keep the Alley temper in check. Small boys scatter as he strides through the South Gate down the hill to George's grave to bare his soul to his friend. What price your optimism now, George? What price my own?

Rewi takes no pleasure in Japan's humiliation. His tirades against the Japanese have always been directed at its imperial leaders, not the people (though, as we've seen, his spoken words don't always tally with his written statements. Near the end of his life he warned my journalist cousin Philip Somerville 'never to trust' the Japanese). But there is no ambiguity around his outrage at America's use of atomic weapons. The Japanese people were being burned alive, while the emperor and his imperial advisers stayed safe in their palaces, protected by the mighty US. Meanwhile China, now in the hands of Chiang and his powerful ally, looks set to become a capitalist state modelled on and subservient to the US. Is this what we fought Japan for? he asks himself bitterly.

Then, from one day to the next, comes news that blows Rewi's bitterness away. Alan and Mike are alive! I see my cousin, struggling to hold back tears, running down the hill to the grave site to share the news with George, assuring him that with the war over it's only a matter of time before there's equally good news of Lao Da and Lao Er.

Rewi doesn't write about his joy at being united with Alan in Shandan, nor his surprise at discovering his Number One son is married. Like his grief at the death of George, his feelings go too deep for words.

*

'It was perfectly clear to us that if we told the Japanese to lay down their arms immediately and march to the seaboard, the entire country would be taken over by the communists. We therefore had to take the unusual step of using the enemy as a garrison until we could airlift Chinese National troops to South China and send marines to guard the seaports.'[3] President Truman's words leave no doubt as to the nature of America's agenda following the Allied victory over Japan. The nuanced views of President Roosevelt, Joe Stilwell, Evans Carlson and others were consigned to history. The future, as decreed by the US, belonged to Chiang Kaishek. Never mind that the communists had fought harder and longer than the KMT. Never mind that the Red Army had opposed the policy of appeasement from the beginning. They were communists, so they must be destroyed. Better to leave the Japanese, war crimes and all, to hold the line against Mao's peasant army than sit back and watch China turn Red.

At first there is a semblance of unity. The 'Double Tenth Agreement', signed on 10 October 1945 by both Chiang and Mao, secures a promise from both sides that they will seek peaceful reconstruction. It doesn't last. Skirmishes break out; full-scale battles follow. Fifty thousand US marines are sent to fight alongside the KMT. The first transfer of what will become over US$5 billion in aid is paid into the Central Bank of China. With the military might of America lined up against them, and the Soviet Union staying on the sidelines, the communists are out-gunned and friendless.

Rewi, following developments with increasing apprehension, does his best to keep things calm. As Chiang's forces move closer, Shandan village, now grown to the size of a town, begins to fill with Ma Bufang's soldiers, eager to ally themselves with the advancing army. Never has Rewi been more grateful to the townsfolk for spreading the rumour that the school is heavily armed. When Ma's soldiers try to help themselves to its trucks and equipment, the students, acting as if they have an entire armoury at their backs and not a mere handful of rifles, put up such a show of force the soldiers melt away.

Likewise when a KMT general turns up, demanding that the school move to a 'safer site', Rewi, recognising the ruse for what it is – an attempt to take over the school – summons his 'troops'. Putting their dramatic skills to good use, the boys soon have the general scurrying back to his base.

In July 1946 Chiang tears up the Double Tenth Agreement and launches a full-scale assault on communist territory in northwest China. For the next three years China will be ravaged by civil war. Shandan, on the edge of the Silk Road, is never far from the line of fire. Now when the students sing their guerrilla songs they know the enemy is close. Close enough to burn down their school, conscript the older students and kill their teachers.

'Of course I was not scared of being killed,' Rewi said, when asked how he'd felt during this time. 'I'd been through all that in World War 1. But a lot of kids depended on me. If I had been shot it would have been chaotic.'[4]

Slowly, painfully – the death toll will end in the millions – the communists start to regain the territory the American-backed KMT had taken from them. Lacking the sophisticated weaponry of the enemy, much of it purloined from the Japanese, the Reds do have one huge advantage – the support of the peasants. The nationalists favour a return to the old landlord system. The communists are promising land reform, giving peasants the right for the first time in history to farm their own land. With that promise ringing in their ears, China's vast, hitherto silent majority will eventually carry the day.

For Rewi and the students of the Shandan Bailie School, liberation comes on 19 September 1949, 'a beautiful day, warm and still, with the best weather of the autumn … Everything … working normally. The water wheel churning, factories humming, heads bent over books in classrooms, flour mill grinding flour, apples being picked in the orchard, leather-workers putting soles on felt boots for winter … Suddenly a lone PLA [People's Liberation Army] soldier appears on the horizon. He strolls casually across the fields towards the East Gate, stopping to ask the boy whose job it is to mind the stud rams grazing on wheat stubble, if there are any KMT soldiers in the town. The boys answers, "Meiyou!" [None] The soldier turns and walks back the way he came … Soon a rider on horseback comes along the road telling the people to be calm, that the place has been liberated. Another rider asks one of the boys, "Has your headmaster run away?" "Hao hao" [Good good] he says, when the reply comes that no one in the school has run anywhere.'[5]

The following day the school's trucks – which Rewi had ordered the transport boys to dismantle to prevent them falling into the hands of the

KMT – are reassembled, ready to take part in the liberation of the Yumen oilfields. At the same time, barrels of diesel, stored out of sight in the coal mine, are manhandled up from the shaft. Finally Rewi, like the corporal he once was, assembles the transport boys and instructs them on the best way to assist the PLA in this next stage of the liberation struggle. By sunset the convoy is ready to depart. Standing on the *lei tai*, watching the trucks, red flags fluttering, snaking through the East Gate, Rewi feels like a proud father watching his sons graduate. Joseph Needham, you should be here, he thinks. Knowing the oilfields as you do, you should be part of that convoy … Then he thinks of George. As he does every day, many times a day. You, more than anyone, should be seeing this, George. This day belongs to you …

*

On 1 October 1949 Mao Zedong leads his victorious People's Liberation Army into Peking (it will not become Beijing until 1958). Standing on the steps of Tiananmen Gate he proclaims the New Republic. The atmosphere, captured on film, is electric. Mao's speech is unimpressive but that hardly matters. Surrounded by his closest comrades, including Soong Chingling and Zhou Enlai, Mao could have spoken in Esperanto and the reaction would have been the same. After half a century of warfare, China is at peace.

Only it isn't. Not yet. Parts of China are still in enemy – that is, warlord – hands. In one of my lost letters from Rewi, I recall him saying that there were places in the mountains that were still 'unsubdued'. Until I read Gao Xingjian's *Soul Mountain* I assumed he was talking about Tibet, a divisive subject that will set Alley whānau tongues wagging the day we visit a Tibetan embroidery co-operative. But I think now he may have been writing about something more elusive: the persistence of ancient ways of living in some of China's remote mountain villages.

*

Did Rewi know, in the days following the departure of the convoy, that his days at Shandan were numbered? The PLA was making its presence felt in Shandan. He was no longer in control. Surely he sensed something? But the record is silent. His memoir records the streams of singing, laughing peasants carrying red banners, making their way across the fields to celebrate 'peace and emancipation': 'The old dragons on the temple roofs, the dropping tiles, the whole process of gentle decay seemed to be arrested by those voices, as if some powerful hand were sweeping the scattered pieces back into order again, back into meaning.'

I imagine the students, now numbering well over 600, singing the songs George has taught them as the soldiers of the victorious PLA move around the school. The students are as certain as the soldiers that the future belongs to them. And for a few months it seems it does. Classes go on as before, only now there is no fear, no need for vigilance. Then, early in 1950, Rewi is summoned to a meeting with the local military commander. Compliments are exchanged, gratitude expressed, but when Rewi asks about funding for the school – whether he should still be accepting donations from ICCIC and Corso – there's an ominous silence. Three months later, the school is placed under the control of the army. Rewi is allowed to stay on as headmaster, but he will not be in the driving seat. What is taught at the school, how it is taught, will be decided by the government.

The writing is on the wall. Rewi can no longer pretend otherwise. Sitting on the *lei tai*, gazing out at the mountains that become, in the blink of an eye, the mountains of his childhood, the sadness he feels is so profound he can only express it obliquely. 'One does die quite a number of times before the actual demise. We go in stages I guess …'[6]

In July 1951 the school is brought under the umbrella of the Northwest Oil Bureau – a department of the Ministry of Fuel. The government is not interested in having the students make pots or paper, blankets or soap, glassware or leather goods; it wants technicians who can work in the oil industry. Everything else is superfluous.

From this time on the blows come thick and fast. Corso announces that because Rewi's school is now being supported by the communist government it will no longer be sending funds or supplies. According to Rewi's SIS file, supplies were still being sent as late as 1953, but because their 'nature and extent' could not be verified the conclusion was that these deliveries were simply a last-ditch attempt on the part of Corso to keep the school in business.[7] The mood in New Zealand has changed. Rewi's poetry collection, *This is China Today*, published by the Caxton Press in Christchurch in 1952, attracts hostile criticism not so much for the quality of the poetry as for its celebration of the communist way of life.

By the end of 1952 it's all over. In fact it had been over, in real terms, since June 1951, when the new government ordered the winding up of the international committee of Gung Ho. From this time on there was nothing for Ida Pruitt, or any of Gung Ho's American benefactors, to do. Deprived of funding, sidelined by the new government, the co-operative movement staggers on for a few more years before finally giving up the ghost. It will be 30 years before Gung Ho is a reality in China again.

As for the school, it's not just the changes to its structure and purpose that Rewi has to deal with. It's rumours and false accusations, fuelled by a former KMT officer posing as an ardent supporter of the new regime. At 'struggle meetings' – part of the apparatus of the new government – two of Rewi's best students are accused of being 'tigers', the name given to the hated money-squeezers of the past. Not for the first time, and certainly not for the last, Zhou Enlai comes to the rescue, and Rewi's reputation, along with the school, is saved.

But the reprieve is temporary. Towards the end of 1952 Rewi is ordered to move the school, lock stock and barrel, to Lanzhou. ('Seems Rewi's been moved on, or the school has …' Words overheard six decades ago making sense at last.) Rewi will play no part in the running of what is now the Lanzhou Petroleum School, an institution committed solely to the training of workers for the oil industry. For some in the Party it's enough that Rewi was once associated with the KMT, conveniently forgetting that so too was their leader, Mao Zedong. He hasn't been publicly disgraced. Or forced into exile, like so many. But he is no longer wanted as an educator.

In the years that follow, the school at Shandan will become a ruin. Even had the earthquake of 1954 not happened, the swirling Gobi desert winds would have done the work of destruction. Classrooms, factories, dormitories, basketball court, orchards, gardens, the clinic where wounded Red Army soldiers were treated, George Hogg's lovingly tended grave: all were doomed, like the cities of old, to be reclaimed by the relentless desert.

CHAPTER FIFTY-ONE

So has one met the lonely Western exile
Planted – by war, so little understood, in
This China; home and all that home means,
In the vague uncertain rear ...
'What a goddamned country! Why the hell ...'
And so one wonders anew, why one loves it so well ...[1]

FOR the first two years after his banishment from Shandan Rewi will live, courtesy of the new government, in the Peking Hotel in Beijing. He may not be doing what he wants, but he has plenty to occupy him. 'Quite busy with this and that, reading and writing and so on,' he writes to Pip. 'On living – one does not worry much. If there is work, there will be food. I have some books and some shirts and shorts for summer, cadre uniform for the winter and a room to live in. A typewriter and some paper.'[2]

The Cold War (the term was coined by Bernard Baruch, an adviser to President Truman) is at its height. On the Korean peninsula, on China's northeastern border, a war as cruel and intimate as any in China's recent history is waging. In speech after speech, poem after poem, Rewi will rage against US imperialism. His anger is visceral, fuelled, I can't help thinking, by his inner torment at the loss of his 'home' in Shandan.

I was at primary school when the Korean War broke out. New Zealand, as a loyal American ally, lost no time answering the call to send troops to fight alongside the US. I assumed we were fighting for decency and democracy, that the 'enemy' was just another manifestation of the wickedness of the Nazis. I knew the word communism, but in my mind there were good communists (Uncle Rewi and the whole of China) and bad ones (Stalin, the USSR, North Korea). I hadn't read what Rewi was writing about the Korean War, and wouldn't for many years. Now that I have read his words, as well as other more nuanced assessments, I have a different view of what happened on that troubled peninsula from 1950 to 1953.

Following the Allied victory in 1945, Korea was artificially divided by the infamous 38th Parallel (brainchild of US Secretary of State John Foster Dulles). When war broke out between the two Koreas, it seemed to many in the West to be the perfect location for the battle between capitalism and communism. People would be killed, but they wouldn't be Europeans and they wouldn't, on the whole, be Americans. No one in the wake of Hiroshima and Nagasaki wanted a hot war. But that didn't mean America was prepared to sit back and watch Soviet power and influence extend south of the 38th Parallel.

The irony in this situation was that Japan, Korea's traditional enemy, was now an ally of the US. The Japanese, who'd occupied Korea for most of the twentieth century, knew better than anyone that the population of North Korea was largely made up of soldiers who'd led the fierce guerrilla campaign against them. Now, five years after Japan's defeat in World War II, the sabre-rattling of the Cold War has brought destruction back to the peninsula, and the Korean people are once again caught up in a war most see as not of their making. It began with a boast: Syngman Rhee, president of South Korea, boasted that he was about to invade the North. The North responded by invading first.

For Rewi the war was a turning point. He had responded to the destruction of Hiroshima and Nagasaki with anger and disgust, but his long association with the US, source of much of the funding for Gung Ho, and his friendship with many Americans, kept alive for him the possibility that the America of President Roosevelt had not entirely disappeared. American carpet-bombing of North Korea would put an end to that. 'Extermination passed over this land,' the French filmmaker Chris Marker declared after visiting the country in 1957. 'Who could count what burned with the houses? … When a country is spilt in two by an artificial border, and irreconcilable propaganda is exercised on each side, it's naive to ask where the war comes from: the border is the war.'[3]

Rewi visited North Korea in 1956. He was used to scenes of carnage and destruction but he could still be shocked at the evidence of what war does, especially when it is waged from the air. 'It was a Korea empty of buildings, a wilderness of shell holes and battered army equipment, a Korea that wiped away its tears and blood, and buried its dead.'[4]

For more than a decade Rewi's anti-Americanism would burn red-hot, stoked not only by the United States' bellicose foreign policy but by its treatment of his friends: Agnes Smedley and Ed Snow forced into exile; war heroes Evans Carlson and Joe Stilwell accused of betraying their country; Joseph Needham blacklisted; Anna Louise Strong barred from returning to her homeland. But it was America's possession of the nuclear bomb that most disgusted him. He told the overseas students who visited him in 1967 that the only people who could be trusted with the nuclear bomb were the Chinese![5]

'It's the American century,' Henry Luce, the most influential private citizen in America of his day, and a supporter of Gung Ho, boasted in an editorial in *Life* magazine.[6] Rewi was having none of it. Within months of the start of the Korean War his characterisations of the US as 'the chief enemy of mankind', a 'force for evil', a 'government of slaves of imperialism, riddled with corruption' would appear in both his prose and his poetry with the regularity and monotony of cliché. In an interview published in New Zealand, he warned his fellow Kiwis that 'slavish following of America would mean being dragged into one adventure after another, all for the purpose of enslaving foreign people to American commercial power.'[7] He followed this with a live broadcast from Beijing, in which he painted a grim picture of what would happen in New Zealand if, as in Korea, the North (Island) were to go to war against the South. 'It is the duty of everyone to try and stop this war,' he maintained. 'The boys at my school have volunteered to go to Korea … If you ask the government to withdraw the troops [they] will not have to stand and be mowed down by machine gun fire, or buried in a Korean cemetery … Wake up down there, you can yet be in time.'[8]

His words, and in particular his claim that the Americans were engaging in germ warfare in North Korea, did not go down well with the New Zealand press. 'Propaganda from Rewi Alley' was the headline in the *Dominion Post* on 1 June 1952. New Zealanders had been proud to be associated with the work of Rewi Alley in China, but not any more. The 'recent cabled report of his descent again into the political arena as a propagandist for Communist actions' had made clear that his entry into politics was the 'price of his continued residence among the Chinese people.'[9] Other reactions went further: 'Worse than any of Hitler's broadcasts.' 'Rewi Alley is China's Goebbels.' 'Alley is clearly a Moscow agent on a propaganda mission.'[10]

There's no doubt that Rewi was stung by these reports. In his reply to the article in the *Dominion Post* he wrote: 'It is interesting that you feel a good New Zealander should not be mixed up in politics. One usually hears the term mixed up in politics being applied to the man on the other side. The man on one's own side is usually an able statesman, a clear thinker, outstanding personality etc. Yet everything concerned with peace and better livelihood is so highly political I am proud to be mixed up in such …'[11]

From now on Rewi would be a person of particular interest to the SIS, which characterised him as a member of a 'subversive group' with links to a person of 'security significance' (Mao Zedong).[12] On his four visits to New Zealand in the 1960s and early 70s, travelling on his Peking Citizen's Certificate, he was shadowed by agents wherever he went. Among the recently declassified files (eight remain classified) is a four-page summary of Rewi's life and work up to 1954.[13] The tone is moderate, confined to the presentation of facts rather than their interpretation. One enlightened New Zealand consulate official even described Rewi as 'a minor Albert Schweitzer ... a holy fool'.[14]

(In a recent interview with the SIS I learned that the reason for its interest in Rewi Alley during the Cold War period had more to do with instructions from New Zealand's two main allies – Britain and the US – than any sense that he was a threat to his native land. In the paranoid atmosphere of the time, both Australia and New Zealand were regarded by the Americans and the British as potential seed beds for communism. The 1954 defection from the Russian embassy in Canberra of the spies Evdokya and Vladimir Petrov merely confirmed the American view that no country was immune to the cancer of communism. So when, in the wake of the Hungarian Revolution of 1956, the Communist Party of New Zealand (CPNZ) opted to follow the Chinese line, interest in the Kiwi who was a friend of China's leaders increased, as did the pressure on New Zealand's fledgling secret service, which had come into being that year. From then on, until New Zealand established diplomatic relations with China in December 1972, the SIS, obeying orders from its allied agencies, kept Rewi on its radar.)

What struck me as I read through Rewi's files was the repeated mention of China's claim that the Americans were not only engaged in germ warfare in North Korea, they were also dropping napalm. At the Asia-Pacific Peace Conference in Beijing in October 1952 Rewi was one of the signatories of a declaration that: 'The people of China and Korea have indeed been the objective of bacteriological warfare ... We are all convinced that the findings of the International Scientific Commission are correct.'[15] (The conclusion was subsequently supported by Joseph Needham.) Given the extensive use of napalm by US forces in Vietnam only a few years later, I'm inclined to give some credence to the claim.

When Rewi visited New Zealand in 1960, the SIS commented on his 'considerable gift for evading difficult questions'.[16] But there were no evasions when it came to discussions of the war in North Korea. 'I have never betrayed New Zealand,' Rewi insisted. 'What I betrayed was the idea many New Zealanders had of what a Kiwi should be and what was right and wrong in the political world. There is a very big difference. Successive New Zealand governments have tried hard to discredit me, as if I was some sort of communist threat to them or a traitor. Well I am a communist, but I am not a traitor. I have always loved New Zealand. I just said what I thought was important and true.'[17]

'Don't believe printed matter about me either good or bad,' he wrote to his family. 'I am a very ordinary person.'[18] But it was too late. The traitor label had been attached to him with super-glue. And I would have the first of several fights in the school playground because of my 'commie uncle'.

Towards the end of his life Rewi would concede that the attacks on him in New Zealand were not as widespread as he had first thought. There were many, even at the highest level, who took a different view of him. Prime Minister Walter Nash, quietly ignoring US policy, agreed to meet him during his 1960 visit – anticipating New Zealand's decision three decades later to defy the US and implement a nuclear-free policy. In a letter to Rewi's brother Pip, the prime minister wrote: 'I shall continue to do what I can at the most expedient moment to help achieve recognition of the Government of the mainland of China.'[19] When Alfred Kohlberg, an ally of US Senator Joseph McCarthy who led the witch-hunt against communists in the 1950s, asked the New Zealand government to put a stop to Rewi's propaganda work, this was the official response: 'Mr Kohlberg is not the type who appreciates that the NZ Government has no control over the utterances of Mr Rewi Alley, and much less responsible for them [sic]. Mr Kohlberg is quite capable of communicating to some Senate committee the poems of Mr Alley and of alleging, if he receives no further communication from us, that the Government of NZ has taken no steps to repudiate the sentiments of these poems.'[20]

What Rewi would never concede was that his view of America and American foreign policy at the time was wrong. (In a July 1953 letter he described the Americans in Korea as 'a treacherous lot of scamps'.[21]) His warning to New Zealand about the risk of slavishly following the American lead on Korea was followed by a letter, signed by all the foreign teachers at the Shandan school, to the American prisoners of war held captive by the Chinese, denouncing America's aims. The Americans were bombing northeast China where Rewi's foster son, Lao San, was living. 'Why do they come?' Lao San wrote to Rewi. 'It's just like the Japanese bombing us in Baoji during the war.'[22] Had the war in Korea not already cemented Rewi's anti-Americanism, the war that broke out in the early 60s in Indochina would assuredly have done so. Like so many around the world he deplored the US's determination to dominate Vietnam. He no longer even referred to the basic goodness of the American people. The whole nation, in his opinion, was contaminated by the lust for power and money.

> Into Vietnam after French
> failure, were dumped
> US draftees
> US air strength
> US weaponry
> US navies
> US dollars, all
> on the same savage
> mission to break the spirit
> of Vietnam …[23]

Not great poetry but there's no denying the white heat in which the words were penned. What Rewi made of the 1972 visit to China of President Nixon (whom he'd nicknamed 'Richard the Sly'), a visit partly engineered by Edgar Snow, is not recorded. The Cultural Revolution was in full swing so Rewi was effectively gagged, but when it came to toeing the Party line on Vietnam no gag was needed. Here was the man whom he held responsible for the worst abuses of that war now being received with full diplomatic honours in Beijing. 'Lies are bullets that usually miss their mark,' he wrote in a poem titled 'Defeat'.[24] So who was telling lies now? Mao? Nixon?

The visit of the American table-tennis team the year before Nixon's visit, when 'ping pong balls flew and eighteen thousand spectators applauded as young Americans played Chinese', must have alerted Rewi to the way the wind was blowing.[25] But could he make such a change himself? Could he go along with this 'ping-pong diplomacy'? He didn't really have a choice. In 'The Strongest Note for Peace', one of the many contemporary poems he translated at this time, the America of Walt Whitman and the American Constitution is compared with the America of President Truman, the first man in history to authorise the use of the atom bomb. 'I seem to hear your ancestors weeping under the sod,' the poet writes.[26] Whether Rewi wept for the loss of America's innocence was not the issue. If he wanted to go on writing about the 'paper tiger' after the Nixon visit, he would have to find a new language – *that* was the issue.

With the rise to power of Deng Xiaoping in 1978, the first decisive steps were taken towards a rapprochement with the West. Anti-American rhetoric didn't disappear overnight but the language became softer, less provocative. Deng had made up his mind. China was to be opened up to the West. In the new China there would be 'Socialism with Chinese Characteristics'. In other words, capitalism was to be allowed to play a part in reinvigorating the sluggish Chinese economy. Rewi put his reservations aside. Deng Xiaoping was his friend. If letting in capitalism was the price to be paid for keeping the 'ultra-leftists' at bay, then so be it. 'The Nixon visit,' he wrote retrospectively, 'led to a great reaching out to the American people by Chinese, and a great desire on the part of ordinary American people for new understanding of China.'[27]

Towards the end of his life, in conversation with David Mahon, Rewi's restless mind had moved in yet another direction. 'They [Deng's reforms] worry me. They will let the capitalists back in and so much of what we fought for will be undone ... I must admit socialism has not worked. People in the end want money and power and they forget the ideas they once stood for.' Mahon recorded that at this point Rewi looked 'sad, defeated'. 'You can't force a revolution on anyone,' was his unhappy conclusion. Later, in an unconscious acknowledgment of the idea that seeded his humanitarianism, he expressed an even deeper distress: 'Human nature isn't up to Christianity and it isn't up to communism – so institutions grow where once there was just this one shining idea ... and the idea turns toxic.'[28]

CHAPTER FIFTY-TWO
18 April 2017

WE are back on the Alley Whānau bus. Shandan is far behind us now. Our destination is a Tibetan Embroidery Co-operative.

'For me Sandan is a place of surging memories,' Rewi wrote in 'Sandan Return 1973'. But it was more than that, far more. It was the place where he found himself, where the fragmented parts of himself – the lonely boy, the soldier, the farmer, the humanitarian, the man who longed for a family – came together, and he was whole. What he left behind, when the leaders of China's Brave New World decided he was no longer needed, was his soul.

'First eat bitterness then the good times will come,' the old Fujianese folk song promises. On that final day as Rewi turns for a last look at the *paifang* he and the boys had erected, the Gung Ho motto shining through the early-morning mist, he tries to tell himself good times will come again. But his heart is too heavy to believe it.

Dave is talking to us about Tibet. He's being careful. He understands that many of us will have strong feelings on the subject. Some of us have walked on marches in support of Tibetan freedom. A few have travelled there. All of us are aware of the mystique surrounding the Dalai Lama. As I listen to Dave explaining the long history of China's relations with Tibet I realise how little I know about this remote mountain nation.

I have a memory – a suspect one, since I can't place it at a time when Rewi was back in New Zealand – of him showing me the skullcap of a murdered Tibetan peasant attached to his belt, evidence, according to him, of the cruelty of Tibet's former feudal overlords. (That he did possess such as thing has been confirmed by others, so at least that part is true.) Inclined as I have been since childhood to take Rewi's part in any debate, I had made an exception of Tibet. The prevailing view in the West – that Tibet is a victim of Chinese imperialism – seemed to me self-evident. Chinese troops were in the streets; protest was stamped out; the Dalai Lama was in exile. Rewi told a different story, one that chimes with what Dave is telling us now. In this narrative the Chinese marched into Tibet to liberate, not to impose their authority on a subject people. Their mission was to free the peasants from centuries of feudalism. In the wake of their 'invasion' Tibet would have healthcare, education, roads, airports, bridges, dams …

I have to wait until I'm back in New Zealand to make some sort of sense of all this conflicting information. I read books on Tibetan history, articles, travelogues, political commentaries … Dave's words, hastily jotted down, become part of a complex story of border disputes, imperial claims, communist ambitions and Tibetan intransigence.

Tibet, surrounded on three sides by China, bordered on its fourth by India, Nepal and Bhutan, has always attracted the attention of its larger, more powerful neighbours. It may not share a border with Russia but when, at the beginning of the twentieth century, Russia began making inroads into the Hindu Kush – a mountain region on the border of Pakistan and Afghanistan – the British, determined to safeguard their Indian empire, decided to take action. A force under the command of Colonel Younghusband was mounted and sent into Tibet, ostensibly to solve a border dispute but in fact to take control. Some accounts estimate that more than 5000 Tibetans, most of them monks armed with hoes, swords and flintlocks, were killed during the campaign. The total number of British casualties was five.

But the British didn't have control for long. The trade agreement they forced on the Tibetans sparked a rebellion, giving the neighbouring Chinese – still ruled by the Qing – an excuse to come to their aid. Anxious not to upset the Chinese, whose acquiescence in matters of trade had been filling government coffers for decades, Britain saw sense and withdrew. When the Qing, in their turn, were overthrown, Tibet was sidelined. The shaky new republic, despite Sun Yatsen's dream of presiding over a united China, was too busy fighting internal battles to bother about fewer than two million Buddhists living on its farthest borders. Tibet, for so long the site of power struggles involving the British, Japanese, Russians, Indians and Chinese, was left to enjoy de facto independence.

Three decades passed before the situation changed. Sun Yatsen's 1912 declaration that all minority peoples – Mongols, Manchus, Tibetans, Uyghurs, Buddhists, Moslems, Taoists, Christians – were Chinese had not been translated into reality. At his death in 1925 China was as divided as ever. But the seeds had been sown. Post-Liberation, when communist troops marched into the Tibetan capital Lhasa, they were not just marching to the communist drum, they were keeping faith with the Father of the Republic.

The arrival of the PLA signalled change on a scale hitherto unknown in Tibet. For centuries, regardless of whoever had ultimate control, it had operated as a feudal, theocratic society. Power rested with the *lamas*

(Buddhist monks) and with the major landowning families. The peasants had no rights. There was no health service, no running water, no electricity. The only schools were those run by the *lamas*. Literacy hovered around five per cent. When Rewi visited in 1939 (and was declared a Living Buddha), there were only a dozen or so cars in the entire country. There was no airport; not even a landing strip. Nor were Tibetan rulers any kinder than their Chinese counterparts. Cruel and inhuman punishments, along with summary executions, were commonplace.

The communists would change all that. They would abolish serfdom, reallocate land, reduce taxes and build roads, schools and hospitals. What they did not do, Dave assures us, is interfere with Tibetan culture. Tibetans were free to follow the rituals and practices that had been part of their lives for centuries.

'So why doesn't the Dalai Lama live there?' someone asks. 'If it's such a Utopia.'

'What you have to decide,' Dave says, answering the question by posing one of his own, 'is whether you think China "invaded" Tibet or "liberated" it. If the Free Tibet campaigns run in the West were to be successful it wouldn't only be the Dalai Lama who would return, it would be the landowners and the wealthy *lamas*. Every uprising that's occurred within Tibet has been supported by the CIA. So America would be pulling the strings. Would that be better for Tibet? I know what I think ...'

If I hadn't lost Rewi's letters I would be going to them now, checking what he wrote about this disputed nation. Because he wrote a lot! 'That Tibetan Dalai Lama hoax is something,' he complained in a 1970 letter to Pip. 'He keeps his brother in the US with plenty of money.'[1]

Again I had to wait until I got back to New Zealand to make sense of what I was hearing. Dave was right about the CIA backing the 1959 Tibetan uprising (it had also, as Rewi had claimed, arranged for the Dalai Lama's brother to flee to the US), but its involvement in Tibetan affairs ended with Nixon's visit to China in 1972. So the second uprising in 2008 cannot be blamed on America.

Whether ordinary Tibetans are better off under Chinese rule than under the old feudal order is a matter for debate. Monasteries have been destroyed, as have temples, but the destruction has been piecemeal, not part of a wider plan to destroy Tibetan culture. Ever since the reforms of Deng Xiaoping, the Chinese leadership has held to the belief that economic prosperity will eventually not only stifle opposition, it will end the need for religion. So Xi Jinping, who justifies his clampdown on dissent by claiming he has lifted millions out of poverty (he has), orders the deployment of troops to Tibet (ostensibly to conduct military exercises, but really to reinforce Chinese control) as part and parcel of the same programme. China's 10-year struggle, post-1949, to subdue Tibet, is said to have cost 1.2 million Tibetan lives. The Chinese would argue that that is the price that had to be paid to liberate this once-backward nation.

We're a thoughtful bunch as we pile out of our bus into the metaphorical arms of the smiling women running the Tibetan Embroidery Co-op. An ambush of goodwill follows. First a tray of small glasses is brought out and we are all invited to down – at 10.30 in the morning – a drink that causes even my cousin Ross to gasp. 'Fire coming out of my ears,' he wails.

Next, long-fringed white silk scarves are draped around our necks – another gift to take home, but one so light no one's tempted to abandon it. A tour of the workshop follows with much smiling and nodding and handling of goods. The shoppers among us chatter excitedly. Many purchases are made – gaily embroidered bags, scarves, cushion covers … The atmosphere is so seeped in goodwill it would be impossible to leave empty handed, so I buy cushion covers for my daughter and a bag for a friend. Out in the courtyard we're offered more drinks – not the firewater this time but warm yak's milk (an acquired taste!) – accompanied by Tibetan breads baked on the premises. The farewells are prolonged and heartfelt. None of us wants to leave. Perhaps we are all inwardly processing not just yak milk and firewater, but the complex picture of Tibet Dave has left us with. Our hosts could not have looked happier or healthier. But I know better than to reach a conclusion on the basis of one carefully choreographed experience.

CHAPTER FIFTY-THREE

SOMETHING has happened to my appetite. I've lost it. Enchanted with Chinese food in our first week I find myself longing for toast and vegemite, anything that doesn't contain oily vegetables and hidden lumps of unidentified fish and meat. Boiled eggs – a staple of most breakfasts – suddenly take on life-saving properties. I wonder if I can stow some in my bag and avoid attending another banquet.

Our destination is Lanzhou, capital of Gansu province, the city Rewi's Shandan school was shifted to on the orders of Mao. We are to travel by train – the famous bullet train traversing the Old Silk Road – but this time we will be travelling soft class. The train will pass through a tunnel hollowed out of the Qilian mountains. By the time we emerge on the other side, Shandan will have taken on the shape created not by its reality but by memory.

Rewi wrote a poem about Lanzhou, celebrating its 'rich orchards' and 'bending ears of millet', but this is not the city we arrive in.[1] Smoke hovers over the uneven roofs of a vast industrial hub. Cranes pierce the skyline. The noise of traffic is as loud and constant as the roar of the sea.

Our hotel is called the Hampton by Hilton, but what it is really by is the Yellow River. I stare down at 'China's sorrow' and think of Rewi, knee deep in its mud, helping to construct the canal designed to prevent further flooding. Even from eight storeys up I can see the movement of its treacherous currents. Yellow is not the word I would use to describe it. Khaki comes closer, tinged with grey. Somewhere out of sight is the old iron bridge where George Hogg, on his epic journey moving pupils and equipment from Shuangshipu to Shandan, crossed by pontoon.

Gazing down on this noisy, modern, industrial city it's hard to hold on to the past. An hour later, meeting Rewi's American grandson Duan Hailong, who has travelled to Lanzhou especially to see us, the past recedes even further. Hailong, or Mike as he likes to be called, is Alan's eldest son. Having lived for 18 years in Los Angeles, he seems more American than Chinese. Rewi didn't live to see Hailong move to the States, but it's not hard to imagine what he would have said to his grandson had he known what he was planning. When younger son Mike's two children, Bao Bao and Mao Mao, announced their decision to emigrate to America, Rewi recorded the fact in a single stark sentence. America, 'the Utopia for so many youth of their time', had won out over China.[2]

I will meet my cousin Hailong again at the family reunion in Christchurch, but it's this first talk with him in Lanzhou that has stayed in my mind. Mike may have decided to live in America but he hasn't broken his ties with China. He returns every year to see his mother and his siblings. He has set up a 'Foundation for Rewi Alley', with the aim of bringing people to and from China. Like his grandfather he believes in 'cultural diplomacy'. Like his grandfather's friend, Zhou Enlai, he knows that countries, every bit as much as people, need friends. ('A man cannot live without friends,' James Bertram records Zhou as saying in *Return to China*. 'And neither can a country. To close your door is to block progress.')

*

That evening we are to attend an event – a live performance in honour of Rewi – at the Lanzhou TV studios. But before that we are taken to a five-star hotel whose gilt and glitter would be right at home in Trump's America. Informed that it was built as a villa for Mao Zedong, my initial response is disbelief. When did Mao stop living like the peasant he was and become the man who saw it as his right to live in the style of the emperors he had worked so hard to overthrow? 'Power corrupts: absolute power corrupts absolutely'. British parliamentarian Lord Acton penned those words in the nineteenth century. They have been quoted so often they have become part of the vernacular. What is less familiar is the rest of the quotation: 'Great men are almost always bad men.'[3] But not all great men, I hear Rewi qualify ...

> Chou En-lai, people's leader ... his
> love for them expressed in service
> to them, and in his common touch;
> he in his modesty and plain style
> of living an example to us all ...'[4]

After yet another sumptuous banquet, hosted by Lanzhou City University – we have learned by now to put only one thing on our plates at a time: how greedy we must have seemed in those first days when we helped ourselves to every passing dish – we leave the hotel I have re-named 'Liberace Hall' and drive to the TV studios. Three of us will be actively participating in tonight's show: Christine will read out Rewi's last will and testament; Jocelyn and Ross, brother and sister, will read the poem 'Beyond the Withered Oak Ten Thousand Saplings Grow'. All the rest of us have to do is sit back and watch.

Had we still needed proof that Rewi's name is legendary in China, that evening would have provided it. We are reminded of his 'glorious achievements', and his role in laying the foundations for New Zealand's eager support of China's flagship trading policy, Belt and Road (New Zealand was the first Western country to sign up to it). We watch a series of films, accompanied by commentary, portraying the highlights of Rewi's journey from New Zealand to China. It's hard not to be impressed. This is a live TV show viewed by millions. When a choir of Chinese students gathers to sing our nation's favourite song 'Pokarekare Ana' (the words written by Māori MP Sir Āpirana Ngata), I give in to tears. Two and half hours later, exhausted and emotional, we are ferried back to our hotel.

Next day is a whirlwind. Photos, speeches, gifts, interviews with the local media, more bowing. Rewi is everywhere: statues; banners; the story of his life carved in 80-metre bas relief, the work of Lu Bo, wife of Rewi's foster son Deng Bangzhen. We're invited to place white chrysanthemums on the plinth in front of his statue. 'Bloody relatives first,' the speaker instructs (I assume he means 'blood relatives'). We are made 'Special Consultants of the Rewi Alley Research Centre'. Certificates bound in red velvet are handed out.

At last we are freed to think our own thoughts. We break up into groups and wander through Lanzhou's famous waterwheel park, marvelling at the huge wooden waterwheel, still fully operational, built during the Ming dynasty. I think of Joseph Needham and his admiring pursuit of China's technological and scientific inventions. I see Rewi bending down to pull a neolithic fragment from the dust of Shandan. I hear George Hogg's snorting laugh as first Lao Si then Lao San jump into his arms. I see a procession of students in white shirts and blue shorts marching through the *paifang* on a summer evening, singing the school song. I think of E.M. Forster's words – 'only connect' – and for a few precious moments past and present are one, and I am a privileged witness to both.

CHAPTER FIFTY-FOUR

WE are in Beijing. Our second visit. The date is auspicious – 21 April, the day, 90 years ago, when Rewi arrived in China. My mother was born, five years earlier than Rewi, on 25 April. Same star sign, Taurus. Positive attributes – stability, trustworthiness, humanity, love of the arts, loyalty: negative attributes – laziness, stubbornness, prejudice, possessiveness. The novelist in me wants to make something of this. Astrology is respected in China. But I know better than to go down that road. My mother loved her cousin, whom she thought of as a brother (and I still think of as an uncle), that's all. The stars have nothing to do with it.

'Men need to wear a suit or at the very least a smart jacket and tie. Women will need to wear a cocktail dress or an outfit you'd wear to a smart wedding.' Those are our instructions, printed in the itinerary. We are to attend a 'Rewi Alley Forum' in the Great Hall of the People, followed by a banquet lunch. Our host will be the vice-president of China, Li Yuanchao.

Forty years ago Rewi was honoured in this same Great Hall (the name that serves for the many halls within this one building) on the occasion of his eightieth birthday. Swings and roundabouts. The Rewi who was quietly but firmly dismissed from control of the Bailie Schools in 1952, whose books were banned during the Cultural Revolution, whose organisation, Gung Ho, was mothballed for 30 years, was restored to official favour in 1977, a year after the downfall of the Gang of Four. Now we, his heirs, are being asked to pay homage in China's most important meeting place to the 'Great Revolutionary Fighter and International Friend of China'. But the Rewi I am thinking about as we reunite with Michael Crook and Lao San and take our seats in the Great Hall, is the exile in his Beijing apartment, typing furiously, producing book after book, poem after poem, some of it in the cause of peace, his new official 'job', but most of it, directly or indirectly, his way of holding on to his Shandan years.

> Hee haw, hee-haw
> Two heaps of straw,
> Two donkeys and one tether
> Should not pull against each other,
> Co-operate and feed together.[1]

The chant Rewi taught his Shandan students is stuck in his memory as firmly as the lessons learned by rote as a child. Other verses will slip in and out, but those lumpy rhythms and easy rhymes are there to stay. Living in China's capital, watching not just one but many phoenixes rise from the ashes, Shandan feels both near and far. He's comfortable in his hotel room, and later in the apartment the government assigns to him in the Old Italian Legation. Within the limits of his new role as a peace ambassador he's able to write more or less what he likes. What he can't do, what he longs for every day, is to be back on the *lei tai* listening to those chanting voices – 'Hee-haw, hee haw ...'

*

... fingers still fall
on keys, trying to tell of the people
and all they do ...[2]

It wasn't just Shandan Rewi hadn't wanted to leave, it was the northwest, his 'home away from home'. He hadn't wanted the school to move, or to become a university for oil workers. He most certainly hadn't wanted the 500,000 Gung Ho co-operatives spread across China to be downgraded to 'handicraft co-operatives'. He may not even have wanted to become a peace envoy, the only job, along with writing about the New China, now on offer to him. Rewi loved peace, but he had seen too much of human nature to believe peace was here to stay. In his mind he was, and always would be, a soldier.

Rewi would tell anyone who asked that it's perfectly possible to be both a soldier and an ambassador for peace. His brief dalliance with pacifism in his early years in China had left him convinced there were times when armed resistance was the only possible response to injustice and aggression. Learning – from what he rejected as much as from what he took on – to know himself, he had come to accept that he was by nature a fighter. He was 'not scared' of dying because he was 'just one more soldier marching on'.

So how could this man who liked to get his hands dirty go on fighting when all he had now was his pen and his voice? 'The pen is mightier than the sword.'[3] Of course he wanted to believe that, who wouldn't? But when he thought of Shakespeare, Dickens, Goethe, Dante, he had to admit their words, their glorious, eternal words, had done nothing to stem the tide of human violence. Greed was not banished. The lust for power did not disappear behind a cloak of humility. Inflicting pain was as popular a pastime as ever. So what on earth could he hope to achieve with his flow of words? 'All this indelible

311

ink, written on the parchment of one's skull,' he wrote after witnessing the executions in Wuxi in 1929.[4] They were the only words he could summon in the face of such senseless butchery (a paralysis familiar to many writers who've struggled to tell stories about the Holocaust). So wouldn't it be better now just to say, 'I don't care' and leave it at that?

'It's not over, Rewi,' his friend and soon-to-be editor Shirley Barton urges. 'Gung Ho was – is – bigger than both of us. So write about it. You say you miss the rough and tumble of Shandan, that you can only write when your hands are calloused from hard work, but you are a poet. You've always been a poet. Who will tell Gung Ho's story if you don't?'[5]

So Rewi starts writing. And writing. And writing … Until the day he dies only his peace work, travelling all over Asia and beyond, plus his four visits to New Zealand, will stop him. Sitting at his desk, watched over by a sixth-century Buddha he picked up in a market in Xi'an, he writes till his fingers, black with carbon, stiffen, forcing him to stop. Beside his typewriter are two porcelain pen holders, a gift from Chingling. If what he has been writing is a letter (his to me were usually typed) he will use a pen taken from one of those holders to scrawl his familiar signature.

But the sense of impotence remains. 'I guess us foreigners who have chosen this world have to pay in a measure for the sins of those who once ruled the roost to the East,' he writes to Kathleen Hall, after her return to New Zealand.[6] The woman who'd declared herself 'married to China', who'd vowed to return as soon as her health improved, has ended up having to take care of her elderly mother. 'If she'd been a man she'd have been famous long ago,' Rewi is reported to have said, presumably in some anger.[7]

On Rewi's not infrequent trips to hospital – recurring malaria, skin cancer, a heart condition, arthritis, gout, warts that have to be burned off ('Had my konk frozen to remove a growth,' he writes to his sister Kath[8])– a desk will be set up in his room so he can continue writing. As the years go by his prose writing dwindles and he turns more and more to poetry. He is 'crazy with it' as he was once crazy for Gung Ho.[9] He translates poets from the Tang, Song and other dynasties. 'I like the old Chinese poets,' he tells the international students who visit him in 1967. 'Tu Fu especially, famous poet of the Tang.'[10]

Tu Fu, writer of poems whose lines
will last as long as time …
Tu Fu who has tasted
the bitterness of poverty, the loneliness

of long roads; his own child dying
because there was not food enough …[11]

Reading Rewi's poetry I can't escape the feeling – despite my belief that in a different time and place he might have lived the life of an artist – that it's not art he's aiming for but an outlet for his frustration. It's as if he's punishing himself for not being in Shandan, not doing the hard physical work of a peasant. He's taken to the typewriter with a vengeance, punching holes in the paper, if Anna Louise Strong is to be believed. Complaining about his lot is not his style, but he can act as a ventriloquist for poets who had no such qualms. Perhaps that's why his translations are often so much better than his original work. They've been described as unorthodox, particularly in his awkward use of line breaks, but what he sacrifices – beauty of expression – is offset by what he gains – a voice that feels both contemporary and true to its origins. 'If any attempt is made to use poetic rhyming or academic language, the translation will fall flat … Language must … flow easily like a stream running over round stones.'[12]

Thin reeds, and from the land
A soft breeze; our mast stands
Tall and stark in the night
And I am alone; stars hang
Over the great plain, and
The moon moves with the flowing river …
It seems I am but as a sand bird
Blown before the elements.[13]

Rewi was not unusual in writing poetry. It's what educated people in old China did. Almost every condemned man, like Walter Raleigh in the Tower, wrote a poem on the eve of his execution. 'When a man is going to be killed, he seems to always write poetry and leave it somewhere or other', Rewi wrote.[14] For him the spur was not the prospect of imminent execution but the desire to 'transmit the poet's ideas in a language which would enable the ordinary people of the English-speaking world to understand the message – whether or not they were in the habit of reading poetry or were familiar with the long history of China'.[15]

The task he set himself was a formidable one – to translate not just the poets of China's dynastic past but her contemporary poets as well. The latter

– following Mao's instructions to soldiers at the Yan'an Forum on Literature and Art in 1942, to write poetry – seldom rise above the level of propaganda, but Rewi would not have considered that a fault. For so many, including himself, poetry was an organ of record. Its value went far beyond mere aesthetics. So in three different collections, *The People Speak Out* (1954), *Poems of Revolt*, published eight years later, and *Light and Shadow Along a Great Road* (1984), he 'transmits the ideas' of those obedient soldier-poets, whose stories – and their attendant propaganda – chimed with his own. One contemporary writer – He Jingzhi – described the deluge of work that followed Mao's dictum as a 'huge almost unmanageable opus'.[16] To Rewi that opus was a challenge. A chance to prove his loyalty.

But one thing is missing – the deeper resonance with his inner life that illuminates the best of his translations from the Tang. There is irony here. Rewi the worker-poet had to go to the art of pre-communist China to find answers to the questions politics had no language for.

The Cultural Revolution will silence Rewi's public voice in China. Though it's hard to discover exactly what happened – was his library destroyed as he subsequently claimed? – it's clear that at least some of his translated works were pulped. (In the Chinese documentary, *Rewi Alley*, the story is told of Red Guards declaring *The Eighteen Laments of Tsai Wen-Chi*, which Rewi had translated, a 'poisonous weed'. Since all existing copies were subsequently pulped, it's reasonable to assume other books of Rewi's suffered the same fate.) Thanks to Pip and Caxton Press in Christchurch several books of poetry and prose were published in New Zealand, but the only book published in China in the years 1966–76 was the one he wrote to order, *Travels in China 1966–71*. 'These people [Tu Fu and others] were writing for the old cultured class,' he tells the visiting students in 1967, donning his apologist hat. 'For the Chinese today … there's nothing so much to them … The new poetry coming out is extremely good poetry. Chairman Mao himself is a poet. In fact, in China, you know, practically everybody writes poetry. All the revolutionary martyrs have written poetry.'[17]

What he doesn't tell them is that he can no longer publish his own poems in China, or work as a translator. His Chinese collaborator cannot afford to be seen associating with him. By the end of that terrifying decade Rewi will be restored to favour but by then he has forgotten many of the old imperial characters. Translating, always a demanding task, will prove more difficult than ever.

CHAPTER FIFTY-FIVE

To get the feel of real Peking,
Ride your bicycle through the streets
before a winter's dawn.
… Walk any
afternoon in a park where there is a lake,
watch youngsters skate …
the little ones
joyously riding toboggans. Visit
the railway station and look at the stream
of country folk coming in to enjoy
the sights of Peking – palaces, markets,
the zoo …[1]

REWI, in his banishment in Beijing, is making the best of things. 'I am middle-aged, fat, with various ailments which I treasure like the people in our family have always done,' he writes to Gwen.[2] He loves to walk by the lake in the Summer Palace, especially during the Qing Ming Festival when people come to sail their paper boats. The families sweeping their ancestral tombs, leaving ghost money on graves, are his people now. A few years later, when he takes a nine-year-old orphan boy – the seventh child to call him Dad – to the same lake, he watches in amazement as the boy captures the scene with a few quick strokes of his pencil. Deng Bangzhen will go on to draw, for his foster father, the mountains, rivers, factories and temples of Shandan. He will draw George Hogg in Yan'an, and Rewi talking with the old Chinese doctor. He will sketch tea shops and markets and people doing tai-chi-chuan, a practice Rewi has been persuaded to take up by his friend Sid Shapiro. Eventually Bangzhen will move to New Zealand with his wife, sculptor Lu Bo, creator of the Amberley memorial. 'Go to New Zealand,' I imagine Rewi advising the two artists. 'Paint its beauties and bring them back to China. Then do the same in reverse. The more art ambassadors we have in this world the better.'

Every time Rewi comes to the Summer Palace he marvels at the change that has come over China. Even after the fall of the Qing ordinary Chinese people couldn't walk here. As a foreign concession governed by the British and the French, it was the preserve of Europeans. Now look at it. Old, young, families, lovers, students, workers, playing and relaxing in the soft spring sunshine. Homesick for Shandan he may be, but this sight cheers. On fine days he'll walk up to the raised marble dais at the southern end of the park and gaze out over the blue tiled temples nestling in groves of old cypress trees. New Zealand, he was told as a kid, is the most beautiful country in the world. Not true, he thinks as he looks down on the park. Not true at all.

*

October 1952. Rewi has attended his first peace conference. Now that China has assumed leadership of the World Peace Council (founded in 1950 by the Soviet Union, so not exactly bi-partisan) his role is an important one. In the years to come he will attend conferences in Finland, Sweden, Poland, Japan, Vietnam, Indonesia, the Philippines, India, Korea and Cuba. (In the documentary *Rewi Alley*, the Chinese commentator jokes that Rewi had visited every continent in the world except Antarctica.) He will rage against American aggression. 'The US is getting madder than several adders' he will complain to Pip in a 1960 letter, as the war in Korea is followed by a longer, even more devastating, war in Vietnam.[3] He will send letters to the New Zealand Peace Council, addressing them as 'fellow workers for peace': 'In all the years I have lived with this great people [the Chinese], there has never been a time when the pestilence of war and its accompanying horrors have not overshadowed their lives ... New Zealand can only live with peace. There is no other way for her. Just as Britain is geographically tied to Europe, so is New Zealand to Asia' – a statement decades ahead of its time.[4]

Living for the first few years, post-Shandan, in the Peking Hotel, Rewi is comforted by the presence of friends, Chinese and European, with whom he can share meals and walks. Ma Haide lives nearby as, now, does Chingling. His Jewish friends – Israel Epstein, Sid Shapiro, Ruth Weiss – are constants in his life, as are Manny and Grace Granich who join him for meals, often with Hans Mueller, the old Eighth Route Army doctor and his wife, in tow. Best of all he is now a grandfather. Alan and his wife Alia will go on, in this pre-one-child-policy period, to have six children. Younger son Mike will have two. Alan lives in faraway Lanzhou, so Rewi has to make do with letters and the occasional visit. But Mike is in Beijing. His regular Sunday visits with his wife and babies are the highlight of his week.

Soon visitors from overseas start arriving, the first for decades (though this will stop during the Cultural Revolution). 'Do not worry about a trip to

China now,' Rewi will write to Pip in 1969, by which time the revolution has been raging for three years. 'Ed Snow who has done so very much cannot get an invite yet and says he has given up hope.' (Rewi, however, did not give up hope. A year after that letter to Pip his behind-the-scenes efforts paid off and Snow was invited back. It would prove to be a history-changing visit.) 'Guess in politics one should not let personal things, emotions and what not, interfere with basic principles,' he tells Pip. 'Revolutions are never simple things.'[5] Advice aimed, I can't help thinking, not at his brother but at himself.

*

1952 is not a good year for Rewi. His future is uncertain, his banishment from Shandan still an open wound. But that is not all. A telegram arrives. His mother has died. The shock is violent: a seizure that grips his muscles and won't let go. Why did he not see this coming? She who has always supported him, loved him, validated him. But then who sees an earthquake coming, or a flood? The land is supposed to be eternal, like the rivers and the ocean. Like a mother … An ache sets in around his heart and stays there.

'It's no joke to be an old bachelor,' he writes to Pip as he struggles with renewed attacks of homesickness in the wake of his mother's death. He should have gone back. He very nearly did. 'If the trail leads to a bachelor's two rooms down by Dad's old WC at the end of the orchard then that is that.'[6]

Now that his mother is dead, Pip is his lifeline. It's to him he confesses that he's not writing poetry any more. He's doing translations, but the inspiration needed to write his own poetry seems to have dried up. (The drought doesn't last long). I wonder if he also confessed that he'd turned down a knighthood? Pip more than anyone else in the family would have understood that decision. Having dismissed the whole business from his mind as speedily as he dismissed the offer itself, Rewi is surprised to find himself thinking about it four years later. Clark-Kerr, as ambassador, must have made the recommendation, but Rewi would bet his bottom dollar the idea was put into his head by Sir John Hope-Simpson, the man in charge of the dyke repairs at Wuhan. Rewi had liked Sir John – 'one of the better type of conservative Englishmen'[7] – sensing in him a loneliness not unlike his own. But when he was shown the report Hope-Simpson had written about his work on the dykes – 'Alley is a most remarkable man and his work at Hankou has been beyond praise'[8] – he dismissed it as tommy rot, just as he dismissed the subsequent League of Nations assessment that his actions in moving refugees away from the threat of execution had saved thousands of lives.

'I am pig-headed rather than clever,' he writes to Pip, elaborating on his decision to stay in China. 'I like people and production and to me China is part of my being.'[9] Whatever doubts he may have had, by the end of 1952 they have been resolved. Like Kathleen Hall, he sees himself as 'married' to China. What he's committed himself to is not communism but the people. 'Life is mostly about courage,' he'll tell David Mahon years later. 'Live dangerously or else do not live at all.'[10]

According to the British chargé d'affaires based in Peking in 1952, Rewi chose China not because he saw her as a Great Power in the future, but because he believed the Chinese people deserved better and he thought he could be of help. (Britain had recognised Communist China in 1950, but China refused to exchange ambassadors until the British consulate in Taipei was withdrawn. The British finally conceded in 1972.) From 1952 on, Rewi's expressed wish was to 'serve the revolution in the best way possible.'[11] Like others of his generation of fighters and revolutionaries, he had moved too far from his homeland, geographically, politically, intellectually, to believe there was a place for him there.

> Living in China through the years
> has brought the bitter with the sweet …
> Though living in Peking
> brings solid comfort
> and a quiet compound
> of trees and grass in which to work,
> parks, gardens, museums,
> exhibitions for the afternoon
> stroll, yet always there is the lure back
> among villages where people
> face so much together …
> … the beauty
> of the Chilien and Tienshan alps.[12]

CHAPTER FIFTY-SIX

HAVING made the decision to stay in China, Rewi manages to get back to New Zealand four times, in 1960, 1964–65, 1971–72 and 1973. Kathleen Hall is at the airport to meet him in 1960 but by 1971 she has died. All four visits will see him shadowed not just by the SIS, but by absence – his mother gone; Westcote sold; his siblings scattered; Moeawatea abandoned to the bush.

> And as I slip back
> into the comfort of
> lovely New Zealand today,
> and in view of the fact
> that two-thirds of the
> world is hungry, exploited,
> struggling, I can but
> wonder whether
> the folk of my homeland
> still sleep ...[1]

He cannot forgive his country for its support of the US in the war in Korea (just as many people cannot forgive him for his 'treason') but his experience during his visit in 1960, when his movements were tracked not just by the SIS but by an often hostile press, tempered his enthusiasm for public speaking in his homeland. When he visits at the end of 1964 he keeps his head down. This time he just wants to be a family member. He hasn't enjoyed being painted as an enemy of the country he loves and has continued to celebrate (and scold!) in his poems. The explanation provided by the SIS for the silencing of this former firebrand is interesting – they describe him as 'older and much sicker' (could they be describing depression?) than when he visited in 1960. They also point out that he has 'lost favour' with the New Zealand public. Whatever the reasons, over the two months of that mid-sixties visit, Rewi 'neither attracted much public attention nor sought it'.[2]

His next visit, in 1971, is book-ended by the twin horrors of the Cultural Revolution and the war in Vietnam. This time he is not silent. He gives press interviews, addresses meeting of the CNZFS and the CPNZ, and is guest speaker at a public meeting in Auckland chaired by the mayor. The SIS reports that he 'spoke well, in a straightforward manner (and) seemed extremely alert mentally'.[3] He addresses other public meetings in Christchurch and Nelson, as well as talking to schools, Rotary clubs and trade unions. But he has not entirely done away with the caution he exercised on his previous visit. He refuses to answer questions from the floor, stipulating that they must be provided to him in writing before each meeting.

As he moves through the country, staying with family, catching up with friends, he's encouraged by signs that the winds are changing in the land of his birth. Ten years have passed since his cordial meeting with Prime Minister Walter Nash. The prime minister in 1971 is Keith Holyoake, leader of the National Party. An invitation from that quarter is unlikely! But his meetings with other officials – mayors, councillors, community leaders – have reassured him that the Kiwi ability to think outside the box is alive and well. Maybe New Zealand will not be such a willing servant of US imperialism in the future …

Two years later he is back. Invited by the Ministry of Foreign Affairs to give his impressions of contemporary China, he accepts gladly. I wonder if they had any inkling of what they were letting themselves in for? As expected, he waxes lyrical about China's progress in industry and agriculture, but it's when he moves on to talk about China's 'internal dissensions' and its troubled relationship with the USSR that eyebrows start to rise. Describing Russia as an 'arrogant super-power' intent on discrediting China, Rewi, warming to his theme, deplores the 'constant fusillade of rubbish' directed at Beijing by Moscow.[4] He puts the blame for this on Lin Piao (Lin Biao), the celebrated marshall from the civil war, whose attempts to take China into the Soviet camp led to the excesses of the 'Ultra Left'. That Rewi in 1973 should have been so outspoken in his condemnation of 'Ultra Leftism' rather gives the lie to the accusation that he only began to acknowledge the crimes of the Cultural Revolution when it was safe to do so.

But there is a personal note, detectable even in the unemotional language of the SIS. 'The aim of the Ultra Leftists, according to Alley, was to smash everything and everybody around Chou En-lai … The attacks almost drove him mad.' Had Zhou been purged, as might well have happened, it would have been the end of Rewi's China dream and probably of Rewi himself. 'Between 1967 and 1969 there were 11 so-called suicides in the foreign-language press,' Rewi tells the ministry officials. 'Notices were put out in Beijing accusing one of my sons of selling government secrets for tens of thousands of dollars …'[5]

His final remarks constituted a challenge, one which will prove prescient given New Zealand's later defiance of the US over nuclear power and nuclear weapons. 'It's time you established your own embassy in China,' he says – or rather I imagine him saying, since not all his words were recorded. 'Don't rely on the Australians. New Zealand may be a small country but that doesn't mean it can't have a big voice. You should be operating your own foreign policy independent of both Australia and the US.' His advice is taken. At the end of that year New Zealand announces that it has established diplomatic relations with China. At the same time, with Rewi's help, a New Zealand embassy is opened in Beijing.

Rewi will not live to see the Free Trade Agreement between New Zealand and China signed in 2008, the first such agreement involving a nation from the developed world, but his fingerprints are all over it. I try to imagine his feelings were he to learn that he is even more use to New Zealand (and to China) now he is dead. Tony Browne, New Zealand's ambassador to China 2004–09, spoke of his 'great mana' in Beijing, describing him as a man who 'still supports and benefits New Zealand and China today'.[6] Perhaps Rewi would simply be amused by this reversal of fortunes. But I like to think there would be more. 'Now for me China and New Zealand have crossed that bit of water that separates us geographically and are one,' he wrote in the preface to *Beyond the Withered Oak Ten Thousand Saplings Grow*. Words that go to the heart of his longing to see the two countries he called home united in friendship.

(There's a postscript to this. On 29 May 2018 the *Guardian* published a report claiming that the New Zealand government's relationship with China had 'come under the spotlight' of the CIA after an analyst suggested that the country's 'participation in the Five Eyes intelligence alliance needs to be reconsidered'. 'What did I tell you?' I hear Rewi whisper in my ear. 'Up to their old tricks!')

*

If Rewi ever regretted the decision to stay in China he gave no sign of it. But he never lost touch with his family or his friends.

'I have always been and will always be a New Zealander,' he told the students who visited him in 1967, 'although New Zealand has not always seen me as that. The buggers even refused to renew my passport at one point and they treated my adopted son very badly. Despite New Zealand being basically a good country populated by a just and practical people, there's a fascist streak there. I remember as a boy, I was walking along the beach near Christchurch and there was a group of men coming back from a strike, or a picket of some kind. Suddenly, out of the dunes came police on horseback and they rode into these unarmed workingmen, swinging their clubs as if they were culling seals. I will stand up against such forces as long as I can stand.'[7]

His foster son Deng Bangzhen, recalling Rewi in old age when he sometimes had trouble remembering his English, said he thought his father had forgotten he was a New Zealander. Rewi would refute this. Questions about his identity always resulted in the same answer: he was a New Zealander but he had become Chinese too. As someone who has lived in and identified with a different country and culture from the place where I was raised, I understand that duality. 'Geographic schizophrenia', a phrase I adopted to express my sense of identity with two widely separated nations, may sound like a disease but it can also be a cure – a remedy for the resurgent tribalism we are witnessing in so many parts of the world today. The Chinese celebrate Rewi as a Great Internationalist. The dream he shared with his friends Zhou Enlai and Soong Chingling was not one of domination of one country over another, but of friendship between nations. Rewi was often lonely but he never gave up on that dream, not even when, along with his adopted country, he was shunned and isolated.

'I imagine Gwen would be embarrassed to get a letter from China,' he writes in a 1969 letter to Pip, hinting at his sadness at being estranged from his favourite sister. 'I will not write her as she would be embarrassed with my postage stamp.'[8] Nostalgia for family was never far from the surface.

'It's nice to think back on Mother,' he wrote in 1970 on the anniversary of Clara's death. 'What a terrific person she was, with such a reserve of sweetness and understanding. How she made that old house and garden so beautiful and brightened up so many lives that came into contact with her …'[9]

In 1986, the year before he died, he received news that his youngest sister Joy was coming to visit. His grandson Hailong (Mike), who was living with him at the time, describes him as being 'happy as a child' and 'counting the days' till her arrival.[10] The death in May 1978 of Pip, his greatest supporter in the family, had hit him hard. As had the fact that his brother Geoff never visited, despite being invited several times. Joy's visits – there were two – cheered him immensely. 'Hope you have told her [Gwen] all about it,' he writes to her after the first visit. 'Have nothing to send her but my love.'[11] In a later letter, presumably after yet another Alley family falling-out, he writes, 'Do not worry too much about the little shafus [sic] that arise in the best regulated homes', scribbling at the bottom, 'My love to you sweet old dear.'[12]

CHAPTER FIFTY-SEVEN

Across the moat
the old great wall of the Imperial City
stands dark against a night sky, while
across at Tien An Men heavens are lit
by bursting fireworks, their colours
reflected in the waters below us; and
through the maze of courtyards
comes the sound of the music which
this night the thousands dance dance
for the May Day that is so surely theirs ...[1]

REWI in 1953 is making the best of things. He's stayed in China because he believes he can help the Chinese people, but he's not living among them any more, he's living in what would, for a Chinese peasant, be unbelievable comfort. But comfort is powerless to heal the pain of loneliness. Wherever he looks he is surrounded by absence: his sons far away, Jim Bertram and Nurse He back in New Zealand, Agnes Smedley and the Snows enduring the slings and arrows of Cold War America, his New Zealand family and friends – some of them anyway – expressing dismay at his outpourings on Korea. Not that he's completely alone. Ma Haide is still in Beijing, as are Israel Epstein, Ruth Weiss, Hans and Kyoto Mueller, Manny and Grace Granich. But the gaps are there. I try to imagine his feelings when Chingling moves to Beijing – the comfort that must surely have flowed from knowing she was close. But this is a man who keeps his promises. The number of words he will write about his friendship with Susie, his 'everlasting flower', will barely cover a page.

But the greatest gap in Rewi's life is Shandan. Early in 1953 he is appointed honorary headmaster of the renamed Lanzhou Oil and Technical School, but it's a sinecure, he has no power. When his son Alan is offered the job of actual headmaster he urges him to take it. It's a good position. Alan and his growing family with thrive.

'It will never be possible to think of Shandan without emotion,' he writes to a former Shandan colleague. 'There has been so much that has been rich in that seemingly poorest of places.'[2] His longing to be back in the bare, hard

Jialing Valley, surrounded by mountains that change from purple to red in the setting sun, will never leave him. Some nights he imagines he can smell the pungent odour of the burning *kangs*, so different from the sweet smells of his Beijing garden. He hears the cries of wolves and jackals, the braying of camels, the croaking of frogs, Skimpy's excited barking, the slow swish of the water wheel, the shouts of boys and girls playing basketball. His mouth and nose fill again with Gobi desert dust. Ancient pagodas, complacent Buddhas, workshops, playgrounds, classrooms, chimneys belching smoke, hungry boys wolfing down millet patties, the swimming hole, a gibbous moon playing hide and seek with racing Mongolian clouds ... These scenes will never leave him.

In order to stay on in China, Rewi has had to apply to the Peking Foreign Affairs Bureau for a permit. This must have been galling for him, but he says nothing. His public utterances remain relentlessly upbeat. He celebrates the new building going on all around him. He applauds the students marching through the streets wearing their Pioneer kerchiefs, chanting 'Taiwan must be liberated!' When Stalin dies in March he joins the vast crowd gathered in Tiananmen Square. The atmosphere is solemn, as befits the occasion. China's leaders stand to attention at Tiananmen Gate while troops from the army, navy and air force parade past. Factory sirens sound, artillery guns fire a salute.

Making the best of things means making the best of each day. So Rewi goes out into the streets, seeking inspiration for his poetry, hunting for treasures. He haunts the markets in Liulichang, the old second-hand book and antiques district, picking up books on Sui and Tang music from the People's Bookstore, discovering, to his delight, an illustrated manual for children full of advice about factory safety. Antique shops are a magnet. He picks through their wares, seizing on anything that might turn out to be a treasure – a surgical instrument from the Tang; a measuring spoon from the Han; a bronze horse from the Song; a pottery camel from the Three Kingdoms. At the Chinese medicine shop the proprietor, who's been there since before the Japanese invaded, tells him a story of how acupuncture was first practised in the sixth century BC. 'If kids don't run around naked for the first 10 years of their lives their last 20 will be full of ills,' the old man says, when his rambling tale has come to an end. 'Kids need yang to grow and the sun is yang.'

Rewi, who collects these old Chinese sayings in the same way he collects artefacts, decides to have a bit of fun at the shopkeepers's expense. Most of the people he's encountered in this line of work are vegetarian. 'Yes, and if you don't eat meat at the New Year you will not pass 56,' he teases.

'But I am already 79,' the old man answers solemnly.[3]

Rewi does some research. Discovers that as far back as the eleventh century the Chinese had a vaccination for smallpox. The more he learns about the past, the more humbled he feels. How pale and paltry a thing European history seems when compared to the wonders of this ancient civilisation.

His favourite market is the Dongdan, now renamed the People's Market. To his great delight he discovers he can buy marmalade there. He can even buy real coffee, left behind, like the tins of marmalade, by the departing Americans. When that runs out he has to rely on foreign visitors. A modest list is circulated round the family. Marmalade, preferably Oxford, is top; Nescafé a close second.

He goes to the dentist. A lot. Like so many of his generation of New Zealanders he has notoriously poor teeth. Apart from the regular appointments to have skin cancers burned off his face, visits to the doctor can be staved off more easily, though in the end he's forced to admit that his years of yellow-fishing across China, staying in inns that would fail every health and safety regulation in the West, have compromised his health.

As word spreads abroad that the civil war really is over, foreigners who are not diplomats or embassy officials looking for trade deals start to appear. Many of these – British, Americans, Canadians, Australians, New Zealanders – come because they've heard of Rewi Alley. After Edgar Snow's articles – published in the *Saturday Evening Post* at the time of the founding of Gung Ho – brought Rewi to the attention of Americans from the president down, his fame has spread around the world. 'Talk to Rewi Alley,' travellers from the West are advised. 'He's the man to see.'

To escape Beijing's 'tiger heat', which never fails to bring him out in a rash, Rewi spends as much of the summer as he can at the seaside resort of Beidahe, accompanied, whenever it can be arranged, by one or other of his sons and assorted grandchildren. Ma Haide and his wife are often there as well. In the winter Rewi dons padded clothes and forces himself out for his daily constitutional, often again with George as companion, in temperatures many degrees below freezing.

In 1955 Rewi meets the French existentialist writer Jean Paul Sartre. ('I come from a West that is increasingly concerned with the thought of Death,' Sartre will write. 'I find here six hundred and fifty million people entirely taken up with the idea of Life.'⁴) The following year he meets British MP Tony Wedgwood-Benn. If Rewi gets tired of the endless calls on his hospitality he never lets on. He sees it as his job to promote the New China in whatever way he can.

> I pull out the card index
> of addresses around the world –
> … a Parisian
> lady who travelled with me
> and took such wonderful pictures
> of ordinary folk …
> I go on, flicking cards,
> so that others come out to drop
> into the waste paper basket.
> Always life is like this, ending,
> then beginning again …⁵

In October 1956 Rewi joins the crowds protesting in Tiananmen Square against the British and French invasion of Suez. In the same year he visits Korea. Taken to see the ruins of Sunchun, where Christians lived in a peaceful community, the Alley temper flares as the survivors ask him to explain how Christians could bomb fellow Christians.

And still the poems keep coming. 'I have written another slug of poems,' he writes to Pip, who, as often as not, is left to find a publisher for them.⁶

> Red cheeks, grey beard
> this is me half drunk with years gone by …
> but still I am good
> at poetry, as if crazy
> with it …⁷

*

Until the outbreak of the Cultural Revolution, Rewi's path, while not exactly strewn with roses, is pleasant enough. He attends May Day celebrations in Tiananmen Square, returning every 1 October to celebrate the anniversary of China's Liberation. He entertains foreign visitors. He travels the globe as an envoy of peace.

In 1958 he moves into the apartment that will be his home for the rest of his life. Thanks to the cook he shares with Anna Louise, he eats well. Visitors describe him as 'plump'. ('I am busy and too fat,' he writes in a 1960 letter to Pip.[8]) He and Ma Haide meet regularly at the famous Mutton Grill by the Drum Tower. They speak English. But when Rewi visits his friend's home they speak Mandarin out of respect for George's wife Su Fei. Like Chingling, George is a soul mate, the only man, now that the other George is dead, with whom he feels completely at ease.

A devotee of the Peking Opera, Rewi is often to be seen in the company of Chingling, sitting in the stalls, a rapt expression on his face, as the story unfolds in music and dance and a display of costumes so opulent he wonders how the actors manage to move, let alone sing. He's not particular in his taste. He appreciates the old stories of monkey-kings, dragons, emperors and sky gods as much as the more recent tales of struggle and liberation. One does become a favourite, though – *The Western Tower* – a story from his beloved northwest in which a sing-song girl and the son of a puritanical Confucian official fall in love …

In 1962 he travels to Cuba at the invitation of Che Guevara. But by then China is in the middle of another catastrophe.

CHAPTER FIFTY-EIGHT

1958, the year Rewi moves into his final Chinese home, is not a good year for China. Mao Zedong, committed to transforming the country's agrarian economy and proving to his increasingly irksome Russian allies that he is in charge, launches the disastrous five-year programme known as The Great Leap Forward. As many as 55 million are estimated to have died as a direct result of this policy of forced collectivisation and industrialisation. Even conservative estimates put the number at 18 million. (As with so many things relating to government policy in China it's almost impossible to verify the facts.)

I found Rewi's book about this period – *China's Hinterland in the Leap Forward* – almost unreadable. It troubles me that he turned a blind eye to what was happening, glossing over the facts even when Geoff Chapple interviewed him in 1979. He could hardly claim ignorance so long after the event. Any comparison between Rewi's published writings and the reports of his private conversations shows that he tended to let his guard down when talking with people he trusted. Geoff was a man he trusted with the story of his life, so why did he 'lie low' when this particular issue was raised?[1] A year later Rewi publishes another almost unreadable book – *Struggle Around the Central Plains: A story of Honan province* – in which he celebrates the outpouring of poetry that accompanied the announcement of the Great Leap Forward.

> Barren mountains, don't
> frown at us; today
> we shall give your face
> a new make-up; putting on you
> a green gauze hat, a bracelet
> of red flowers ....
>
> The forests we have planted
> are more lovely than heaven
> ... everywhere
> rise sounds of joy at the richness
> of the crop that is coming in ...[2]

This is not the place for an analysis of Mao's failed attempt to bring China's industry and agriculture into the modern age. Suffice it to say that the answers as to why such an apparently well-intentioned policy caused so much suffering are neither obvious nor straightforward. Almost every official associated with the programme, from the top levels of society to the bottom, lied about the results. Time and again Mao was told what he wanted to hear – that the harvests were a success, that the communes were thriving, that productivity was up. Rewi, catching the echoes, would have been caught in the same web of lies and half truths as everyone else.

So he kept his head down. Toed the line. China was still finding its feet. Criticisms from a *yang guizi* would not be appreciated. Perhaps he told himself the Great Leap Forward was none of his business. Mao was in charge and what he'd seen of Mao in the war years had convinced him he was the right leader for China. Or perhaps he simply said, 'I don't care …'

Eventually he could no longer ignore the evidence. But his acknowledgement in his memoir – so far as I know the only one he made in writing – about the 'extravagances' of the 'ultra-left' during this time feels like too little, too late.

*

The Cultural Revolution takes Rewi by surprise. No one, except perhaps Mao himself, has seen it coming. It starts innocuously enough. A play, *Dismissal of Hai Rui from Office*, written by Wu Han, the mayor of Beijing, is staged by Peking Opera. It tells the story of a Ming official who dares to criticise the emperor and so is dismissed from office. Something about it draws in the crowds. It's more than probable Rewi saw it. He enjoyed theatre almost as much as opera. If he did, and recorded his thoughts, then that document, like so many letters written and received at this time, has been destroyed. Did Mao, the poet manqué, see the play or was he merely informed of its content? The answer is irrelevant because what happened subsequently was so catastrophic the play and its unfortunate author were forgotten.

Mao is convinced the play is an attack on him. Since the failure of the Great Leap Forward, his power within the Party has been waning. Now here is a play suggesting a high official has been dismissed from office for daring to criticise the country's leader. Mao is not the only one to see in this drama a reflection of his own dismissal, six years earlier, of Peng Dehuai, the official who publicly rebuked him for the Great Leap Forward during the Lushan

Conference of July–August 1959. The play closes. The author, one of the first victims of the Cultural Revolution, is purged, dying in prison in 1969.

(Twenty years later the same fate awaits Gao Xingjian, author of *Soul Mountain*. His work is deemed counter-revolutionary by the Party. With the threat of imprisonment hanging over him, he escapes to Paris in 1987. A decade later artist and writer Ma Jian, following his imprisonment during the Anti-Spiritual Pollution Campaign of 1983 and the subsequent banning of his books and paintings, moves first to Germany then to Britain. He was invited to attend the Hong Kong literary festival in November 2018 to talk about his novel *China Dream*, but the invitation was revoked on the orders of the Beijing government.)

On 16 May 1966 Mao issues a notification. In it he claims the Party has been infiltrated by revisionists and counter-revolutionaries. 'Representatives of the Bourgeoisie have sneaked into the Party, Government, Army, Literary and Art circles,' he declares.[3] First to be hit are the ministers and leading officials in the Ministry of Culture (this, after all, is a 'Cultural Revolution'). Next on the list are university professors, teachers and intellectuals. Some are dismissed, some arrested, some simply disappear. A few commit suicide. The economic disaster, waiting in the wings, will take longer to appear, but for those first few confusing months it's the thinkers and artists, the upholders of the traditional art forms so beloved of the Chinese people, who suffer.

Mao has been here before. His 'Hundred Flowers' campaign in 1957 was designed with exactly the same end in mind – to flush out dissident intellectuals and artists. The difference now is that the net will be cast far wider. And the consequences will devastate lives across the whole of China. Just as in the Great Leap Forward, years of economic stagnation will follow, adding to the miseries of a people all too familiar with suffering.

There's no way of knowing when Rewi becomes aware of this new revolution, but he's living in Beijing where it's all happening so it can't have taken long for news to reach him and Anna Louise. Mao has ordered the schools to be shut down. Who could not be aware of that? To the delight of many, young would-be scholars are freed from the classroom and organised into Red Guard bands. Their job is to hunt out 'revisionists', subject them to 'struggle meetings', then march them off to prison. Cities first, then countryside. 'Like the red sun rising in the East the Great Proletariat Cultural Revolution is illuminating the land with its brilliant rays,' the Big Character Posters announce.[4] The death toll will reach into the millions.

If you are only out
for face, or fame or fortune,
if you make mistakes
refuse to let them be
pointed out to you,
try to shift the blame on to others ...
set out to build
a cosy little control group
that you can dominate
to hold privilege
for your own sweet self –
why then you will
meet trouble in one
high wave or other of China's
revolution ...[5]

Rewi wrote these lines in August 1967, a year into the revolution. The 'cosy little control group' refers to the officials in the Ministry of Culture where Mao's purge began. He will go on justifying Mao's orders, oblivious to the rumours that must have reached him not just from Beijing but from all over China (though not entirely ignoring them, as we know from his remarks to the ministry officials in New Zealand). He will say nothing publicly about the arrest and imprisonment of David and Isabel Crook, Sid Shapiro, Israel Epstein, Ruth Weiss ... ('It was terrible,' Shapiro will tell the *Los Angeles Times* when it's safe to speak again. 'The thing that kept me going was that it was so stupid and obviously wrong that it had to end any day.'[6])

'How could Mao do this?' Ma Haide is reported as saying. Like Rewi he was not arrested. As Mao's Red Army doctor he was exempt from the worst of the Red Guard's abuses. But, again like Rewi, all he could do was complain in private. To speak out in public would have been to sign his own death warrant.

'Foreigners at the time were just ignored or not wanted,' Rewi wrote, unconvincingly, in a letter to Pip. 'I was very small potatoes, a subsidiary out on the edge. You couldn't say I was a target.'[7] But he was. Gung Ho and the co-operative ideas it championed had been discredited, along with its leaders. Collectivisation was the drum China marched to now.

But what hurt Rewi most was the treatment meted out to his sons. Both were arrested and imprisoned. Makeshift cells known as 'cowsheds' had been erected all over China expressly to house people like Mike and Alan who had come under political suspicion. Mike – like his brother, separated from his wife and family – dug ditches for two years. Alan was sent to a particularly harsh prison where he was repeatedly beaten. Eventually he escaped, though his freedom was short-lived. Not wanting to endanger his father, he took refuge with Ma Haide. George, saying nothing to Rewi, took Alan in and treated his wounds. He then took the bold step of writing to Zhou Enlai, knowing if it backfired he could suffer the same fate as Alan. Riding to the rescue once again, Zhou replied that while he couldn't authorise a release for Alan he could arrange for him to be sent to a prison where they didn't beat the prisoners. But even when that sentence was served Alan was still not free. For the remainder of that terrible decade he was in a re-education camp, working as a manual labourer in the mornings, studying Mao Tse-tung Thought in the afternoons.

Mao knew his history. The French Revolution may have brought the Ancien Régime to an end but it failed in its attempt to transform French society. With the fall of Robespierre and the Jacobins, power returned to the property-owning classes, where it has stayed. Mao was determined not to let that happen in China. Rather 'continuous revolution' than see the bureaucrats of the old Mandarin class restored to power. Rewi would have agreed. He had no time for bureaucrats, with their 'fat little bottoms stuck to their swivel chairs'.[8] Whether he knew Mao's other reason for starting the revolution – the need to shore up his own position within the Party – is a question I can't answer.

That Rewi, who knew about revolution both from history and from experience, would have supported what was happening, for a time at least, strikes me as obvious. But as one arrest followed another his unease grew. New Zealand had taught him what it was like to be under surveillance. Now he was learning the same lesson in China. What pathos the word *home* must have had for him in those years. He'd kept his mouth shut during his 1965 visit to New Zealand, but in 1971 he found his voice again, at what personal cost I can only imagine. He was sure of his brother Pip, and of my mother, but of how many others, apart from the members of the CPNZ? Not even the SIS doubted his love for New Zealand – he never renounced his citizenship – but they did question his loyalty. 'While the policies of the New Zealand Government are based on opposition to Communism, Alley's loyalty is more likely to lie with his adopted country, China, than with the country of his birth,' was the conclusion they reached at the time. Describing him as having 'the closest relationship of any European (with the exception of Edgar Snow) with Chairman Mao', they were concerned that he might be couriering confidential papers from the CPNZ to the Chinese Communist Party. The consensus today is that this was unlikely. The general secretary of the CPNZ, Victor Wilcox, made several visits to Beijing. If documents were couriered they were far more likely to have been carried by him than by Rewi Alley.[9]

There's no way Rewi could have known that the lens through which he was being seen in New Zealand, far from revealing him as a dangerous Red, revealed him – if my interpretation of those SIS files is correct – as a man in thrall to an idea which had its roots in humanitarianism. The reason eight files are still classified is not because there's something there the SIS doesn't want people to see, it's because they contain material relating to the US and UK agencies, the ones calling the shots at the time, and their permission would have to be obtained before any documents could be released – a long, drawn-out and possibly fruitless process.[10]

'Of course a great deal of dirt has come out in the washing,' Rewi told the visiting students in 1967. 'Whole things have been found to be going on that people didn't know about and the revolution, of course, is not a bed of tulips … It's a rough-and-tumble and some of these people who had exercised big authority were not above using their authority to get workers to do things that the workers didn't really understand … That is revolution. It's not so simple. In many parts of China, we have things happening. China is so huge. Way back in Tibet and Xinhai [Qinghai] and Xinjiang you've got all kinds of conditions. They are not quite so easy to deal with, you know …'[11]

What I feel as I re-read the material from this time – Rewi's conflicted words, the SIS reports, the letters and transcripts of conversations – is a sense of a man being slowly tortured, isolated from the people closest to him (his sons in particular); cast, metaphorically speaking, into the equivalent of my mother's wardrobe. For a man trained in emotional reticence those 10 terrible years must have finally turned the key on his heart. He did many good and brave things after 1976, keeping his own kind of faith, but he was a quieter, sadder version of the man he had been.

*

So do I slip another sheet
into my battered typewriter,

veteran of so many roads
over which the old poets once rode ...
below me an accompaniment of sound
of a spring day in Peking; street cars
rollicking past, the hooting of horns;
all the sounds of construction ...
a lot of old books
toppling off my bookshelf ...[12]

Trying to imagine Rewi writing during these years I see the faces of other writers – Solzhenitsyn, Milan Kundera, Ivan Klima – struggling to express themselves within repressive regimes. I think of the writers who are in prison today in Egypt, Turkey, Israel, Russia ... The list, which includes China, is long. Does Rewi belong in their company? Are the gaps in his work to be accepted without criticism because of the conditions he was writing under? Why, for example, did he not write about his son Alan's dramatic escape from prison? Was he embarrassed that it was his friend Ma Haide who saved his son and not himself? Like their father, both Alan and Mike were restored to favour after 1976, but the scars remained. Rewi may have deplored his grandchildren's decision to emigrate to the States but he must, deep down, have understood it.

*

On 21 October 1976 the Cultural Revolution comes to an end. Mao is already dead, his place taken by the now notorious Gang of Four led by Mao's widow, Jiang Qing. The internal coup which brings them down is bloodless. China breathes a collective sigh of relief.

At last Rewi can say what he thinks. He doesn't need to blame Mao for what happened. Like everyone else he can blame the Gang of Four. Hearing that what he called a 'criminal gang' posing as revolutionaries has been overthrown, he lets out a whoop of joy. Minutes later he is sitting at his desk, two fingers typing madly.

As the news spread ... Peking
along with sister cities, became
ablaze with joy ...
banners drums and clashing cymbals ...[13]

This is how Han Suyin described the final moments of that tyrannous decade: 'An emergency session of the Politburo was to take place in the Great Hall of the People that evening. Their [the Gang of Four's] presence was required ... As they passed through the swinging doors into the entrance lobby, they were apprehended and led off in handcuffs. A special unit then went to Madam Mao's residence at No. 17 Fisherman's Terrace and arrested her ... All was done with quiet and efficiency.'[14]

CHAPTER FIFTY-NINE

IT'S not just the Cultural Revolution that ends in China in 1976, it's the lives of three of the heroes of the revolution that brought the communists to power. In July the death of Zhu De, the peasant boy from Sichuan who became commander in chief of the Red Army (and the subject of Agnes Smedley's book *The Great Road: The life and times of Chu Teh*), is announced. Described by Evans Carlson as a man with 'the kindness of a Robert E. Lee, the tenacity of a Grant, and the humility of a Lincoln', Chu is mourned throughout China.[1] The man who led the PLA to victory was also a poet who spun, wove, grew and cooked his own food, and ordered his troops to attend women's classes on how to preserve vegetables. Rewi, who met him on several occasions, knows there will never be another like him:

> The sturdy old tree
> that has stood against
> so many a storm has fallen …[2]

Then in September comes news of the death of Mao. Rewi's response is interesting. Of course, like every other man, woman and child in China, he feels the shock, the sudden absence, the vacuum that has opened up. Everything stops. Schools and factories from Yunnan in the south to Xinjiang in the north close their gates. Streets are decked in white, the Chinese colour of mourning. But when Rewi comes to write the obligatory poem his words, like Macbeth's welcoming Duncan to his castle, are stilted:

> Ever does the old
> give way to the new.
> A giant of his age accepts
> the verdict of life
> and passes on, leaving
> a people who have started
> to think in a new way
> because of him …[3]

A month after Mao's death the Cultural Revolution is over. Gradually the old patterns begin to reassert themselves. The guard disappears from the gate of Rewi's compound. Chingling comes to tea. The two old friends talk in low voices, not yet convinced that the danger has passed. Rewi and Ma Haide, walking in the grounds of the Temple of Heaven for the first time in years, move through their old haunts like ghosts.

Slowly, in ones and twos, then in larger groups, foreigners, including Americans, start to appear again in Beijing. But the three Americans dearest to Rewi – Edgar Snow, Agnes Smedley, Evans Carlson – are all dead. The last time Rewi saw Ed was in December 1970 after the invitation he'd been agitating for was finally approved, and Ed became one of the few Westerners permitted to visit China at that time. Invited by Mao to call at his office before dawn, Ed found himself locked into a wide-ranging discussion that lasted over five hours. Though he would not live to see China again, he would live to see the fruits of that five-hour discussion – a thawing in the China–US relationship that would lead, two years later, to the visit of President Nixon, the first American leader to set foot on Chinese soil. Rewi's reaction on being told that Mao was willing to invite Nixon to China was mixed. Of course he agreed that improved relations between China and the US were a good thing. But Richard the Sly? Couldn't they wait till a better president had been elected?

Edgar Snow died in Switzerland on 15 February 1972, right in the middle of the Nixon visit. The doctors attending him – one of whom was Ma Haide – had been sent by Zhou Enlai, who knew how impoverished his old friend was. Ed's last wish was that half his ashes be scattered in the homeland he'd been forced to leave, and half in the land he considered his second home. 'I love China. I would like a part of me to stay here after death as it always did during life,' he wrote. 'To rest with her tawny hills, her terraced emerald fields, her island temples seen in the morning mist.'[4]

'China's so big. How can you ever tell it?' Ed had said to Rewi when they first met.

'Start at the beginning and keep going,' Rewi had replied.[5]

After Ed's death Rewi's ties to America, fragile at the best of times, snap. 'I belong to the same family as the Chinese – the human family,' Ed had insisted.[6] But Rewi isn't so sure about the human family any more. ('Human nature isn't up to Christianity and it isn't up to communism …') Have I really been chasing windmills all this time? he asks himself. Well, if I have, so be it.

Better that than lording it over other people. 'I have always been a terrier and will continue to be a terrier all the way through.'[7]

But it was not Ed's death, or Zhu De's, or Mao's that had the most profound effect on Rewi; it was the loss, at the beginning of that cataclysmic year, of his friend Zhou Enlai. I imagine Rewi, hearing the news on the radio, letting out a howl of anguish. His secretary, thinking he's been taken ill, jumps up from his desk and runs to his side. Rewi waves him away. The announcer's voice sails on, confirming what Rewi never wanted to hear, what, in his loving foolishness, he had never imagined happening. 'He could love all right,' he'd written after the death of George Hogg.[8] And so could you, Enlai, he says to himself as the awful news sinks in. And so could you …

The phone rings. It's Chingling.

'Rewi,' she says.

'Chingling …'

'Oh Rewi …'

'I know,' he answers.

*

It was a paper flower,
merely a paper flower, white with big
green leaves; yet her old fingers
had fashioned it, making it
a true piece of art, so big it covered her breast; firmly she held it
in front of her with one hand
while with the other she led a grandchild
carrying a small flower, coming
on to Tien An Men Square on the tiny feet
of the other day … and so with
her old face set, she went forward
to add her offering to the vast
bank of flowers. And then from her
I looked back behind to the red and gold
Tien An Men gate, and seemed to see
the spare erect figure of Chou En-lai
still standing here … a little smile
playing around his lips …[9]

CHAPTER SIXTY
21 April 2017

THE event in the Great Hall of the People was always intended to be the high point of our journey. What greater honour could be bestowed on us than a private audience with the vice-president, followed by a ceremony celebrating the life of our relative? Here we all are, in best bib and tucker, seated in a room that would not have been out of place in an imperial palace: thick elaborately patterned carpet underfoot, a vast crystal lamp overhead that fills the room with creamy light, a painting of one of China's many mountains covering the wall in front of which Vice-President Li Yuanchao and other dignitaries are seated. One by one our names are called and we are introduced to the vice-president. Having once gone through a similar ceremony in Buckingham Palace I am for a disorientating moment tempted, when my turn comes, to curtsy.

At the end of the proceedings we are led through to another even grander room with the title 'Western Hall'. I assume we're in this hall and not the Shanghai, Taiwan or Beijing Halls out of deference to Rewi's work in the northwest. Sinking into a huge golden armchair with my name on it, the thought of sleep briefly surfaces. With only a small adjustment I could curl up as comfortably as if I were in bed. Beside us on decorated lacquer tables are lidded mugs of tea, tea-leaves floating worryingly – are we meant to swallow them? – on the surface. Above us another elaborate light arrangement spreads out from the centre of the ceiling, like a flower seen under a magnifying glass. Luxury, comfort, power – all are signalled in this room, as they were in the one we have just left. A huge screen on the front wall alerts us to the fact that we are in for yet another video of the main events of Rewi's life.

We listen to the speeches telling us things we've heard many times before about Rewi Alley, the 'Internationalist and Great Friend of China', applauding when appropriate, fighting the desire, on my part anyway, to shout 'Up yours too, squire!' I want to believe there is sincerity in the by-now familiar words, but what I'm seeing clashes with what I'm hearing. Emperor's new clothes, I think, as I look up at the illuminated flower. It's as if the dust of Shandan has settled over my eyes, altering what I see, stripping it of its gloss and glitter, leaving behind the China Rewi loved.

('In China compliments and flattery are an aspect of social courtesy. They are intended as gifts and often have little if any relationship with reality.'[1] Reading these words of David Mahon's, several months later, I would take a kinder view of the ceremony. The praises heaped on Rewi were not signs of a growing veneration – though in his last years he was known as *Ai-lao*, a living treasure – they were gifts to us, his family, ones we could carry home easily.)

At last it's over. Cousin Maurice has spoken on behalf of the family, we've sung our waiata (reasonably well now that we've had more practice), the dignitaries have filed out, and we can go.

'Come and meet Isabel,' Dave Bromwich says as we emerge into the entrance hall.

Isabel Crook, Michael's mother, still beautiful despite her years, is warm, welcoming, and sharp as a pin. She answers my questions with ease and good humour, assuring me that her imprisonment during the Cultural Revolution did her no harm at all. On the contrary, she learned a lot from the experience, as did her husband. 'I was let go at first,' she tells me. 'The Red Guards who arrested me took me to Security, but when no evidence was found against me I was released. That same day I was re-arrested and taken straight to a Red Guard gaol where I remained for the next two years. I was well-treated. I have no complaints.'

'Yes, I have heard these things,' she says in response to my expression of incredulity. Well treated? Did she not know how many were beaten, tortured, killed? 'But I was allowed to have books, writing materials. I didn't go hungry.'

I could have spent hours talking with this remarkable woman, whose personal story, like Rewi's, is also China's story … but we have a train to catch.

'It helps to be mad in China,' Rewi wrote in his 1934 diary.[2] Waiting interminable hours in searing heat on Beijing's packed railway station for our long-delayed train, the suspicion that I've been time-travelled back to an outpost of Bedlam creeps into my mind. By the time we reach Shanghai I don't care if it is Bedlam I'm in, so long as the first part of the word is true, and there's a bed.

*

We are back where it all started for Rewi, in Shanghai. It's our last full day. Emotions are running high. Most of the group are eager to explore the Bund, as famous today as it was when Rewi gaped in amazement at its hotels,

bars, theatres, nightclubs, movie houses and opium dens. I opt out. I want
to stay with the Shanghai Rewi knew, the Shanghai of Ma Fan-to, one of
the contemporary poets he translated, whose rage against oppression and
sympathy with the downtrodden resonated so powerfully with him.

> One could knock on numberless doors
> finding each one closed so tightly
> and behind each door would be people
> upon whom one has no claim;
>
> one could glance over numberless rice bowls
> seeing each bowl clutched so firmly,
> each single bowl with so many dependents
> guarded so carefully from being snatched away;
>
> Shanghai the vortex drawing in people from all sides,
> bits of timber that were floating in the sea
> with the bitterness of winter and the cold north winds –
> how many hundreds frozen to death today?
>
> One could ask numberless people
> who in this China has happiness and freedom?
> And the reply would be dead silence
> broken only by the sound of weeping.[3]

On my return home Peter will send me a story about his Uncle Rolla who
worked in Shanghai for 27 years, serving, as Peter put it, 'opposite economic
interests' from Rewi's. Rolla worked for the Imperial Chinese Maritime
Customs, an organisation set up to collect taxes on behalf of the nationalist
government. Peter thinks he must have arrived in Shanghai about the same
time as Rewi. His salary was generous, he paid no income tax and lived in
great comfort, attended by many servants, in the Customs Mess. Every three
years he was given six months' overseas leave on half pay. A wonderful life,
which, according to his nephew, he thoroughly enjoyed. When it all came
to an end in 1949 he was one of the lucky ones who got out with his money.

Trying to imagine what these two men – Rewi and Rolla – might have
had to say to one another is not as difficult as it might sound. According to
Peter his uncle loved the Chinese and regarded the work he was doing as for

and on behalf of the people. After the 1911 revolution the new republic was obliged to borrow large sums in order to re-build the country in the wake of Manchu misrule. The revenue gathered by officials like Rollo played a vital part in securing those loans. But Rolla knew all was not as it should be in Chiang Kaishek's government. He spoke often about corruption, complaining that the big wigs in the KMT stole what they could, without caring for those lower down the social scale. That in itself would have been enough to start a conversation with Rewi.

'A man is good if he makes life better for his fellows.' An old Chinese saying which I hear Rewi quoting in the conversation I am imagining ...

*

'Europeans always feel at home in Shanghai,' our guide tells us as we drive away from the Hongkou Fire Station where Rewi, the would-be soldier and eager young adventurer, had his first Chinese job. A collective exhaustion hangs in the air like a miasma, but we are a tight-knit group now. We've shared our frustrations over internet access, streaming sinuses, cracked lips and the lack of soap and toilet paper. We've laughed and danced, coughed and spluttered and, on occasion, thanks to Ross's skill on the piano, sung our way around China. We have finally, under Jocelyn's tutelage, sung in public. Miraculously, considering the Alley reputation for quarrelling, there have been no fallings-out. Lionel, husband of Carole, fell ill while we were in Shandan, but quickly recovered thanks to a doctor we didn't even know was travelling with us. We've shared anti-histamine pills, tissues, hand sanitiser, water bottles, throat lozenges and stories. We've drunk tea and beer and tortured ourselves with memories of cappuccinos and flat whites. We've eaten far too much. I look around at the familiar faces and feel sure I am not the only one dreading tomorrow's goodbyes.

Our last official function is at the New Zealand Shanghai Consulate. Another banquet. More speeches. This time it's Carole's turn to reply to the inevitable plaudits. I feel nervous for her. The stop-start speaking required when you have a translator at your elbow is not easy at the best of times. Harder still when faced with a jaded audience of family and friends.

Carole starts out at a gallop, leaving no time for the translator. She is full of praise for the way we have been treated in China. Her words of thanks are heartfelt. As she slows down at the translator's request, I wait for her to bring things to a close – she has more than fulfilled what was required of her – but this is not what she does. Leaning forward, not quite pointing a finger but almost, she starts to address China as if it were a person in the room. 'There are too many rich people in your country,' she says. 'The gap between your rich and your poor is too large ... Don't be like New Zealand,' she admonishes, warming to her theme. 'We have the fastest-growing gap between rich and poor in the OECD. Please don't copy us. Find your way back to your vision of a country where no one is poor and everyone is free ...'

Did the translator faithfully represent what Carole said? I have no way of knowing. But the stunned silence that follows the end of her speech gives way seconds later to a standing ovation, not just from the whānau but from our Chinese hosts.

It was a great note to end on.

CHAPTER SIXTY-ONE

1980, the Year of the Monkey, is ushered in with the usual chaos, fanfare and celebration. Shops, offices, schools, universities close so that family members can spend time together. Millions of city workers jam trains, planes and buses in a nation-wide surge to reunite 'refugees' with their families and villages. Overnight, red lanterns appear in streets and doorways. Money is put in red envelopes and given to family members, friends and employees. The amount must be an even number and not contain the number four (because the word for four sounds like the word for death). If you are born in a monkey year you will be eloquent, smart, quick-witted, sociable, agile mentally and physically, creative, innovative and competitive. You may also be snobbish, egotistical, overly optimistic, impatient, reckless, inquisitive and vain.

Rewi, struggling with his translations, working behind the scenes to get Gung Ho up and running again after its 30 years in the wilderness, looks up from his typewriter for a moment and thinks how nice it would be to be on a train or plane headed for Shandan, his true home in China. Or if not Shandan then New Zealand, where so much of him still belongs. 'Just finkin', he says out loud.

He's 83 years old. There's a lot wrong with him. Apart from his ongoing chronic conditions, he has cataracts, arthritis, gout, varicose veins, heat rash and recurring shingles: 'My skin is worse than ever,' he writes to his sister Joy. 'All sorts of complications. Never mind. I don't care.'[1] In his diary he will confess, 'This disease of getting old is a great nuisance.'[2]

He finally gets to Shandan in June 1982. He's there to see the official opening of the Exhibition of Cultural Relics that he himself has donated. Eventually his entire collection will be housed in the new Shandan Alley Memorial Hall. On this memory-soaked visit Rewi is also taken to see the newly restored grave of George Hogg. He and the students of the rebuilt school gather around the grave to sing the old school song. 'I don't think I ever met anyone who could enter into others' lives as George could,' Rewi had written in the lonely weeks after George's death.[3] The words come back to him as he stands at the graveside. Well, you entered into mine all right, George, he acknowledges. You with your big heart and your great snorting laugh …

The following year Gung Ho splutters into life again. 'My old dream had come true,' Rewi writes in his memoir. This time the dream will last. Today there are close on two million co-operatives, including the ones we visited, operating throughout China.

Qi lai, Zhong-guo-de gong-ren,	Rise up, Chinese workmen,
Qi lai, Zhong-guo-de gong-ren!	Rise up, Chinese workmen,
Xi'ang-xin ni zi-ji, zai mo-yao	Trust in yourself, no more hesitation!
pang-huang,	Come together as a team
Kuaikuai tuan-jie qi-lai,	Join in production,
Can-jia gong-he yun-dong!	Join the cause of Gung Ho
	'one for all and all for one!'[4]

In 1984 Rewi will make one more visit to Shandan, his last.

*

Rewi's diary for the last few years of his life tells a mostly family story. Alan and his family come down from Lanzhou for an extended visit. 'What a lovely bunch of children. It's going to be fun living together. I've taken a bigger house for the summer …'[5]

Nothing more is said about Bao Bao and Mao Mao, now living in the US. (Bao Bao's parting from her grandfather was acrimonious. She accused him of selfishness, refusing to believe that he was powerless to help her. In a December 1978 letter to Shirley Barton, a heart-broken Rewi could hardly disguise his anguish. His adored granddaughter had believed he only had to say 'the magical word' for the gates to her 'desired illusory heaven' to open. Even when she substituted New Zealand for the US he still insisted there was nothing he could do. She and her brother had turned their backs on him, eventually finding another way to reach their chosen paradise.[6])

Perhaps, having been comforted for so many years by memories of his mother, Rewi took comfort now from the memories of the many Sundays he'd spent with his beloved grandchildren in Beijing. Whether Mike went to the US at the same time as his wife and children is not clear. He was in China when Rewi died, but the trail, once the family has emigrated to the States, runs cold. Efforts on the part of Alan's children and grandchildren to locate their cousins have drawn a blank.

As Rewi's health begins to fail, the four Nie brothers, closer at hand than Alan and his family, take it in turns to visit their foster father. Often Lao Si's children, Ya Ya and Xiao Long, come along as well. 'I have the usual Sunday invasion,' Rewi writes in a letter home. 'Kids opening bottles of Coca Cola.'[7] Others who come to visit are treated with a display of the laconic Alley humour. 'I'm not dying,' he jokes, 'but you know what they say: it's time to go and meet Marx.'

By this time Rewi is an old hand at playing host to world leaders – not that he ever gives them more than a passing mention in his diary: 'Pierre Trudeau came to lunch last week'; 'Edward Kennedy popped in'; Gough Whitlam seemed 'quite an interesting bloke'.[8] He writes more when it's a friend who's come to see him – Han Suyin, for instance. ('Suyin came and saw and conquered as usual.'[9] 'I wish I could express the deep feeling of love, respect and admiration I have for you,' Suyin wrote to him after one such visit.[10]) Her insistence that it was Rewi who helped her more than any other person to understand the meaning of the revolution is followed, despite his protests, with heartfelt words of thanks for the support he gave her when her marriage became violent. 'You were so patient with me,' she acknowledges, 'and so kind.' ('Rewi was no untouchable saint,' she will write in her 1994 tribute to him, 'but if he ever were to have a halo he would wear it askew with that humour that is so deeply his.'[11])

Each birthday is celebrated as if it might be his last. At his eightieth he is presented with a card from Chairman Hua Guofeng, the man who succeeded – briefly – the Gang of Four. He also receives a telegram from New Zealand's controversial right-wing prime minister, Robert Muldoon, whom he had met when Muldoon visited China in 1976. To everyone's astonishment the two men had got on famously. 'Muldoon said all the right things and said them well,' Rewi had written to his sister Kath in the wake of that visit.[12] 'On behalf of the Government and People of New Zealand I want to offer you warm congratulations on your eightieth birthday. The work you have done during your 50 years in China has contributed greatly to the development of understanding and friendship between our two countries. We are proud of you.'[13]

His eighty-third birthday is hosted by Soong Chingling. Six months later she is dead. Rewi doesn't record his feelings when he learns that the friend closest to his heart has gone. His only comfort is that he was able to say goodbye to her.

His eighty-fifth, attended by Deng Yingchao, widow of Zhou Enlai, is marked by a ceremony conferring on him the honorary citizenship of Beijing. In his speech, Mayor Jiao Ruoyu refers to 'Comrade Rewi Alley' as 'a revolutionary veteran and a down-to-earth doer'.[14] And that is not all. Deng Xiaoping, by now elevated to the top job, acknowledges China's debt to 'Comrade Rewi ... To have done so much for the Chinese people for more than 50 years, whether in the years we experienced untold difficulty [a reference to the Cultural Revolution] or when we were fighting for the victory of the Revolution, or in the post-victory years ... was no easy thing ... Comrade Alley is a fine son of the New Zealand people.'[15]

'My 55 years in China have brought me much happiness,' Rewi says in response. 'The thrill of watching many dreams come true, the joy of seeing two blades of grass grow where but one grew before ...'[16] Later he will tell the man who interviews him for the Chinese documentary, *Rewi Alley*, 'China gave me a life of wonder'.[17]

Three years later, when Rewi turns 88, he is in hospital. Seated in a wheelchair, wearing his familiar Uyghur cap, he receives the congratulations of Vice-Chairman Huang, one of a small number of high-profile guests crowded into his room. Cameramen jostle for position as the short ceremony is filmed for showing that evening on national television.

'I'm like an old vintage vehicle,' Rewi tells the New Zealand journalist Anthony Hubbard, who interviews him in hospital. 'I go into hospital for a while, come out again, go on again ...' But he is firm in his support of Deng Xiaoping. 'I have a great deal of faith in the present leadership. They don't want to have palaces, face, fame and fortune. I think they are all tested old revolutionaries without any personal axes to grind.' (With a skill honed over the years he has disguised his reservations about Deng's reforms in his writings about the revival of Gung Ho.) 'I don't believe in allegiances and all that crap,' he concludes, with just a hint of the Alley temper. 'I think you become a citizen of the world and you are one of the world.'

Hubbard, picking up on Rewi's homesickness for New Zealand, describes him as 'a battered old eagle swooping between two worlds'.

'I won't spend another month in this beautiful place,' Rewi announces when the interview is over. 'All hospitals stink.'[18]

So the 'battered old eagle', whose face bears the scars of flying too close to the sun, discharges himself and goes on with his life. He goes swimming, takes afternoon walks in nearby Bamboo Park, has tea with friends – George and Sufei Hatem, Sid Shapiro, Han Suyin, Grace and Manny Granich, Israel Epstein. Grandchildren come and go. Sons stay overnight. He writes to his sister Joy asking her to send pruning shears and vitamin C powder; in return he will send her the lacebark seeds he promised. He works on plans for the building of a new Bailie School in Shandan. He has suggested harnessing wind power to make electricity, leaving coal, of which there is plenty, to supply heating. But he's anxious about the curriculum, insisting that the study of ecology be prioritised. Ahead of his time in this as in so many things – he's already predicted the rise of robots – he spells out the need for forestry to be given the same status as agriculture and animal husbandry. Without trees the northwest will sink back under its blanket of Gobi desert sand.

Meanwhile Rewi's son Alan has been co-opted to translate *Yo Banfa!* and *The People have Strength* into Chinese, while Rewi himself pens a little book titled *China's Industrial Cooperatives and Why They Should be Revived*. Gung Ho is on the move again.

The pile of books beside his bed grows. There is never enough time to read. The New Zealand ambassador Lindsay Watt has given him a copy of the Booker Prize-winning novel *The Bone People*. Did he read it? If he did, he never said anything. But we do know what he thought of Robin Hyde's *Dragon Rampant*, read so many years after his meeting with the author in Peking: 'Surprisingly lucid since she was nutty.'[19]

In October 1986, the year before his death, he meets the Queen. They discuss the medal he's wearing. 'She does her job well,' he will write in a letter to Joy. 'I suppose she loves the Duke. He looks the typical Red Tab officer to me.'[20] Surrounded by his Chinese family, Rewi's thoughts keep straying to his family and friends on the other side of the world. The best days are those in which letters arrive from New Zealand.

'Please thank the 23-year-old who mows your lawns for his effort to give me religion,' he writes to Joy in March 1984. 'I did go through that stage myself until the world began to open out in front of me in all its complications.'[21]

In the last months of Rewi's life, the Nie brothers take it in turn to spend the night at No. 1 Tai Ji Chang. Lao Si, interviewed for the Chinese documentary on Rewi, records, 'Forty years ago, when I had pneumonia, I slept by his side on the *kang*; now he has pneumonia and I am sleeping at his side.'[22]

Rewi celebrates his eighty-ninth birthday. 'I have eaten the food of the Chinese people and experienced the privilege of working together with them,' he says. 'China is a land of wonders, of magnificent scenery, of glorious mountains and fascinating streams …'

'Love, love again,' he signs his letters to Joy. 'It's been a stinger of a summer [his last] but my walnut tree has survived. There is still so very much to be done …'[23]

The final entry in his diary is about Chingling. He doesn't believe in life after death, but since her spirit is with him night and day he believes that when his time comes to 'go and meet Marx' she will be with him. He dies on 27 December 1987. At his request, his ashes are scattered over the red earth of Shandan.

When I was young I left my home.
When I was old I returned again …
The children saw me and they looked at me,
laughing and they said,
'Old man where do you come from?'[24]

GLOSSARY OF MĀORI WORDS AND NEW ZEALAND SLANG

chooks	hens
creek	stream
dunny	outside lavatory
haka	Māori ceremonial war dance
morepork	night owl, ruru
Pākehā	New Zealander of European descent
pā	fortified settlement
poutama	stepped pattern symbolising genealogies and/or levels of learning
to shout	to treat (as in pay for)
tucker	food, usually a meal
tūī	native bird with a melodious call
whānau	extended family/friends
whare	house/dwelling place

NOTES

I apologise for the incomplete information in some of these endnotes. This is not an academic book and I am not an academic writer, but I have been persuaded of the value of providing as much information as possible about my source material. I hope readers will forgive any omissions and shortcomings.

Abbreviations

Alley, Diary Rewi Alley Diary, ABHS W4627 950 Box 1481, 58/264/6, Archives New Zealand

Alley, Memoirs Rewi Alley, *At 90: Memoirs of my China years* (Beijing: New World Press, 1986)

ANZ Archives New Zealand

ATL Alexander Turnbull Library, National Library of New Zealand, Wellington

MFAT Ministry of Foreign Affairs and Trade

NZE New Zealand Embassy

NZSIS New Zealand Security Intelligence Service

Epigraph
1. MFAT file 58/264/6 Part 1 – New Zealand Affairs: External Relations/China/ Rewi Alley 1973–1985.
2. Diary, RA Papers, MS-Papers-6533-340, ATL

Prologue
1. Gwendolen Somerset, *Sunshine and Shadow*, New Zealand Playcentre Federation, 1988.

Chapter Two
1. Rewi Alley, 'Autobiography' in *Gung Ho: Poems by Rewi Alley*, Christchurch: Caxton Press, 1950.
2. Somerset Family Papers, RA Papers, 84-181-3/16, ATL.
3. Alley, *Memoirs*.
4. Gwendolen Somerset, *Sunshine and Shadow*, New Zealand Playcentre Federation, 1988.
5. Ibid.
6. Ibid.
7. Diaries and memoir relating to China, Freer, Warren Wilfred (Hon), 1920– 2013, MS-papers 11634, ATL.
8. Alley, *Memoirs*.

9. Rewi Alley, *Struggle Around the Central Plains: A story of Honan province*, Beijing: New World Press, 1980.

10. Rewi Alley, 'Kazak', in *Beyond the Withered Oak Ten Thousand Saplings Grow*, Christchurch: Caxton Press, 1962.

11. Somerset, *Sunshine and Shadow*.

12. Citation for honorary degree. 'Rewi Alley is undoubtedly one of our most famous sons. He is a man of great personal modesty, who throughout his life has shunned public honours. He was reluctant to accept even such tribute as we offer tonight to his literary achievement and to his life of service. He was recently in New Zealand on the longest visit he has made to his country in over forty years, and it had been our hope that he might be present to receive this degree in person. Since that has not proved possible the degree must be conferred *in absentia*.

   'It is therefore with great pleasure, Mr Chancellor, that I place before you the name of Rewi Alley, holder of the Military Medal, author, poet, translator, and interpreter of China to other nations, for the degree of Doctor of Literature *honoris causa* in this University.'

   From the Council minutes, 24 April 1972:

   'The Vice-Chancellor read a letter dated 6 April 1972 from Mr Alley, accepting the offer of an Honorary degree, but regretting that he would not be able to be present at the Graduation Ceremony as his age prevented his travelling to Wellington.

   'The Chancellor said that it was proposed to confer the degree in absentia at the next Graduation Ceremony and that a public announcement of the award would be made on the night of the Graduation Ceremony.'

   From the Council agenda, 26 June 1972:

   'From Mr Rewi Alley, 17.5.72: "1 Yung Ke Road, Peking, May 17th, 1972. D.B. Taylor, Esq., Victoria University of Wellington, Wellington, NEW ZEALAND. Dear Mr Taylor: Thank you for sending me the degree certificate and copies of the oration read at your capping ceremony on 4th of May, 1972. I am, of course, slightly overwhelmed by the honour, and the kind words spoken. I hope very much that the University's action in this matter will lead to better relations between New Zealand and this part of the world. Should I be able to visit New Zealand again, I will certainly pay you a visit. I am glad too, to have the page you sent from "Salient" the student newspaper. Yours sincerely, Rewi Alley"'. Papers of James and Jean Bertram, 93-103-04, ATL.

13. Edgar Snow, 'China's blitzbuilder Rewi Alley', *Saturday Evening Post*, 8 February 1941.

14. Edgar Snow, in Secretariat of the National Committee for the Commemoration of Rewi Alley's 75th birthday, *Rewi Alley Seventy-five*, Hamilton, 1972.

15. Geoff Chapple, *Rewi Alley of China*, Auckland: Hodder & Stoughton, 1980.

16. Somerset, *Sunshine and Shadow*.

17. Ibid.

18. Both quotations from Alley, *Memoirs*.

19. Letters to family members, RA Papers, MS-Papers 11775-1, ATL.
20. Family story.
21. Letters to Pip, October 1964, RA Papers, 74-047-4.09, ATL.
22. Somerset, *Sunshine and Shadow*.
23. Alley, *Memoirs*.

Chapter Four

1. James Bertram, *Capes of China Slide Away: A memoir of peace and war 1910–1980*, Auckland: Auckland University Press, 1993.
2. Han Suyin, *Eldest Son: Zhou Enlai and the making of modern China*, London: Pimlico, 1994.
3. Ibid.
4. 'In Memoriam – Chou En-lai', in Rewi Alley, *Snow Over the Pines*, New Zealand–China Friendship Society and Progressive Book Society, 1977.
5. James Bertram Papers, MS-Group 0216, ATL.

Chapter Five

1. James McNeish, *Dance of the Peacocks: New Zealanders in exile in the time of Hitler and Mao Tse-Tung*, Auckland: Vintage, 2003.
2. Alley, *Memoirs*.
3. 'Autobiography', in Rewi Alley, *Gung Ho: Poems*, Christchurch: Caxton Press, 1948.
4. NZ Defence Force Personnel File, WWI R2 4095751, NZ Defence Force Archives.
5. Geoff Chapple, *Rewi Alley of China*, Auckland: Hodder & Stoughton, 1980.
6. Alley, *Memoirs*.
7. Ibid.
8. Chapple, *Rewi Alley of China*.
9. Agnes Smedley, *Chinese Destinies*, Beijing: Foreign Languages Press, 2003.
10. Online Cenotaph Records, Auckland War Museum: www.aucklandmuseum.com
11. Letters to family members, RA Papers, MS-Papers 117751, ATL.
12. Willis Airey, *A Learner in China: A life of Rewi Alley*, Christchurch: Caxton Press, 1970.
13. 'Who Will Build Anew?', in Rewi Alley, *Poems for Aotearoa*, Auckland: New Zealand–China Friendship Society and Progressive Book Society, 1972.
14. 'On Training Puppets for Cambodia', in Alley, *Poems for Aotearoa*.

Chapter Six

1. Reported in *Christchurch Boys' High School Magazine*, no. 104, December 1941, RA Papers, 74-0471/06, ATL.
2. In a letter to Roger Duff, director of the Canterbury Museum, entitled 'One thing leads to another' (8 July 1975), Francis Shurrock described how he came to make

the bust, having first met Rewi's brother Geoff: 'I was invited to Westcote to meet Geoff's people and on the 2nd occasion Rewi Alley was home on leave from the Shanghai Fire Brigade ... Rewi and myself became friends & I asked him if he would pose for a modelled portrait but he would have none of it. I noticed there was a particular bond between Rewi and his mother so I suggested that I should do the modelling & if she didn't like it, the clay head could be thrown back in the clay bin. The bargain was made & Mrs Alley was brought to see the modelling & we left her alone with it for a while. She made no comment on going away: I was most disappointed. However 2 days later I received a wonderful letter from her telling me how she had always thought of Rewi as a dear kind boy but had not noticed the strength of character. So there it was I had won my bargain. The clay head was moulded & cast in plaster & this plaster head was in due course sent to London to be cast into bronze, accepted & exhibited in the Royal Academy Annual Exhibition.'

Chapter Seven
1. Alley, *Memoirs*.
2. New Zealand Defence Force Personnel file WW1 55386 R24095751, ANZ.
3. 'Foreclosure', Geoff Chapple, *Rewi Alley of China*, Auckland: Hodder & Stoughton, 1980.
4. Untitled NZSIS document, part of which has been withheld, dated 14 April 1951. Declassified 11 November 2009.
5. Somerset Family Papers, RA Papers, 84-181-3/40, ATL.
6. Philippa Reynolds, *Rewi Alley from Canterbury to China*, Christchurch: Christchurch–Gansu Friendly Relations Committee of the Christchurch City Council, 1997.
7. Rewi Alley, 'Little Red Devils', in Rewi Alley (trans.), *Poems of Revolt: Some Chinese voices over the last century*, Beijing: New World Press, 1962.
8. 'Seen in Nanking', in ibid.
9. 'Autobiography', in Rewi Alley, *Gung Ho: Poems*, Christchurch: Caxton Press, 1948.
10. Alley, *Memoirs*.

Chapter Eight
1. New Zealand Defence Force Personnel file WW1 55346 R24095751, ANZ.
2. Ibid.

Chapter Nine
1. Statement made by Lady Caroline Lamb about the English poet Lord Byron.
2. A law passed in 2018 designed to make cremation mandatory has led to a wave of suicides among elderly people determined to be buried in the traditional way before the law comes into effect. Other acts of resistance, particularly in rural areas, continue to disrupt the government's 'zero burials' campaign.

3. Interview in *New Zealand Listener*, 1 April 2017.
4. David Mahon, 'Afternoons with Rewi Alley', *North & South*, October 2013.
5. Interview with Dave Harré, 12 September 2017.

Chapter Ten
1. Alley, *Memoirs*.
2. Willis Airey, *A Learner in China: A life of Rewi Alley*, Christchurch: Caxton Press, 1970.
3. W.H. Auden and Christopher Isherwood, *Journey to a War*, New York: Paragon House, 1990.
4. Airey, *A Learner in China*.
5. Alley, Diary, 58/264/6, ANZ.

Chapter Eleven
1. Rana Mitter, *A Bitter Revolution: China's struggle with the modern world*, Oxford: Oxford University Press, 2004. Mitter makes the point that the KMT every bit as much as the CCP regarded itself as a revolutionary party – the word Kuomintang means 'national' or 'country people' party. Both sides in China's bitter civil war called themselves heirs of Sun Yatsen, citing his Three Principles of the People – Nationalism, Democracy, Welfare – as central to their vision of a New China. Mao, in the years before the communist victory, frequently used the word democracy, but he was no more an advocate of pluralist policies than his arch-enemy Chiang Kaishek. Democracy would be allowed at grassroots level, but that, in the minds of both leaders, was as far as it would go. At every other level of society political orthodoxy would reign.
2. Anne-Marie Brady, *Friend of China: The myth of Rewi Alley*, London: Routledge Curzon, 2003.

Chapter Twelve
1. James MacManus, *Ocean Devil: The life and legend of George Hogg*, London: Harper Perennial, 2010.
2. 'Fruition', in Rewi Alley, *Fruition: The story of George Alwin Hogg*, Christchurch: Caxton Press, 1967.
3. Told to me in China.
4. Han Suyin, *A Mortal Flower*, London: Jonathan Cape, 1966.
5. http://nzchinasociety.org.nz/wp-content/uploads/2013/11/Transcription-of-Peter-Lyness-Tapes-Rewi-Alley_091113v2.pdf
6. Alley, Memoirs.
7. 'Advice to Myself', in Rewi Alley, *73 Man to Be*, Christchurch: Caxton Press, 1970.
8. David Mahon, 'Afternoons with Rewi Alley', *North & South*, October 2013.
9. RA Papers, 84-181-3/16, ATL.

Chapter Thirteen

1. Alley, Diary, RA Papers, MS-Papers, 0424-08, ATL.
2. Alley, Diary, 58/264/6, ANZ.
3. Ibid.
4. Edgar Snow, 'China's blitzbuilder Rewi Alley', *Saturday Evening Post*, 8 February 1941.

Chapter Fourteen

1. Stuart Reynolds Schram, 'Mao Zedong Chinese Leader': www.britannica.com
2. 'At Tu Fu's "Tsao Tang", Chentu', in Rewi Alley, *Beyond the Withered Oak Ten Thousand Saplings Grow*, Christchurch: Caxton Press, 1962.
3. 'Eunuch's Cemetery – Pa Li Chuang', in Alley, *Beyond the Withered Oak*.

Chapter Fifteen

1. Alley, Diary, 58/264/6, ANZ.
2. Letters to Mother and Siblings, RA Papers, 74-047-3/09, ATL.
3. Willis Airey, *A Learner in China: A life of Rewi Alley*, Christchurch: Caxton Press, 1970.
4. Letters to Pip, 58/264/6, ANZ.
5. David Mahon, 'Afternoons with Rewi Alley', *North & South*, October 2013.
6. Rewi Alley, *Yo Banfa!* (*We Have a Way*), Shanghai: China Monthly Review, 1952.

Chapter Sixteen

1. 'Problems of War and Strategy', in *Selected Works of Mao Tse-Tung*, vol. II, Beijing: People's Publishing House, 1965.
2. Edgar Snow, *Red Star Over China*, New York: Grove Press, 1968.
3. James Bertram, *Capes of China Slide Away: A memoir of peace and war 1910–1980*, Auckland: Auckland University Press, 1993.
4. 'Report on an Investigation of the Peasant Movement in Hunan', in *Selected Works of Mao Tse-Tung*, vol. I, Beijing: Foreign Languages Press, 1965.
5. RA Papers, 84-181-3/16, ATL.

Chapter Seventeen

1. Alley, *Memoirs*.
2. Letter to Alan, 8 July 1952, Shirley Barton Papers, MS-Papers 6533-043, ATL.
3. Willis Airey, *A Learner in China: A life of Rewi Alley*, Christchurch: Caxton Press, 1970.
4. The correspondence between Rewi and Shirley Barton, held in the ATL, gives some credence to the rumour that she too, along with Ida Pruitt and Agnes Smedley, was in love with him and those feelings may have been reciprocated. Describing Shirley as 'wonderful', 'terrific', 'magnificent', in a letter written in February 1962, Rewi chides her for not writing often enough. 'I write 5 letters

to your every one. How can you doubt I love you?' In a later letter, written in January 1969, he goes further: 'I have often kicked myself for ever letting you go, but actually did save you many a heartbreak, I'm sure.' As for Shirley, in a letter of August 1972 she claimed to have learned to distrust 'emotions and personal attraction', insisting that it was the cause Rewi represented she was devoted to, not the man himself. Even if Rewi believed her, others close to her did not. 'My years in China and meeting you Rewi were the highlight of my life,' she'd written in an earlier letter. Finally, just before she died, her words barely legible as they trailed across the page, she wrote, 'Don't worry about me and remember China, and your friendship and inspiration, has been the greatest experience of my life.' Shirley Barton Papers, MS-Papers 6533-028 and -031, ATL.

5.   A conversation between Madame Soong Chingling and Da Jitao, journalist, politician and author of a book on the philosophy of Sun Yatsen, reported in *China Tomorrow*, vol. 1, no. 12, 20 October 1929 (Yenching University).
6.   Rewi Alley (trans.), *Poems of Revolt: Some Chinese voices over the last century*, Beijing: New World Press, 1962.
7.   'Kansu Peasant Bridge Builders', in Rewi Alley, *This Is China Today*, Christchurch: Caxton Press, 1951.
8.   Diary, RA Papers, MSX-5290, ATL.
9.   'Soong Ching Ling – In Memoriam', RA Papers, MS-Papers 4697, ATL.
10. Diary, RA Papers, MS-Papers 0424-08, ATL.
11. James McNeish, *Dance of the Peacocks: New Zealanders in exile in the time of Hitler and Mao Tse-Tung*, Auckland: Vintage, 2003.
12. Rewi Alley, *Six Americans in China*, Beijing: International Culture Publishing Corporation, 1985.
13. Han Suyin, *A Mortal Flower*, London: Jonathan Cape, 1966.
14. McNeish, *Dance of the Peacocks*.
15. 'Soong Ching Ling', in Rewi Alley, *Beyond the Withered Oak Ten Thousand Saplings Grow*, Christchurch: Caxton Press, 1962.

Chapter Eighteen

1.   'For October the First 1975', in Rewi Alley, *Snow Over the Pines*, Auckland: New Zealand–China Friendship Society and Progressive Book Society, 1977.
2.   Jung Chang, *Wild Swans: Three daughters of China*, London: Harper Collins, 1991.
3.   Han Suyin, *A Mortal Flower*, London: Jonathan Cape, 1966.
4.   James McNeish, *Dance of the Peacocks: New Zealanders in exile in the time of Hitler and Mao Tse-Tung*, Auckland: Vintage, 2003.
5.   Alley, Diary, 58/264/6, ANZ.
6.   Ibid.
7.   Han Suyin, *A Mortal Flower*.
8.   'One Remembers So Well', in Rewi Alley, *Gung Ho: Poems*, Christchurch: Caxton Press, 1948.

Chapter Nineteen

1. Rewi Alley (trans.), in *Light and Shadow Along a Great Road: An anthology of modern Chinese verse*, Beijing: New World Press, 1984.
2. Rewi Alley (trans.), *Tu Fu: Selected poems*, Peking: Foreign Languages Press, 1964.
3. The story of Rewi's 'cultural diplomacy' is told in James Beattie and Richard Bullen, *New China Eye Witness: Roger Duff, Rewi Alley and the art of museum diplomacy*, Christchurch: Canterbury University Press, 2017. The story is not only unique – after 1952 no artwork older than 80 years could be legally exported from China – it provides a window into the extraordinary place Rewi, and by association New Zealand, occupied in mid- to late twentieth-century China. That New Zealand still holds a special place in Chinese affections is due in part to this behind-the-scenes contact. Because it wasn't all one way. Rewi's gifting of artworks to the Canterbury Museum triggered a corresponding traffic in the other direction. Over the years New Zealand donated many works of Māori and Polynesian art to the Imperial Palace Museum in Beijing. 'It's hard to understand why Rewi was considered such a threat,' a New Zealand diplomat admitted to David Mahon ('Afternoons with Rewi Alley', *North & South*, October 2013): 'He is our greatest asset now … Frankly there would be few diplomats who would not squirm at that shameful episode [SIS surveillance of Rewi]. The Cold War … was about absolutes. In the "them and us" scenario, few cared who Alley actually was, they just wanted to break what he stood for.'
4. Alley, *Tu Fu*.
5. RA Papers, 74-047-3/08, ATL.

Chapter Twenty

1. Edgar Snow, *Journey to the Beginning: A personal view of contemporary history*, New York: Random House, 1958.
2. Alan's Memories of Rewi, RA Papers, MS-Papers 5792, ATL.
3. Lois Wheeler Snow, *Edgar Snow's China*, London: Orbis, 1981.

Chapter Twenty-one

1. Rewi Alley, *Leaves from a Sandan Notebook*, Christchurch: Caxton Press, 1950.
2. Family story.
3. Essay on Anna Louise Strong, in Rewi Alley, *Six Americans in China*, Beijing: International Culture Publishing Corporation, 1985.
4. David Mahon, 'Afternoons with Rewi Alley', *North & South*, October 2013.
5. *Gung Ho: Rewi Alley of China*, a documentary, directed by Geoff Steven, 1980, ANZ.
6. Told to me while travelling in China. On further investigation it turns out to be a phrase used by Mao to describe Dr Norman Bethune (possibly re-used later to describe Rewi) in his 1939 article 'In Memory of Norman Bethune' (*Selected Works of Mao Tse-Tung*, vol. II, Beijing: Foreign Languages Press, 1965). Later it would be used by Deng Yingchao, wife of Zhou Enlai, writing about Rewi in the

preface to the 1987 edition of his autobiography published by Gansu People's Publishing House.
7. http://nzchinasociety.org.nz/wp-content/uploads/2013/11/Transcription-of-Peter-Lyness=Tapes-Rewi-Alley_091113v2.pdf
8. Shirley Barton Papers, MS-Papers 6533-042, ATL.
9. NZSIS document: copy of *Truth* article, 'Idol might leave red-faced', 16 April 1968. Declassified 11 November 2009. Part of document withheld.
10. Ibid.
11. NZSIS file: Rewi Alley, 3 October 1968. Declassified 11 November 2009. Part of document withheld.
12. Steven, *Gung Ho: Rewi Alley of China*.
13. Essay on Anna Louise Strong, in Alley, *Six Americans in China*.
14. Shirley Barton Papers, MS-Papers 6533-043, ATL.
15. RA Papers, 74-047-4/11, ATL.
16. RA Papers, 84-181-3/16, ATL.
17. Brady, *Friend of China*.
18. Family story.
19. RA Papers, 58/264/6, ANZ.
20. David Mahon, 'Afternoons with Rewi Alley', *North & South*, October 2013.
21. Roderick MacFarquhar and Michael Schoenhals, *Mao's Last Revolution*, Cambridge, Mass: Harvard University Press, 2008.
22. Shirley Barton Papers, MS-Papers 6533-042, ATL.
23. Somerset Family Papers, 84-181-3/38B, ATL.
24. Steven, *Gung Ho: Rewi Alley of China*.

Chapter Twenty-two

1. Rewi Alley, *A Highway, and an Old Chinese Doctor*, Christchurch: Caxton Press, 1973.
2. Rewi's great-granddaughter, Luyi Duan, a university teacher, lawyer and mother, explained Alan's naming of his children in an email to me in November 2018: 'My grandpa Alan named the name of his six children because of his delight in the ocean when he and Rewi travelled back to New Zealand, but their names do not all means different seabirds. Each of their given names contains two different Chinese characters. The characters in the middle are all the same. It means ocean in Chinese and is pronouced Hai. The last characters are different. Haiying means the sea-hawk, but it may not really fit a girl, so Alan chose another character instead which is more feminine. Haiyan means the petrel. Hailu means sea and the land. Hailong means seadragon. Haijun does not mean any of the sea animals, jun means handsome. Maybe Alan wished my dad to be a handsome boy and he really is. Haiou means seagull.'
3. 'Dedication', a poem written for his mother, in Rewi Alley, *Leaves from a Sandan Notebook*, Christchurch: Caxton Press, 1950.
4. Paraphrased from Alley, *Memoirs*.

Chapter Twenty-three

1. Barbara W. Tuchman, *Stilwell and the American Experience in China, 1911–45*, London: Macmillan, 1971.
2. Diary, RA Papers, MS-Papers 0424-08, ATL.
3. Alley, *Memoirs*.
4. Letter from Ida Pruitt to Rewi, in Anne-Marie Brady, *Friend of China: The myth of Rewi Alley*, London: Routledge Curzon, 2003.
5. Essay on Agnes Smedley, in Rewi Alley, *Six Americans in China*, Beijing: International Culture Publishing Corporation, 1985.
6. Correspondence to Mrs Alley, RA Papers, 74-047-2/10, ATL.
7. Alley, Diary, 58/264/6, ANZ.
8. Essay on Ma Haide, in Alley, *Six Americans in China*.

Chapter Twenty-four

1. Letters to Pip, RA Papers, 58/264/6, ANZ.
2. John Fraser, *The Chinese: Portrait of a people*, Toronto: Collins, 1980.
3. Rewi Alley, *Yo Banfa!* (We Have a Way), Shanghai: China Monthly Review, 1952.
4. Airey, *A Learner in China*.
5. 'Wuhan Reverie Spring 1972', in Rewi Alley, *Over China's Hills of Blue*, Christchurch: Caxton Press, 1974.
6. *Quotations from Chairman Mao Tse-Tung*, (The Little Red Book), Peking: Foreign Languages Press, 1966.
7. MFAT file 58/264/6 Part 2 – New Zealand Affairs: External Relations/China/Rewi Alley 1986–1987.
8. MFAT file 58/264/6 Part 3 – New Zealand Affairs: External Relations/China/Rewi Alley 1973–1985.
9. From Xi Jinping's speech to the National Conference on Religion, Beijing, 22–23 April 2016, reported in *South China Morning Post*, 21 November 2017.

Chapter Twenty-five

1. Rewi Alley, *Human China: A diary with poems*, Christchurch: Caxton Press, 1957.
2. 'On Love', in Rewi Alley, *Poems of Protest*, Christchurch: Caxton Press, 1968.

Chapter Twenty-six

1. Rewi Alley, *Fruition: The story of George Alwyn Hogg*, Christchurch: Caxton Press, 1967.

Chapter Twenty-seven

1. Han Suyin, *A Mortal Flower*, London: Jonathan Cape, 1966.
2. Ibid.
3. Essay on Ma Haide, in Rewi Alley, *Six Americans in China*, Beijing: International Culture Publishing Corporation, 1985.

4. 'Care of the Taiping Soldiers Longer than the Chien River', in Rewi Alley (trans.), *Poems of Revolt: Some Chinese voices over the last century*, Beijing: New World Press, 1962.

5. James MacManus, *Ocean Devil: The life and legend of George Hogg*, London: Harper Perennial, 2010.

6. Suyin, *A Mortal Flower*.

7. Letter dated 5 January 1930, in *Selected Military Writings of Mao Tse-Tung*, Beijing: Foreign Languages Press, 1963.

8. Edgar Snow, *Red Star Over China*, New York: Grove Press, 1968.

9. 'The Long March', in Rewi Alley (trans.), *Light and Shadow Along a Great Road: An anthology of modern Chinese poetry*, Beijing: New World Press, 1984.

Chapter Twenty-eight

1. Mark Twain, *Personal Recollection of Joan of Arc, by the Sieur Louis de Conte*, US: Harper, 1896.

2. Essay on Edgar Snow, in Rewi Alley, *Six Americans in China*, Beijing: International Culture Publishing Corporation, 1985.

3. James McNeish, *Dance of the Peacocks: New Zealanders in exile in the time of Hitler and Mao Tse-Tung*, Auckland: Vintage, 2003.

4. James Bertram, *Capes of China Slide Away: A memoir of peace and war 1910–1980*, Auckland: Auckland University Press, 1993.

Chapter Twenty-nine

1. Letter from Eric Livingstone to Alison Horn, 27 July 2017.

2. MFAT file 58/264/6 Part 2 – New Zealand Affairs: External Relations/China/Rewi Alley 1986–1987

3. NZE to MFAT Cabinet Office, 'Rewi Alley and Presentation of QSM', 27 December 1985, 26/1/4 NZE.

4. Ibid.

5. Ibid.

6. MFAT file BEI-CH/NZ3/6 Part 2 – Beijing Post Files/China/New Zealand Bilateral Relations/Social Issues/People to People Links/Including Rewi Alley 2003–2004.

7. Letter to the *Dominion Post*, Wellington, 1 June 1952.

8. Deuteronomy 15:8.

9. 'Never Realising', in Rewi Alley, *Snow Over the Pines*, Auckland: NZ–China Friendship Society and Progressive Book Society, 1977.

10. MFAT file 58/264/6 Part 1 – New Zealand Affairs: External Relations/China/Rewi Alley 1973–1985.

11. Ibid.

12. David Mahon, 'Afternoons with Rewi Alley', *North & South*, October 2013.

13. 'Which Side of the Fence', in Rewi Alley, *73 Man to Be*, Christchurch: Caxton Press, 1970.

Chapter Thirty

1. James Bertram, *First Act in China: The story of the Sian mutiny*, New York: Viking, 1938.

Chapter Thirty-one

1. 'SS PA Weekend', in Rewi Alley, *Leaves from a Sandan Notebook*, Christchurch:. Caxton Press, 1950.
2. Tom Newnham, 'Kathleen Hall: Dr Bethune's angel', *China Today*, 1997: http://nzcfs.adminmouse.co.nz/wp-content/uploads/2010/10/kathleen-hall-tom-newnham.pdf
3. Adrienne Clarkson, *Norman Bethune*, Toronto: Penguin Books, 2009. It's tempting to see Rewi and Bethune as cut from the same cloth. Clarkson's claim that the Chinese loved Bethune because they saw his impatience as 'unlimited eagerness', his stubbornness as 'unequivocal determination' and his dominance as 'unshakeable commitment' could as easily have been written about Rewi. Both men loved art. Both were poets. Bethune was a gifted painter. But perhaps what connects them most closely is that both suffered neglect in their home countries because of the difficulty their compatriots had – and, in Rewi's case, continue to have – accepting the veneration in which they are held in China.
4. www.nzedge.com/legends/rewi-alley/
5. Willis Airey, *A Learner in China: A life of Rewi Alley*, Christchurch: Caxton Press, 1970.
6. James MacManus, *Ocean Devil: The life and legend of George Hogg*, London: Harper Perennial, 2010.

Chapter Thirty-two

1. Deng Xiaoping, 'Building socialism with a specifically Chinese character', *People's Daily*, 1 October 1984.
2. Speech given by President-in-waiting Xi Jingping in January 2013, reported by Xinhua, the State News Agency.
3. Mao Zedong's description of the Communist Party strategy of infiltrating institutions so as to control them. Quoted in *Philippine Daily Enquirer*, 22 November 2017.
4. Mao's speech 'On the Correct Handling of Contradictions Among the People', 27 February 1957, cited in *Quotations from Chairman Mao Tse-Tung*, Peking: Foreign Languages Press, 1966.
5. Reported in translator's note to Yan Lianke, *The Day the Sun Died*, London: Chatto & Windus, 2018.
6. Eric X Li: www.ted.com, TED Global, 2013.
7. Introduction to Ma Jian, *China Dream*, London: Chatto & Windus, 2018.

Chapter Thirty-three
1. Jung Chang, *Wild Swans: Three daughters of China*, Pymble: Harper Perrenial, 1991.
2. Han Suyin, *Birdless Summer*, London: Jonathan Cape, 1968.
3. Christopher Isherwood and W.H. Auden, *Journey to a War*, New York: Paragon House, 1910.
4. Helen Foster Snow, *Inside Red China*, New York: Da Capo Press, 1979.
5. David Mahon, 'Afternoons with Rewi Alley', *North & South*, October 2013.

Chapter Thirty-four
1. Geoff Chapple, *Rewi Alley of China*, Auckland: Hodder and Stoughton, 1980.
2. 'Autobiography 11', in Rewi Alley, *Beyond the Withered Oak Ten Thousand Saplings Grow*, Christchurch: Caxton Press, 1962.
3. Willis Airey, *A Learner in China: A life of Rewi Alley*, Christchurch: Caxton Press, 1970.
4. *Selected Military Writings of Mao Tse-Tung*, Beijing: Foreign Languages Press, 1963.
5. In 'Autobiography', in *Gung Ho: Poems* (Christchurch: Caxton Press, 1948), Rewi describes himself as 'midwife to the infant Gung Ho'.

Chapter Thirty-five
1. Robyn Hyde, *Dragon Rampant*, London: Hurst & Blackett, 1939.
2. In 'Afternoons with Rewi Alley' (*North & South*, October 2013) David Mahon quotes Rewi describing Hyde as 'a stupid selfish woman' for ignoring the advice she was given.
3. Story told in www.nzedge.com/legends/rewi-alley/. 'An Indian journalist wrote this account of a stoic Alley in Chongqing, China's wartime capital in 1939: As the bombs were crashing all over the city, the two hundred-odd people in the restaurant sat or stood with tense and strained expressions. Chopsticks were dropped, the soup grew cold in the bowls. Who could think of eating at such a time? Unhurriedly, as if no bombs were crashing around, he [Alley] was eating his food. And as he ate he was calmly reading his newspaper.'

Chapter Thirty-six
1. Rewi Alley, *Fruition: The story of George Alwyn Hogg*, Christchurch: Caxton Press, 1967.
2. RA Papers, 740-047-6/22, ATL.
3. 'Gung Ho', in Rewi Alley, *Fragments of Living Peking*, Christchurch: New Zealand Peace Council, 1955.
4. Rewi Alley, *Leaves from a Sandan Notebook*, Christchurch: Caxton Press, 1950.

Chapter Thirty-eight

1. Diary, RA Papers, MS-Papers 0424-08, ATL.
2. George Hogg's words quoted in James MacManus, *Ocean Devil: The life and legend of George Hogg*, London: Harper Perennial, 2010.
3. Song Chiu-Chia, 'The Conscript' in Rewi Alley (trans.), *Peace Through the Ages: Translations from the poets of China*, Beijing: Rewi Alley, 1954.

Chapter Thirty-nine

1. Philippa Reynolds, *Rewi Alley from Canterbury to China*, Christchurch: Christchurch–Gansu Friendly Relations Committee of the Christchurch City Council, 1997.
2. 'Shangshipu Return', in Rewi Alley, *Beyond the Withered Oak Ten Thousand Saplings Grow*, Christchurch: Caxton Press, 1962.

Chapter Forty

1. 'Report on an Investigation of the Peasant Movement in Hunan', *Selected Works of Mao Tse-Tung*, vol. I, Beijing: Foreign Languages Press, 1965.
2. RA Papers, 74-047-6/22, ATL
3. Willis Airey, *A Learner in China: A life of Rewi Alley*, Christchurch: Caxton Press, 1970.
4. Ibid.
5. *Guardian* interview with Alice O'Keefe, 15 January 2017.

Chapter Forty-two

1. Preface to Rewi Alley, *Snow Over the Pines*, Auckland: NZ–China Friendship Society and Progressive Book Society, 1977.
2. James Bertram, *Return to China 1957*, London: Heinemann, 1957.
3. Willis Airey, *A Learner in China: A life of Rewi Alley*, Christchurch: Caxton Press, 1970.
4. Both letters quoted in James McNeish, *Dance of the Peacocks: New Zealanders in exile in the time of Hitler and Mao Tse-Tung*, Auckland: Vintage, 2003.
5. Essay on Agnes Smedley, in Rewi Alley, *Six Americans in China*, Beijing: International Culture Publishing Corporation, 1985.
6. McNeish, *Dance of the Peacocks*.
7. Nicholas Jenkins with Katherine Bucknall, *Auden and Spain*, Oxford: Clarendon Press, 1990.
8. James Bertram Papers, MS-group 1277, ATL.
9. From Rudyard Kipling, *A Song of the English*, New York: Doubleday & Co, 1909.
10. MFAT file 58/264/6 Part 3 – New Zealand Affairs: External Relations/China/Rewi Alley 1973–1985.
11. Letter to the *Dominion Post*, 19 June 1952.
12. McNeish, *Dance of the Peacocks*.

13. Edgar Snow, *Journey to the Beginning: A memoir*, New York: Random House, 1958.
14. James Bertram Papers, MS-group 1277, ATL.
15. Anne-Marie Brady, *Friend of China: The myth of Rewi Alley*, London: Routledge Curzon, 2003.
16. McNeish, *Dance of the Peacocks*. Bertram's unhappy assessment of what had happened to the Chinese revolution was echoed 20 years later in Douglas Martin's obituary for Israel Epstein, published in the *New York Times* on 5 June 2005: 'Perhaps the most loyal Communists today are foreigners, veteran fellow travellers from a vanished era of idealism,' he wrote, a view now held by many around the globe.
17. 'Home', in Rewi Alley, *The Freshening Breeze*, Beijing: New World Press, 1977.

Chapter Forty-three
1. 'Yellow Fish', in Rewi Alley, *Gung Ho: Poems*, Christchurch: Caxton Press, 1948.
2. NZSIS file P.F. 206, Personal Particulars File Rewi Alley. Declassified 11 November 2009.

Chapter Forty-four
1. Geoff Chapple, *Rewi Alley of China*, Auckland: Hodder and Stoughton, 1980.
2. Roel Sterck, 'In the fields of Shennong: An inaugural lecture delivered before the University of Cambridge on 30 September 2008 to mark the establishment of the Joseph Needham Professorship of Chinese History, Science and Civilisation', Cambridge: Needham Research Institute, 2008.

Chapter Forty-five
1. 'Sandan Five Years After', in Rewi Alley, *Beyond the Withered Oak Ten Thousand Saplings Grow*, Christchurch: Caxton Press, 1962.
2. 'The Assyrian came down like the wolf on the fold', the opening line of Byron's 'The Destruction of Sennacherib'.
3. James MacManus, *Ocean Devil: The life and legend of George Hogg*, London: Harper Perennial, 2010.

Chapter Forty-six
1. Family papers.
2. Rewi Alley, *Six Americans in China*, Beijing: International Culture Publishing Corporation, 1985.
3. 'On Discovering the Site of a Neolithic Workshop', in Rewi Alley, *Leaves from a Sandan Notebook*, Christchurch: Caxton Press, 1950.
4. Letters to Pip, RA Papers, 58/264/6, ANZ.
5. Rewi Alley, *A Highway, and an Old Chinese Doctor*, Christchurch: Caxton Press, 1973.

6. Rewi Alley, *Peking Opera*, Beijing: New World Press, 1954 and 1981.
7. Ibid. (1981 edition).
8. Letters to Pip, RA Papers, 58/264/6, ANZ.
9. Diary, RA Papers, MS-Papers 6533-340, ATL.

Chapter Forty-seven

1. Both quotes from James MacManus, *Ocean Devil: The life and legend of George Hogg*, London: Harper Perennial, 2010.
2. 'The Guerillas' Song', written and composed by He Luting.
3. Rewi Alley (trans.), *Light and Shadow Along a Great Road: An anthology of modern Chinese poetry*, Beijing: New World Press, 1984.
4. MacManus, *Ocean Devil*.
5. David Mahon, 'Afternoons with Rewi Alley', *North & South*, October 2013.
6. New Zealand China Council, Rewi Alley Frogcast: www.youtube.com/watch?v=Ga5CmOshkMw, 90th anniversary of Rewi Alley's arrival in China.

Chapter Forty-eight

1. From Percy Bysshe Shelley, 'Ode to the West Wind', in *Prometheus Unbound: A lyrical drama in four acts*, Montana: Kissinger Publishing, 2004.
2. Correspondence to Mrs Alley, RA Papers, 74-047-2/10, ATL.
3. 'Yellow Fish', in Rewi Alley, *Gung Ho: Poems*, Christchurch: Caxton Press, 1948.

Chapter Forty-nine

1. Rewi Alley, *Two Years of INDUSCO Chinese Industrial Co-operatives*, Hong Kong: Hong Kong Promotion Committee, 1940.
2. Essay on Evans Carlson, in Rewi Alley, *Six Americans in China*, Beijing: International Culture Publishing Corporation, 1985.
3. Stilwell's regular reports to Roosevelt on the status of the United Front were uncompromising. Appointed Chiang's chief of staff, he was in a unique position to see what was really going on. Making no secret of his contempt for his Chinese boss – whom he called 'The Peanut' – his reports are full of complaints about KMT corruption, Chiang's recklessness and arrogance, and the insubordination of many of the KMT's top officials. Chiang was 'dumb ignorant', indifferent to the welfare of his soldiers, and capable of acts of great cruelty. His soldiers weren't soldiers at all but 'speculators'. Lois Wheeler Snow (ed.), *Edgar Snow's China: A personal account of the Chinese Revolution*, New York: Random House, 1981.
4. James MacManus, *Ocean Devil: The life and legend of George Hogg*, London: Harper Perennial, 2010.
5. Rewi Alley, *Fruition: The story of George Alwin Hogg*, Christchurch: Caxton Press, 1967.
6. 'Proudly the Peaks', in ibid.
7. RA Papers, 74-047-4/11, ATL

Chapter Fifty

1. 'Dedication', in Rewi Alley, *Leaves from a Sandan Notebook*, Christchurch: Caxton Press, 1950.
2. 'Presidential Speeches/Harry S. Truman Presidency, August 6, 1945: Statement by the President Announcing the Use of the A-Bomb at Hiroshima': https://millercenter.org/the-presidency/presidential-speeches/august-6-1945-statement-president-announcing-use-bomb
3. Harry S. Truman, *Memoirs of Harry S. Truman: 1945 year of decisions*, New York: Doubleday, 1955.
4. www.nzedge.com/legends/rewi-alley/
5. Alley, *Memoirs*.
6. Philippa Reynolds, *Rewi Alley from Canterbury to China*, Christchurch: Christchurch–Gansu Friendly Relations Committee of the Christchurch City Council, 1997.
7. NZSIS file titled 'Rewi Alley', August 1973. Declassified 11 November 2009.

Chapter Fifty-one

1. 'So Has One Met the Lonely Western Exile', in Rewi Alley, *Gung Ho: Poems*, Christchurch: Caxton Press, 1948.
2. Letters to Pip, RA Papers, 74-047-3/21, ATL.
3. Bruce Cummings, 'A murderous history of Korea', *London Review of Books*, 18 March 2017.
4. Alley, *Memoirs*.
5. http://nzchinasociety.org.nz/wp-content/uploads/2013/11/Transcription-of-Peter-Lyness-Tapes-Rewi-Alley_09113v2.pdf
6. Henry Luce, the founder of *Time* and *Life*, was an enthusiastic supporter of Gung Ho. Born in China to missionary parents, he became one of Gung Ho's principal donors. Rewi, while happy enough to take Luce's money, refused to go along with his view of America. In a 1968 letter to Pip, Rewi recalls sitting next to Luce at a dinner in Chunking. Luce, having reiterated his claim that it was the American century, invited Rewi to 'come in with us and we will make you'. Rewi's reply is not recorded.
7. NZSIS document, 14 April 1951. Declassified 11 November 2009.
8. Inward Correspondence and other papers, RA Papers, 88-191-8, ATL.
9. *Dominion Post*, 1 June 1952.
10. Willis Airey, *A Learner in China: A life of Rewi Alley*, Christchurch: Caxton Press, 1970.
11. *Dominion Post*, 19 June 1952.
12. NZSIS file titled 'Rewi Alley', August 1973. Declassified 11 November 2009.
13. The SIS's explanation for withholding eight files relating to Rewi Alley was conveyed to me in a letter dated 16 April 2018 from Rebecca Kitteridge, director-general of security: 'The bases for withholding information are sections 6(a) (prejudice security), 6(b) (prejudice entrusting of information),

9(2)(a) (protect the privacy of natural persons including that of deceased natural persons) and 18(c)(i) of the OAI, because the making available of the information requested would be contrary to the provisions of a specified enactment, namely section 227 of the Intelligence and Security Act 2017.'

14. Untitled NZSIS document, part of which has been withheld, dated 14 April 1951. Declassified 11 November 2009.

15. 'Response to the Report of the International Scientific Commission for the Investigation of the Facts Concerning Bacterial Warfare in Korea and China', Beijing, 1952: https://mronline.org/wp-content/uploads/2017/09/ISC-Executive-Report-on-Biological-Warfare-in-Korea_pp1-61.pdf

16. NZSIS document 'Rewi Alley's Visit to New Zealand 1960'. Declassified November 2003.

17. Geoff Chapple, *Rewi Alley of China*, Auckland: Hodder and Stoughton, 1980.

18. Ibid.

19. Walter Nash, letter to Pip, June 1952, in RA Papers, 74-047-4/05, ATL.

20. MFAT file 58/264/6 Part 1 – New Zealand Affairs: External Relations/China/Rewi Alley 1973–1985.

21. Letters to Pip, RA Papers, 74-047-3/21, ATL.

22. Inward Correspondence Guangtao Nie, RA Papers, 6533-208, ATL.

23. 'All in Seventy Years', in Rewi Alley, *Upsurge: Asia and the Pacific*, Christchurch: Caxton Press, 1969.

24. 'Defeat', in Rewi Alley, *Winds of Change*, Christchurch: Caxton Press, 1972.

25. 'Table Tennis Match in Peking', in ibid.

26. Rewi Alley (trans.), *Peace Through the Ages: Translations from the poets of China*, Peking: Rewi Alley, 1954.

27. Rewi Alley, *Taiwan: A background study*, Auckland: New Zealand–China Friendship Society and Progressive Book Society, 1972.

28. David Mahon, 'Afternoons with Rewi Alley', *North & South*, October 2013.

Chapter Fifty-two

1. Letters to Pip, RA Papers, 58/264/6, ANZ.

Chapter Fifty-three

1. 'New City', in Rewi Alley, *Human China: A diary with poems*, Christchurch: Caxton Press, 1957.

2. Alley, *Memoirs*.

3. Letter from Lord Acton to Bishop Mandell Creighton, April 1887: www.phrases.org.uk/meanings/absolute-power-corrupts-absolutely.html

4. 'None Can Forget', in Rewi Alley, *Snow Over the Pines*, Auckland: NZ–China Friendship Society and Progressive Book Society, 1977.

Chapter Fifty-four

1. 'Autobiography', in Rewi Alley, *Gung Ho: Poems*, Christchurch: Caxton Press, 1948.
2. 'Chunking 1955', in Rewi Alley, *Fragments of Living Peking*, Christchurch: New Zealand Peace Council, 1955.
3. From *Richelieu; Or the Conspiracy*, a play by Edward Bulwer-Lytton, 1839.
4. Willis Airey, *A Learner in China: A life of Rewi Alley*, Christchurch: Caxton Press, 1970.
5. Shirley Barton Papers, MS-group 2275, ATL.
6. Papers relating to Kathleen Hall, MS Papers 11164, ATL.
7. Tom Newnham, *He Ming Qing: The life of Kathleen Hall*, Beijing: New World Press, 1992.
8. RA Papers, MS-Papers 4698-02, ATL.
9. 'About Myself', quoted in Geoff Chapple, *Rewi Alley of China*, Auckland: Hodder and Stoughton, 1980.
10. http://nzchinasociety.org.nz/wp-content/uploads/2013/11/Transcription-of-Peter-Lyness-Tapes-Rewi-Alley_091113v2.pdf
11. Lines written at Tu Fu's '"Tsar Tang", Chengdu', in Shirley Barton Papers, MS-group 2275, ATL.
12. Duncan M. Campbell, 'Labouring in the "Sheltered Field" of Rewi Alley's translations from the Chinese', *New Zealand Journal of Asian Studies 16*, December 2014.
13. Tu Fu, 'Night Thoughts of a Traveller', in Rewi Alley (trans.), *Tu Fu: Selected poems*, Beijing: Foreign Languages Press, 1964.
14. Alley, *Memoirs*.
15. Rewi Alley (trans.), *The People Speak Out: Translations of poems and songs of the people of China*, Beijing: Rewi Alley, 1954.
16. He Jingzhi, author of the 1945 song-drama 'The White-Haired Girl', quoted in Hong Zicheng (trans. Michael M. Day), *A History of Chinese Literature*, Beijing: Peking University Press, 1999.
17. http://nzchinasociety.org.nz/wp-content/uploads/2013/11/Transcription-of-Peter-Lyness-Tapes-Rewi-Alley_091113v2.pdf

Chapter Fifty-five

1. 'Peking Winter Scene' in Rewi Alley, *Snow Over the Pines*, Auckland: NZ–China Friendship Society and Progressive Book Society, 1977.
2. RA Papers, 844-181-3/16, ATL.
3. Letters to Pip, RA Papers, 58/264/6, ANZ.
4. NZSIS file, 'Rewi Alley's Letter to New Zealand, Peking 25 March 1951'. Declassified 11 November 2009.
5. Letters to Pip, RA Papers, 58/264/6, ANZ.
6. Letters to PJ Alley, RA Papers, 74-047-3/2, ATL.
7. Alley Diary, RA Papers, MS-Papers 0424-08, ATL.

8. Geoff Chapple, *Rewi Alley of China*, Auckland: Hodder and Stoughton, 1980.
9. Letters to PJ Alley, RA Papers, 74-047-3/21, ATL.
10. David Mahon, 'Afternoons with Rewi Alley', *North & South*, October 2013.
11. Alley Diary, MS-Papers 6533-339, ATL.
12. 'Living in China', in Rewi Alley, *Winds of Change*, Christchurch: Caxton Press, 1972.

Chapter Fifty-six

1. 'Contradictions', in Rewi Alley, *Poems for Aotearoa*, Auckland: NZ–China Friendship Society and Progressive Book Society, 1972.
2. NZSIS inter-office memorandum, 2 February 1965. Declassified 11 November 2003.
3. NZSIS file, 'Rewi Alley's Visit to NZ 23rd October 1971–15th March 1972'. Declassified 11 November 2009.
4. NZSIS file, 30 January 1973, 58/264/6, MFAT.
5. NZSIS document, 'Annexure to 21/43/1', 7 March 1973. Declassfied 11 November 2009.
6. 'Rewi Alley New Zealand and China's Shared Son': https://media.stuff.co.nz/video/production/1492908233531-NZ%20China.mp4
7. http://nzchinasociety.org.nz/wp-content/uploads/2013/11/Transcription-of-Peter-Lyness-Tapes-Rewi-Alley_091113v2.pdf
8. Letters to Pip, RA Papers, 58/264/6, ANZ.
9. Ibid.
10. Conversation with Mike (Duan Hailong) in China, 2017.
11. Rewi Alley letters to family members, RA Papers, 11775-1, ATL.
12. Ibid.

Chapter Fifty-seven

1. 'Peking May Day 1953', in Rewi Alley, *Fragments of Living Peking*, Christchurch: New Zealand Peace Council, 1955.
2. Anne-Marie Brady, *Friend of China: The myth of Rewi Alley*, London: Routledge Curzon, 2003.
3. Rewi Alley, *A Highway, and an Old Chinese Doctor*, Christchurch: Caxton Press, 1973.
4. Wu Gefei, 'Sartre's Encounter with China: Discovery and reconstruction of the human paradigm in new-era Chinese literature', Xuzhou, Jiangsu: China University of Mining and Technology, School of Foreign Studies, 2007.
5. 'Card Index', in Rewi Alley, *Over China's Hills of Blue*, Christchurch: Caxton Press, 1974.
6. Letters to Pip, RA Papers, 58/264/6, ANZ.
7. 'About Myself', in Geoff Chapple, *Rewi Alley of China*, Auckland: Hodder and Stoughton, 1980.
8. Letters to Pip, RA Papers, 58/264/6, ANZ.

Chapter Fifty-eight

1. 'As to Rewi not saying anything about the GLF famines,' Geoff Chapple wrote to me in an email on 20 October 2017, 'I'm absolutely sure he would not have said there was no famine. He never did lie. But he just would have avoided the subject, and talked about the positive aspects of that Maoist programme, decentralisation of industry from the cities, etc …'
2. A Leap Forward song about afforestation quoted in Rewi Alley, *Struggle Around the Central Plains: A story of Honan province*, Beijing: New World Press, 1980.
3. Circular of the Central Committee of the Communist Party of China on the Great Proletarian Cultural Revolution, 16 May 1966: www.marxists.org/subject. china/documents/cpc/cc_gpcr.hfm
4. 'In praise of the Red Guards', *Peking Review*, vol. 9, no. 39, 23 September 1966.
5. 'To Rebel is Justified', in Rewi Alley, *Upsurge: Asia and the Pacific*, Christchurch: Caxton Press, 1969.
6. Aljazeera American obituary for Sid Shapiro, 20 October 2014: http://america. aljazeera.com/articles/2014/10/20/sidney-shapiro-usborntranslatorchinesecitiz endiesat98.html
7. Rewi Alley letters to family members, RA Papers, 11775-1, ATL.
8. Alley, Diary, 58/264/6, ANZ. Rewi's contempt for bureaucrats is given free rein in the diaries. The officials he dealt with in the course of his Gung Ho work are dismissed as 'little bureaucrats sitting in restaurants, idling …'
9. NZSIS document, 'Rewi Alley', August 1973. Declassified 11 November 2003.
10. Explanation given to me by the SIS during an interview on 15 May 2018.
11. http://nzchinasociety.org.nz/wp-content/uploads/2013/11/Transcription-of-Peter-Lyness-Tapes-Rewi-Alley_091113v2.pdf
12. 'On a Spring Afternoon in Peking', in Rewi Alley, *Fragments of Living Peking*, Christchurch: New Zealand Peace Council, 1955.
13. 'China and the Clear Road Forward', in Rewi Alley, *Snow Over the Pines*, Auckland: NZ–China Friendship Society and Progressive Book Society, 1977.
14. Han Suyin, *Eldest Son: Zhou Enlai and the making of modern China*, London: Pimlico, 1994.

Chapter Fifty-nine

1. Rewi Alley, *Six Americans in China*, Beijing: International Culture Publishing Corporation, 1985.
2. 'Chu Teh – A Tribute', in Rewi Alley, *Snow Over the Pines*, Auckland: NZ–China Friendship Society and Progressive Book Society, 1977.
3. 'In Mourning: Mao Tse Tung', in ibid.
4. Essay on Edgar Snow, in Alley, *Six Americans in China*.
5. Alley, *Memoirs*.
6. Lois Wheeler Snow (ed.), *Edgar Snow's China: A personal account of the Chinese Revolution*, Random House, 1981.
7. Alley, *Memoirs*.

8. Rewi Alley, *Fruition: The story of George Alwin Hogg*, Christchurch: Caxton Press, 1967.
9. 'On Tien An Men Square, January 18th, 1976', in Alley, *Snow Over the Pines*.

Chapter Sixty
1. David Mahon, 'Afternoons with Rewi Alley', *North & South*, October 2013.
2. Alley, Diary, 58/264/6, ANZ.
3. From Alley (trans.), *The People Speak Out: Translations of poems and songs of the people of China*, Beijing: Rewi Alley, 1954.

Chapter Sixty-one
1. Rewi Alley letters to family members, RA Papers, 11775-1, ATL.
2. Alley, Diary, 58/264/6, ANZ.
3. Rewi Alley, *Fruition: The story of George Alwin Hogg*, Christchurch: Caxton Press, 1967.
4. Words provided by Michael Crook, chair of the International Committee for the Promotion of Chinese Industrial Co-operatives.
5. Rewi Alley letters to family members, RA Papers, 11775-1, ATL.
6. Shirley Barton Papers, MS-Papers 6533-042, ATL.
7. Letters to Pip, RA Papers, 74-047-4/09, ATL
8. RA Papers, MSX-5290, ATL.
9. RA Papers, MSX-5293, ATL.
10. RA Papers, Inward Correspondence Han Suyin, 74-047-7114, ATL.
11. 'Han Suyin remembers Rewi Alley', *New Argot*, 1994.
12. RA Papers, MSX-5289, ATL.
13. File 118/13/101/2 Part 1, ANZ.
14. MFAT file 58/264/6 Part 3 – New Zealand Affairs: External Relations/China/Rewi Alley 1973–1985.
15. Ibid.
16. Ibid.
17. New Zealand China Council, Rewi Alley Frogcast: www.youtube.com/watch?v=Ga5CmOshkMw, 90th anniversary of Rewi Alley's arrival in China.
18. MFAT file 58/264/6 Part 2 – New Zealand Affairs: External Relations/China/Rewi Alley 1986–1987.
19. Ibid.
20. Rewi Alley letters to family members, RA Papers, 11775-1, ATL.
21. Ibid.
22. New Zealand China Council, Rewi Alley Frogcast.
23. Rewi Alley letters to family members, RA Papers, 11775-1, ATL.
24. Eighth-century poem by He Zhizhang, translated by Rewi Alley.

BIBLIOGRAPHY

Books written or translated by Rewi Alley

73 Man to Be, Christchurch: Caxton Press, 1970

A Highway, and an Old Chinese Doctor: A story of travel through unoccupied China during the War of Resistance, and some notes on Chinese medicine, Christchurch: Caxton Press, 1973

At 90: Memoirs of my China years, Beijing: New World Press, 1986

Beyond the Withered Oak Ten Thousand Saplings Grow, Christchurch: Caxton Press, 1962

Children of the Dawn, Beijing: New World Press, 1957

China's Hinterland in the Leap Forward, Beijing: New World Press, 1961

Chinese Children (Photographs), Christchurch: Caxton Press, 1972

Fragments of Living Peking, Christchurch: New Zealand Peace Council, 1955

Fruition: The story of George Alwin Hogg, Christchurch: Caxton Press, 1967

Gung Ho: Poems, Christchurch: Caxton Press, 1948

Human China: A diary with poems, Christchurch: Caxton Press, 1957

Journey to Outer Mongolia, Christchurch: Caxton Press, 1957

Land and Folk in Kiangsi – A Chinese Province in 1961, Beijing: New World Press, 1962

Leaves from a Sandan Notebook, Christchurch: Caxton Press, 1950

Light and Shadow Along a Great Road: An anthology of modern Chinese poetry (trans.), Beijing: New World Press, 1984

Man Against the Floods, Beijing: New World Press, 1956

Not a Dog: An ancient Tai Ballad (trans.), Beijing: New World Press, 1962

Our Seven – Their Five: A fragment from the story of Gung Ho, Beijing: New World Press, 1963

Over China's Hills of Blue, Christchurch: Caxton Press, 1974

Peace Through the Ages: Translations from the poets of China (trans.), Beijing: Rewi Alley, 1954

Beijing Opera, Beijing: New World Press, 1954 and 1981

Poems for Aotearoa, Auckland: New Zealand–China Friendship Society and Progressive Book Society, 1972

Poems of Protest, Christchurch: Caxton Press, 1968

Poems of Revolt: Some Chinese voices over the last century (trans.), Beijing: New World Press, 1962

Prisoners: Shanghai 1936, Christchurch: Caxton Press, 1973

Refugees from Vietnam in China, Beijing: New World Press, 1980

Rewi Alley on Gung Ho, Beijing: Review Press, 1989

Sandan: An adventure in creative education, Christchurch: Caxton Press, 1959

Six Americans in China, Beijing: International Culture Publishing Corporation, 1985

Snow Over the Pines, Auckland: New Zealand China Friendship Society and
   Progressive Book Society, 1977
Spring in Vietnam: A diary of a journey, Christchurch: Raven Press, 1956
Stories out of China, Beijing: New World Press, 1958
Struggle Around the Central Plains: A story of Honan province, Beijing: New World
   Press, 1980
Taiwan: A background study, Auckland: New Zealand–China Friendship Society
   and Progressive Book Society, 1972
The Eighteen Laments of Tsai Wen-Chi (trans.), Beijing: New World Press, 1963
The Freshening Breeze, Beijing: New World Press, 1977
The Mistake, Christchurch: Caxton Press, 1965
The People Have Strength, Beijing: Rewi Alley, 1954
The People Speak Out: Translations of poems and songs of the people of China,
   Beijing: Rewi Alley, 1954
The Rebels, Auckland: New Zealand–China Friendship Society and Progressive
   Book Society, 1973
This is China Today, Christchurch: Caxton Press, 1951
Three Conferences: Cairo, New Delhi, Bandung, Christchurch: Caxton Press, 1961
Today and Tomorrow, Christchurch: Caxton Press, 1975
Towards a People's Japan, Christchurch: Caxton Press, 1960
Travels in China 1966–71, Beijing: New World Press, 1973
Tu Fu: Selected poems (trans.), Beijing: Foreign Languages Press, 1964
Two Years of INDUSCO Chinese Industrial Co-operatives, Hong Kong: Hong Kong
   Promotion Committee, 1940
Upsurge: Asia and the Pacific, Christchurch: Caxton Press, 1969
What is Sin?, Christchurch: Caxton Press, 1967
Winds of Change, Christchurch: Caxton Press, 1972
Yo Banfa! (We Have a Way), Shanghai: China Monthly Review, 1952

Other books

Airey, Willis, *A Learner in China: A life of Rewi Alley*, Christchurch: Caxton Press,
   1970
Beattie, James and Richard Bullen (eds), *New China Eye Witness: Roger Duff, Rewi
   Alley and the art of museum diplomacy*, Christchurch: Canterbury University
   Press, 2017
Bertram, James, *Capes of China Slide Away: A memoir of peace and war 1910–1980*,
   Auckland: Auckland University Press, 1993
____, *First Act in China: The story of the Sian mutiny*, New York: Viking, 1938
____, *Return to China 1957*, London: Heinemann, 1957
Brady, Anne-Marie, *Friend of China: The myth of Rewi Alley*, London: Routledge
   Curzon, 2003
Buck, Pearl S., *The Good Earth*, New York: Washington Square Press, 1931

Capon, Edmund, *Tang China: Vision and splendour of a golden age*, London/Sydney: MacDonald Orbis, 1989

Chang, Jung, *Wild Swans: Three daughters of China*, Pymble: Harper Perennial, 1991

Chapple, Geoff, *Rewi Alley of China*, Auckland: Hodder and Stoughton, 1980

Clarkson, Adrienne, *Norman Bethune*, Toronto: Penguin Canada, 2009

Dai Sijie, *Balzac and the Little Chinese Seamstress*, New York: Anchor Books, 2000

Farquhar, Roderick and Michael Schoenhals, *Mao's Last Revolution*, Cambridge, Mass: Harvard University Press, 2008

Feigon, Lee, *Demystifying Tibet*, London: Profile Books, 1999

Fraser, John, *The Chinese: Portrait of a people*, Toronto: Collins, 1970

Han Suyin, *A Mortal Flower*, London: Jonathan Cape, 1966

____, *Birdless Summer*, London: Jonathan Cape, 1968

____, *Eldest Son: Zhou Enlai and the making of modern China*, London: Pimlico, 1994

____, *Han Suyin's China*, London: Phaidon, 1987

Hitchens, Christopher, *The Missionary Position: Mother Teresa in theory and practice*, London: Atlantic, 1995

Hong Zicheng, *A History of Chinese Literature* (trans. Michael M. Day), Beijing: Beijing University Press, 1999

Hyde, Robin, *Dragon Rampant*, London: Hurst & Blackett, 1939

Isherwood, Christopher and W.H. Auden, *Journey to a War*, New York: Paragon House, 1990

Jin Yong, *A Hero Born: Legends of the condor heroes*, vol. 1 (trans. Anna Holmwood), London: MacLehose Press, 2016

Liu Heng, *The Obsessed*, Beijing: Chinese Literature Press, 1991

Johnson, Ian, *The Souls of China: The return of religion after Mao*, London: Allen Lane, 2017

MacManus, James, *Ocean Devil: The life and legend of George Hogg*, London: Harper Perennial, 2010

Ma Jian, *China Dream*, London: Chatto & Windus, 2018

Makine, Andreï, *The Woman Who Waited*, London: Hodder and Stoughton, 2006

Mao Tse-Tung, *Selected Military Writings of Mao Tse-Tung*, Beijing: Foreign Languages Press, 1963

____, *Selected Works of Mao Tse-Tung*, vol. I, Beijing: Foreign Languages Press, 1965

____, *Selected Works of Mao Tse-Tung*, vol. II, Beijing: Foreign Languages Press, 1965

____, *Selected Works of Mao Tse-Tung*, vol. III, Beijing: Foreign Languages Press, 1967

____, *Selected Works of Mao Tse-Tung*, vol. IV, Beijing: Foreign Languages Press, 1971

McNeish, James, *Dance of the Peacocks: New Zealanders in exile in the time of Hitler and Mao Tse-Tung*, Auckland: Vintage, 2003

Mitter, Rana, *A Bitter Revolution: China's struggle with the modern world*, Oxford: Oxford University Press, 2004

Newnham, Tom, *He Ming Qing: The life of Kathleen Hall*, Beijing: New World Press, 1992

____, *Interesting Times: A Kiwi chronicle*, Auckland: Graphic Publications, 2003

Quotations from Chairman Mao Tse-Tung (The Little Red Book), Beijing: Foreign Languages Press, 1966

Reynolds, Philippa, *Rewi Alley from Canterbury to China*, Christchurch: Christchurch–Gansu Friendly Relations Committee of the Christchurch City Council, 1997

Schmitz, Rob, *Street of Eternal Happiness*, New York: Penguin, 2016

Secretariat of the National Committee for the Commemoration of Rewi Alley's 75th Birthday, *Rewi Alley Seventy-Five*, Hamilton, 1972

Smedley, Agnes, *Battle Hymn of China*, New York: Da Capo Press, 1975

____, *Chinese Destinies*, Beijing: Foreign Languages Press, 2003

____, *Daughter of Earth*, New York: Coward-McCann, 1929

Snow, Edgar, *Journey to the Beginning: A personal view of contemporary history*, New York: Random House, 1958

____, *Living China*, London: Harrap, 1936

____, *Red China Today: The other side of the river*, New York: Random House, 1971

____, *Red Star Over China*, New York: Grove Press, 1968

____, *Scorched Earth*, London: Victor Gollancz, 1941

Snow, Helen Foster, *Inside Red China*, New York: Da Capo Press, 1979

Snow, Lois Wheeler (ed.), *Edgar Snow's China: A personal account of the Chinese Revolution*, New York: Random House, 1981

Somerset, Gwendolen, *Sunshine and Shadow*, Auckland: NZ Playcentre Federation, 1988

Spender, Stephen and David Hockney, *China Diary*, London: Thames and Hudson, 1982

Truman, Harry S., *Memoirs of Harry S. Truman: 1945 year of decisions*, New York: Doubleday, 1955

Tuchman, Barbara W., *Stilwell and the American Experience in China, 1911–45*, New York: Macmillan, 1971

Yan Lianke, *The Day the Sun Died*, London: Chatto & Windus, 2018

Xiaolu Guo, *Nine Continents: A memoir in and out of China*, New York: Grove Atlantic, 2017

Zhou Erfu, *Doctor Norman Bethune*, Beijing: Foreign Languages Press, 1982

Articles and papers

Barker, Miles, 'Robin Hyde, Rewi Alley and the varieties of "Mahi Tahi"', Paper delivered at the National Conference of the NZCFS, Hamilton, May 2018

Chinese Literature: Essays, Articles, Reviews (CLEAR), vol. 36, December 2014: www.jstor.org/stable/i40138442

Mahon, David, 'Afternoons with Rewi Alley', *North & South*, October 2013

New Zealand Journal of Adult Learning, vol. 34, no. 1, 29–47

New Zealand Journal of Asian Studies, December 2014

Papers tabled at the Rewi Alley 120th Anniversary Symposium, Christchurch, 1
December 2017

Taylor, Evan, 'The Chinese Industrial Cooperative, the China Defense League and
Internationalism in the Sino-Japanese War', *Journal of the Royal Asiatic Society
of China*, vol. 78, no. 1, 2018

Wu Gefei, 'Sartre's Encounter with China: Discovery and reconstruction of the
human paradigm in new-era Chinese literature', Xuzhou, Jiangsu: China
University of Mining and Technology, School of Foreign Studies, 2007

Archives
Documents generously provided by NZSIS

James Bertram Papers, Alexander Turnbull Library, MS-group 1277

MFAT file 58/264/6 Part 1 – New Zealand Affairs: External Relations/China/Rewi
Alley 1973–1985

MFAT file 58/264/6 Part 2 – New Zealand Affairs: External Relations/China/Rewi
Alley 1986–1987

MFAT file 58/264/6 Part 3 – New Zealand Affairs: External Relations/China/Rewi
Alley 1973–1985

MFAT file BEI-CH/NZ3/6 Part 2 – Beijing Post Files/China/New Zealand Bilateral
Relations/Social Issues/People to People Links/Including Rewi Alley 2003–2004

Rewi Alley Diary, ABHS W4627 950 Box 1481, 58/264/6, Archives New Zealand

Rewi Alley Papers, 58/264/6, Archives New Zealand

Rewi Alley Papers, Alexander Turnbull Library, 70-047 and MS-group 0809

Shirley Barton Papers, Alexander Turnbull Library, 87-038 and MS-group 2275

Magazines and newspapers
New Zealand
Auckland Weekly News
Dominion Post
Herald
New Zealand Listener
North & South
Otago Daily Times
Sunday Times

China
China Reconstructs
China Today
China Weekly Review
Eastern Horizon (Hong Kong)
Global Times
People's Daily
Voice of China

United States
Christian Science Monthly
Far East Reporter
Saturday Evening Post
Time

Britain
Daily Herald
Daily Pioneer
News Chronicle
The Telegraph
The Times

Films and documentaries

Eric and Rewi Alley: Great war story, produced by Anna Cottrell, NZ On Air Ngā Kōrero a Ipurangi o Aotearoa: https://nzhistory.govt.nz/media/video/eric-and-rewi-alley-great-war-story
From Scratch, Geoff Chapple, Phil Dadson, Wayne Laird, Don McGlashan, 1980: www.sonicsfromscratch.co.nz
Gung Ho: Rewi Alley of China, produced by John Maynard, directed by Geoff Steven, 1980: www.nzonscreen.com/title/gung-ho-rewi-alley-of-china-1979
Mao Zedong at his Cave House in Yan'an, China in 1944: www.criticalpast.com/video/65675046859_Mao-Zedong_Edgar-Snow_reporters_interpreter
New Zealand China Council Rewi Alley Frogcast: www.youtube.com/watch?v=Ga5CmOshkMw, 90th anniversary of Rewi Alley's arrival in China
Rewi Alley and David Lange, Beijing, 1986, produced by Carl Worker: www.youtube.com/watch?v=SYXdXwIh6f8
Rewi Alley – Early Years: www.youtube.com/watch?v=2PHZrKMNlXM
Rewi Alley – 10 Years in Shanghai: www.youtube.com/watch?v=khIccY_UzGM
Adopted Son Recalls Life of New Zealand's Rewi Alley, Old Friend of China: www.youtube.com/watch?v=3mpicq8nPA0
Rewi Alley – Immersion in Gong He: www.youtube.com/watch?v=XA-qK1EAtfM
Rewi Alley – Bailie Schools: www.youtube.com/watch?v=P3J4n_Q7OsI
Rewi Alley – In New China: www.youtube.com/watch?v=xM1pihyKCps
Rod Alley on Rewi Alley (filmed on George Andrews' phone at a function organised by the NZ China Council in Auckland, December 2017): www.youtube.com/watch?v=vwPce15YQMc&t=109s
The Second Blade of Grass, Dawn Productions: David Harré and Geoff Chapple, 1987 (not available to the public)

ACKNOWLEDGEMENTS

WRITING books can be a lonely experience, or so it has proved for me in my life as a novelist. Not so with the writing of this book. So many people – friends, family, colleagues – have accompanied me, giving advice, providing information, lending or giving books and photos, raising funds to offset the costs of travel to China and the many books I have had to buy in the course of my research – that I have sometimes wondered if I can truly claim sole authorship. To all those enablers I give my warmest thanks.

My largest debt is to the Simon Deng Li Fund and the New Zealand–China Friendship Society (NZCFS) for making possible the journey to China in April 2017. I am also indebted to Consul General Jin and the Chinese Consulate in Christchurch for the provision of additional funds. This book would never have been written had that journey not taken place.

I owe a similar debt to Geoff Chapple, whose biography of Rewi Alley has been my bible, and whose generosity in sharing his stories has provided not just encouragement but inspiration. Thank you, Geoff.

To my cousins – Jocelyn Watkin, who first suggested the book to me and has since provided invaluable help and support, and Maurice Alley, who lent books, answered questions and opened doors – my heartfelt thanks. Thanks also to Carole Magee, Alison Horn and Sarah Stuart for the loan of precious books; Judith Chisnall for her generous gift of books; Christine Rogers who printed out the family tree; Tony Browne, executive chair of the New Zealand Contemporary China Research Centre, for valuable insights; David Mahon, whose published conversations with Rewi brought him vividly alive for me; and Bruce Somerville for permission to read his father's letters.

To all family members who shared their stories and answered my questions, particularly Sarah who facilitated the family reunion in Christchurch, and Dorothy Waymouth who photocopied Rewi's family letters, making my task so much easier, I give my warm thanks.

Support in all sorts of ways was given by Dave Bromwich, George Andrews, and Eric Livingstone of the NZCFS. Dave's help, freely and generously given, in tracking down sources and correcting my use of Chinese words and phrases has been invaluable. Any mistakes are mine, not his.

Warm thanks to the Rewi Alley 120th Anniversary Committee for enabling me to attend the celebrations in Christchurch in December 2017; to

Liu Guozhong, deputy general of ICCIC and senior lecturer at the Shandan Bailie School, for identifying sources; to Tony Eyre of Dunedin who helped in my search for books; and to Christopher Pugsley who put me right on matters military.

To the trustees of the Robert Lord Cottage in Dunedin, Claire Matthewson and Gay Buckingham in particular, I say a grateful thank you for providing me with a quiet place to write. My two and a half months in Dunedin were very happy and very productive. I would also like to acknowledge the help and advice of the officials I encountered at the Ministry of Foreign Affairs and Trade, New Zealand Security Intelligence Service, Archives New Zealand and the National Library. I am particularly indebted to Charlotte McGillen, research assistant at MFAT, for her careful examination of the material I have used and for pointing me in the direction of additional files.

This book would not be in the shape it is without the involvement of my editor Jane Parkin, whose ability to see the larger picture, aligned with her eye for detail, has made an immense difference to the text. My debt to Jane is incalculable.

To my publisher, Rachel Scott, heartfelt thanks for her patience, wisdom, guidance and encouragement.

Warm thanks also to my friend Robert Smellie, whose kindness has supported me at every stage during the writing of this book.

Finally I would like to thank all the people in China – family, guides, officials – who did so much to make our journey the remarkable experience it was. I would especially like to thank Wang Fang, our guide for the latter part of the journey, who also provided valuable help via video link. To my Chinese cousins – Rewi's wonderful granddaughters and other family members, also Lao San, Hailing (Mike) Duan and Luyi Duan – I offer warm thanks for so generously sharing your time and your stories. The same warm thanks are due to Michael Crook, chair of the International Committee for Promotion of Chinese Industrial Co-operatives, and his mother Isabel, part of our journey and part of this book. Michael made me feel I could ask him anything and for that I was and am deeply grateful.

INDEX

Page numbers in **bold** refer to images.